KOREAN YEARBOOK OF
INTERNATIONAL LAW

KOREAN YEARBOOK OF INTERNATIONAL LAW

Volume 10
2022

PARKYOUNGSA

THE KOREAN BRANCH OF THE INTERNATIONAL LAW ASSOCIATION

KOREAN YEARBOOK OF
INTERNATIONAL LAW

Copyright ⓒ The Korean Branch of the International Law Association 2023
Published by PARKYOUNGSA

PARKYOUNG Publishing&Company
210-ho, 53, Gasan digital 2-ro, Geumcheon-gu, Seoul, 08588, Korea
Tel 82-2-733-6771
Fax 82-2-736-4818

First published 16 October 2023
Printed in Seoul, Korea
ISBN 979-11-303-4542-0 93360

For subscriptions to this Yearbook, please contact the sole distributor, PARKYOUNG Publishing&Company
210-ho, 53, Gasan digital 2-ro, Geumcheon-gu, Seoul, 08588, Korea
Tel 82-2-733-6771 Fax 82-2-736-4818 E-mail: pys@pybook.co.kr

THE KOREAN BRANCH OF
THE INTERNATIONAL LAW ASSOCIATION

PRESIDENT

LEE Chang-Wee

HONORARY PRESIDENT

LIMB Thok-Kyu

VICE-PRESIDENTS

JO Hee-Moon

KANG Junha

LEE Gyooho

SHIM Sangmin

SECRETARY-GENERAL & TREASURER

SHIM Sangmin

MEMBERS OF EXECUTIVE COUNCIL

HONG Seong-Keun

JO Hee-Moon

KANG Junha

LEE Chang-Wee

LEE Gyooho

LEE Jee-Hyung

SHIM Sangmin

SON Hyun-Jin

WON Jae-Chun

SUPPORTING MEMBERS

All correspondences concerning the Yearbook should be sent to:
Secretary-General, Korean Branch, ILA
#422, Jamsil REZION Officetel, 87, Ogeum-ro, Songpa-gu, Seoul, Korea
E-mail: ilakoreanbranch@gmail.com / Homepage: http://www.ilakorea.or.kr

CONTENTS

A Dedicated Scholar's Contribution to the Development of Korean International Law: A Tribute to the Late Professor Choi Seung-Hwan

The sudden death of Choi Seung-Hwan, the first president of the Korean Branch of the International Law Association and an emeritus professor at Kyunghee University Law School, came as a great shock and was met with sorrow by everyone who knew him. He left us early because of his failing health, although he should have been active as a scholar for many more years.

He reorganized the Korean Branch of the ILA in 2014 to put it on firmer academic footing than ever. Under his leadership, the Korean Branch published the Korean Yearbook of International Law every year and held a wide range of academic events.

He contributed greatly to exchanges between Korean international law scholars and overseas scholars by attending the biennial International Law Conferences of the International Law Association alongside many other scholars and experts. The development of the Korean Branch of the ILA today would not have been possible without his dedication and efforts.

His family and friends universally describe him as a gentle and caring person. Scholars and colleagues who worked with him will never forget his academic sincerity and commitment to the ILA. We deeply grieve that we have been forever parted from the man who was loved and respected by his family, friends and colleagues.

It is also thanks to Professor Choi that the Korean government and various public institutions fully supported the Korean Branch.

Thanks to his efforts, the Korean Branch will develop further and be more active than ever in its academic endeavors. The members of the Korean Branch who miss him will follow his wishes and devote ourselves to the development of the Korean Branch.

Though he is no longer with us, he will never be forgotten. May his memory be forever held in the pages of this book.

LEE Chang-Wee, JO Hee-Moon, LEE Gyooho,
KANG Junha, SHIM Sangmin, Won Jae-Chun,
HONG Seung-Keun, SON Hyun-Jin

EDITORIAL NOTE

The Korean Yearbook of International Law has reached its tenth volume, and as will sometimes happen over the course of a decade, we have suffered a loss within our community. Professor Choi Seung-Hwan of Kyunghee University Law School, the first President of the Korean branch of the International Law Association, passed away suddenly while this volume was being prepared. A driving force behind the publication of the Yearbooks, he is and will be much missed. For more, please refer to the Editorial Board's moving tribute to Professor Choi in the beginning of this volume.

As we carry on with Professor Choi's vision to continue and improve the yearbook as a reference abroad for Korea's international legal practice, the current volume has come together under a broad theme of risk to international exchange. Navigation, trade, business, and immigration across borders create bounties of opportunity. At the same time, these interactions and interfaces are also sources of legal, health, environmental, and other risks.

International law, both public and private, is a major means of managing and mitigating the risks that arise out of international exchange and cross-border issues. The current collection of articles and reports delve into this role of international law in a variety of contexts and circumstances.

The article *Legal Status of Marine Scientific Research in the Law of the Sea* by Professor Lee Chang-Wee examines the Law of the Sea rules applicable to marine scientific research and the conflicts over these rules, most prominently between China and the United States, for a dynamic view of these much-contested rules. Marine research is a leading example of an activity rife with both opportunities (scientific and economic) and risk (security and military), and state behaviors surrounding the international law in this area demonstrate the high stakes of deciding how international law will manage the risks.

The Meaning of "Service" as One of the Requirements for Recognition and Enforcement of Foreign Judgments by Judge Kim Young-Seok looks at service of process in international litigation. Litigation across borders, along with the recognition and enforcement thereof, is a vital means of managing cross-border risks, while service of process allows individuals to be notified of and respond to the legal risk that such litigation raises in turn. Judge Kim gives a thoughtful and nuanced exploration of a landmark decision by the Korean Supreme Court in this field, in the process making the crucial distinction between legality of the service of process itself under domestic law (Korean law, in this case) and its being a requirement for recognition and enforcement.

Judge You Jung Hwa's article, *Private International Law Issues in Joint Venture Agreements and Shareholders' Agreements Governed by Korean Law*, takes a look at the sometimes tangled issues that arise in the interface between different jurisdictions, and proposes several strategies for the advance separation of contract and corporate legal aspects to manage disputes that may arise out of joint venture agreements.

Attorney Han Mino's article, *Revisiting Optional Arbitration Clauses Before the Korean Courts*, critiques a major Korean Supreme Court judgment that deemed optional arbitration clauses ineffective unless both parties consent. Attorney Han then goes on to argue that courts should take a more pro-arbitration stance to resolve practical confusion over the validity of these clauses. Expanding the effectiveness of optional arbitration clauses would certainly change the calculus of dispute and legal risk management, and it remains to be seen if the Korean courts will listen to these calls.

Dr. Chung Min Jung opens the Special Reports section with a breakdown of the Constitutional Court's 2020 decision on renunciation of nationality by Koreans who hold multiple nationalities. The balance between individual rights and the need for a large, ready military force through mandatory military service has always been a delicate one in Korea, yet the thorough treatment by the Special Report shows that individual rights and practicality are not necessarily in tension: The Constitutional Court's reasoning is clear that disallowing the relinquishment of Korean nationality after the nationality selection period not only causes undue hardship for the multiple nationality holders, but is also impractical for military purposes.

The subject of Professor Lee Jang-Hie's report, the Inter-Korean Basic Agreement of 1991, may be characterized as a major push by the two Koreas to manage and mitigate perhaps the single greatest geopolitical risk on the Korean peninsula and the surrounding region: that of military tension and, at the extreme, another Korean War. By examining both the substance of the Agreement in its usefulness to building a framework for Korean peace, and its form which Professor Lee argues meets the requirements of a binding international treaty, the conclusion is reached that the Agreement should be implemented by both Korean governments and leveraged as a foundation for lasting peace.

Professor Lee Gyooho's special report on industrial security laws in the Republic of Korea outlines the state of the law on industrial security and argues for greater coordination with Japanese law, as South Korea and Japan are two of the states most affected by security concerns in their high-tech industries. This may be an emerging area of cooperation and coordination to manage security risks in these industries.

In a special report on the normalization of Korea-Japan relations in the Yoon Suk-Yeol administration, Professor Hong Sungkee makes comparisons between the Korea-Japan relations policies of the current administration an past ones, and argues for a productive way forward for the two countries beyond historical gridlock based on the foundational legal principle that a contract must be honored.

Dr. Doh See-Hwan, a recurring and valued contributor to the Yearbooks, contributed a special report on the invasion of Dokdo and the Korea-Japan treaty in 1905 through the lens of the San Francisco Peace Treaty in 1951. Dr. Doh argues that Korea's sovereignty over Dokdo and the illegality of Japan's annexation of Korea are confirmed by the San Francisco Peace Treaty, making a firm grounding in international law a vital part of East Asian peace and justice going forward.

In the Recent Development section, Professor Lee Seok-Yong comments on military activities in other states' exclusive economic zones (EEZs), which is all the more interesting read together with Professor Lee Chang-Wee's article on the legal aspect of marine scientific research. Military activities in EEZs are reasonably viewed as another front in the struggle between states over the law of the sea, which is not an abstract academic argument but often a matter of security and even survival.

Dr. Chung Min Jung reported on the Korean National Assembly's international law resolutions taken in 2022 and added insights such as the decrease in the quantity of international law resolutions undertaken by this body, including human rights resolutions. The five international law resolutions by the Assembly in 2022 mainly concerned geopolitical issues, marking a departure from prior years when human rights resolutions were more dominant.

Professor Won Jae-Chun provided a timely report on the international investor arbitration tribunal ICSID's decision in *Lone Star Holdings vs. Republic of Korea*, pointing out where the decision fell short and presenting directions the Korean government could seek in the rectification proceedings. Investor claims like the Lone Star Holdings case represent a major risk for states in their government policy and enforcement actions, and these experiences along with commentary on them will prove valuable going forward.

In Contemporary Practice and Judicial Decisions, Judge Hong Eungi presents judicial decisions in public international law, including the arrest of foreign nationals and their right to be notified of the right to have the consuls of their country of nationality notified; the legality of a deportation order of a refugee that does not specify the country of repatriation; and the recognition of gender change for transgender people with minor children.

This final section is rounded out by translations of the Quarantine Act, Framework Act on Carbon Neutrality and Green Growth, and Space Development Promotion Act, together with Judge Jang Jiyong's summary of judicial decisions in public international law including the applicability of the CISG, assumption of obligations, formation of marriage, and recognition of a threefold damage awarded by a foreign court.

The depth and breadth of the articles and reports in this volume come together to form a picture of Korean international legal practice in 2022 of responding to new and known risks at all levels, through the international legal process, legislation, litigation, diplomacy, judgments, resolutions, and more. This is a truly dynamic and multilayered process that no one book can hope to capture the entirety of, but the Korean Yearbook of International Law delivers at least one slice of this organic, pulsing process for a year. Though I may not agree with all the selections and some of them have contrasting viewpoints, perhaps this, too, is a reflection of the contradictions and strife inherent in the course of international law.

This volume also marks the end of the tenure of the current editorial team led by Professor Lee Gyooho, including myself as the Executive Editor. Professor Lee and the team, including the tireless Ms. Choi Ji-in as the staff editor, deserve all accolades for their energetic dedication and unending patience. For myself, it has been a privilege working with the scholarly output of so many talented scholars and practitioners. I wish the succeeding team every success in continuing this important work.

LEE Jee-Hyung
Executive Editor
Korean Yearbook of International Law

ARTICLES

Legal Status of Marine Scientific Research in the Law of the Sea: Conflicts over Codification and Policy—Oriented Jurisprudence as a Solution*

LEE Chang—Wee
Professor
University of Seoul, Law School, Seoul, Korea

Abstract

Marine Scientific Research (MSR) has been one of the most controversial issues between maritime powers and coastal states since the second World War. As developed countries invested heavily in pure and applied scientific research on the sea in the 1950s and 1960s, newly independent developing states grew concerned about the possibility of being placed at a disadvantage in the exploitation of marine resources. There was also a concern that MSR could have military repercussions.

Both sides have long been opposed to each other over the legal status of the MSR regime since the beginning of the third UN Conference on the Law of the Sea. As a result, no definition of MSR was stipulated in the 1982 UN Convention on the Law of the Sea (LOSC). Given the wide gap between the viewpoints of the two groups, conflicts over MSR activities in the areas under national jurisdiction are not expected to be settled in the near future. In the long run, these kinds of conflicts should be understood in the context of maritime policy implementation and policy-oriented jurisprudence.

Taking into account state practice, this article addresses relevant issues regarding conflicts over MSR between the two sides. Specifically, it examines several issues, including the relevant provisions in the 1982 LOSC, as well as the conflicting positions of coastal states and maritime powers. A future prospect is added as a concluding remark.

The United States and China are mentioned as an example of conflicts between maritime powers and coastal states along with Korea and Japan. The United States has been a traditional maritime power since the late nineteenth century, while China has been considered a continental power for a long time. However, with China's recent been transformation into a maritime power, it remains to be seen how China could make alterations to its maritime policy.

Key Words

marine scientific research, maritime powers, coastal states, policy oriented jurisprudence

I. Introduction

The UN Convention on the Law of the Sea (UNCLOS) does not accurately define the concept of Marine Scientific Research (MSR). Considering the fact that the Convention contains numerous articles that deal with MSR, this lack of definition is unusual, and raises many questions. Especially, as MSR is an essential regime for the efficient protection of the marine environment and management of marine resources, this lack of definition in the Convention can be noted as a critical lacuna.

Maritime powers emphasize the freedom of the sea, but coastal states stand in opposition to this view. Conflicts between the two sides started in the Age of Exploration in the 15th century and have continued to the present day. MSR has been a demonstrative case of these conflicts in the 21st century and has become another tinderbox between the two sides.[1]

Since the entry into force of the UNCLOS, coastal states have been unable to extend their jurisdiction beyond the limits of the Exclusive Economic Zone (EEZ). In the 1990s, Chile attempted to extend its jurisdiction beyond the 200-mile EEZ by introducing the concept of "presential sea." They suggested that adjacent to the EEZ lies the presential sea, a contiguous zone in turn adjacent to the territorial sea in which coastal states can regulate other states' fisheries, MSR and use of natural resources. However, this failed to gain the recognition of other states,[2] leading the coastal states to confront the maritime powers by using the concept of "thickening jurisdiction" in the EEZ. Through thickening jurisdiction, a new stage of conflict evolved which permitted stronger jurisdiction for the coastal states, leaving the maritime powers in a relatively weak position in the EEZ.[3]

Conflict between the two sides regarding MSR and the EEZ grew into a particularly serious issue in relation to the conduct of military surveys. Differing understandings of the two sides regarding the legal characteristics of the EEZ as a symbolic system of the extension of maritime jurisdiction is an example of conflict regarding the strengthening of maritime jurisdiction. This conflict, along with different interpretations of MSR, have in turn generated other, more intricate forms of conflict. Until recently, the U.S. and China have vigorously confronted each other in regards to military and hydrographic surveys.[4] The interpretation of MSR has been the key issue in conflicts between the deep-water fishing states and the maritime powers. For example, Japan went through a series of conflicts with Australia and New Zealand after stating that its test fishing of highly migratory species and marine mammals was legitimate.[5] Such severe conflicts would not have arisen, or at least would have unfolded differently, had there been an international consensus on MSR.

Taking into account what has been mentioned above, this article will deal with legal and political issues regarding MSR, especially in relation to conflicts between maritime powers and coastal states. Specifically, this paper will first address related articles in the UNCLOS and the stances of international organizations, and then investigate the national conduct of the U.S, China, Japan and Korea. The confrontation between the U.S. and China is one lens through which to view conflicts between maritime powers and coastal states. Looking at the ways in which Korea and Japan have dealt with this issue is also meaningful because they, too, have struggled over consensus regarding the MSR. Furthermore, China and Japan have also had their differences in viewing MSR, making it necessary to study their stances. In conclusion, in the context of maritime policy implementation and policy-oriented jurisprudence, this paper will examine the gap between normative aspects and practical matters of MSR and seek solutions for their discordance.

II. Qualified Consent Regime

1. Absence of Definition of Marine Scientific Research

Detailed regulations on MSR are contained in Part XIII of the UNCLOS. Throughout the 28 articles in the UNCLOS from Article 238 to Article 265, there are elaborate regulations for conducting MSR. Other than Part XIII, there are related rules in the relevant parts or sections covering territorial seas, the EEZ, the high seas, deep seabeds, the development and transfer of marine technology, and regimes for disputed settlements. This is due to the advance of technology in developing ocean resources and demonstrates the significance of MSR in the international law of the sea.[6]

MSR became more crucial due not only to the increase in demand for resources but also due to the increase in military needs.[7] Maritime powers supported freedom of MSR in this context, whereas coastal states agreed on more regulation of MSR in the context of expanding jurisdiction.[8] The former claim that MSR will promote marine science and will eventually benefit the entire international community, while the latter state that MSR will only result in the monopolization of marine resources by maritime powers. Coastal states in particular stress that MSR is directly related to marine exploration, and should therefore be regulated. Due to this vital difference in viewing MSR, no written agreement was made in defining MSR in the UNCLOS. However, it can be asserted that basic frameworks established in the 1958 Law of the Sea remained unchanged.[9]

The failure to codify a definition for MSR is due to the vagueness of the boundary between pure and applied scientific research. For example, if certain survey results were used for life science, it would be difficult to distinguish whether the survey represented pure or applied scientific research. It is suggested the same applies to submarine geologic surveys for hydrocarbon resources. The thin line between military and hydrographic surveys makes it still more difficult to establish a definition for MSR.

Since the UNCLOS does not explain the definitions of military or hydrographic surveys, the U.S. recognizes the freedom of states to navigate and conduct military and hydrographic surveys in the EEZ as long as they are conducted in accordance with the related provisions of the UNCLOS.[10] However, China and other coastal states claim that the concepts of hydrographic and military surveys which maritime powers speak of are basically indistinguishable from the concept of MSR, and that therefore none of the three practices shall be conducted in the EEZ. This disagreement between the two sides began from the UN Law of the Sea Conference and has continued to the recent confrontations between the U.S. and China.[11]

For this reason, the UNCLOS did not state the exact definition of MSR. Nonetheless, the UNCLOS attempts to distinguish between the concepts of pure and applied scientific research with regard to MSR conducted in the EEZ and on the continental shelf of other countries by referring to the approval of coastal states. This is because it states that coastal states do not approve of scientific research conducted for the purpose of resource development, but can approve MSR conducted for purely scientific purposes.[12] However, this regulation, which only indirectly distinguishes between the two, cannot provide sufficient grounds to define the concept of MSR.

Conflict between maritime powers and coastal states over MSR and the UNCLOS's unclear definition appear specifically in the provisions on the EEZ and the continental shelf. This is because these provisions are included for the purpose of the exploration, exploitation and conservation of marine resources. Compared to territorial seas and the high seas, the nature of the EEZ and the continental shelf is rather functional. This makes conflict inevitable due to their legal status, and MSR represents a demonstrative case of this conflict.

2. Conflicts in Codification

Along with the protection and preservation of marine environments, and with the establishment and use of artificial islands, installations and structures, the UNCLOS approves MSR as one of the rights of coastal states to exercise their jurisdiction in the EEZ.[13] This was codified at the UN Law of the Sea Conference due to the need to enhance the management of marine resources. Article 246 in Part XIII of the Convention stipulates in detail that coastal states, in the exercise of their jurisdiction, have the right to regulate, authorize and conduct MSR in the EEZ. According to Article 246, this also applies to MSR on the continental shelf. Confrontation between the two sides is noticeably seen in related UNCLOS articles.

The main purport of Article 246 is that MSR can be conducted by foreign countries in the EEZ and on the continental shelf according to the approval of the coastal states. Although the UNCLOS does not clearly stipulate it, part XIII includes extensive scientific activities in the sphere of MSR. Thus, although not as absolute as their jurisdiction over territorial seas, coastal states have discretion over regulating and allowing MSR by other states in the EEZ and on the continental shelf.

However, the UNCLOS states that coastal states shall grant their consent for MSR projects by other states or international organizations in their EEZ or on their continental shelf to be carried out for peaceful purposes, specifically if its purpose is to increase scientific knowledge of the marine environment for the benefit of all mankind. This limits the discretion of the coastal states.[14] This regulation stipulates the argument of maritime powers that MSR should be conducted easily at least in the EEZ and on the continental shelf. Moreover, the UNCLOS states that "coastal States shall establish rules and procedures ensuring that such consent will not be delayed or denied unreasonably" to strengthen the intent of this regulation.[15]

However, coastal states have the right to withhold their consent to MSR projects if they directly influence the exploration or exploitation of natural resources, whether living or non-living, or if they are related to drilling into the continental shelf, the use of explosives, or the introduction of harmful substances into the marine environment. They can also withhold consent to MSR if it involves the construction, operation or use of artificial islands, installations or structures, as referred to in Articles 60 and 80, or if the coastal states giving the consent is notified with inaccurate or insufficient information, or if the state or competent international organization planning to conduct the research has not performed its relevant duties during previous research.[16] Therefore, it can be said that in certain cases this provision allows broad discretion to the coastal states.

We can assess such a "qualified consent regime" as a major step forward from the related provisions of the 1958 Convention on the Continental Shelf. The Convention on the Continental Shelf left open the possibility of subjective interpretation of the difference between pure and applied research. Indeed, related rules from the UNCLOS do leave room for controversy. However, it is important to note that, compared to the past, the UNCLOS has reduced uncertainty by introducing a detailed dispute settlement regime.[17]

Disapproval of MSR projects which are related to the exploration or exploitation of natural resources, whether living or non-living, can raise serious conflicts between coastal states and researching states. In the past, conflicts between maritime powers and coastal states were not as serious. Developments in MSR technology that were unexpected in the 3rd UN Law of the Sea Conference made interpretations of MSR based on life science very difficult.[18] This ambiguated the boundary between pure and applied scientific research even further, making it more difficult to define the concept of MSR in the UNCLOS.

Besides, there are various rules for MSR in the UNCLOS. Examples of such MSR regulations include limitations on the discretion of coastal states regarding MSR projects on the continental shelf conducted 200 nautical miles beyond the EEZ,[19] MSR projects undertaken by or under the auspices of international organizations,[20] the duty to provide information to coastal states,[21] the duty to comply with certain conditions,[22] implied consent,[23] and the suspension or cessation of MSR activities.[24]

These regulations were created to properly allocate rights among maritime powers and coastal states regarding MSR.[25] Coastal states can approve or regulate MSR but this is not absolute, and there are certain constraints on international organizations and maritime powers conducting MSR in the jurisdictional areas of coastal states. Therefore, the power which coastal states have over their jurisdictional areas other than their territorial seas cannot be exercised unconditionally or recklessly. For the sake of the public interest of the international community, certain regulations are given positive consideration when other countries make requests to conduct MSR projects.

3. Guidelines of International Organizations

The United Nations Division for Ocean Affairs and the Law of the Sea at the Office of Legal Affairs provides detailed guidelines on the performance of MSR. It provides a supplementary interpretation and general implementation of the related provisions of the UNCLOS to promote convenience in states' compliance and their conduct of MSR. As these guidelines are given by the UN, which is a highly authoritative international organization, they have become important for the conduct and regulation of MSR.[26]

The guidelines explain why the UNCLOS could not provide a definition of MSR, and also describe the definitions suggested by participating countries during the UN Law of the Sea Conference. By examining their suggestions and objections, we can understand the background and context of the conflicts between the participating countries. We should note that the 1976 Informal Single Negotiating Text (ISNT) of the conference defines the meaning of MSR. In this draft, MSR is defined as "any study or related experimental work designed to increase mankind's knowledge of the marine environment."[27] According to Florian H. Th. Wegelein, even though the UNCLOS does not define the concept of MSR, this draft provides a direction in figuring out a definition.[28] Yet the draft definition was deleted when the 1977 Informal Composite Negotiating Text (ICNT) was adopted in the conference.

Part 1 of the guidelines stipulates provisions of the Convention related to MSR, including a brief history of the provisions of MSR of the Convention, general aspects of MSR under the Convention, MSR in related jurisdictional areas, MSR in the ABNJ, scientific research installations or equipment, development and transfer of maritime technology, protection and preservation of the marine environment, responsibility and liability, and settlement of disputes. Part 2 prescribes procedures for states to implement the provisions of the Convention related to MSR, while Part 3 specifies practical guidance on the implementation of the provisions of the Convention on MSR.[29]

Although this legal regime is not completely stable, based on these guidelines and the Intergovernmental Oceanographic Commission's activities, MSR is being conducted in ocean areas around the world. It would be desirable for coastal states who support regulation of MSR to agree on the legal status of these guidelines, which would facilitate the mediation of conflicts between the two sides regarding the strengthening of maritime jurisdiction in the EEZ. However, as in many cases, if the regulatory or normative power provided by the international organization is weak, a country will not easily give up its national interests. We should understand the conflicts between these two sides in this context.

III. Conflicts between Maritime Powers and Coastal States

1. The U.S.

The U.S. is a prototypical maritime power that strongly supports freedom of MSR. Even when the UNCLOS downsized the area of the high seas where such freedom is approved, the U.S. claimed that freedom of MSR should be respected. The U.S. prefers that coastal states under normal circumstances approve MSR conducted by foreign countries in the EEZ or on the extended continental shelf. Although the U.S. did not ratify the UNCLOS, it interprets the rules of MSR based on its views on customary international law.[30]

In 1983, the U.S. government announced that it would not claim jurisdiction over MSR within their EEZ. At that time, President Ronald Reagan announced a statement that respecting freedom and removing unnecessary regulations would promote national interests.

However, the U.S. also stated that it would acknowledge the coastal states' jurisdiction claims when they are under international laws.[31] The U.S.'s intention was confirmed once more by an official document written for the purpose of ratifying the UNCLOS and sent by the Department of State to the Senate in 1994, and its stance remains unchanged to this day. Currently, consistent with former President Reagan's announcement and relevant national laws, MSR is conducted freely in most EEZs. However MSR in U.S. territorial seas requires the prior permission of the U.S. government.[32]

Although the meaning of MSR is not stated in the UNCLOS, the U.S. government claims that MSR increases knowledge of marine environments. Also, as a concept separate from MSR, the U.S. has introduced "Marine Data Collection," which includes research and exploration of natural resources, hydrographical surveys, military activities such as military research, laying and management of submarine cables, environment monitoring, marine pollution assessment and marine weather data collection.[33] The U.S.'s intention in introducing Marine Data Collection as a distinctive concept was to create leeway in avoiding the regulation of MSR by coastal states. If these various activities at sea can be classified as Marine Data Collection, then the ability of coastal states to exercise jurisdiction will be reduced.

As the world's most powerful maritime power, the U.S. emphasizes freedom of MSR and takes this stance domestically as well. The U.S.'s basic marine policy principle is to promote national interests through the performance of maritime activities. The U.S. has a unique perspective on jurisdiction over the ocean that differs from the framework of jurisdiction under the Law of the Sea. The U.S. sees the high seas, EEZs and contiguous zones as international waters, and differentiates these areas from territorial seas and archipelagic waters. The U.S. supports the freedom of MSR and military activities through this integrated approach.[34] Thus, it is important to understand the U.S.'s strong support of the freedom of MSR in the context of its marine policy.

2. China

China, in contrast to the U.S., is a prototypical coastal state that advocates strict regulation and management of MSR. Since the beginning of the 3ʳᵈ UN Conference on the Law of the Sea, China has been insisting that prior approval of coastal states is essential, and that the domestic laws of coastal states must be complied with when MSR is conducted in jurisdictional sea areas. China submitted a joint proposal with developing countries during the 3ʳᵈ UN Conference making it clear that requirements for coastal states' approval of MSR conducted in jurisdictional sea areas should be explicitly stated in the Convention.[35]

The reason behind China's support of strict regulation and management of MSR is its objection to the monopolistic use of the sea by maritime powers. China claims that maritime powers have infringed upon the rights of coastal states by performing MSR and hydrographical surveys. It maintains that historical proof of imperialist nations' invasions by sea demonstrate the validity of this statement. To protect the rights and safety of coastal states, China emphasizes the principle of acquiring approval for MSR within jurisdictional sea areas.[36]

During the UN Law of the Sea Conference, the opinions of China and other coastal states, including developing countries, were accepted and incorporated into the UNCLOS. Developing countries, using their numerical superiority, codified their stance on the extension of maritime jurisdiction, and maritime powers were left with limited control over the agendas of coastal states. As a result, the UNCLOS lacked any definition of MSR and was left open to ambiguous interpretation of the relevant articles.[37]

China then completed its national legislative processes on the subject of MSR. In 1996, China enacted "Regulations on the Management of Foreign-Related Marine Scientific Research" as a State Council decree consisting of 15 provisions.[38] It should be noted that China regulated MSR with a decree, which is a legal norm of lower status than statute. Furthermore, the "Act on the Exclusive Economic Zone and Continental Shelf Law" of 1998 clearly stipulates jurisdiction over MSR. China's enactment of domestic laws and regulations related to MSR prior to the establishment of the EEZ and continental shelf is similar to that of Korea.

China incorporated relevant provisions of the UNCLOS into domestic law. However, the Chinese government strictly underlines the obligation of other states to conduct joint research with China in internal waters and territorial seas. It also stresses Chinese military authorities' right to intervene in research applications and China's control of the usage of research outcomes, which has sparked international controversy. They state the rights of coastal states more powerfully than the UNCLOS. This means that, unlike Korea, China strictly opposes freedom of MSR and is not hesitant to portray this stance in its domestic law as well.[39]

Specifically, the purposes of this legislation are to strengthen management of foreign MSR within China's jurisdictional sea areas, to accelerate international cooperation on MSR, and to strengthen national security, as well as to protect their rights at sea. It is noteworthy that China emphasized security as a value of priority during the UN Law of the Sea Conference.[40] This legislation applies to internal waters, territorial seas and other jurisdictional areas of China, including the EEZ and continental shelf.[41] This legislation clearly states that exploration of marine mineral resources should comply with the related laws and administrative decrees of China, which applies to marine oil resources, surveys of fishery resources, and observation of marine wild animals under protection.[42]

The institutions controlling MSR are the State Council, related agencies, and China's competent state administrative authority for marine affairs.[43] According to the legislation, within internal waters and territorial seas, only joint research with China is allowed, while in the EEZ and on the continental shelf, both joint research and unilateral research by foreigners are permitted.[44] If a foreigner desires to conduct unilateral research, an application must be submitted through diplomatic routes to the competent state administrative authority for marine affairs six months prior to the estimated research commencement date, and the competent authority for marine affairs is obligated to report this to the State Council to acquire ratification.[45] In the case of joint research, China can apply on behalf of the other researching state to receive permission to conduct MSR. In this case, the Ministry of Foreign Affairs, military authorities and the State Council jointly evaluate the application.[46] A distinctive feature of this regulation is that China's military authorities take part in the screening process to assure national security. This legislation also prescribes in detail the usage of research materials, forbidden activities, cessation of research activities, and penalties for violation.

3. Japan

Unlike Korea and China, Japan has not enacted any national laws or regulations for MSR. In other words, they did not adhere to Article 3, subparagraph 1 of the EEZ and Continental Shelf Act, where it is stated that Japan's national law applies to MSR in the Japanese sea areas. Instead, Japan enacted "Guidelines for Conducting the MSR in Areas under the National Jurisdiction of Japan" in 1996.[47]

These guidelines, comprising three provisions, were enacted to avoid unfair delays or rejections of foreigners' applications for scientific research in their jurisdictional areas and to promote the utilization of research outcomes.[48] Foreign nationals or institutions planning to conduct MSR in the Japanese EEZ or on the Japanese continental shelf are requested to submit a formal request of consent six months prior to the expected research commencement date through a diplomatic route and must receive approval from the Japanese government.[49] According to the applicable laws, if the research involves the capture, collection or exploration of marine animals or plants, then approval from the Minister of Agriculture, Forestry and Fisheries is required. In the territorial seas, activities involving capture or collection are not permitted.[50]

The Japan's reasoning for only announcing guidelines instead of legislating domestic laws for MSR is understood as an expression of its intention to follow the tendency of maritime powers to minimize regulation of MSR.[51] Japan claims that even in intermediate zones where the delimitation of maritime boundaries is not complete, the management of marine resources and the protection of marine environments should be carried out through MSR.[52]

Korea and Japan went through a serious conflict in 2006 concerning MSR in the area surrounding Dokdo, which conflict was subsequently settled for the time being. The concern of the Korean government is to block all possible direct or indirect influence of Japan on the territoriality of Dokdo.

China and Japan have also been in conflict for a long time over MSR. The two countries exchanged diplomatic notes verbally in February of 2001 regarding advanced notice for MSR in the East China Sea, but it has become a meaningless agreement which is not being adhered to.[53] In this situation, conflict over MSR in the areas around Diaoyudao or Okinotorishima can reignite any time.

4. Korea

Korea has taken an active position on MSR from a relatively early period. Prior to the introduction of the EEZ regime in the seas around the Korean peninsula, it enacted the Marine Scientific Research Act on January 5, 1995, fully regulating issues related to marine scientific research. This Act was originally intended to prescribe the procedures necessary for foreigners or international organizations to conduct MSR in the jurisdictional sea areas of Korea, and to contribute to the promotion of marine science and technology through efficient administration and release of the research data resulting from MSR conducted by Korean nationals.

The Act was overhauled on August 13, 2013, and entered into force on November 14, 2013. Although the Act had been amended several times over the past fifteen years, only technical issues had been dealt with in prior revisions to maintain coherence and consistency with other legislation. In this context, the revision of 2013 is noteworthy in many ways. The Korean government amended the Marine Scientific Research Act with a view to promoting efficient implementation of the relevant policies.

The main reasons for amending the Marine Scientific Research Act were as follows: First, the Korean government clarified the scope of foreigners permitted to conduct MSR in the jurisdictional sea areas of Korea so as to minimize unnecessary diplomatic friction over MSR issues. That is, any person of dual nationality as stipulated under the Nationality Act, or any juridical person incorporated under the laws of Korea which has its head office or principal office in a foreign country or in respect of which more than half of the stock or equity shares are owned by foreigners, has come to be defined as a foreigner.[54]

Second, the government sought to prevent future illegal MSR in the jurisdictional sea areas of Korea by stipulating that any MSR vessel in the charge of a foreigner seeking to call at a port of Korea that has not obtained permission or consent to conduct MSR shall obtain permission from the Korean government.[55]

Third, foreigners shall have the obligation to ensure fair sharing of the benefits accrued as a result of their MSR. This is meant to set a domestic legal basis regarding the sharing of benefits generated from the results of MSR conducted with the permission or consent of the Korean government.[56]

Fourth, penal provisions for acts of violation have been amended to more reasonable levels, and all legal terms written in Chinese characters have been converted into Hangul (the Korean alphabet) in principle. In addition, in order to make the Act more understandable to the general public, difficult terminology has been replaced with simpler terms, and long, complex sentences have been made more concise.

Due to the Act, however, the differences between MSR, hydrographic surveys and military surveys have become ambiguous since it only provides a broad definition of MSR as "the act of researching or exploring, etc., the seabed, subsoil, the waters superjacent to the seabed, and the adjacent atmosphere for the purpose of studying and clarifying the natural phenomena of the oceans and seas."[57] For example, if a vessel of a foreigner intending to perform hydrographic surveys in the EEZ of Korea submits an application for MSR, the Act may provide weak grounds for the Korean government to decline the grant of consent.[58] The government may argue that it is possible to decline the application on the grounds that research and surveys are distinct from each other under domestic law.

The Territorial Sea and Contiguous Zone Act of Korea, incorporating the relevant provisions in the UNCLOS, specifies the "carrying out of research or survey activities" as an act prejudicial to the peace, good order or security of the Republic of Korea.[59] It may be controversial, however, whether this provision can be applied to MSR or hydrographic surveys conducted in the EEZ since the territorial sea and the EEZ differ significantly in the level of sovereignty exercised. Furthermore, the 2009 Measurement, Hydrographic Surveys and Cadastre Act regulates hydrographic surveys and hydrographic measurement separately.[60]

As regards the MSR issues of Korea, research conducted in intermediate zones under the Korea-Japan Fisheries Agreement and the Korea-China Fisheries Agreement are of major significance. The Korean government made its own declaration on optional exceptions in accordance with the dispute settlement procedures of the UNCLOS in 2006. These issues are not likely to be resolved until maritime boundary delimitation between neighboring states is completed around the Korean peninsula. Until then, the Korean government should take a cautious approach to MSR issues considering the harmonization and coherence between domestic and international law. The Korean government has incorporated the provisions of the UNCLOS related to the EEZ and MSR into domestic law by means of the Marine Scientific Research Act and the EEZ Act.[61] The Marine Scientific Research Act of 2013 was partially revised in 2020 in relation to "marine scientific research in waters under foreign jurisdiction or areas beyond national jurisdiction."

IV. Policy-Oriented Jurisprudence

In order to protect and preserve marine environments effectively, an evaluation of the effects of scientific research on marine environments is needed. In particular, to prevent planet-wide marine pollution, the full cooperation of the international community is crucial. On a related note, the preamble of the UNCLOS declares the establishment of a legal order for the seas and oceans to accelerate the study, protection and preservation of marine environments. Furthermore, its articles stipulate that states shall endeavor to participate actively in regional and global programmes to acquire knowledge for the assessment of nature and to investigate the extent of pollution and our exposure to it, as well as its pathways, risks and remedies.

However, maritime powers and coastal states are still in serious conflict regardless of normative justifiability. Maritime powers emphasize the use and exploitation of the sea, stressing the development of the entire international community as the rationale, while coastal states disagree with the maritime powers' arguments in order to protect their own rights and security. Surely neither side can approach this problem merely by considering the functional use of the oceans or legal appropriateness. Development of the law of the sea is a process of compromise between maritime powers and coastal states, and it is of limited utility to view both sides' policies of protecting their national interests solely from a legal perspective. It is rather more useful to understand these issues in the context of policy-oriented jurisprudence, which emphasizes the political aspects of the law.

From the perspective of policy-oriented jurisprudence, international public order or world public order can be established by guaranteeing the minimum exclusive interest and the maximum comprehensive interest. The common interest or community interest can be derived through this process. According to Myres S. McDougal, the top authority on policy-oriented jurisprudence, the historical function of effective international law is to protect the interest of the international community and to maintain public world order by eliminating excessive exclusive interest.[62] McDougal lists the principles involved with the freedom of the high seas as a demonstrative case regarding comprehensive interest, and provides the principles of coastal states' security related to the law of the sea as an example of exclusive interest.[63] Therefore, conflict between the two sides regarding MSR is due either to collision between exclusive interests or to collision between exclusive interest and exclusive interest disguised as common interest. Until the two sides give up their exclusive interests to make concessions, there is still a long way to go before real settlement of the conflict can be reached.

Conflicts such as those between Korea, China and Japan can be reduced if we stress the common interest or common society interest as described by policy-oriented jurisprudence. There are ways of conducting MSR in the intermediate zones or provisional zones established by the three fisheries agreements of Northeast Asia, such as joint performance of MSR, MSR carried out under the condition of prior notice, or the introduction of specific zones for MSR. If these three countries consider military or hydrographic surveys to be different from MSR activities, as the U.S. does, then conflict over MSR can ease.

Conflicts between maritime powers and coastal states are, however, a current reality. The U.S. and Japan understand MSR from the perspective of maritime powers, while China understands it from the view of coastal states. The U.S. and China continue to remain in conflict over exploration of the sea as manifested in the conduct of MSR. Disputes over the sovereignty of Diayudao/Senkaku Retto and maritime boundary delimitation between China and Japan have become more evident through conflicts over MSR. What would Korea's position be in such conflicts? The stance of the Korean government on this issue will be evaluated based on management of the revised MSR statutes. Rumination on the meaning of international law is needed in the context of the harsh reality of international politics.

Notes

* This article has been written with updates and changes based on the author's Korean article, "Conflicts over Marine Scientific Research between Maritime Powers and Coastal States" in the Korean Journal of International Law, Vol.60, No.3, 2015

1. David Freestone, "The Law of the Sea Convention at 30: Successes, Challenges and New Agendas," *The International Journal of Marine and Coastal Law 27* (2012), pp.679 –680

2. Then Chilean navy commodore Jorge Martinez Bush suggested that, in order to regulate fisheries and MSR activities, as well as exploration and exploitation of mineral resources in the broad high seas adjacent to the EEZ in the near future, they should have an embryo of sovereignty. Yet his statement was unsuccessful (José Antonio de Yturriaga, *The International Regime of Fisheries: From Unclos 1982 to the Presential Sea*, (The Hague, Boston, London, Martinus Nijhoff Publishers, 1997), pp.227-232).

3. Stuart Kaye, "Freedom of Navigation in a Post 9/11 World: Security and Creeping Jurisdiction," David Freestone, Richard Barnes and David M Ong (eds), *The Law of the Sea: Progress and Prospects*, 2006, pp.347-349

4. The U.S. and China were in serious conflict due to the collision of a U.S. EP-3 reconnaissance plane and a Chinese F-8 combat plane which occurred in April 2001 in the air above the sea 87 nautical miles southeast of Hainan Island. The two countries confronted each other regarding the USNS Bowditch incident in the Yellow Sea in March 2001 and the USNS Impeccable incident in the South China Sea in March 2009 over the legality of the collection of military information in the EEZ. The two countries were also in confrontation over the aircraft carrier USS George Washington sailing into the EEZ during the Korea-U.S. joint military exercises after the shelling of Yeonpyeong Island in November 2010 (Yu Zhirong, "Jurisprudential Analysis of the U.S. Navy's Military Surveys in the Exclusive Economic Zones of Coastal Countries," Peter Dutton (ed) *Military Activities in the EEZ: A U.S.-China Dialogue on Security and International Law in the Maritime Commons*, 2010, pp.37-39; Jerome A. Cohen and Jon M. Van Dyke, "Limits of Tolerance," South China Morning Post, December 7, 2010).

5. The most controversial issue in the Southern Bluefin Tuna Case and the Whaling Case was the legitimacy of Japan's right to conduct scientific research on living marine resources (Barbarak Kwiatkowsk, "Southern Bluefin Tuna (Australia and New Zealand v. Japan). Jurisdiction and Admissibility," *American Journal of International Law, Vol 95 No.1*, 2001, pp. 165-167; Donald R. Rothwell, "The Whaling Case: Australian Perspectives," *Kokusai Mondai*, No.636, November 2014, pp.8-9).

6. Myron Nordquist, Shabtai Rosenne and Alexander Yankov, *United Nations Convention on the Law of the Sea 1982 A Commentary Vol. IV*, 1990, pp.429-431

7. Florian H. Th. Wegelein, *Marine Scientific Research: The Operation And Status of Research*

Vessels And Other Platforms in International Law, (Leiden/Boston: Martinus Nijhoff Publishers 2005), pp.25-26

8. Marine scientific research has been developed from experimental maritime research, which was traditionally conducted in certain sea areas. After WW II, the purpose of MSR was not limited only to pure scientific research, but expanded to include research on marine resources and the protection of marine environments. This was when conflict between maritime powers and coastal states started. As maritime powers invested heavily in applied scientific research, increased numbers of independent developing countries strongly opposed the monopolistic use of the sea by maritime powers (Donald Rothwell and Tim Stephens, *The International Law of the Sea* (Oxford and Portland, Oregon, Hart Publishing, 2010), pp.322-323).

9. The 1958 Convention on the High Seas comprehensively yet not explicitly includes MSR in the freedom of the seas (Article 2), and the Convention on Fishing and Conservation of the Living Resources of the High Seas states the importance of MSR related to the management of fisheries based on scientific findings (Article 7(2)). The Convention on the Continental Shelf considers the interests of coastal states and maritime powers and states that research on the continental shelf requires the consent of coastal states, while also stating that coastal states should not disapprove of scientific research of a purely physical or biological nature (Article 5(8)).

10. Article 58(1); David Freestone, *op. cit.*, pp.680–681

11. Yu Zhirong, *op. cit.*, pp.37-39

12. Article 246(3)(5)

13. Article 56(1)(b)(ii)

14. Article 246(3)

15. *Ibid.*

16. Article 246(5)

17. For example, the UNCLOS states that disputes over MSR should be resolved through compulsory procedures. It states that in the case of (i) exercise by the coastal state of a right or discretion in accordance with Article 246; or (ii) a decision by the coastal state to order suspension or cessation of a research project in accordance with Article 253, disputes concerning the interpretation or application of the provisions of this Convention with regard to MSR do not have to be settled in accordance with Section 2 (Article 297 (2)(a)). Additionally, a dispute arising from an allegation by the researching state that with respect to a specific project the coastal state is not exercising its rights under Articles 246 and 253 in a manner compatible with this Convention shall be submitted, at the request of either party, to conciliation under Annex V, Section 2, provided that the conciliation commission shall not call into question the exercise by the coastal state of its discretion to designate specific areas as referred to in Article 246(6), or of its discretion to withhold consent in

accordance with Article 246(5) (Article 297(2)(b)). It also states that a state may declare optional exceptions to the compulsory procedures regarding disputes concerning military activities, including military activities by government vessels and aircraft engaged in non-commercial service, and disputes concerning law enforcement activities in regard to the exercise of sovereign rights or jurisdiction excluded from the jurisdiction of a court or tribunal under Article 297(2) or (3) (Article 298(1)(b)). Therefore, there are several ways to avoid the compulsory dispute settlement process.

18. Donald Rothwell and Tim Stephens, op. cit., pp.328-329

19. UNCLOS Article 246(6)

20. UNCLOS Article 247

21. UNCLOS Article 248

22. UNCLOS Article 249

23. UNCLOS Article 252

24. UNCLOS Article 253

25. For example, with regard to pure scientific research or elementary level scientific research, states and competent international organizations should respect the coastal state's right to participate in the research and to send a representative, should provide the coastal state with a preliminary report and the final results after the research has been concluded, should allow the results to be made available internationally through appropriate channels as quickly as possible, and should remove installations or equipment used for the research after the research is completed (Article 249(1)).

26. United Nations Division for Ocean Affairs and the Law of the Sea, Office of Legal Affairs, *Marine Scientific Research: A revised guide to the implementation of the relevant provisions of the United Nations Convention on the Law of the Sea*, (United Nations, New York 2010).

27. The Informal Single Negotiating Text 18, which was issued in 1976, provides in Part III, Art. 48 of its draft that: "[f]or the purpose of this Convention, 'marine scientific research' means any study or related experimental work designed to increase mankind's knowledge of the marine environment" (*Ibid.*, pp.5-6).

28. Florian H. Th. Wegelein, *op. cit.*, pp.11-12

29. Marine Scientific Research: A revised guide to the implementation of the relevant provisions of the United Nations Convention on the Law of the Sea (http://www.ioc-unesco.org/, last visit on October 2019)

30. J. Ashley Roach, "Marine Scientific Research and the New Law of the Sea," *Ocean Development & International Law 27* (1996), pp.59-60

31. President's Ocean Policy Statement, March 10, 1983, *Public Papers of the Presidents: Ronald Reagan*, pp.378-379

32. Authorization is required for surveys in areas within the EEZ that are designated as "marine protected areas" such as "national marine sanctuary" or "marine national monument." Surveys in areas related to other living resources or dumping also require authorization. (https://www.state.gov/marine-scientific-research-consent-overview/) (Last visit in October 2019)

33. https://www.state.gov/marine-scientific-research-consent-overview/ (Last visit in October 2019)

34. Sam Bateman, "Security and the Law of the Sea in East Asia: Navigational Regimes and Exclusive Economic Zones," David Freestone, Richard Barnes and David M Ong (eds), *The Law of the Sea: Progress and Prospects*, 2006, pp.379-380

35. Working Paper on Marine Scientific Research submitted by the Chinese Delegation, 19 July 1973 (A/AC.13S/SC.III/L.42; A/AC.138/SC.III/L.55)

36. Zou Keyuan, "Governing Marine Scientific Research in China", *Ocean Development & International Law, 34(2003)*, pp.1-3

37. Disputes may easily arise between the two sides over interpretation of Article 246, which gives authority to coastal states in regulating MSR on the continental shelf and in the EEZ, where coastal states can exercise their discretionary power, and of Article 251, which provides general standards and guidelines.

38. Regulations on the Management of Foreign-Related Marine Scientific Research, See, Zou Keyuan, *China's Marine Legal System and the Law of the Sea*, (Leiden/Boston: Martinus Nijhoff Publishers, 2005), pp.289-311

39. Articles 4, 5, 7, 10, 13, Regulations on the Management of Foreign-Related Marine Scientific Research

40. *Ibid.* Article 1

41. *Ibid.* Article 2

42. *Ibid.* Article 2

43. *Ibid.* Article 3

44. *Ibid.* Article 4

45. *Ibid.* Article 4

46. *Ibid.* Article 5

47. Masahiro Miyoshi, "Research Activities in the EEZ," Tadao Kuribayashi and Takamine Sugihara (eds), *The Law of the Sea and Japan*, (Tokyo: Yushinto, 2010), pp.175-177

48. Article 1, Guidelines for Conducting the MSR in Areas under the National Jurisdiction of Japan

49. *Ibid.* Article 2

50. *Ibid.* Article 3

51. Atsuko Kanehara, "Marine Scientific Research in the Waters Where Claims of the Exclusive Economic Zone Overlap between Japan and the Republic of Korea - Incidents between the Two States in 2006," *The Japanese Annual of International Law* No.49(2006), pp.104-105

52. *Ibid.*, pp.115-122

53. Masahiro Miyoshi, *op. cit.*, pp.177-178

54. Article 2(3), Marine Scientific Research Act

55. *Ibid.*, Article 15-2

56. *Ibid.*, Article 10(1)①

57. *Ibid.*, Article 2(1)

58. *Ibid.*, Article 7(4)

59. Article 5(2), Territorial Sea and Contiguous Zone Act

60. The Measurement, Hydrographic Surveys and Cadastre Act defines hydrographic surveys as hydrographic measurement, oceanographic observation, sea lane surveys and oceanographic name surveys whose purpose is to prevent marine disasters, maintain maritime traffic safety and the preservation, use, or development of the sea, or secure maritime jurisdiction, thus defining hydrographic surveys more broadly than hydrographic measurements (Part 2). This is a typical example of local legislation that does not reflect the standards of international law.

61. Korea's Marine Scientific Research Act stipulates the need for authorization from the Minister of Oceans and Fisheries regarding applications for MSR within the territorial sea, and requires consent for research in the EEZ and on the continental shelf (Articles 6 and 7). On the other hand, the UNCLOS stipulates the need for the consent of coastal states regarding MSR conducted in the territorial sea, in the EEZ, or on the continental shelf (Articles 245 and 246).

62. Myres S. McDougal and William Burke, *The Public Order of the Oceans - A Contemporary International Law of the Sea*, 1987, pp.1-3

63. *Ibid*, p.10

The Meaning of "Service" as One of the Requirements for Recognition and Enforcement of Foreign Judgments

-Focusing on the Supreme Court of Korea 2017-Da-257746 Judgment-

KIM Young-Seok
Research Judge
Supreme Court of Korea, Seoul, Korea

Key Words

2017-Da-257746, Recognition and Enforcement of Foreign Judgment, substituted service, Hague Service Convention, Civil Procedure Act, Hague Judgments Convention

1. Overview

In principle, a judgment rendered in a foreign country is effective only within the country, thus whether to recognize or enforce the judgment must be in accordance with the laws of the recognizing and enforcing country. In this regard, Article 217(1) of the Civil Procedure Act of the Republic of Korea (hereinafter the "CPA") provides for four requirements: (1) Jurisdiction, (2) service (excluding service by public notice and similar types of service), (3) public policy, and (4) reciprocity. The judgment discussed in this paper,

Supreme Court of Korea 2017-Da-257746 Judgment (hereinafter "the Judgment"), deals with the "service" requirement.

The Judgment concluded that service to a person who has a certain personal relationship with the recipient (hereinafter "substituted service"[1]) is legitimate service as a requirement for recognition and enforcement. It held that substituted service is not similar to "service by public notice," and repealed all existing precedents that took a different position. The Judgment is meaningful, legally valid, and consistent with the practice of cross-border transactions, in which service abroad is frequently performed.

2. The Judgment

2.1. Facts

2.1.1. Service of process in Korea at the request of New Zealand court

In February 2013, the plaintiff (a bank incorporated under the laws of New Zealand, hereinafter "P") brought an action against the defendant (a person doing business in New Zealand, hereinafter "D") in a New Zealand court (Auckland High Court) seeking performance of a loan and guarantee obligation.

On February 27, 2013, P applied to the New Zealand court for extraterritorial service of documents like complaint, notice of action, and interim motion for summary judgment (hereinafter 'the documents') on the grounds that D was residing in the Republic of Korea (hereinafter 'Korea'). Subsequently, D's husband instead of D received the documents at their apartment (D's residence) on May 1, 2013 through the following route:

New Zealand court ➡ Ministry of Justice of New Zealand ➡ Embassy of New Zealand in Korea ➡ Ministry of Foreign Affairs of the Korea ➡ Court Administration Office of the Supreme Court of Korea ➡ Seoul Central District Court (=Korean court with jurisdiction over D's residence) cooperated (Cooperation No. 2013-185, Case No. 2013-Ruh 51) ➡ Documents were served on D's husband on May 1, 2013 [substituted service].

2.1.2. New Zealand court Judgment

On May 1, 2013, the New Zealand court was notified that the case documents had been served on D through the same reverse process as above. On August 15, 2013, the court held a hearing for summary judgment, and entered judgment (hereinafter the "NZ Judgment")[2] in favor of P on the same day, ordering the payment of NZ$8,336,110.71 plus delay damages, which was confirmed as such on September 12, 2013.

2.1.3. Application for the Enforcement of the NZ Judgment in Korea

On June 23, 2014, P filed an action in the Seoul Central District Court seeking a judgment for the enforcement judgment of the NZ Judgment. The first instance court (Seoul Central District Court, 2014GaHap544291) and the appellate court (Seoul High Court, 2016Na2052577) judged in favor of P, finding that substituted service was legitimate under Article 217(1)2 of the CPA.

The courts reasoned that substituted service gives a party more chances to become aware of the documents and prepare for the lawsuits, which is different from service by public notice carried out by posting on the court's bulletin board. Also, the growing importance of international cooperation and coordination in the field of justice was cited as one of the main bases for the conclusion.

D appealed the appellate court judgment and the case was heard by the Supreme Court of Korea as case number 2017-Da-257746.

2.2. Overview of the Court's Reasoning in 2017-Da-257746

The Supreme Court of Korea held that substituted service is legitimate under Article 217(1)2 of the Civil Procedure Act largely for the following reasons, and overruled all previous Supreme Court of Korea judgments, such as Supreme Court of Korea Judgment 92-Da-2585, Supreme Court of Korea Judgment 2008-Da-65815 (hereinafter collectively referred to as "existing precedents") to the extent that they were inconsistent with the Judgment (Supreme Court of Korea 2017-Da-257746.)

(1) Korea acceded to the Hague Service Convention[3] in 2000, but New Zealand has not.[4] Accordingly, service of process in Korea upon the request of New Zealand is governed by the International Judicial Mutual Assistance in Civil Matters Act (hereinafter "IJMA"), Article 15[5] of which stipulates that the service of process requested by a foreign country is governed by the laws of Korea. Substituted service is one of the lawful services prescribed by the CPA, making it legal under Korean law.

(2) Article 217(1)2 of the CPA aims to protect defendants who lose a lawsuit without having the opportunity to defend themselves.[6] The method of substituted service, which allows the documents to be served to a person who has the intelligence to discern the matter, such as his clerk, employee or cohabitant, is much less likely to deprive the defendant of the opportunity to exercise the right of defense. This is not like the service by public notice which gives effect to service by just posting on the court bulletin board.

(3) Existing precedents holding that substituted service is not

proper under Article 217(1)2 of the CPA did not directly address the legitimacy of substituted service, but merely referred the service as a "general theory" of proper service.[7] In addition, the provision only excludes service by public notice and "similar types of service," and does not specifically limit other methods of service.

(4) If the position of the existing precedents is maintained, service of process for foreign trials becomes more stringent. In particular, disallowing substituted service would mean that the documents would have to be delivered directly to the representative of the corporation where the defendant is a corporation, which would lead to unfair results.[8]

(5) International trust in the judicial process may be undermined if the existing precedents were to be maintained, and Korea may be perceived as acting in a contradictory manner because substituted service is valid under its own laws.

3. Review

3.1. Recognition and Enforcement of Foreign Judgments and Service of Process

In a modern world where individuals and entities frequently control foreign assets, the recognition and enforcement of foreign judgments has naturally become a part of legal practice. This is because a plaintiff who obtains a winning judgment has no choice but to seek enforcement of the judgment in the country of the defendant's property if there is no property of the defendant in the forum state.

However, in principle, a judgment rendered in a foreign country is only effective in the country that rendered the judgment, so whether the judgment is recognized and enforced is determined by the courts of the country where recognition and enforcement are requested. Article 217 of CPA provides for four requirements, with the subparagraph relating to service quoted below:

Article 27 of the Civil Enforcement Act (Enforcement Judgment)
(2) An application for an enforcement judgment shall be dismissed where it falls under any of the following subparagraphs:
1. When the conditions of Article 217 of the CPA are not met
Article 217 of the CPA (Recognition of Foreign Judgments)
(1) A final judgment of a foreign court or any decisions having the same effect (hereinafter referred to as "final judgment, etc.") shall be recognized where all of the following requirements are met.:
2. The losing defendant has been served with the complaint or equivalent document and the due date notice or order in a lawful manner with time for defense (excluding service by public notice and similar types of service,) or would have responded to the lawsuit even if not served

---

3.2. Purpose of Exclusion of Service by Public Notice

3.2.1. Legality under the *lex fori* principle

According to the *lex fori* principle,[9] the legality of service made in the forum state (country A) is judged based on the law of that country A. For example, service by public notice available under the laws of country A is a legitimate service. If the defendant resides in another country (country B) and the service is made in country B as requested by the courts of country A, the law of country B functions as a criterion for determining the legality of service along with the law of country A.[10] Therefore, the court of the recognizing and enforcing country (country C) cannot treat the service by public notice made under the law of either country A or country B as improper just because documents were served by public notice.

The European Court of Justice held that service by public service (Öffentliche Zustellung) under the German Civil Procedure Act (Gerichtsverfassungsgesetz)[11] in German Court was not unlawful because every effort had been made to determine the location of the other party in accordance with the principles of diligence and good faith.[12] The Supreme Court of Korea has also found that service cannot be said to have been made in a proper manner within the meaning of Article 217 of the CPA, where the manner and procedure for service did not follow the law of the forum state (see Supreme Court of Korea Judgment 2008-Da-31089).[13]

3.2.2. Purpose of the Exclusion of Public Notice

However, it is the right of a sovereign state to take the position that it will not recognize and enforce foreign judgments where the losing defendant's right to defend has been violated in substance, even if the service delivered in the trial is legal. This is where the legality and timeliness of service comes into play via the Article 217 of CPA.[14] Legality and timeliness have been described as requirements to ensure the right to "due process" under Anglo-American law or the right to "rechtliches Gehör" under German law.[15]

Service by public notice is not limited to public notice under Korean law (Article 194 of the CPA), but also refers to any type of public notice available in accordance with the laws of individual countries, including ① public service under Article 185 of the German Civil Procedure Act discussed above, ② service for inspection (remise au parquet) under Article 684 of the French Code de procédure civile,[16] ③ public service under Article 110 of the Japanese Code of Civil Procedure.[17] The foregoing are summarized in the following table:

Classification	Trial Court (Country A)	Process of Service (Country B)	Recognizing and Enforcing Country (Country C)
Example 1	Service of process in Country A is made in accordance with A's laws	n/a	· Service itself is legal in Country A. · However, if the service falls under any category of improper service, Country C may refuse to recognize and enforce under its laws
Example 2	Country A requests extraterritorial service in accordance with A's laws	Country B (requested by Country A) serves documents in accordance with B's laws	· Country A's request for cooperation & Country B's service of process are legal. · However, if service was improper, Country C may refuse to recognize and enforce under its laws
Notes	If Country C does not have a provision excluding service by public notice as the requirement for recognition and enforcement of foreign judgments like Article 217(1)2 of the CPA ➟ C cannot refuse recognition and enforcement on the grounds of improper service issue		

3.3. Reasonable Conclusion Considering the Particularity of This Case

3.3.1. The particularity of this case

This case is unusual in that it involves Korea as the recognizing and enforcing country as well as the country of service following a request for cooperation from a New Zealand court. In other words, according to the table above, Korea is both country B and Country C. If the country of service (Country B) were a third country (other than New Zealand or Korea), the Korean court would have had to figure out the specific regulations or rules of the third country, but in this case, Korean courts were relieved of that difficulty because the country of service was also Korea.

If a defendant does not have an adequate opportunity to present its defense in the process of substituted service, it would fall under the definition of "similar types of service" in Article 217(1)2 of the CPA, and would not meet the requirements for foreign recognition and enforcement. This is the position taken by previous Supreme Court of Korea precedents. However, the Judgment (Supreme Court of Korea 2017-Da-257746) changed the existing precedent by holding that substituted service not included in the "similar types of service."

3.3.2. The Judgment is reasonable

Service of process is the act of notifying parties and other litigants in order to give them an opportunity to be informed of the contents of the documents in a lawsuit.[18] Substituted service is a variant of service of process which is not directly delivered to the litigant, so it is closer to the service by public notice. It is therefore possible to treat substituted service like service by public notice and as illegitimate in terms of the recognition and enforcement of foreign judgments.[19] However, unlike service by public notice which is processed with the court's bulletin board only,[20] substituted service is based on a reasonable expectation that documents are likely to be delivered to the defendant based on the relationship between the defendant and the recipient.

In the modern world where documents cannot always be delivered to the parties directly, substituted service is a significant part of practice and disallowing it in litigation is not practical at all, especially for overseas corporations. As the effectiveness of substituted service can be limited through established legal principles, it cannot be said that there is significant harm to the parties. Therefore, the Judgment's conclusion that substituted service constitutes proper service as a requirement for recognition and enforcement of a foreign judgment is valid.[21]

3.4. Critical Review

Despite the correct result, the Judgment was rendered without clearly distinguishing between the legality of service of process itself and the legality of service of process as a requirement for recognition and enforcement.

3.4.1. Confusion between service per se and the service as a requirement for recognition and enforcement

First, the Judgment held that "service of process in Korea is governed by the laws of Korea (Article 15 of the IJMA), and substituted service, being one of the legitimate methods of service prescribed by Article 186 of the CPA, should be considered legitimate service." Yet, the issue in this case is not whether the service was lawful, but whether, even if the service was lawful, it could be assessed as sufficiently guaranteeing the defendant's right to defense. In other words, it is not whether the service itself was lawful under the laws of the forum state (Country A, New Zealand in this case) or process of service (Country B, which is Korea), but whether the defendant's right to defense was violated in substance by the service in the recognizing and enforcing country (Country C, which is also Korea).

Accordingly, it is difficult to agree with the Judgment's reasoning that the legal service requirements for recognition and enforcement are satisfied if it is legal under the laws of the country of service of process (Country B). Such logic leads to the conclusion that even a document is served by public notice in Korea would meet the legal service requirement for recognition and enforcement. It is, after all, one of the legitimate services under the CPA, which is permitted by the IJMA. The reasoning above of the Judgment is, therefore, flawed.

3.4.2. Lack of logical consistency

Secondly, the Judgment also reasoned that it would be logically inconsistent for a Korean court to deny the legality of substituted service delivered in Korea. This argument is understandable and desirable for international comity, but it could be misconstrued to mean that any form of service done in Country B will always be recognized as legitimate in Country C where a specific country has the status of both Country B and Country C, even if it substantively violates the defendant's right to defend.

For example, it seems that service by public notice in Japan (Country B) will be judged to have failed to meet the requirements of recognition and enforcement by Korea (Country C). It is not reasonable to treat the same service differently just to avoid logical contradictions. From the point of view of the losing defendant, the infringement of its defense rights is the same, and it is only disadvantaged by the coincidental circumstance that the country of service and the country of recognition and enforcement are the same. Therefore, this reasoning is also flawed.

4. Conclusion

The Judgment concluded that substituted service, like regular service, constitutes "lawful service" under Article 217(1)2 of the CPA as a requirement for recognition and enforcement of a foreign judgment, and changed all existing precedents that took a different position to the extent that they were inconsistent with the Judgment. The author believes that it is a significant judgment in line with cross-border transaction practice, where service abroad is frequently an issue.

Although not directly stated in this case, it should be noted that foreign court's direct service to a domestic resident through postal channels without going through diplomatic channels, including the Hague Service Convention, is not proper service of process for purpose of recognition and enforcement. Supreme Court of Korea Judgment 92-Da-2585, which limited the scope of consular service to its own citizens, is still effective in this respect.

In addition, in a situation where there is no choice but to serve a document by public notice in Country B, it is preferable for Country B to reply to Country A with "undeliverable status" rather than give such public notice, which might result in embarrassment to Country B as an enforcing and recognizing country in the future. If electronic service of process is introduced, the existing foreign service system established under Hague Service Convention will be revolutionized. Thus, it is necessary to pay attention to the electronic service of process currently being considered in the EU and Anglo-American countries. Also, in insolvency cases where efficient and collective debt-restructuring is required, the situations where public notice is allowed for service should be expanded beyond the very limited circumstances where it is currently allowed.[22]

Compared to the past practice, where service abroad was uncommon and difficult in practice to accomplish,[23] Korea's service system has come a long way. We look forward to the establishment of a more effective service of process system that is both efficient and protective of the rights of the parties in the modern world, where foreign creditors and assets located abroad are common.

Notes

1. "Substituted Service" originally refers to diverse methods of service, but the term is used as above in this article.

2. Summary judgment is rendered in a judicial proceeding in which cross-examination is guaranteed, and therefore subject to due recognition and enforcement, which is the difference between summary judgments and confession judgments. For reference, the Supreme Court of Korea, in 2009-Da- 68910 Judgment, held that a confession judgment is registered by reviewing only a few documents without proceeding further trial or examination upon the plaintiff's petition, and therefore not subject to recognition and enforcement. For details, see Ja-Heon Koo, "Meaning of a Foreign Court Judgment Subject to Enforcement Judgment," Supreme Court of Korea Case Law Commentary No. 83, Court Library (2010), p. 318 et seq.

3. Hague Convention on the Service Abroad of Judicial and Extrajudicial Documents in Civil and Commercial Matters.

4. Korea acceded to Hague Service Convention on January 13, 2000 (effective August 1, 2000), but New Zealand had not acceded to the Convention until now. Since its entry into force on February 10, 1969, about 79 major countries, including the United States, the United Kingdom, Germany, France, China, and Japan, have acceded to Hague Service Convention, and Korea joined the Convention in 2000. https://www.hcch.net/en/instruments/conventions/status-table/?cid=17 (last visited June 7, 2022). For details, *See* HccH Permanent Bureau, *Practical Handbook on the Operation of the Service Convention* (4th Ed.), HccH (2016).

5. Article 15 (Proper Law) The matters entrusted by a foreign country shall be implemented in conformity with the laws of the Republic of Korea: Provided that in a case where the foreign court requests to implement it through a specified way, if such a way is not contrary to any law of the Republic of Korea, the implementation shall be made in such a way.

6. *See* the Supreme Court of Korea Judgment 2015-Da-207747. The text of Article 217(1)2 of the CPA does not directly provide for the requirement of "guaranteeing the right to defense," so there is room to treat a violation of the right to defense that occurs when the legality and timeliness of service are not met as a violation of public policy under the Article 217(1)3. However, service of process has been understood as an aspect of the exercise of sovereignty in Korea, a country of continental law, and is treated as more important requirement compared to Anglo-American law. Thus, treating it as an issue under the Article 217(1)2 is more consistent with the Korean legal system. Kwang-Hyun Suk, International Civil Procedure, Private International Law (Procedure), Park Young-Sa (2012), p. 375 explains public policy issues are concerned where excessive punitive damages are awarded, where the trial is obtained by fraud, and where the evidentiary process under foreign law is conducted in a way that infringes on sovereignty.

7. The effectiveness of consular service was addressed in the Supreme Court of Korea Judgment 92-Da-2585, and whether the person actually served with the documents was entitled to receive service on behalf of the defendant was addressed in the Supreme Court of Korea Judgment 2008-Da-65815. These cases did not deal directly with substituted service.

8. Since the litigation actions that will influence a legal entity should be done against the natural person representing the legal entity, documents such as complaints, summonses, and judgments must be served on the representative of the legal entity (Supreme Court of Korea Judgment 76-Da-170). However, in practice, it is common for documents sent to the address of a corporation to be received by its employee rather than its *representative*. Accordingly, it is inconsistent with the practice of service of process to exclude substituted service.

9. This is a general principle of private international law that proceedings are governed by the law of the forum. For details, see Kwang-Hyun Suk, Commentary on Private International Law, Park Young-Sa (2013), p. 24.

10. Lawrence Collins (eds.), *Dicey, Morris and Collins, The Conflict of Laws*, Sweet & Maxwell Ltd (15th Ed.) (2012), para. 8-065, clearly points this out, stating that if service is made abroad, it cannot be lawful if it is contrary to the law of the place where service is made. Kwang-Hyun Suk, supra note 4, at 363, and Young-Il Yoo, "Legality of Service as a Requirement for Recognition of Foreign Judgments," International Case Law Studies, Vol. 2, Seoul Institute of International Law (2001), at 226 explain in the same way. The lawfulness of service is primarily a matter of the law of the country of the judgment and, in the case of foreign service, the law of the country of service is also relevant.

11. Article 185 of the German Civil Procedure Act (Zivilprozessordnung) lists four cases in which the court may make public service: (1) If the residence of the person to be served is unknown and it is not possible to serve him or her or his representative or receiver, (2) the address of a legal entity registered in the commercial register or a person authorized to receive service is not known; (3) service abroad is not possible or cannot be expected to be successful; or (4) service is made on a person who is not subject to the jurisdiction of a German court pursuant to the Court Organization Act (Gerichtsverfassungsgesetz), such as diplomats and their families.

12. Case C-292/10 (Cornelius de Visser), ECLI:EU:C:2012:142, para. 59.

13. In this case, the Supreme Court of Korea held that it was unlawful to serve a summon on a defendant with only a 20-day response period instead of the 60-day prescribed by the State of Washington's service rules. It can be said that the Supreme Court of Korea correctly pointed out that the standard for judging the legality of service should be the law of the trial state (Washington).

14. For details on the legality and timeliness of service of process through Article 217(1)2 of the CPA, see Won-Yeol Jeon, Lectures on the Civil Procedure Act, Park Young-Sa (2020), p. 497. According to Kwang-Hyun Suk, "Legislative Theory on the Recognition and Enforcement of Foreign Judgments," in International Law and International Litigation, Vol. 1, Park Young-Sa (2001), pp.

418, 432, legality and timeliness have been enacted following a proposal by Professor Kwang-Hyun Suk during the amendment of the CPA in 1999.

15. Kwang-Hyun Suk, supra note 7, at 362. Han, Ae-Ra, "Requirements and Procedures for Recognition and Enforcement of Judgment under the Lugano Convention," Status and Prospects of International Norms, Administrative Office of the Courts (2008), p. 309 also notes that the Lugano Convention does not examine the formal legality of service of process, but rather whether the service actually ensured the defendant's right to defense. It should be noted that the U.K. has attempted to rejoin the Lugano Convention post-Brexit and follow the framework established by the Brussels Regulation between the EU Member States, Switzerland, Iceland and Norway, but this is unlikely to be possible due to opposition from the EU Commission.

16. Article 684 of the French Code de procédure civile provides that service of documents required to be served abroad is deemed to be accomplished by delivery to a public prosecutor in France. However, it is important to note that the above article does not apply to cases where direct service is required under EU regulations, or under treaties/conventions signed by France.

17. Article 110 of the Japanese Code of Civil Procedure categorizes the cases in which public notice can be made into four categories, and in particular, the fourth category establishes a flexible system for public notice by stating that it can be used in the event of a delay in foreign service.

Article 110 (Requirements for Public Service) ① In the following cases, the trial court may, upon application, make public service:
1. The address, residence or other place of service of a party is unknown;
2. When service cannot be made in accordance with the provisions of Article 107 (1);
3. When it is recognized that service cannot be made in accordance with the provisions of Article 108 for service to be made in a foreign country or that service cannot be made in accordance with the provisions of Article 108; or
4. If a document certifying delivery has not been received within six months after requesting a competent public institution in a foreign country in accordance with the provisions of Article 108.

---

18. Si-Yoon Lee, New Civil Procedure Law, 15th Edition, Park & Young (2020), p. 432.

19. Moon-Hyuk Ho, Civil Procedure Law, 14th ed. (2020), p. 732; Myung-Hwan Lee, "Effect of Foreign Judgments," Commandment Law Review 9 (2005), p. 9.

20. Supreme Court of Korea 99-Da-3150 Judgment makes this point by stating that it is rare for a defendant to actually become aware of documents through public notice.

21. Jeong-Hyun Pi, "Recognition and Enforcement of a Foreign Court's Final Judgment - Focusing on Service Abroad", Law Review No. 2246, Law Review (1993), had already expressed the opinion that "substituted service should be fall under proper service as a requirement for recognition and enforcement of a

foreign judgment" at the time the Supreme Court of Korea 92-Da-2585 Judgment was handed down.

22. For example, in the Korean insolvency proceedings of Hanjin Shipping, there were a large number of foreign creditors, but since the addresses of the foreign creditors were not precisely known, it was not possible to directly serve the documents on each of them. Most of the proceedings were conducted through the "public notice in lieu of service" permitted by Article 10 of the Debtors Rehabilitation and Bankruptcy Act. In such a situation, let's say that a foreign creditor claims that it has lost the opportunity to participate in the Korean insolvency proceedings against Hanjin Shipping just because it was not properly informed of the Korean insolvency proceedings and claims that the foreign country should deny the validity of the order confirming the plan or discharge order rendered in Korea. If this argument is accepted without restriction, Hanjin Shipping would still be liable to certain foreign creditors in the foreign country, leaving the door open for individual enforcement actions against the debtor's assets in the foreign country and preventing the debtor from forming a sound financial structure and resuming business activities in the foreign country. For details, see Young-Seok Kim, "A Study on the Foreign proceedings and the Recognition and Enforcement of Insolvency-related Judgments in Cross-Border Insolvency Matters," Ph.D. dissertation, Seoul National University (2022), at 297 et seq.

23. Hyung-Du Nam, "Haehoo," The Way, Korean Bar Association (2012), provides an anecdote about the difficulty of serving documents to a US-based defendant in a Korean case in 1994.

Private International Law Issues in Joint Venture Agreements and Shareholders' Agreements Governed by Korean Law

YOU Jung Hwa
Judge
Seoul Eastern District Court, Seoul, Korea
Ph.D Candidate in International Business Transactions Law, College of Law, Seoul National University, Seoul, Korea

Abstract

To come up with an effective and tangible resolution to the disputes arising out of company-type joint venture agreements, it would be beneficial for the parties to carefully analyze the nature of each issue in the fields of contract and corporate law. A strategic approach can be made to minimize the legal risks in advance when in-house counsel or external counsel representing the parties conduct a thorough analysis as early as possible in the contract drafting stages regarding (i) international jurisdiction agreements, (ii) choice-of-law agreements, and (iii) arbitration agreements.

Key Words

Joint Venture Agreement, Shareholders' Agreement, Korean Law, Korean Court Precedent, International Jurisdiction, Governing Law, Arbitration, Korea's Amended Act on Private International Law of 2022

1. INTRODUCTION

When a joint venture company is established between two parent companies with different citizenship (nationality), the legal relationships among these parties have foreign elements and are associated with private international law (i.e., conflict of laws) issues. Joint venture agreements usually accompany shareholders' agreements, and the validity of these agreements may be up for discussion with regard to clauses that can be construed in a manner inconsistent with the corporate law of the jurisdiction under which the joint venture company is established.

For a successful joint venture investment in Korea, it is worth discerning the relevant issues that are frequently triggered in Korean law when it is the governing law of joint venture agreements, shareholders' agreements and the joint venture company. Further, to ensure foreseeability for the resolution of the disputes arising out of the joint venture relationship or the company, the parties are potentially required to grasp the rules and principles of international jurisdiction recognized by Korean courts or those for the interpretation of arbitration agreements. The aim of this paper is to provide brief coverage of the major issues or relevant rules and principles in Korean private international law with an analysis of several major Korean court precedents and arbitration cases. The body of this paper focuses on the contractual issues in (i) international jurisdiction agreements, (ii) choice-of-law agreements, and (iii) arbitration agreements contained in the joint venture agreements or shareholders' agreements.

Two major terms are defined for the sake of the ensuing discussion. Parent companies conclude shareholders' agreements (abbreviated as "SHAs") to govern the control structure of the organs, execution of the voting rights, disposition of the shares and operation of their subsidiary company. SHAs are widely used by the parent companies, which are the parties to joint venture agreements (abbreviated as "JVAs") as a device to establish and operate their subsidiary company as a joint venture company.

A joint venture is arranged by a meeting of the minds between the parties to pool their resources for the purpose of accomplishing a specific task. To establish a joint venture in the form of an incorporated company, the JVAs involve an arrangement to establish and organize a project company. When a project company is established, the parties to JVAs often become the shareholders of the project company. These shareholders mutually reach an agreement on how to operate the company, which is called a shareholders' agreement, and in such a case, a joint venture agreement is construed as including or being treated the same as a shareholders' agreement.[1]

2. LEGAL ISSUES WITH INTERNATIONAL JURISDIC-TION AGREEMENTS

2-1. GENERAL PRINCIPLES IN THE ACT AND JURISPRU-DENCE

Article 2 of Korea's Amended Act on Private International Law of 2022 ("the Act" or "KPILA")[2] sets forth general principles of determining which forum has the international jurisdiction over a certain case.[3] Supreme Court Decision 2002Da59788, rendered on January 27, 2005, put forward an abstract interpretation of the general principles in Article 2 of the Act, stating that "The determination of international jurisdiction should follow the basic idea of aiming to achieve impartiality between the parties, appropriateness, speediness and economy of adjudication, and should, more concretely, take into account not only *private interests* such as impartiality between the parties, convenience and predictability, but also *interests of the court* as well as *of the state* such as appropriateness, speediness and efficiency of adjudication, and effectiveness of judgment. The issue of which interest among such diverse interests deserves protection should be determined reasonably, applying *in each individual case* the objective criteria of substantial relationship between the court and the parties, and substantial relationship between the court and the case in dispute."[4]

This case-by-case approach means the legal practice with regard to JVAs should be taken into careful consideration. Generally, almost all the JVAs contain dispute resolution clauses in the form of international jurisdiction agreements when the parties wish to resolve a dispute through litigation. A typical example is as follows: "Article 24.2 Any dispute, controversy or claim arising out of or relating to this joint venture agreement, including its conclusion, interpretation, performance, breach, termination or invalidity, shall be finally settled by the courts of the U.S. District Court for the Southern District of New York which will have exclusive jurisdiction."[5]

The activities under the JVAs in international transactions should be highly protected and promoted as joint ventures accompany corporate law issues that might hinder the stability of collective legal relationships. To ensure such protection, Korean courts appear to hold that international jurisdiction clauses should be deemed valid whenever possible absent extraordinary circumstances, as shown in the Seoul High Court Decision below.[6]

2-2. HOW THE NATURE AND VALIDITY OF INTERNATIONAL JURISDICTION AGREEMENTS IN JOINT VENTURE AGREEMENTS ARE DETERMINED IN KOREAN COURTS: SEOUL HIGH COURT DECISION 2014NA16489

2-2-1. FACTUAL BACKGROUND

The Plaintiffs established D Co., Ltd. ("D Corp.") on April 12,

2005 to pursue the Jeju E Development Project. On September 3, 2009, the Plaintiffs and D Corp. signed the First Joint Venture Agreement ("JVA 1") with the Defendant, a Chinese corporation, that the Defendant would invest CNY 2 billion in D Corp. in the form of a loan and acquire 70% of D Corp.'s issued shares at face value. The Plaintiffs and D Corp. signed the Second Joint Venture Agreement ("JVA 2") with the Defendant on January 28, 2010. The key clauses of JVA 2 are as follows:

Article 11 (Other)

This Agreement shall be effective upon signature and seal of the parties. In order to prove the conclusion of this Joint Venture Agreement, this Agreement shall be prepared in two languages, Chinese and Korean, and one copy shall be kept by each of the two companies from the date of signing. If the content of the Chinese version and the Korean version do not match, the content of the Chinese contract shall prevail.

Article 12 (Resolution of Disputes)

12.1 The laws and regulations of China shall apply to this Joint Venture Agreement. The activities for management after the establishment of a Joint Venture Company between the two parties shall be governed by laws and regulations of the Republic of Korea.

12.2 For the purpose of amicable cooperation, the parties negotiate and resolve disputes arising out of the matters not agreed upon under this Agreement. If a settlement is not reached between the parties, the people's court in the place where the Defendant is located shall have jurisdiction.

On December 5, 2010, the Plaintiffs signed a new Shareholders' Agreement with the Defendant that the Defendant would take over 80% of the issued shares of D Corp. at face value instead of repaying 80% of the debt of D Corp. The dispute resolution clause of the Shareholders' Agreement is as follows:

> Article 20 (Dispute Resolution) If a dispute between the parties under this Agreement is contested by a lawsuit, the court with jurisdiction over the location of the Defendant (meaning the person to be sued) shall have jurisdiction.

According to JVA 2, D Corp. carried out a paid-in capital increase on January 1, 2011, changing its capital to KRW 300 million and its total number of issued shares to 60,000 (each share's face value of KRW 5,000). The Defendant acquired 48,000 shares (the Stock) at face value and became a major shareholder with an 80% stake. The Defendant's chairman F was appointed as the CEO of D Corp., and the Defendant's representative G was appointed as an auditor. The Defendant remitted only USD 50 million in total to D Corp. (= USD 5 million on July 6, 2010 and USD 45 million on November 8, 2010).

On June 22, 2012, the Plaintiffs requested that the Defendant to fulfill its investment obligations pursuant to Article 21 of the Shareholders' Agreement, and notified that the Agreement would be automatically terminated without a separate termination notice if the Defendant does not fulfill the obligations within 30 days from the day it received the request.

2-2-2. DEFENDANT'S DEFENSE ON THE LACK OF JURISDIC-TION

The Defendant argued that the Korean court lacks jurisdiction over this case referring to the exclusive international jurisdiction agreement (Article 20 of the Shareholders' Agreement) between the Plaintiffs and the Defendant.

2-2-3. RULING AND TAKEAWAY

Seoul High Court accepted the Defendant's defense prior to the merits and dismissed the Plaintiffs' appeal (that is, the first instance court's judgment that the Plaintiffs' lawsuit lacks jurisdiction and should be dismissed was affirmed). Seoul High Court used a twofold approach when deciding on this argument as follows:[7]

2-2-3-1. THE LEGAL NATURE OF A JURISDICTION AGREEMENT

First of all, regarding the criteria for distinguishing between an exclusive jurisdiction agreement and an additional jurisdiction agreement, Seoul High Court saw it as a matter of interpreting the parties' intention, holding that the agreement would be construed as an exclusive jurisdiction agreement if the court designated by the agreement is one of the several courts that can be deemed to have jurisdiction over the case, whereas the agreement would be construed as an additional jurisdiction agreement if the court designated by the agreement does not originally have jurisdiction but is newly granted jurisdiction by the parties through the agreement.

Seoul High Court paid particular attention to the following circumstances: (i) According to the Korean and Chinese civil procedure codes, both Korean and Chinese Courts have jurisdiction over the disputes between the parties under the SHA; (ii) The Plaintiffs and the Defendant must have foreseen that various problems with regard to the jurisdiction may be triggered in the event of a legal dispute arising out of the SHA, and that is why the parties decided in advance that the court with jurisdiction over the location of the Defendant (meaning the person to be sued) shall have jurisdiction in Article 20 of the SHA; and (iii) if the jurisdiction agreement in question were to be construed as an additional jurisdiction agreement, the agreement becomes meaningless since both Korean and Chinese courts already have jurisdiction without such an agreement. Thus, since the Defendant in this lawsuit is a Chinese corporation, it is concluded that the Chinese court has exclusive jurisdiction over this case.

Seoul High Court's above ruling seems to have been based on a reasonable interpretation of the parties' intention to reach such an agreement in light of the purpose and motivation of the international jurisdiction agreement in Article 20 of the SHA.

2-2-3-2. THE VALIDITY OF A JURISDICTION AGREEMENT

Further, Seoul High Court ruled that in light of the requirements confirmed by Supreme Court Decision **2010Da28185** rendered on August 26, 2010, the jurisdiction agreement is valid. In addition to the nature of the jurisdiction agreement decided earlier above, Seoul High Court gave weight to the following circumstances: (i) The Defendant is a Chinese corporation established under Chinese law, its CEO is also a Chinese person domiciled in China, and the Defendant must obtain approval from the Chinese authorities to invest money in foreign countries. The purpose of the lawsuit was to resolve the issue of whether the Defendant had fulfilled its investment obligations under the SHA, which were closely related to JVA 2. The governing law for the JVA 2 was Chinese law. Considering these factors, this lawsuit was found to have a reasonable connection with the Chinese court as well as the Korean court; and (ii) if the Defendant had filed a lawsuit against the Plaintiffs, it would have had to do so with the Korean court according to the jurisdiction agreement in question. Likewise, the jurisdiction agreement is not unilaterally disadvantageous to the Plaintiffs, and it cannot be deemed that the jurisdiction agreement is so remarkably unreasonable and unfair so as to be against the public order.

Part (i) above shows that Seoul High Court deemed the requirement of rational relevance between the case and foreign courts has been fulfilled, and part (ii) above shows that the Court deemed the agreement not to be contrary to the public order.

In furtherance of the spirit of the above ruling, it can be said that Seoul High Court has properly and thoroughly reviewed whether there exists a reasonable connection between the lawsuit and China. The conclusion of the above Seoul High Court ruling is desirable in that it has implemented predictability and legal stability that the parties in international business transactions intend to achieve through international jurisdiction agreements by respecting the private autonomy of the parties.

3. LEGAL ISSUES WITH CHOICE-OF-LAW AGREEMENTS

The parties in drafting and concluding an international contract pursue legal stability and predictability by choosing the applicable law. If the parties do not make such a choice, the law of the country most closely related to the contract generally becomes the governing law by the conflict of laws principles. The parties may explicitly or implicitly choose the governing law of the contract, and according to Article 45, Paragraph (1) of KPILA,[8] the implied choice of the governing law can be recognized if the content of the contract and all other relevant circumstances support it.

The parties establish and operate a joint venture by executing a JVA. In a JVA made in international transactions, it is necessary to separately consider the issue of the law applied to the relationship between the parties to the joint venture (i.e., the governing law of joint venture agreements) and the law associated with a joint venture company.

3-1. GOVERNING LAW OF THE LEGAL RELATIONSHIPS UNDER JOINT VENTURE AGREEMENTS

The Supreme Court of Korea defined the legal nature of JVAs as partnership agreements, so-called *johap* contracts. In the leading case of Supreme Court Decision 2005Da38263, rendered on September 6, 2007, where the joint venture agreement with a bankruptcy termination clause is deemed essentially a *johap* contract, Supreme Court ruled that "The joint venture agreement refers to a partnership agreement (*johap* contract), which means for two or more parties to make mutual contribution and establish and operate a company. The parties have completed the performance of their obligations for the formation of a partnership by making mutual contribution and establishing a joint venture company. *Accordingly, as provided in the agreement, the obligation to cooperate with each other for the corporate activities of the established joint venture company, i.e., the exercise of voting rights or the formation of the board of directors, still remains and is imposed on the parties.*"9

Thus, a company-type joint venture in Korea can be seen as an internal *johap* (*Projektinnengesellschaft* in German law) without its own property, and it is worth noting that this JVA remains valid even after the establishment of a joint venture company, which is a project company, and the parties have the status of shareholders of the that company.10

As to whether Article 30 of KPILA on the governing laws of corporations11 can be applied to a JVA treated as a partnership contract under Korean civil law, scholars suggest several different views. Some say that since a partnership is a contract under Korean civil law, the internal relationship between the partners should be governed by Article 45 of KPILA on contracts and other provisions, but Article 30 of KPILA on corporations can be applied to a partnership if it has its own organs under the agreement. On the other hand, some opine that the internal relationship of a partnership is to be governed by the agreement itself and the partnership's external relationship shall be governed by Article 30 of KPILA. However, there is little practical merit in distinguishing between treating the joint venture as a corporation under Article 30 of KPILA or a contract under Articles 45 and 46 of KPILA, since both approaches are based on the principle of party autonomy.[12] Considering that the legal relationships of a legal entity as an organization should be determined by its substance, and that if, under Korean civil law, such an entity has more of a collection of legal personalities of individual members with a weak collective nature rather than a corporation which has a strong collective nature, it would be reasonable to identify such an entity as a contractual relationship and resolve it in accordance with Articles 45 and 46 of KPILA. Therefore, in the end, as long as a JVA has the nature of a partnership under civil law, it is a contractual relationship subject to Articles 45 and 46 of KPILA rather than Article 30. Therefore, as in the above Supreme Court Decision 2005Da38263, the obligation imposed on the partners to a JVA to cooperate with each other for the established joint venture company shall be viewed from a contract law perspective and thus be governed by the Korean Civil Code or Korean Commercial Code when legal issues arise associated with the failure to perform this obligation.

In practice, the fact that JVAs in international transactions usually have the following governing law provision can be seen as a result of naturally presupposing the application of Article 45 of KPILA: "Article 20. Governing Law. This Joint Venture Agreement shall be governed by and construed in accordance with the laws of Delaware without giving effect to the conflict of laws rules thereof."[13]

3-2. GOVERNING LAW OF THE JOINT VENTURE COMPANY

The governing law of a joint venture company is the law

applicable to the establishment (not the law applicable to the principal place of business) in accordance with Article 30 of KPILA. This approach adopted by KPILA takes into account the advantages of securing legal stability, and it respects the intentions of the founder and promoter because it is easy to confirm the law applicable to the companies (*lex societatis*) which is always fixed.[14]

Meanwhile, as a matter of international transactions, if the parties to a JVA establish a joint subsidiary for the original purpose of carrying out specific projects (i.e., in the case of a company-type joint venture), a multinational business group may be formed. At this point, in a situation where it is questionable whether to apply the law applicable either to the parent company (i.e., parties to the JVA) or to the subsidiary (i.e., joint venture company), the prevailing view prioritizes the protection of shareholders and creditors.[15] For example, if the transfer of the whole or a substantial part of the business of the joint venture company to the parent company (Article 374 (1) 1 of the Korean Commercial Code puts forth this matter as an agendum for special resolutions at the general shareholders' meeting), the law governing the subsidiary applies. On the other hand, if the soundness of the parent company's capital is at issue, e.g., the acquisition of shares of the parent company by a subsidiary, the law governing the parent company applies. It appears that this approach has the advantage in being reasonable from the perspective of applying the most closely related law as the governing law to the legal relationships of these companies.

3-3. PRACTICAL COMPLEXITIES

In some cases, due to the discrepancy between the law applicable to the parties' relationships to the joint venture (i.e., the governing law of the JVA) and the law applied to the joint venture company, the parties are confronted with disputes that they could not have predicted at the time they executed the contract. Further, there may be cases where the JVA was originally drafted supposing that it would be governed by Country A's law, but only the governing law provision of the agreement is changed to Country B's law at the very last minute of the negotiations and concluded likewise. In such a case, unpredictable problems may arise in contract interpretation due to the mismatch between the understanding intended by the contractual parties and that under the governing law.

One typical example is as follows: A Corp., a German company, and B Corp., a Korean company, have decided to cooperate in Korea in a form of joint venture. During the negotiation process, the two companies decided that instead of establishing a new joint venture company, the shareholders of B Corp. would sell some of their holdings to A Corp. and operate B Corp. as a joint venture company. A Corp. and B Corp. signed a technical support agreement to provide A Corp.'s know-how and technology to B Corp., but A Corp. refused on several occasions to comply with B Corp.'s request to provide know-how on new product development. Two months before the expiration of the agreed contract period, B Corp. notified A Corp. that it would terminate the technical support contract due to A Corp.'s *material breach*. A Corp. filed a request for arbitration to the International Court of Commerce ("ICC"), claiming that the termination made by B Corp. is invalid. It was agreed that the governing law of the above JVA would be German civil law.[16]

The main dispute in the above example was whether A Corp.'s contract violation constitutes a *material breach*. According to the German Civil Code, which is the governing law, continuous contracts can be terminated if there is a *serious cause* while general contracts that are not continuous can be terminated if there is a *material breach*. Furthermore, the German Civil Code does not explicitly define the meaning of a "material breach" as an independent concept, but there is a reference to "*serious cause*" in a case where a party cannot reasonably expect to maintain the contract until the agreed expiration date despite contract violation.

B Corp. argued that, although the technical support agreement was a continuous contract, the criteria for determining whether A Corp.'s contract violation constitutes a basis for B Corp.'s termination should be that of "material breach," not "serious cause" under the German Civil Code, in that the term "material breach" was used in the wording of the termination clause. The arbitral tribunal ruled that simply using the term "material breach" in English could not be construed as the parties' intention to exclude the application of the "serious cause" provision to the termination of a continuous contract under the German Civil Code. In the end, whether A Corp.'s breach of contract constitutes a basis for B Corp.'s termination should be determined in line with whether it constitutes a "serious cause" under the German Civil Code. In this case, considering the circumstances, it was found that B Corp. could expect to maintain the contract for the remaining period, invalidating the termination of contract by B Corp.

The above example suggests that if contract provisions (e.g., termination clause) are prepared without sufficient and profound consideration of the potential ripple effect of governing law, disputes that had not been previously predicted may be triggered or become complicated out of control. Therefore, it appears that unnecessary disputes can be prevented if in-house counsel or retained external counsel exhaustively analyze potential risks harbored in the law which is highly likely to be designated as governing law from the early stages of negotiation when preparing and drafting a JVA. In practice, one should bear in mind that depending on the negotiating power of the two parties, the law applicable to the legal relationships under the JVA may differ from the law applicable to the joint venture company, and at some point one should prepare strategies to respond to the disputes deriving from such discrepancy.[17]

Further, if a new joint venture company is established in Korea when a foreign company A and a Korean domestic company B decide to cooperate in Korea, it is likely that both the governing law of the JVA and the governing law of the joint venture company will be designated as Korean law. However, the term "material breach" in English or in a translated expression in Korean is often used in a contract termination clause because English is generally chosen as the official language of a JVA. The term "material breach" is a legal concept developed under Anglo-American law (especially in M&A-related contracts) and is a foreign legal concept unfamiliar to Korean law, resulting in contrasting views on how to interpret this term under Korean law.

Some may assert that when "material breach" is interpreted literally, it refers to a "significant violation," so in light of Korean legal principles, its definition should be limited to a violation of major obligations. This is because Korean courts use such expressions as "major obligation" or "ancillary obligation" as addressed in the Supreme Court Decision 2001Da20394, rendered on November 13, 2001; Supreme Court Decision 2005Da53705, rendered on November 25, 2005, etc., but when Korean Courts determine the validity of contract termination, the legal test is whether the parties can achieve the purpose of the contract despite one party's breach of contract, regardless of whether the breached obligation is major or ancillary.[18]

However, a JVA is essentially a continuous contract that is expected to continue for a long time as the joint venture is designed to operate for a certain period of time (i.e., usually for decades). In this case, even if a certain obligation appears to be a relatively ancillary one (e.g., parties' obligation to cooperate to facilitate performance of a project through a joint venture), it is reasonable to interpret this obligation as a "significant violation" that constitutes a "material breach," considering all the circumstances surrounding the joint venture relationship and its spirit.

4. LEGAL ISSUES WITH ARBITRATION AGREEMENTS

When a joint venture company is established as a result of concluding a JVA, various contracts such as Memorandum of Understanding (MOU), shareholders' agreements, equity sale and purchase contracts and licensing contracts are usually signed together, and each of these contracts has a dispute resolution clause. These accompanied contracts may be concluded simultaneously, but in some cases, the parties to each contract may be represented by different legal counsel and these contracts are concluded sequentially with some time gap. Thus, the dispute resolution clause of each contract may differ with various means (i.e., litigation or arbitration). On the other hand, in the event of a dispute over the dissolution of a joint venture, the dispute is not resolved simply by the termination of the JVA; rather, various other contracts signed in relation to the joint venture have to be resolved together consistently, resolving the contract violation disputes serially like a row of dominoes.

If the contracts have different dispute resolution provisions, it may be difficult to achieve a unified resolution of this series of disputes, or the parties are forced to suffer the perplexing problem of having to file claims or defend in multiple jurisdictions. To minimize these risks, not only joint venture agreements but also all related agreements need to have a unified dispute resolution clause "to refer disputes arising out of the contract to international arbitration" where the same arbitration agencies (e.g., the ICC), arbitrators and governing law are arranged among these agreements to be mutually consistent. At minimum, it would be beneficial for the parties to agree in advance that the dispute resolution procedures agreed upon in the JVA, which would be the basis of all other contracts, can be applied ahead of other clauses in the event of a dispute. Conversely, contract drafters should always keep in mind the possibility that even if disputes under some contracts are designed to be resolved through other arbitration proceedings, depending on the arbitral tribunal's view, the JVA is likely to be perceived as an umbrella agreement by the arbitral tribunal, and the disputes may be comprehensively integrated and be uniformly subject to the arbitration provision of the JVA.

However, when corporate issues are subject to dispute resolution, hearings may have to be conducted through litigation at the court where the company is located, rather than through arbitration. In such case, the parties should conduct a comprehensive review of how to coordinate multiple arbitration proceedings advantageously and take a strategic approach accordingly. For example, if a foreign company G Corp. and a Korean domestic company H Corp. decide to cooperate and establish a new joint venture in Korea, whether the joint venture has taken proper procedural steps to establish itself in Korea or whether the resolution of the general shareholders' meeting or the board of directors' meeting have been validly formed are typical matters of corporate legal dispute. It would be inappropriate to leave the decision on these corporate issues to the disposition of the parties, which might undermine the public order of Korean corporate system by bypassing the mandatory regulations set forth in the Korean Commercial Code.[19] Considering the foregoing, it would be favorable for G Corp. and H Corp. to draft the dispute resolution provision of the JVA in the first place to designate a Korean court with an exclusive international jurisdiction, resolving these corporate issues by litigation.

In light of the author's experience working as counsel in several ICC international arbitration cases, in practice, technology transfer contracts and exclusive supply contracts are often signed in conjunction with JVAs, and the governing laws and dispute resolution methods between the JVAs and other contracts often vary and agreed upon in a diverse manner. As a result, inconsistent or even conflicting judgments or arbitral awards may be drawn from various courts or arbitral tribunals, resulting in an astronomical increase in legal costs. Therefore, as technology transfer contracts or exclusive supply contracts are eventually concluded to facilitate the implementation of JVAs, if the disputes are not limited to attached contracts such as technology transfer contracts or exclusive supply contracts (e.g., delay in performance of specific technology transfer obligations) but rather associated with the purpose and spirit of the joint venture (e.g., one partner of the joint venture dumps its shares of the joint venture company to the third party and leaks crucial know how of the joint venture), those disputes would better be heard through the proceedings agreed upon under the umbrella of the JVA.

5. CONCLUDING REMARKS

JVAs or SHAs in international transactions are located at the intersection of private contracts (international contract law) and collective legal entities (corporate law). Thus, these agreements, in practice, are followed by conflicts between the principles built up in the field of corporate law, i.e., the principle of shareholder equality, majority voting, the distribution of authority among the organs and the right to represent a company, and the principle of private autonomy, i.e., freedom of contract.

On the other hand, JVAs or SHAs play a role in making up for the shortcomings of unified legal relations under corporate law, and can lead to the promotion of investment and the assurance of efficiency in financing.

To achieve a solid resolution to disputes arising out of the JVAs, especially in the case of joint ventures where the parties to the agreements form a project company, it is advisable to carefully categorize the nature of each issue (i.e., characterization or classification in private international law) considering both contract law and corporate law aspects as described above. In addition, since most disputes are subject to resolution by litigation or arbitration unless successful settlements are achieved beforehand, it will be cost-effective and effort-effective to prevent disputes in advance with careful drafting of international jurisdiction agreements or arbitration agreements with clear wording that reflects the parties' intentions.

Notes

This article is based on the author's recent article in Korean titled "Private International Law Issues in Joint Venture Agreements and Shareholders' Agreements Governed by Korean Law: Focused on Jurisprudence and Cases in Practice", Current Issues and Future Tasks of International Business Transactions Law and Private International Law, Liber Discipulorum SUK Kwang-Hyun, 2022, pp. 139-179.

1. CHEONG Jae Oh, "Zusammenfassung Eine Untersuchung über Joint Ventures", Ph.D Dissertation Paper, College of Law, Seoul National University, 2016, pp. 79-81.
2. Korea's Amended Act on Private International Law was amended as a whole on January 4, 2022 and came into effect from July 5, 2022.
3. Article 2, Paragraph (1) provides that "The court of the Republic of Korea (hereinafter referred to as "court") shall have international jurisdiction where a party or a case in dispute has *a substantial connection with the Republic of Korea*. In determining whether any substantial connection exists, the court shall adopt reasonable principles, compatible to the ideology of the allocation of international jurisdiction, which aims to achieve *impartiality between the parties, appropriateness, speediness, and economy of adjudication.*", and Paragraph (2) provides that "Where there is no provision regarding international jurisdiction in this Act or in any other statutes or regulations, or treaties of the Republic of Korea, the court shall determine whether it has international jurisdiction, *in consideration of the provisions of the domestic laws on jurisdiction*, but shall *give full consideration to the special nature of international jurisdiction*, in light of the purport of Paragraph (1)" (emphasis added).
4. Supreme Court Decision 2002Da59788, rendered on January 27, 2005. In this case of Supreme Court Decision 2002Da59788, the Supreme Court recognized that the courts of the Republic of Korea have international jurisdiction over the litigation on the ground that the content of the dispute is substantially related to Korea, where a person domiciled in Korea and operating a business therein challenges the decision rendered by the US National Arbitration Forum ordering transfer of his domain name which he registered at a US registrar for domain names and possessed.
5. Paraphrased from an excerpt of International Trade Centre, "ITC Model Contract for an International Corporate Joint Venture", Geneva, 2010, p. 34.
6. Professor SUK Kwang-Hyun has opined that international jurisdiction agreements arising out of the international business transactions between enterprises should be respected by the Korean courts, which means that "a substantial connection" requirement should not be considered by the Korean courts when deciding the validity of the agreement unless the agreements are seriously irrational and impartial. *See* Suk Kwang-Hyun, Korea, "Requirements of Exclusive International Jurisdiction Agreements to Be Valid", Commentaries on Court Cases, Law

Times, May 27, 2004.

7. Seoul High Court Decision 2014Na16489, rendered on September 5, 2014. This judgment was confirmed as final and conclusive by the Supreme Court's decision to discontinue trial, 2014Da68624.

8. Article 45 (Party Autonomy) of KPILA (1) A contract shall be governed by the law chosen, explicitly or implicitly, by the parties: Provided, That the implicit choice shall be limited where reasonable recognition can be achieved, in consideration of the content of the contract and all other circumstances.

9. Supreme Court Decision 2005Da38263, rendered on September 6, 2007.

10. CHEONG, *supra* note 1, pp. 201, 271.

11. Article 30 (Corporations and Organizations) of KPILA
Corporations and organizations shall be governed by the law applicable to the establishment thereof: Provided, That where corporations or organizations established in foreign countries have their principal offices located in the Republic of Korea or conduct their principal business activities in the Republic of Korea, such corporations and other organizations shall be governed by the law of the Republic of Korea.

12. *See* SUK Kwang-Hyun, Commentary on KPILA, Parkyoungsa, 2013, p. 210.

13. This phrase of "without giving effect to the conflict of laws rules thereof" is to avoid *renvoi* and to specify that the contract law, which is the substantive law of Delaware (not the conflicts of law of Delaware), becomes the governing law. See Article 22 of KPILA for further information.

14. *See* SUK, *supra* note 15, p. 203.

15. *See* KIM Taejin, "Special Feature: Legal Issues of Foreign Companies: International Organizational Change of Companies - Focusing on Cases Involving Foreign Companies", BFL Vol. 42, 2010, p. 22.

16. This example is a paraphrased version of the one in CHUNG Kyo-Hwa (Liz), "Various Exit Strategies of Joint Venture and Dispute Resolution by International Arbitration", Korean Journal of International Trade and Business Law Vol. 21, No. 1, 2012, pp. 14-15.

17. *See* CHUNG, *supra* note 17, p. 15. In the same context, see KIM Byung Tae, "Legal Problems Arising from International Joint Venture Agreement and Joint Venture Company - Promotive Perspective of the Foreign Direct Investment for Local Economy", Korean Journal of International Trade and Business Law Vol. 18, No. 2, 2009, p. 188, fn. 16. KIM explains as follows: "In joint venture agreements, the governing law may be freely agreed upon by the parties, and the law of the country of a foreign investor or domestic investor or the law of a third-party country can be determined as the governing law. However, when a joint venture is established in Korea for the purpose of conducting business in Korea, it is common to designate Korean law, the law of the local country where the joint venture is established, and this is desirable for a smooth resolution of disputes arising out of the joint venture agreement."

18. The author's view on this point is in line with KIM Sungmin, "Study on the

Material Breach Clause in Contracts", Justice Vol. 157, 216, Section IV. 3. KIM opines as follows: "The distinction between major and ancillary obligations adopted by the Korean Supreme Court is not consistent with the criteria of reviewing whether fulfillment of such obligation is essential to achieve the purpose of the contract in the stage of seeking compensation or termination of the contract for non-performance. In particular, Korean courts do not deem the termination of the contract valid in case of an incidental non-performance, whereas they deem that the contract may be terminated if the purpose of the contract cannot be achieved due to the failure to perform (or there is a special agreement). This indicates that the distinction between the major obligation and ancillary obligation is not decisive. Therefore, distinguishing between major and ancillary obligations is not a useful way to decide whether termination of a contract is valid, and such an approach is not desirable especially in international arbitration or before foreign courts who are exposed to the risks of deriving a wrong interpretation of the terms 'major obligation' and 'ancillary obligation.'"

19. *See* SUK Kwang-Hyun, "Comment on a Lower Court Judgment Dealing with Law Applicable to International Acquisition Agreement - Are the Provisions of the Korean Commercial Code Requiring Resolution of Special Shareholders' Meeting Internationally Mandatory Rules?", Kyung Hee Law Journal Vol 53, No. 2, 2018, p. 138.

Revisiting Optional Arbitration Clauses Before the Korean Courts

HAN Mino
Senior Associate
Peter & Kim, Seoul, Korea

YOO Eun Kyung (Jennifer)
Senior Associate
Peter & Kim, Seoul, Korea

Abstract

This paper examines the Korean courts' long-established position concerning optional arbitration clauses, manifested in the Supreme Court Judgment Case No. 2003Da318. According to this judgment, optional arbitration clauses are ineffective as arbitration agreements unless both parties consent to the arbitral process, for instance by failing to challenge the validity or existence of an arbitration agreement by a certain time. This paper aims to revisit this position. Korean courts should adopt a more pro-arbitration interpretation towards optional arbitration clauses, consistent with the approach taken by other Model Law jurisdictions. Furthermore, optional arbitration clauses are commonly used in energy, construction and EPC contracts involving Korean parties, and are in fact boilerplate clauses for construction, supply and engineering contracts entered into by the Korean government or state-owned companies. Departing from the courts' traditional position will assist in resolving the practical confusion that frequently arises with respect to the validity of these clauses.

Key Words

Optional arbitration clauses, Arbitration agreements, Pro-arbitration, Party autonomy, Korean Supreme Court Judgment Case No. 2003Da318

1. INTRODUCTION

Optional arbitration clauses (OACs) are provisions which set out arbitration as an alternative or optional means of dispute resolution, but do not require mandatory submission of disputes to arbitration.[1] The use of such clauses is usually not recommended, as they cause procedural uncertainty in Korea and may themselves become a source of dispute.[2]

The reality, however, is that OACs are frequently seen and used in practice, particularly in energy, construction and EPC contracts. Also commonly used are multi-tier dispute resolution clauses – these are similar to OACs in that they provide for several dispute resolution methods, but in "tiers" so that parties are required to attempt other methods of dispute resolution prior to commencing arbitration.[3] Therefore, it seems that these clauses, and the potential problems associated with them, are here to stay for the time being.

Korean companies are active players worldwide in the energy and construction industries, and are no strangers to OACs (or multi-tier dispute resolution clauses). Therefore, the stance of the Korean courts with respect to these clauses holds much practical significance. In this respect, it is necessary to examine the Korean Supreme Court Judgment Case No. 2003*Da*318 ("2003 Supreme Court Judgment"), which manifests the Korean courts' long-standing position on the validity of these clauses.[4] In essence, the Supreme Court held around twenty years ago that OACs are unenforceable in principle as arbitration agreements unless both parties proceed with the arbitration without challenging the validity or existence of an arbitration agreement.[5]

It is suggested that this position be revisited. As will be further discussed below, the Korean courts' position is incongruous with the approach implemented by other jurisdictions having adopted the 1985 UNCITRAL Model Law on International Commercial Arbitration

("Model Law"),[6] and more broadly, with the pro-arbitration policy of other New York Convention[7] member states. This judicial practice also creates unnecessary confusion for contracts involving Korean parties. It is particularly worthy of note in this regard that OACs are in fact used as boilerplate provisions in virtually all construction, supply and engineering contracts entered into by the Korean government or state-owned companies.

This paper proceeds as follows. Section 2 explains the academic discussions in Korea on OACs and the stance of the Korean courts with respect to these clauses. Section 3 summarises the approach taken in other jurisdictions on the validity of OACs. Section 4 argues that the Korean courts' position should be reconsidered, particularly given the practical problems that continue to arise from this position. Section 5 ends with concluding remarks.

As a final point of introduction, it should be noted that the validity of OACs is ultimately a matter to be determined by reference to the law governing the substantive validity of arbitration agreements.[8] However, to simplify matters, this paper will not delve into the complex debate concerning the choice of law governing arbitration agreements. Instead, when discussing the approach of a certain jurisdiction (e.g. Korea), it is assumed that the governing law is Korean law.

2. KOREAN APPROACHES TO OPTIONAL ARBITRATION CLAUSES

2-1. Before the 2003 Supreme Court Judgment

Despite OACs being used widely in practice, it is often unclear whether these clauses are valid and enforceable. Neither the Model Law nor the Korean Arbitration Act expressly addresses the issue of the validity of these clauses. As a result, the enforceability of OACs has been controversial in many countries, including Korea.[9]

In Korea, the majority view amongst jurists has been that OACs are valid. That view is most often based on the definitions of "arbitration" and "arbitration agreement" in the Korean Arbitration Act which do not expressly require the arbitration agreement to be mandatory.[10] As such, construing OACs as invalid would be an unduly restrictive interpretation of the Arbitration Act.[11] In line with this view, it is argued that, although optional, OACs nonetheless set out the intent of the parties to arbitrate their dispute, which is all that is needed for a consent-based arbitration agreement to be deemed valid.[12] They also contend that recognising the validity of OACs is more favourable to the parties, since OACs can offer the parties a variety of ways to resolve their disputes and thereby ensure effectiveness and efficiency in protecting the parties' rights and interests.[13]

There is also a minority view in Korea opining that OACs are invalid. Jurists of this view start from the premise that a proper arbitration agreement must reflect a meeting of minds of the parties to completely waive their right to resort to court proceedings, which is lacking in OACs. In their view, their position is supported by the definition of "arbitration" in the Korean Arbitration Act, which states that arbitration should be "*not by a judgment of a court, but by an award of an arbitrator*".[14] They further contend that, given that arbitration agreements deprive or restrict the courts of their jurisdiction, they must be formulated in a very clear and unequivocal way to have that effect; but OACs do not satisfy this threshold. They also assert that OACs are asymmetrical in that they allow one party to determine the method of dispute resolution, which is unfair and unconscionable to the other party.[15] Additionally, these jurists say that recognising the validity of OACs causes unclarity and uncertainty. For example, the clauses give rise to complex issues concerning the timing for exercising the option to arbitrate, and the potential risk of parallel proceedings before a court and arbitral tribunal.[16]

The Korean case law prior to the 2003 Supreme Court Judgment was unsettled. There only existed lower-level court judgments, which all pointed in different directions.[17] That is, some were in favour of accepting the validity of OACs, some were not.[18] The pro-validity judgments reasoned that there was no basis to restrict valid arbitration agreements to those which provided for arbitration as a mandatory means of dispute resolution, and that such a restrictive interpretation could go against the will of the parties who had agreed to this optional provision. These judgments also made clear that a party could not refuse or avoid arbitration proceedings by simply objecting to it, as that would go against the parties' agreement to arbitrate reflected in the OAC.[19]

The judgments that found against validity took the view that OACs were not valid arbitration agreements. Their logic was that an arbitration agreement ought to contain a waiver or exclusion of the right to rely on court litigation proceedings. Since OACs did not exclude litigation, the judgments did not construe OACs as operative arbitration agreements. They found it more sensible to treat OACs as merely providing for the possibility that the dispute may be resolved by arbitration, only if and to the extent that no party objected to doing so.[20]

As the foregoing judgments were all lower court judgments, there was no single prevailing authority on the topic of the validity and enforceability of OACs.[21] It was against this background that the 2003 Supreme Court Judgment was issued.

2-2. The 2003 Supreme Court Judgment[22]

This case concerned a contract price dispute between the Republic of Korea and a Korean supplier. The dispute resolution clause in the relevant supply contract set out that the parties shall attempt to

resolve any disputes arising out of the contract amicably by negotiation. In the event negotiation failed, the clause provided that "*the
dispute shall be referred to adjudication/arbitration in accordance with the laws of the
Purchaser* [i.e. the Republic of Korea]*'s country*".

The supplier filed a Request for Arbitration before the Korean
Commercial Arbitration Board (KCAB) seeking additional payment.
In the arbitration proceedings the Republic of Korea consistently
asserted in its Response and other pleadings that the proceedings
should be dismissed for lack of a valid arbitration agreement. The
arbitral tribunal agreed with the Republic of Korea and dismissed the
proceedings.

Subsequently, the supplier filed suit before the Korean courts
seeking to set aside the arbitral tribunal's decision on jurisdiction.
The Republic of Korea also initiated a parallel proceeding, seeking
confirmation of the non-existence of an arbitration agreement.

The Supreme Court's holding can be translated into English as
follows:

> "*An optional arbitration clause shall be deemed to be effective as
> an arbitration agreement only when one party opts for arbitration
> proceedings and demands that the dispute be resolved by that
> process, and the other party participates in the arbitration
> proceedings without raising any objection. In the event one party
> actively contends that an arbitration agreement does not exist and
> objects to resolution by arbitration, the clause cannot be deemed to
> be effective as an arbitration agreement.*"

In short, since the Republic of Korea had objected to the case
being resolved by arbitration, the Supreme Court held that a valid
arbitration agreement did not exist in the matter at hand.

2-3. SUBSEQUENT SUPREME COURT JUDGMENTS

After the 2003 Supreme Court Judgment was rendered, two more Supreme Court decisions followed regarding the issue of the validity and enforceability of OACs.[23] These subsequent judgments were generally in line with the 2003 Supreme Court Judgment.[24]

Supreme Court Judgment Case No. 2004Da42166[25] was a case between the Korea National Railway Authority and several construction companies. At issue was the dispute resolution clause concluded between the parties which provided for negotiation as the first step, but in the event of failure, that the parties shall resolve the matter either by mediation or by arbitration. The clause further provided that, should mediation fail, the matter shall be subject to the decision of the court. Ultimately, the Supreme Court found that a valid agreement to arbitrate did not exist, as the challenge raised by the Korea Rail Network Authority in the KCAB arbitration proceedings rendered the arbitration agreement ineffective.

Supreme Court Judgment Case No. 2005Da12452[26] relied on the same holding as the preceding Supreme Court decisions. However, interestingly the Court reached a different conclusion. The dispute similarly involved the Korea National Railway Authority and a construction company. The relevant dispute resolution clause also provided for negotiation as the first step, followed by either mediation or arbitration as the next step. However, unlike the preceding cases, the respondent (Korea National Railway Authority) did not contest the validity of the arbitration agreement in its Response submitted in the KCAB proceedings. It only raised arguments on the merits until at a much later stage in the proceedings, when it (belatedly) submitted an opinion memorandum challenging the validity of the arbitration agreement. The arbitral tribunal continued with the proceedings and issued a final award on the merits. The respondent then filed suit in Korean court seeking to set aside the arbitral award. The Supreme Court reiterated the holding of the 2003 Supreme Court Judgment, but also pointed out that the Korean Arbitration Act only allows jurisdictional challenges to be raised by no later than the filing of the Response (Answer) to the Request for Arbitration.[27] On that basis, the Supreme Court found that the OAC had become effective definitively upon the submission of the Response that contained no jurisdictional challenge or an objection to the validity of the arbitration agreement.

In short, since 2003, the Korean Supreme Court has consistently held that OACs are invalid unless and until the respondent party also consents to the dispute being submitted to arbitration (including by failing to raise a timely objection).[28] The question at hand is whether this approach ought to be maintained in 2023.

3. OTHER JURISDICTIONS' APPROACHES TO OPTIONAL ARBITRATION CLAUSES

While OACs have been similarly controversial in other countries, most of them have taken an approach to OACs that is largely different from that of the Korean courts. In many instances, the courts have held that an OAC creates an option permitting either party to initiate arbitration, and that, if the option is exercised by either party, both parties are then bound to arbitrate.[29] Indeed, the starting point for the majority of foreign court judgments is that OACs are in principle valid and effective (save for the case where both parties fail to exercise the option to arbitrate), whereas the starting point for Korean court judgments is that OACs are in principle invalid and ineffective (save for the case where both parties consent to arbitrating their dispute).

U.S. courts have consistently held that "*questions of arbitrability must be addressed with a healthy regard for the federal policy favoring arbitration*".[30] In line with this pro-arbitration policy, U.S. courts have upheld the effect of provisions drafted in optional terms, by finding that either the clause was actually a mandatory (not optional) provision;[31] or even if the clause was optional, that it was in any event valid and enforceable.[32] English courts similarly have accepted the validity of OACs, reasoning that once a party exercised the option to commence arbitration the other party was bound by the arbitration agreement.[33]

Likewise, Canadian courts have found OACs to be valid because a binding arbitration agreement would arise whenever one party exercised its option to invoke arbitration.[34] By way of example, in *Mind Star Toys Inc. v. Samsung Co. Ltd.*, a case the Ontario Court decided in 1992, a contract containing a reference to arbitration as well as to a clause granting Mind Star the *"right to sue"* was at issue. Mind Star brought a claim against Samsung before the Ontario Court, and Samsung requested the stay of proceedings claiming that the reference to the *"right to sue"* would not overturn the parties' choice for arbitration. The Court decided in favour of Samsung and the court proceedings were stayed.[35]

Hong Kong courts have reached similar conclusions. For instance, in *William Co. v. Chu Kong Agency Co. Ltd.* decided in 1993, a Hong Kong court upheld the validity of an arbitration agreement with optional language. The relevant bill of lading contained an arbitration clause providing for arbitration in China, but also an exclusive jurisdiction clause in favour of Chinese courts. The plaintiff filed a suit in Hong Kong court, and the defendants sought a stay of proceedings in favour of arbitration in China. The Court granted the stay, finding that the arbitration clause constituted a valid agreement to arbitrate, and that the defendants had properly opted for arbitration by applying for the stay of proceedings.[36]

The same approach has generally been followed in civil law jurisdictions. For example, in a judgment dated 18 December 1975, the German Federal Court of Justice concluded that there was no reason to deny the validity of an OAC, in light of the principle of the freedom of contract.[37] There are a number of lower court judgments in Germany which have reached similar conclusions.[38]

There are however countries which have interpreted and construed OACs in a way similar to the Korean courts, namely that the parties will only be bound to an agreement to arbitrate if the parties subsequently consent to doing so. The courts in Russia and China, for instance, appear to have adopted this position.[39]

4. REVISITING THE KOREAN COURTS' APPROACH

4-1. Inconsistency with Party Autonomy, the Model Law and Pro-Arbitration Policy

The first criticism with respect to the Korean courts' approach on OACs is that it is incongruous with the approach taken in numerous other jurisdictions, especially those that have adopted the Model Law. All of the judgments recognising the validity of OACs cited in the preceding Section are from countries which have accepted the Model Law in their domestic legislation.[40] Korea also adopted the Model Law into its Arbitration Act in 1999, and the Act has continued to be amended to more closely follow the Model Law.[41] Yet, the Korean courts' stance with respect to OACs has not kept in line with the tendency of other Model Law jurisdictions.[42]

Another problem with the Korean courts' stance is that it plainly denies the existence of an arbitration agreement even though the parties have expressly provided for arbitration (albeit optionally). In that sense, the Korean courts' stance is incompliant with the principle of party autonomy. By referring to arbitration, the parties have already chosen arbitration as their means of dispute resolution as per the language of the dispute resolution clause that they bargained for.

That intent of the parties should be respected. The reference to arbitration should ordinarily be construed as an agreement to arbitrate, not an agreement to discuss or agree on the possibility of arbitrating – which would serve little, if any, commercial purpose.[43] Yet the Korean courts have taken the contrary approach of denying the validity of OACs in principle, which the authors say would go over and beyond what the parties have already agreed to in their contract.[44]

The Korean courts' approach is particularly concerning in that it discourages the use of arbitration, rather than encouraging it. It goes against the pro-arbitration policy that the Model Law and New York Convention member states seek to uphold.[45] Arguably, the Korean courts' approach may be a reflection of the vague hostility towards arbitration that historically pervaded the courts of many countries, including Korea, prior to or around the year 2000.[46] This is not surprising, from a historical perspective, given that up till the early 2000s when the 2003 Supreme Court Judgment was rendered arbitration in Korea was still in its early stages. However, the Korean arbitration community has become far more sophisticated over time, and the number of arbitration users has grown immensely such that arbitration is not deemed an "exceptional" dispute resolution mechanism any longer. Consistent with this development in Korea, the time seems ripe for the Korean courts to update their approach towards OACs accordingly.[47]

4-2. Practical Issues Arising from the Korean Courts' Approach

There are further practical reasons that the Korean courts' approach may be problematic.

First, the validity of the OAC becomes contingent on not the wording of the clause itself, but on the parties' subsequent conduct – that is, whether the respondent party consents to or challenges the arbitration procedure following its commencement by the claimant party.[48] This means, in practice, that the question of validity can only be determined at the time the respondent submits its Response to the claimant's Request for Arbitration.[49] Until then, the clause remains in a quasi-ineffective state, without knowing whether it may or may not become effective in the future. This gives rise to uncertainty.

For example, there may very well be a situation where the claimant party prepares and files an arbitration, only to find later that it has to start over again before the courts because the respondent party refuses to arbitrate. (Indeed, that is precisely what happened in the 2003 Supreme Court Judgment.) The costs and time incurred in that process may pose a significant burden for the parties.

There is a second point arising from a distinct feature of Korean contract practice, namely that OACs are in fact boilerplate clauses for construction, supply and engineering contracts entered into by the Korean government.[50] The Korean government maintains a suite of General Contracts Terms (계약일반조건) pertaining to each type of contract the government regularly procures, so that they can readily be incorporated by reference when executing contracts. All these General Terms contain OACs (as well as multi-tier dispute resolution provisions).[51] It is not a coincidence, therefore, that a large majority (if not all) of the Korean court decisions on the subject of OACs relate to contracts with the Korean government, including the 2003 Supreme Court Judgment.[52]

The consequence of the Korean courts' position is that virtually all of the construction, supply and engineering contracts concluded by the Korean government or state-owned companies become uncertain in terms of their dispute resolution method. This has led to much criticism.[53] At minimum, this clearly demonstrates that the Korean courts' approach lacks coherence with reality, namely the widespread use of OACs by the Korean government or state-owned companies, which are all major international players in the current world.[54]

5. CONCLUSION

This paper examined approaches to OACs in Korea and in other jurisdictions. It goes without saying that parties should think twice about including an OAC in their contract governed by Korean law, given its inherent ambiguity as compared to a clause providing for a single means of dispute resolution. However, once the parties have decided to include such a clause in their contract, the clause – and the parties' intent behind it – should be respected and upheld in full, consistent with the overarching principle of party autonomy and the pro-arbitration spirit underlying the modern international arbitration regime.

In this context, it is suggested that the Korean courts' stance in respect of OACs be revisited. The jurisprudence set out in the 2003 Supreme Court Judgment denies the effectiveness of OACs unless and until the parties' consent to arbitrate is additionally demonstrated by their subsequent conduct. This appears outdated and inconsistent with the tendency of other leading Model Law jurisdictions. From a practical perspective, it defers the determination of the dispute resolution forum to after the arbitration has been commenced, that is, when the respondent party has filed its Response in the arbitral proceedings one way or the other. Unnecessary costs and time are incurred by the parties in the meantime. Furthermore, this juris-prudence renders virtually all construction, supply and engineering contracts entered into by the Korean government unclear in terms of their dispute resolution method, as OACs are almost always included in those contracts as a boilerplate provision.

The 2003 Supreme Court Judgment may have suited Korean

society two decades ago. However, it is now time for the Korean courts' position to evolve towards a direction which better recognises the parties' agreement to arbitrate, whether optional or mandatory, and thereby ensures that the parties' intent to arbitrate, if so bargained for and expressed in a contract, is fully upheld.

REFERENCES

1. Books

Albert Jan Van den Berg (ed), *Yearbook Commercial Arbitration 1994 – Volume XIX* (ICCA & Kluwer Law International 1994)

SUK Kwang Hyun (석광현), *Kuk-Je-Sang-Sa-Jung-Jae-Yeon-Gu* (국제상사중재연구) [*Essays in International Commercial Arbitration*], Vol. 1 (Pakyoungsa, 2007)

Bae, Kim & Lee LLC, *Arbitration Law of Korea: Practice and Procedure* (Juris, 2012)

Gary B. Born, *International Commercial Arbitration* (2nd ed., Wolters Kluwer, 2014)

2. Journals

Okanunle O. Olatawura, "Managing Multi-Layered Dispute Resolution under the Arbitration Act 1996 – Smashing Bricks of Intention" in 4(3), *International Arbitration Law Review* (2001), 70-73

CHANG Moon Chul, "Seon-Taek-Jeok Jung-Jae-Hab-Ui-Ui Hae-Seok-Gi-Jun (선택적 중재합의의 해석기준) [Standard for Interpreting Optional Arbitration Clauses]" (LAWnB, 2003)

JEONG Sun Ju, "Seon-Taek-Jeok Jung-Jae-Hab-Ui-Ji-Hang-Ui Yu-Hyo-Seong-Gwa Mun-Jae-Jeom (선택적 중재합의조항의 유효성과 문제점) [The Effectiveness and Problems of Optional Arbitration Agreement Clauses]" in 13(2), *Jung-Jae-Yeon-Gu* (중재연구) [*Journal of Arbitration Studies*] (2004), 585-612

YEO Mi Sook, "Seon-Taek-Jeok Jung-Jae-Jo-Hang-Ui Yu-Hyo-Seong (선택적 중재조항의 유효성) [Validity of Selective Arbitration Clauses]" in 27, *Min-Sa-Pan-Lye-Yeon-Gu* (민사판례연구) [*Journal of Private Case Law Studies*] (2005), 774-804

LEE Sang Won, "Seon-Taek-Jeok Jung-Jae-Hab-Ui-Ui Yu-Hyo-Yo-Geon (선택적 중재합의의 유효요건) [Requirements for the Validity of Selective Arbitration Agreements]" in 28, *Min-Sa-Pan-Lye-Yeon-Gu* (민사판례연구) [*Journal of Private Case Law Studies*] (2006), 774-804

KIM Kee Chang, "Arbitration Agreement under Korean Law" in 3, *Korea University Law Review* (2008), 83-102

CHUNG Young Hwan, "Seon-Taek-Jeok Jung-Jae-Hab-Ui-Ui Yu-Hyo- Seong-E De-Han Pan-Lye-Bun-Seok (선택적 중재합의의 유효성에 대한 판례분석) [Analysis of Judgments on the Validity of Selective Arbitration Agreements]" in 19(3), *Jung-Jae-Yeon-Gu* (중재연구) [*Journal of Arbitration Studies*] (2009), 3-24

KIM Ji Suck, "Seon-Taek-Jeok Jung-Jae-Hab-Ui-Ui Yu-Hyo-Seong (선택적 중재합의의 유효성) [The Validity of Optional Arbitration Clauses]" in 28(2), *Jae-San-Beob-Yeon-Gu* (재산법연구) [*Journal of Property Law*] (2011), 355- 376

SHIN Han Dong, "Jung-Jae-Pan-Jeong-I De-Beob-Won-E Ui-He Chwi-So- Doen Sa-Lye Yeon-Gu (중재판정이 대법원에 의해 취소된 사례연구) [A Case Study on the Arbitration Awards Cancelled by Korean Supreme Court]" in 21(1), *Jung-Jae-Yeon-Gu* (중재연구) [*Journal of Arbitration Studies*] (2011), 33-56

KIM Soon Lee, "Seon-Taek-Jeok Jung-Jae-Hab-Ui-Ui Yu-Hyo-Seong-E Gwan- Han Beob-Jeok Yeon-Gu (선택적 중재합의의 유효성에 관한 법적 연구) [A Legal Study on the Validity of Optional Arbitration Agreements]" in 56, *Dong-A-Beob-Hak* (동아법학) [*Dong-A Law Review*] (2012), 325-354

Michelle Kwon, "The Evolving Relationship between the Korean Courts and the Korean Commercial Arbitration Board: An Examination of Optional Arbitration Decisions in South Korea" in 16(2), *Inha Law Review* (2013), 125-152

YANG Seok Wan, "Jung-Jae-Hab-Ui-Ui Yu-Hyo-Seong Da-Tum-Gwa Im-Si- Jeok Cheo-Bun-Ui Heo-Yong Yeo-Bu (중재합의의 유효성 다툼과 임시적 처분의 허용 여부) [Disputes on the Validity of Arbitration Agreements and Whether Interim Measures Are Allowed]" in 14(2), *Beob-Gwa-Jeong-Chaek-Yeon-Gu* (법과정책연구) [*Journal of Law and Politics Research*] (2014), 677-710

CHOI Sung Soo, "Seon-Taek-Jeok Jung-Jae-Jo-Hang-E Dae-Han So-Go (선택적 중재조항에 대한 소고) [An Essay on Optional Arbitration Clauses]" in 38(3), *Beob-Hak-Non-Chong* (법학논총) [*Dankook Law Review*] (2014), 469-501

3. Internet Sources

UNCITRAL Model Law on International Commercial Arbitration 1985: with amendments as adopted in 2006 (United Nations, 2008), available at https://uncitral.un.org/sites/uncitral. un.org/files/media-documents/uncitral/en/19-09955_e_ebook.pdf [Accessed on 11 March 2023]

United Nations Commission on International Trade Law, *Status: UNCITRAL Model Law on International Commercial Arbitration (1985), with amendments as adopted in 2006,* available at https://uncitral.un.org/en/texts/arbitration/modellaw/commercial_ arbitration/status [Accessed on 11 March 2023]

Vasilis F. L. Pappas & Artem N. Barsukov, "Five Years Later: Update on Multi-Tier Dispute Resolution Clauses as Jurisdictional Conditions Precedent to Arbitration" in *The Guide to Energy Arbitrations* (5th ed., Global Arbitration Review, 2022), available at https://globalarbitrationreview.com/guide/the-guide-energy-arbitrations/fifth-edition/article/five-years-later-update-multi-tier-dispute-resolution-clauses-jurisdictional-conditions-precedent-arbitration [Accessed on 12 March 2023]

Zhang Shouzhi, "Arbitration Procedures and Practice in China: Overview" (Practical Law, 2022), available at https://uk.practicallaw.thomsonreuters.com/3-520-0163?transitionType=Default&contextData=(sc.Default)&firstPage=true [Accessed on 11 March 2023]

4. Legislation

Jung-Jae-Beob (중재법) [Arbitration Act], Act No. 16918 as amended on 4 February 2020, effective on 4 February 2020. Korean original at https://www.law.go.kr/lsSc.do?section=&menuId=1&subMenuId=15&tabMenuId=81&eventGubun=060101&query=%EC%A4%91%EC%9E%AC%EB%B2%95 [Accessed on 11 March 2023] Unofficial English translation at https://elaw.klri.re.kr/kor_service/lawView.do?hseq=52916&lang=ENG [Accessed on 26 February 2023]

Gong-Sa-Gye-Yak-Il-Ban-Jo-Gun (공사계약일반조건) [General Terms of Construction Contracts], Ministry of Economy and Finance Contract Regulation No. 581 as amended on 1 December 2021, effective on 1 December 2021. Korean original at https://www.law.go.kr/%ED%96%89%EC%A0%95%EA%B7%9C%EC%B9%99/(%EA%B3%84%EC%95%BD%EC%98%88%EA%B7%9C)%EA%B3%B5%EC%82%AC%EA%B3%84%EC%95%BD%EC%9D%BC%EB%B0%98%EC%A1%B0%EA%B1%B4 [Accessed on 11 March 2023]

Yong-Yeok-Gye-Yak-Il-Ban-Jo-Gun (용역계약일반조건) [General Terms of Contracts for Services], Ministry of Economy and Finance Contract Regulation No. 582 as amended on 1 December 2021, effective on 1 December 2021. Korean original at https://www.law.go.kr/%ED%96%89%EC%A0%95%EA%B7%9C%EC%B9%99/(%EA%B3%84%EC%95%BD%EC%98%88%EA%B7%9C)%EC%9A%A9%EC%97%AD%EA%B3%84%EC%95%BD%EC%9D%BC%EB%B0%98%EC%A1%B0%EA%B1%B4 [Accessed on 12 March 2023].

Mul-Pum-Gu-Mae-Je-Jo-Gye-Yak-Il-Ban-Jo-Gun (물품구매제조계약일반조건) [General Terms of Contracts for the Supply and Manufacture of Goods], Ministry of Economy and Finance Contract Regulation No. 583 as amended on 1 December 2021, effective on 1 December 2021. Korean original at https://www.law.go.kr/%ED%96%89%EC%A0%95%EA%B7%9C%EC%B9%99/(%E

A%B3%84%EC%95%BD%EC%98%88%EA%B7%9C)%EB%AC%BC%ED%9
2%88%EA%B5%AC%EB%A7%A4(%EC%A0%9C%EC%A1%B0)%EA%B3%
84%EC%95%BD%EC%9D%BC%EB%B0%98%EC%A1%B0%EA%B1%B4
[Accessed on 11 March 2023]

5. Korean Case Law

Seoul District Court Judgment Case No. 2000*Gahap*37949 dated 19 September 2000

Daegu District Court Judgment Case No. 99*Gahap*20982 dated 5 October 2000

Seoul High Court Judgment Case No. 2000*Na*51386 dated 24 April 2001

Daegu High Court Judgment Case No. 2000*Na*7654 dated 26 July 2001

Seoul District Court (Eastern Division) Judgment Case No. 2001*Gahap*6334 dated 21 December 2001

Seoul District Court Judgment Case No. 2001*Gahap*54637 dated 5 February 2002

Seoul Central District Court Judgment Case No. 2001*Gahap*15595 dated 2 May 2002

Seoul High Court Judgment Case No. 2002*Na*6878 dated 2 July 2002

Seoul District Court Judgment Case No. 2000*Gahap*96825 dated 25 July 2002

Seoul High Court Judgment Case No. 2001*Na*73093 dated 28 November 2002

Seoul High Court Judgment Case No. 2002*Na*16134 dated 2 April 2003

Seoul District Court Judgment Case No. 2003*Gahap*16783 dated 23 April 2003

Supreme Court Judgment Case No. 2003*Da*318 dated 22 August 2003

Seoul District Court Judgment Case No. 2002*Gahap*44743 dated 4 November 2003

Gwangju High Court Judgment Case No. 2003*Na*5596/5602 dated 21 November 2003

Seoul High Court Judgment Case No. 2003*Na*33112 dated 5 February 2004

Seoul Central District Court Judgment Case No. 2003*Gahap*81152 dated 13 April 2004

Seoul Central District Court Judgment Case No. 2003*Gahap*49684 dated 3 May 2004

Seoul High Court Judgment Case No. 2003*Na*66693 dated 2 July 2004

Seoul Central District Court Judgement Case No. 2004*Gahap*23740 dated 13 August 2004

Supreme Court Judgment Case No. 2004*Da*42166 dated 11 November 2004

Supreme Court Judgment Case No. 2005*Da*12452 dated 27 May 2005

6. Foreign Case Law

Hull Dye & Print Works, Inc. v. Riegel Textile Corp., 325 N.Y.S. 2d 301 (App. Div. 1971)

Moses H. Cone Memorial Hospital v. Mercury Construction Corp., 460 U.S. 1, 24 (1983)

Sablosky v. Gordon Company, Inc, 538 N.Y.S.2d 513 (1989)

Rainwater v. Nat'l Home Ins. Co., 944 F.2d 190 (4th Cir. 1991)

McKee v. Home Buyers Warranty Corp. II, 45 F.3d 981, 983 (5th Cir. 1995)

St. Lawrence Explosives Corp. v. Worthy Bros. Pipeline Corp., 916 F.Supp. 187 (N.D.N.Y. 1996)

Summit Packaging Systems, Inc. v. Kenyon & Kenyon, 273 F.3d 9 (1st Cir. 2001)

Kemiron Atlantic, Inc. v. Aguakem International Inc., 290 F.3d 1287 (11th Cir. 2002)

Dale Wells et al. v. Chevy Chase Bank, F.S.B. et al., 832 A.2d 812 (Md. 2003)

Wash. Mut. Bank v. Crest Mortg. Co., 418 F.Supp.2d 860, 862 (N.D. Tex. 2006)

Tokumaru Kaium Co. Ltd. v. Petredec Ltd [1995] unreported (QB) (English High Ct.)

Lobb Partnership Ltd v. Aintree Racecourse Co., Ltd. [2000] B.L.R. 65 (QB) (English High Ct.)

Mind Star Toys Inc. v. Samsung Co. Ltd., 9 Ontario Reports (3d), 374

Campbell v. Murphy, [1993] CanLII 5460 (Ontario Super. Ct.)

Canadian Nat'l Railway Co. v. Lovat Tunnel Equip. Inc., (1999) 174 D.L.R.4th 385 (Ontario Ct. App.)

William Co. v. Chu Kong Agency Co. Ltd., [1993] HKCFI 215 (H.K. Ct. First Inst.)

OLG Hamburg KTS 1958, 189

OLG Munchen NJW 1959, 2222

OLG Oldenburg KTS 1972, 114

BGH NJW 1976, 852

Presidium of the Supreme Commercial Court of the Russian Federation, Ruling No. 1831 dated 19 June 2012

Notes

1. LEE Sang Won, "Seon-Taek-Jeok Jung-Jae-Hab-Ui-Ui Yu-Hyo-Yo-Geon (선택적 중재합의의 유효요건) [Requirements for the Validity of Selective Arbitration Agreements]" in 28, *Min-Sa-Pan-Lye-Yeon-Gu* (민사판례연구) [*Journal of Private Case Law Studies*] (2006), 774-804; SUK Kwang Hyun, *Kuk-Je-Sang-Sa-Jung-Jae-Yeon-Gu* (국제상사 중재연구) [*Essays in International Commercial Arbitration*], Vol. 1, 132 (Pakyoungsa, 2007); CHUNG Young Hwan, "Seon-Taek-Jeok Jung-Jae-Hab-Ui-Ui Yu-Hyo-Seong-E De-Han Pan-Lye-Bun-Seok (선택적 중재합의의 유효성에 대한 판례분석) [Analysis of Judgments on the Validity of Selective Arbitration Agreements]" in 19(3), *Jung-Jae-Yeon-Gu* (중재연구) [*Journal of Arbitration Studies*] (2009), 3-24; KIM Ji Suck, "Seon-Taek-Jeok Jung-Jae-Hab-Ui-Ui Yu-Hyo-Seong (선택적 중재합의의 유효성) [The Validity of Optional Arbitration Clauses]" in 28(2), *Jae-San-Beob-Yeon-Gu* (재산법연구) [*Journal of Property Law*] (2011), 355-376; KIM Soon Lee, "Seon-Taek-Jeok Jung-Jae-Hab-Ui-Ui Yu-Hyo-Seong-E Gwan- Han Beob-Jeok Yeon-Gu (선택적 중재합의의 유효성에 관한 법적 연구) [A Legal Study on the Validity of Optional Arbitration Agreements]" in 56, *Dong-A-Beob-Hak* (동아법학) [*Dong-A Law Review*] (2012), 325-354; Michelle Kwon, "The Evolving Relationship between the Korean Courts and the Korean Commercial Arbitration Board: An Examination of Optional Arbitration Decisions in South Korea" in 16(2), *Inha Law Review* (2013), 125-152; Gary B. Born, *International Commercial Arbitration*, 789 (2nd ed., Wolters Kluwer, 2014); YANG Seok Wan, "Jung-Jae-Hab-Ui-Ui Yu-Hyo-Seong Da-Tum-Gwa Im-Si- Jeok Cheo-Bun-Ui Heo-Yong Yeo-Bu (중재합의의 유효성 다툼과 임시적 처분의 허용 여부) [Disputes on the Validity of Arbitration Agreements and Whether Interim Measures Are Allowed]" in 14(2), *Beob-Gwa-Jeong-Chaek-Yeon-Gu* (법과정책연구) [*Journal of Law and Politics Research*] (2014), 677-710; CHOI Sung Soo, "Seon-Taek-Jeok Jung-Jae-Jo-Hang-E Dae-Han So-Go (선택적 중재조항에 대한 소고) [An Essay on Optional Arbitration Clauses]" in 38(3), *Beob-Hak-Non-Chong* (법학논총) [*Dankook Law Review*] (2014), 469-501.

2. Born, *supra* note 1, at 789.

3. Vasilis F. L. Pappas & Artem N. Barsukov, "Five Years Later: Update on Multi-Tier Dispute Resolution Clauses as Jurisdictional Conditions Precedent to Arbitration" in *The Guide to Energy Arbitrations* (5th ed., Global Arbitration Review, 2022), available at https://globalarbitrationreview.com/guide/the-guide-energy-arbitrations/fifth-edition/article/five-years-later-update-multi-tier-dispute-resolution-clauses-jurisdictional-conditions-precedent-arbitration [Accessed on 12 March 2023]; Bae, Kim & Lee LLC, *Arbitration Law of Korea: Practice and Procedure*, 113 (Juris, 2012); CHUNG, *supra* note 1; KIM (2012), *supra* note 1; Kwon, *supra* note 1.

4. Supreme Court Judgment Case No. 2003*Da*318 dated 22 August 2003.

5. JEONG Sun Ju, "Seon-Taek-Jeok Jung-Jae-Hab-Ui-Ji-Hang-Ui Yu-Hyo-Seong-Gwa Mun-Jae-Jeom (선택적 중재합의조항의 유효성과 문제점) [The Effectiveness and Problems of Optional Arbitration Agreement Clauses]" in 13(2), *Jung-Jae-Yeon-Gu* (중재연구) [*Journal of Arbitration Studies*] (2004), 585-612; LEE, *supra* note 1; SUK,

supra note 1, at 134; CHUNG, *supra* note 1; KIM (2011), *supra* note 1; SHIN Han Dong, "Jung-Jae-Pan-Jeong-I De-Beob-Won-E Ui-He Chwi-So-Doen Sa-Lye Yeon-Gu (중재판정이 대법원에 의해 취소된 사례연구) [A Case Study on the Arbitration Awards Cancelled by Korean Supreme Court]" in 21(1), *Jung-Jae-Yeon-Gu* (중재연구) [*Journal of Arbitration Studies*] (2011), 33-56; Bae, Kim & Lee LLC, *supra* note 3, at 120; Kwon, *supra* note 1; CHOI, *supra* note 1.

6. *UNCITRAL Model Law on International Commercial Arbitration 1985: with amendments as adopted in 2006* (United Nations, 2008), available at https://uncitral.un.org/sites/uncitral.un.org/files/media-documents/uncitral/en/19-09955_e_ebook.pdf [Accessed on 11 March 2023].

7. Convention on the Recognition and Enforcement of Foreign Arbitral Awards, 10 June 1958, 330 U.N.T.S. 3.

8. SUK, *supra* note 1, at 134.

9. LEE, *supra* note 1; KIM (2011), *supra* note 1; Kwon, *supra* note 1.

10. The current Korean Arbitration Act defines 'arbitration' and 'arbitration agreement' as follows (at Article 3):
    1. "Arbitration" means a procedure to settle a dispute over property rights or disputes based on non-property rights that the parties can resolve through a reconciliation, not by a judgment of a court, but by an award of an arbitrator.
    2. "Arbitration agreement" means an agreement between the parties to settle by arbitration all or certain disputes which have arisen, or which may arise in the future in respect of defined legal relationships, whether contractual or not.
    Jung-Jae-Beob (중재법) [Arbitration Act], Act No. 16918 as amended on 4 February 2020, effective on 4 February 2020. Korean original at https://www.law.go.kr/lsSc.do?section=&menuId=1&subMenuId=15&tabMenuId=81&eventGubun=060101&query=%EC%A4%91%EC%9E%AC%EB%B2%95 [Accessed on 11 March 2023]. Unofficial English translation at https://elaw.klri.re.kr/kor_service/lawView.do?hseq=52916&lang=ENG [Accessed on 26 February 2023].

11. CHANG Moon Chul, "Seon-Taek-Jeok Jung-Jae-Hab-Ui-Ui Hae-Seok-Gi-Jun (선택적 중재합의의 해석기준) [Standard for Interpreting Optional Arbitration Clauses]" (LAWnB, 2003).

12. CHUNG, *supra* note 1; KIM (2012), *supra* note 1; CHOI, *supra* note 1.

13. JEONG, *supra* note 5; LEE, *supra* note 1; KIM (2011), *supra* note 1.

14. Article 3(1) of Jung-Jae-Beob (중재법) [Arbitration Act], Act No. 16918 as amended on 4 February 2020, effective on 4 February 2020.

15. CHOI, *supra* note 1.

16. CHUNG, *supra* note 1; KIM (2012), *supra* note 1; YANG, *supra* note 1.

17. Korea adopts a three-instance judicial system, comprising district courts (serving as courts of first instance), high courts (serving as appeals courts), and the Supreme Court (serving as the second court of appeals and final instance).

18. For more details of key lower court decisions, see JEONG, *supra* note 5.

19. Daegu District Court Judgment Case No. 99*Gahap*20982 dated 5 October 2000; Seoul High Court Judgment Case No. 2000*Na*51386 dated 24 April 2001; Daegu

High Court Judgment Case No. 2000*Na*7654 dated 26 July 2001; Seoul District Court Judgment Case No. 2001*Gahap*54637 dated 5 February 2002; Seoul Central District Court Judgment Case No. 2001*Gahap*15595 dated 2 May 2002; Seoul High Court Judgment Case No. 2002*Na*6878 dated 2 July 2002; Seoul District Court Judgment Case No. 2000*Gahap*96825 dated 25 July 2002; Seoul High Court Judgment Case No. 2001*Na*73093 dated 28 November 2002; Seoul High Court Judgment Case No. 2002*Na*16134 dated 2 April 2003; Seoul District Court Judgment Case No. 2003*Gahap*16783 dated 23 April 2003; Seoul High Court Judgment Case No. 2003*Na*33112 dated 5 February 2004; Seoul Central District Court Judgment Case No. 2003*Gahap*49684 dated 3 May 2004.

20. Seoul District Court Judgment Case No. 2000*Gahap*37949 dated 19 September 2000; Seoul District Court (Eastern Division) Judgment Case No. 2001*Gahap*6334 dated 21 December 2001; Seoul District Court Judgment Case No. 2002*Gahap* 44743 dated 4 November 2003; Gwangju High Court Judgment Case No. 2003*Na*5596/5602 dated 21 November 2003; Seoul Central District Court Judgment Case No. 2003*Gahap*81152 dated 13 April 2004; Seoul High Court Judgment Case No. 2003*Na*66693 dated 2 July 2004; Seoul Central District Court Judgement Case No. 2004*Gahap*23740 dated 13 August 2004.

21. In the Korean law system, court judgments do not have binding, precedential value. However, higher court judgments, especially those of the Supreme Court, are regarded as strong persuasive authority and are typically followed by lower-level courts.

22. Supreme Court Judgment Case No. 2003*Da*318 dated 22 August 2003.

23. Supreme Court Judgment Case No. 2004*Da*42166 dated 11 November 2004; Supreme Court Judgment Case No. 2005*Da*12452 dated 27 May 2005.

24. CHUNG, *supra* note 1.

25. Supreme Court Judgment Case No. 2004*Da*42166 dated 11 November 2004. See also Kwon, *supra* note 1.

26. Supreme Court Judgment Case No. 2005*Da*12452 dated 27 May 2005. See also KIM (2012), *supra* note 1.

27. Article 17(2) of Jung-Jae-Beob (중재법) [Arbitration Act], Act No. 16918 as amended on 4 February 2020, effective on 4 February 2020.

28. JEONG, *supra* note 5; LEE, *supra* note 1; SUK, *supra* note 1, at 134; CHUNG, *supra* note 1; KIM (2011), *supra* note 1; SHIN, *supra* note 5; Bae, Kim & Lee LLC, *supra* note 3, at 120; Kwon, *supra* note 1; CHOI, *supra* note 1.

29. Born, *supra* note 1, at 789.

30. Moses H. Cone Memorial Hospital v. Mercury Construction Corp., 460 U.S. 1, 24 (1983).

31. McKee v. Home Buyers Warranty Corp. II, 45 F.3d 981, 983 (5th Cir. 1995); Rainwater v. Nat'l Home Ins. Co., 944 F.2d 190 (4th Cir. 1991); Wash. Mut. Bank v. Crest Mortg. Co., 418 F.Supp.2d 860, 862 (N.D. Tex. 2006); St. Lawrence Explosives Corp. v. Worthy Bros. Pipeline Corp., 916 F.Supp. 187 (N.D.N.Y. 1996), referenced in Born, *supra* note 1, at 790.

32. Hull Dye & Print Works, Inc. v. Riegel Textile Corp., 325 N.Y.S. 2d 301 (App. Div. 1971); Sablosky v. Gordon Company, Inc, 538 N.Y.S.2d 513 (1989); Kemiron Atlantic, Inc. v. Aguakem International Inc., 290 F.3d 1287 (11th Cir. 2002); Summit Packaging Systems, Inc. v. Kenyon & Kenyon, 273 F.3d 9 (1st Cir. 2001); Dale Wells et al. v. Chevy Chase Bank, F.S.B. et al., 832 A.2d 812 (Md. 2003).

33. Tokumaru Kaium Co. Ltd. v. Petredec Ltd [1995] unreported (QB) (English High Ct.); Lobb Partnership Ltd v. Aintree Racecourse Co., Ltd. [2000] B.L.R. 65 (QB) (English High Ct.), referenced in Born, *supra* note 1, at 791. See also Okanunle O. Olatawura, "Managing Multi-Layered Dispute Resolution under the Arbitration Act 1996 – Smashing Bricks of Intention" in 4(3), *International Arbitration Law Review* (2001), 70-73.

34. Canadian Nat'l Railway Co. v. Lovat Tunnel Equip. Inc., (1999) 174 D.L.R.4th 385 (Ontario Ct. App.); Campbell v. Murphy, [1993] CanLII 5460 (Ontario Super. Ct.), referenced in Born, *supra* note 1, at 791.

35. Mind Star Toys Inc. v. Samsung Co. Ltd., 9 Ontario Reports (3d), 374, referenced in Albert Jan Van den Berg (ed), *Yearbook Commercial Arbitration 1994 – Volume XIX, 265* (ICCA & Kluwer Law International 1994).

36. William Co. v. Chu Kong Agency Co. Ltd., [1993] HKCFI 215 (H.K. Ct. First Inst.), referenced in Born, *supra* note 1, at 791.

37. BGH NJW 1976, 852.

38. OLG Hamburg KTS 1958, 189; OLG Munchen NJW 1959, 2222; OLG Oldenburg KTS 1972, 114.

39. Presidium of the Supreme Commercial Court of the Russian Federation, Ruling No. 1831 dated 19 June 2012, referenced in Kwon, *supra* note 1; Zhang Shouzhi, "Arbitration Procedures and Practice in China: Overview" (Practical Law, 2022), available at https://uk.practicallaw.thomsonreuters.com/3-520-0163?transitionType =Default&contextData=(sc.Default)&firstPage=true [Accessed on 11 March 2023]. See also CHOI, *supra* note 1.

40. United Nations Commission on International Trade Law, *Status: UNCITRAL Model Law on International Commercial Arbitration (1985), with amendments as adopted in 2006*, available at https://uncitral.un.org/en/texts/arbitration/modellaw/commercial_arbitration/status [Accessed on 11 March 2023].

41. CHANG, *supra* note 11; Kwon, *supra* note 1.

42. CHANG, *supra* note 11; KIM (2011), *supra* note 1.

43. Born, *supra* note 1, at 792-793.

44. JEONG, *supra* note 5; CHUNG, *supra* note 1; KIM (2011), *supra* note 1; Kwon, *supra* note 1; CHOI, *supra* note 1.

45. LEE, *supra* note 1.

46. CHANG, *supra* note 11; CHUNG, *supra* note 1.

47. KIM (2012), *supra* note 1.

48. KIM (2012), *supra* note 1.

49. Bae, Kim & Lee LLC, *supra* note 3, at 120.

50. YEO Mi Sook, "Seon-Taek-Jeok Jung-Jae-Jo-Hang-Ui Yu-Hyo-Seong (선택적 중재조항의 유효성) [Validity of Selective Arbitration Clause]" in 27, *Min-Sa-Pan-Lye-Yeon-Gu* (민사판례연구) [*Journal of Private Case Law Studies*] (2005), 774-804; SUK, *supra* note 1, at 132; KIM (2011), *supra* note 1; CHOI, *supra* note 1.

51. For example, Article 51 of the General Terms of Construction Contracts reads as follows: (1) A dispute arising between the parties during the performance of the contract shall be resolved by discussion. (2) If a resolution is not reached by way of paragraph (1), the dispute shall be resolved by a judgment of the court or arbitration under the Arbitration Act. Gong-Sa-Gye-Yak-Il-Ban-Jo-Gun (공사계약일반조건) [General Terms of Construction Contracts], Ministry of Economy and Finance Contract Regulation No. 581 as amended on 1 December 2021, effective on 1 December 2021. Korean original at https://www.law.go.kr/%ED%96%89%EC%A0%95%EA%B7%9C%EC%B9%99/(%EA%B3%84%EC%95%BD%EC%98%88%EA%B7%9C)%EA%B3%B5%EC%82%AC%EA%B3%84%EC%95%BD%EC%9D%BC%EB%B0%98%EC%A1%B0%EA%B1%B4 [Accessed on 11 March 2023].

A similar provision is contained in Article 36 of the General Terms of Contracts for Services, and Article 31 of the General Terms of Contracts for the Supply and Manufacture of Goods.

Yong-Yeok-Gye-Yak-Il-Ban-Jo-Gun (용역계약일반조건) [General Terms of Contracts for Services], Ministry of Economy and Finance Contract Regulation No. 582 as amended on 1 December 2021, effective on 1 December 2021. Korean original at https://www.law.go.kr/%ED%96%89%EC%A0%95%EA%B7%9C%EC%B9%99/(%EA%B3%84%EC%95%BD%EC%98%88%EA%B7%9C)%EC%9A%A9%EC%97%AD%EA%B3%84%EC%95%BD%EC%9D%BC%EB%B0%98%EC%A1%B0%EA%B1%B4 [Accessed on 12 March 2023].

Mul-Pum-Gu-Mae-Je-Jo-Gye-Yak-Il-Ban-Jo-Gun (물품구매제조계약일반조건) [General Terms of Contracts for the Supply and Manufacture of Goods], Ministry of Economy and Finance Contract Regulation No. 583 as amended on 1 December 2021, effective on 1 December 2021. Korean original at https://www.law.go.kr/%ED%96%89%EC%A0%95%EA%B7%9C%EC%B9%99/(%EA%B3%84%EC%95%BD%EC%98%88%EA%B7%9C)%EB%AC%BC%ED%92%88%EA%B5%AC%EB%A7%A4(%EC%A0%9C%EC%A1%B0)%EA%B3%84%EC%95%BD%EC%9D%BC%EB%B0%98%EC%A1%B0%EA%B1%B4 [Accessed on 11 March 2023].

52. Bae, Kim & Lee LLC, *supra* note 3, at 120.

53. KIM Kee Chang, "Arbitration Agreement under Korean Law" in 3, *Korea University Law Review* (2008), 83-102.

54. LEE, *supra* note 1; SHIN, *supra* note 5; CHOI, *supra* note 1.

SPECIAL REPORTS

The Constitutional Court's Decision and Recent Legislation Related to Relief for Elapsing the Period of Renunciation of Nationality by Multiple Nationality Holders

CHUNG Min Jung
Legislative Research Officer
National Assembly Legislative Research Service

Key Words

Constitutional Court, Freedom to renounce nationality, multiple nationality holder, obligation of military service, European Convention on Nationality

1. INTRODUCTION

In September 2020, the Constitutional Court ruled that legislation unilaterally prohibiting multiple nationality holders incorporated into the military service reserve from renouncing the nationality because the period of nationality selection had elapsed did not conform to the Constitution on the grounds that it violated both the principle against excessive restriction and the principle that damage should be minimized. Therefore, the Court made a declaration of constitutional non-conformity premised on improving legislation by September 30, 2022 (2016Hun-Ma889).

Nationality is a legal bond between the individual and the state.

In general, individuals acquire nationality according to the principle of lineage or birthplace at birth, regardless of their free will. States' enactment of laws that permanently bind individuals to their own countries based on their lineage or birthplace did not pose a problem when cross-border population movements were infrequent.

However, as the number of multiple nationality holders surged due to overseas migration and international marriages, the principles of lineage and birthplace could no longer reflect the actual bonds between individuals and countries. Individuals did not consider their parents' country of birth as their own country when they themselves did not reside in that country or enjoy rights as a citizen of that country, yet they were unilaterally granted unwanted nationality as prescribed by domestic law. Accordingly, international law began to see an individual's acquisition and renunciation of nationality not as a matter of state's discretion but as the right of an individual to break the legal bond connected to their country of nationality regardless of their will. The freedom of nationality thus emerged as a principle of international law. In other words, the point is not whether the state can beneficially grant nationality on individuals, but on whether the state is obliged to allow individuals to renounce their nationality in response to the freedom of individual nationality.

In South Korea, which has a conscription system, the issue of nationality renunciation is closely related to the obligation of men with multiple nationalities to serve in the military. Because nationality is a medium for securing human resources for the state to fulfill its obligation of national security, renunciation of nationality according to an individual's voluntary will may conflict with the sovereignty and interests of the national state.

Some multiple nationality holders seek to enjoy the rights derived from holding a Korean nationality while avoiding the obligation of military service as a Korean citizen on the grounds that they have other nationalities. The current Nationality Act therefore allows multiple nationality holders to renounce their nationality only after they have fulfilled their military service obligations. As a result, in specific cases, some multiple nationality holders are unduly considered criminals, although they did not intend to evade military service, and are therefore unfairly forced to fulfill their military service obligations before renouncing their South Korean nationality.

Therefore, to identify appropriate legislation on nationality renunciation in countries with conscription obligations such as South Korea, we reviewed the legislation of the National Assembly after analyzing the decisions of the Constitutional Court.

2. THE CONSTITUTIONAL COURT'S DECISION ON THE RIGHT OF MULTIPLE NATIONALITY HOLDERS TO RENOUNCE THEIR NATIONALITY

2-1. MILITARY SERVICE OBLIGATIONS OF MEN WITH MULTIPLE NATIONALITIES

According to Korea's Nationality Act, multiple nationality holders under the age of 18 living abroad can renounce their Korean nationality by filling in a form.[1] While the state may secure military service resources through a nationality-based system, it is difficult to exercise effective jurisdiction over multiple nationality holders whose lives are based entirely abroad.[2] Therefore, the freedom of multiple nationality holders to renounce their nationality takes precedent to the national interest in securing military service resources. In other words, this provision did not take the military service of multiple nationality holders residing abroad for granted; in fact, the state had already predicted the loss of military service resources due to the renunciation of nationality.

However, the balancing test, which considers an individual's renunciation of nationality to take priority, changes three months after one is in military service reserve.[3] Until then, holders of multiple nationalities residing abroad may renounce their nationality. However, three months after joining the military service in reserve, multiple nationality holders must fulfill their military service obligations before they can give up their nationality. In other words, the fulfillment of military service obligations becomes a prerequisite for the renunciation of nationality. The important criteria for determining whether one can renounce one's nationality without fulfilling the military service obligation are as follows: whether one is incorporated into the military service reserve and whether three months have elapsed since.

2-2. DECISION OF THE CONSTITUTIONAL COURT

On November 26, 2015, the Constitutional Court ruled that Article 12 (2) of the Nationality Act was constitutional.[4] This Act enabled multiple nationality holders to renounce their nationality only after resolving their military service obligation if three months had passed from the date of being incorporated into military service reserve.

The Korean Constitutional Court views the freedom to renounce nationality as a basic constitutional right. In addition, this is not considered a right that directly contradicts the national interest in securing military service resources, but something that can be restrained through the balancing test with seemingly contradictory national values. According to the majority opinion of the five judges, Article 12 (2) of the Nationality Act did not wholly deprive multiple nationality holders of the right to renounce their nationality, and it cannot be considered a violation of the principle against excessive restriction taking into consideration the loss of military service resources, equal military burden, and preventing the evasion of military service.

However, in October 2020, the Constitutional Court ruled that the legislation providing that multiple nationality holders subject to participating in the military service should be unilaterally banned from renouncing the nationality violated both the principle against excessive restriction and the principle of damage minimization (2016Hun-Ma889). According to this decision multiple nationality holders cannot be expected, for reasons such as their residential location, to file nationality renunciation forms in time to renounce their nationality within the period set by the contested provisions. As the requirements were not announced to the respective individuals during the period of nationality selection, disallowing an individual to file for nationality renunciation for not having fulfilled the military service obligation on the ground the period had elapsed greatly limited the claimant's freedom to renounce his nationality, as the claimant was not accountable for his failure to renounce nationality in time.[5]

The Constitutional Court in its 2020 ruling, in other words, reversed its decision of 2015 with a majority opinion of seven judges, concluding that even if the period of nationality selection had passed, if the legislative purpose of securing fairness in military service performance was not objectively damaged because individuals had a valid excuse, the legislation should have provided an exception for the individuals to renounce their nationality. The Constitutional Court ruled that prohibition without recourse from doing so is a violation of the principle against excessive restriction.

In addition, the provisions of the Nationality Act pursue the public interest of the equitable performance of military service obligations. However, multiple nationality holders are unable to enjoy such public interests if they reside abroad and have not registered their birth in the Republic of Korea. As the Korean government cannot recognize them as citizens, they also cannot be incorporated into the military service reserve. Even if they were to be accidentally incorporated, the state could not enforce their military service obligations unless they entered the country. Nevertheless, multiple nationalities holders may still experience disadvantages in their countries of residence. For example, in the United States, multiple nationality holders are restricted from taking office and taking charge of public affairs. Considering these specific circumstances, applying the balancing test showed that the infringement of private interests was substantial.

There were also dissenting opinions of two judges. They argued that, as Korea has a conscription system, there is high public interest in the fair imposition of military service obligations and a great backlash in the event of unfair dealing and that the majority of the Constitutional Court should have taken a cautious approach because the contested provisions of the Nationality Act contain substance directly related to the military service obligation of multiple nationality holders.

3. EVALUATION

Koreans view multiple nationality holders negatively because some seek to behave opportunistically. In particular, Koreans are concerned that multiple nationality holders can abuse their multiple nationalities to avoid military service obligations. A major social issue arises from the fact that more parents seek to leave for the United States so that their children can acquire dual citizenship.[6] Accordingly, the Nationality Act allows multiple nationality holders born while their parents stayed abroad for short-term purposes to renounce their nationality only after their military service obligations are fulfilled.

The problem is that the objective criterion of "three months after incorporation into military service reserve" is insufficient for proving the subjective intention of exemption from military service. In fact, the claimants in the 2013Hun-Ma805, 2014Hun-Ma788, and 2016Hun-Ma889 cases tried to renounce their Korean citizenship to retain their U.S. citizenship, as their lives were based entirely in the U.S. Their only bond with South Korea was that their parents were Korean; they had never actually enjoyed the rights bestowed by their Korean nationality. The Constitutional Court decided that this was unfair for multiple nationality holders, and that it violated the principle against excessive restriction because it did not meet the minimum infringement and legal interest balancing requirements.

3-1. AN EVALUATION OF THE PROVISIONS OF THE NATIONALITY ACT IN TERMS OF LEGISLATIVE PURPOSES

In the 2016Hun-Ma889 decision announced on September 24, 2020, the Constitutional Court stated that the legislative purpose of the provisions of the Nationality Act subject to judgment was to impose military service obligations fairly. To this end, the period of nationality selection is limited so that multiple nationality holders cannot abuse the nationality selection system to evade military service obligations. However, the majority opinion held that this means not directly related to achieving the public interest of the contested nationality law, as multiple nationality holders who had not been registered for birth in Korea were unlikely to be obligated to serve in the military. The state has practical difficulty in recognizing them as citizens, and even if they are included in the military service reserve, they can be legally exempted from military service under the Military Service Act. On the other hand, it is possible to refute the view in that there is still a chance that multiple nationality holders who are obligated to serve in the military will fulfill their military obligations according to changes in circumstances, such as entering the Republic of Korea as long as they maintain Korean nationality.

3-2. EVALUATION OF THE INFRINGEMENT OF FREEDOM OF NATIONALITY

The Constitutional Court ruled that the contested provisions of the Nationality Act were inconsistent with the Constitution because they fail to acknowledge any renunciation of nationality. The issue was not its limitation of the period of nationality selection to a short period, but its failure to acknowledge any exceptions to the renunciation of nationality. This reasoning shows that the Constitutional Court still placed weight on the legislative purpose of the equitable imposition of military service obligations as a crucial value.

One of the main reasons the provisions of the Nationality Act were found to violate the principle against excessive restriction and the freedom to renounce nationality was the practice of nationality selection procedures or restrictions that occurred when the nationality selection period elapsed. It is impossible in practice to provide individual guidance on the selection or renunciation of nationality and difficult to identify citizens the authorities have not registered as residing overseas, especially those with multiple nationalities whose births have not been registered in Korea. Authorities continuously strive to provide guidance regarding the period and procedure for selecting nationality through overseas embassies and consulates. However, this level of guidance cannot replace notifications at the individual level. The expiry of this period can pose serious disadvantages to multiple nationality holders who will be unable to report their renunciation of nationality until the military service obligation is fulfilled. Considering that mandatory military service is usually fulfilled at the age of 36 years, during which citizens are incorporated into wartime labor service under the Military Service

Act, or at the age of 38 years, during which they are exempt (Article 71), the period in which individuals cannot renounce their nationality is burdensome by any standard.

4. AMENDMENT OF THE NATIONALITY ACT TO PROVIDE A REMEDY FOR THE ELAPSE OF THE NATIONALITY RENUNCIATION PERIOD

In the past, the Nationality Act did not allow male multiple nationality holders to renounce the nationality until they were relieved of their military service obligations unless they chose their nationality by the end of March of the year they turned 18 years old. In the 2016Hun-Ma889 decision of September 24, 2020, the Constitutional Court ruled that the provision was unconstitutional because it severely restricted freedom of residence and movement of residence without considering the circumstances that made it infeasible for multiple nationality holders to report their renunciation within the nationality selection period. Accordingly, the National Assembly revised the requirements and procedures to comply with the Constitution so that multiple nationality holders could report their renunciation of nationality if there was a justifiable cause.[7]

Individual renunciation of nationality can only be partially limited based on the principle of preventing statelessness and for the obligation of citizens. In addition, the Constitutional Court ruled in the 2016Hun-Ma889 decision that the unconstitutional legislation should be replaced by exceptionally allowing multiple nationality holders who lived abroad and were unable to file for nationality renunciation within the given time frame to renounce their nationality after the period had elapsed. Accordingly, the 21st National Assembly incorporated amendments to the Nationality Act, which allowed those who were born in a foreign country or who moved to a foreign country under the age of six years to abandon their nationality even after three months had elapsed from the date of incorporation into the military service reserve (Article 14-2). It was promulgated as Act No. 18978 on September 15, 2022, immediately before the expiration of the revised legislative deadline ordered by the Constitutional Court (September 30, 2022). This law became effective on October 1, 2022. In addition, the revised Nationality Act upgraded the Nationality Review Committee, which was previously based on the Enforcement Decree of the same Act, to a legal deliberation body, and added matters on permission to renounce nationality as subjects they were charged with deliberating (Article 22). For multiple nationality holders, Korean nationality is merely granted according to lineage. This review allowed the Committee to investigate whether multiple nationality holders intended to evade military obligations or were unaware of such obligations.

5. CONCLUSION

South Korea follows the principles of parental pedigree in granting nationality, with Article 2 of the Nationality Act granting Korean nationality to children born to Korean nationals on the basis of blood ties. Such Korean nationality is valid simultaneously alongside U.S. immigration law, which follows the principle of birthplace; one can therefore acquire multiple nationalities. However, for South Korean immigrants in the U.S., who only want to acquire and possess U.S. citizenship to incorporate themselves into mainstream U.S. society such as entering public office and military schools, South Korean nationality is overreaching.[8]

Some individuals who were born and resided in the United States might not feel a real bond with South Korea because their only ties with the country were through their Korean parents. In fact, these individuals were unable to enjoy their rights as nationals of the Republic of Korea. Therefore, if only the obligations that follow their nationality are imposed on an individual, the nationality of the Republic of Korea is considered to an overreach. According to the perspective of international human rights norms and the 2020 decision of the Constitutional Court, the Republic of Korea should allow individuals to renounce their nationality to the extent that it does not inherently undermine the fair allocation of military service obligations.[9] Eventually, on September 15, 2022, the 21st National Assembly revised the Nationality Act to grant legislative relief to multiple nationality holders.[10] We hope that the legislation will solve the overreaching problem of Korean nationality for Korean-American residents.

REFERENCES

1. Articles

Gong Jin-sung, "Constitutional Limits and Legislative Improvement Measures for Restrictions on Freedom of Multiple Nationality Holders Incorporated in Military Reserve," Kookmin University, 33(3) *Constitutional Forum*, (2021), pp. 498-542.

Gu Jawan, "Qualification for Restriction of Nationality Renunciation", 27(1), *Constitutional Studies*, (2021), pp. 75-113.

Yang So-yeon, "Citizenship and Multiple Nationality Holders from the Perspective of Basic Rights," 182(1), *Justice*, (2021), pp. 5-44.

2. Working Papers and Reports

Chung Min-jung, "International legal issues and legislative tasks on renunciation of nationality of multiple nationality holders," National Assembly Legislative Research Service, *Issues and Tasks*, No. 1722, (2020).

3. Constitutional Court's Decisions

Constitutional Court of Korea, 2016Hun-Ma889, Decided on September 24, 2020 (S. Kor.).

Constitutional Court of Korea, 2013Hun-Ma805, 2014Hun-Ma788 (merged), Decided on November 26, 2015 (S. Kor.).

Notes

1. Article 12 (1) of the Nationality Act.
2. Gu Jawan, "Qualification for Restriction of Nationality Renunciation," 27(1), Constitutional Studies, (2021), p.88.
3. Article 12 (2) of the Nationality Act.
4. Constitutional Court of Korea, 2013Hun-Ma805, 2014Hun-Ma788 (merged), Decided on November 26, 2015 (S. Kor.).
5. Constitutional Court of Korea, 2016Hun-Ma889, Decided on September 24, 2020 (S. Kor.), Gazette No. 288, pp.1280-1281.
6. Regarding the differences in social class due to multiple nationality holders usually being from wealthy families, the Constitutional Court's November 30, 2006 2005 Constitution 739 ruling reads, "In particular, a majority of dual nationality holders are the children of social leaders and wealthy people; if the State does not regulate their opportunistic military exemptions, the public's distrust in military service will increase and the public will experience a larger burden derived from military obligations. This will ultimately damage the public's overall capability."
7. Gong Jin-sung, "Constitutional Limits and Legislative Improvement Measures for Restrictions on Freedom of Multiple Nationality Holders Incorporated in Military Reserve," Kookmin University, 33(3) Constitutional Forum, (2021), p.538.
8. Yang So-yeon, "Citizenship and Multiple Nationality Holders from the Perspective of Basic Rights," 182(1), Justice, (2021), p.15.
9. On the other hand, statelessness may arise as an issue in various political situations within the context of pedigreeism, and Korean nationality is under-reached to compatriots in other regions who want to acquire and possess Korean nationality.
10. Chung Min-jung, "International legal issues and legislative tasks on renunciation of nationality of multiple nationality holders," National Assembly Legislative Research Service, Issues and Tasks, No. 1722, (2020), p.4.

The Inter-Korea Basic Agreement of 1991 – Its legal nature and its role in the promotion of peace on the Korean Peninsula

Lee Jang-Hie
Emeritus Professor
Hankuk University of Foreign Studies, Law School, Seoul, Korea

Key Words

The Inter-Korea Basic Agreement, Reconciliation, Self-reliance, the tentatively special relations, perestroika, Inter-Korea High-Level Talks, ratification, German Basic Treaty, peaceful coexistence, The West German Constitutional Court, Duality

1. Background to the signing of the Inter-Korean Basic Agreement of 1991(IKBA)

This year (2023) marks the 32nd anniversary of the signing of the Agreement on Reconciliation, Nonaggression and Exchanges and Cooperation between the South and the North ("the IKBA") (on December 13, 1991) and the two Koreas' simultaneous entry into the UN on September 18, 1991.

Thirty one years ago, Mikhail Gorbachev, who was inaugurated in 1985 as the General Secretary of the Communist Party of the Soviet Union as the leader of the Socialist Bloc recognized serious problems in the political and economic system of his country and made serious attempts to implement what came to be known across the world as glasnost (door opening) and perestroika (innovation). The Berlin Wall was demolished in November 1989 and, just one month later, U.S. President George Bush and Mikhail Gorbachev met at a summit held in Malta, a small island in the Mediterranean. At the summit, the two leaders made the Malta Declaration to the effect that the Eastern and Western Blocs were ushering in a new era of cooperation, thus signaling the end of the Cold War period. In reality, the Soviet Union could no longer provide economic support for, or interfere with, the political and military affairs of its satellite countries in Eastern Europe. Likewise, China could no longer provide economic support for, or interfere with, the political and military affairs of its Socialist allies including North Korea. The latter country, feeling a deep sense of crisis concerning its failed system amid international isolation and the ever widening gap with South Korea in terms of its overall national strength, had no choice but to opt for a strategy of peaceful coexistence with the South.

The Malta Declaration of 1989, made jointly by the United States and the Soviet Union, had a great impact on the easing of tensions on the Korean Peninsula. To touch on the situation on the Korean Peninsula a little further, following the emergence of "New Thinking" in the diplomacy adopted by the Soviet Union in 1986, the South witnessed a series of major events linked to a grass-roots democratization movement which had been suppressed by many years of dictatorship and the Cold War system, along with pressure to open the country's doors exerted by factions demanding inter-Korea reunification. Examples include Reverend Moon Ikhwan's visit to the North in 1989 without having obtained a permit from the government; the visit to the North by a student named Im Sugyeong, then leader of the National Association of University Student Representatives (Jeondaehyup), in order to participate in the 13th World Festival of Youth and Students held in Pyongyang; and many other unification activists illegally entering North Korea. On the back of its superior economic strength, which was surpassing that of the North by far, the South's government also took a very positive stance in its relations with the North. The Roh Taewoo government of the South pushed ahead with the July 7, 1988 Declaration, the Korean National Community Unification Formula (1989), the re-establishment of diplomatic relations with the Soviet Union (1990), the two Koreas' simultaneous entry into the UN (1991), and the re-establishment of diplomatic relations with China (1992) as part of its Northern Policy and its efforts to improve inter-Korean relations. These initiatives took place against the backdrop of the general international thawing of the Cold War period, the people-driven democratization movement, the pressure to open the country's doors from factions asking for peaceful re-unification, and the North's favorable response.

After the July 7, 1988 Declaration, President Roh Taewoo started making efforts to re-establish diplomatic relations with former Soviet Bloc countries including Hungary in 1989, followed by Poland, Yugoslavia, Czechoslovakia, Bulgaria, Rumania, and Albania in 1991.

The IKBA was the result of a combination of factors including the gradual international thawing of the Cold War, the North's increasing sense of crisis amid its international isolation, the strong demand for inter-Korean exchange and cooperation from the factions of the South calling for democratization, and the two Koreas' strategies for peaceful coexistence.

The IKBA was signed at the 5th High-Level Talks held in 1991, following a series of meetings between the delegations of the two sides headed by the Prime Ministers, including the first one held from September 4, 1990, some forty-six years after the division of the country into two separate states. The IKBA agreement was made at an official government meeting, the first one of its kind to be held since the country's division. Its form and substance correspond to those of an international treaty and touch on overall inter-Korean relations in a systematic way. At the 6th Inter-Korea High-Level Talks held in February 1992, the two sides reached an agreement on the composition and operation of subcommittees on political and military matters, exchanges, and cooperation in addition to the IKBA. They also made the Joint Declaration on the Denuclearization of the Korean Peninsula.

2. Overview of the Inter-Korea Basic Agreement (IKBA)

The form and contents of the IKBA have the most crucial legal significance among all the agreements reached between the two sides over the past seventy years of division. In form the IKBA is composed of a foreword and four chapters (including 25 articles). It was signed by ROK Prime Minister Jeong Wonsik and DPRK Administration Council Prime Minister Yeon Hyeongmuk, the persons entrusted by those authorized to sign a treaty, and it used the official names of the two sides. It was carried out in accordance with the procedure for signing a treaty, including negotiations, signing, ratification by parliament, registration, and effectuation under the prevailing international law. It met all the requirements for a treaty (such as the capability of the treaty signatory, the person who has the right to sign a treaty, expression of intent without defects, and legitimacy of the contents of the treaty). It is deemed that the IKBA requires the National Assembly's ratification under Article 60 of the Korean Constitution as an international treaty. The IKBA includes the details of the two sides' agreement, structured logically and comprehensively as follows:

The Preamble covers the three leading principles of homeland reunification (self-reliance, peace, and grand national unity) as stated in the July 4, 1972 Joint Declaration and a definition of the tentatively special relations between the two Koreans; Chapter 1 addresses inter-Korean reconciliation; Chapter 2 covers mutual non-aggression; Chapter 3 deals with inter-Korea exchanges and cooperation; and Chapter 4 presents clauses concerning amendment and effectuation. It can be said that all the agreements reached between the leaders of the two sides, including the June 15 (2000) South-North Joint Declaration, the October 4 (2007) Declaration, and the April 27 (2018) Panmunjeom Declaration are more detailed, expanded and developed versions based on the IKBA. Its major points are as follow:

2-1. Preamble

- Re-affirmation of the three leading principles of homeland reunification (self-reliance, peace, and great national unity) stated in the July 4, 1972 Joint Declaration;
- Relations between the two Koreas: Defined as tentatively special relations formed in the process of moving toward reunification, not inter-country relations;
- Reconciliation between the two sides by putting a stop to political and military confrontations;
- Prevention of armed clashes, guarantee of peace, realization of multi-sided exchanges and cooperation, and realization of the common interests of the Korean nation.

* Appraisal: The definition of the legal nature of inter-Korean relations as "tentatively special relations" is thought to have had an impact on inter-Korean relations in general in consideration of the specificity of a divided country.

2-2. Chapter 1 Inter-Korean Reconciliation (Articles 1 to 8)

-Article 1: Mutual recognition of and respect for each other's regime;
-Article 2: Non-interference in each other's internal issues;
-Article 3: No slander or defamation;
-Article 4: No attempt to destroy or overthrow the other side;
-Article 5: Observance of the Armistice Agreement until a stable state of peace is achieved;
-Article 6: No confrontation on the international stage; pursuit of the common interests of the Korean nation;
-Article 7: Establishment of the Inter-Korean Liaison Office at the Panmunjeom;
-Article 8: Composition of the Inter-Korean Political Subcommittee within one month of effectuation of the Agreement and discussion on how to achieve inter-Korea reconciliation.
* Appraisal: Articles 1 to 5 were placed at the top of the North's agenda concerning its need to protect its regime. "The stable state of peace" stated in Article 5 refers to the North's first recognition of the South as a party to the peace issue. Previously, the North recognized the South only as a party to the non-aggression treaty, but not a party to matters related to peace and unification. The Inter-Korea Liaison Office was included only as a body having the function of liaison, not a consular function like that of the Standing Representatives stated in the German Basic Treaty of 1972.

2-3. Chapter 2 Inter-Korean Non-aggression (Articles 9 to 14)

-Article 9: Non-use of military force or aggression. A dual guarantee concerning observance of the Armistice Agreement until a stable state of peace is achieved, and observance of the clause stipulating abstention from the threat or use of force as mandated in the UN Charter, Article 2(4).

-Article 10: Obligation to pursue the peaceful settlement of disputes.

-Article 11: Fixing of each country's border and area for non-aggression as the military demarcation line (MDL) stipulated in the Armistice Agreement and the areas controlled by each side: A proposal for compromise concerning the Northern Limit Line (NLL).

-Article 12: Formation and operation of the Inter-Korean Military Commission within three months of the effectuation of the Agreement in order to guarantee non-aggression toward each other. The Inter-Korean Military Commission is to discuss and promote matters concerning the establishment of military trust (i.e. peaceful use of the DMZ, notice on/control of large-scale relocation of military units and military exercises, exchange of military personnel/ information, realization of phased reduction of arms aimed at the removal of WMDs and a reduction of large-scale attack capability, and verification thereof).

-Article 13: Installation of a direct phone line linking the military authorities of the two sides.

-Article 14: Composition of the Inter-Korea Military Subcommittee as a consultative body for observance of execution of the Agreement within one month of effectuation of the Agreement.

* Appraisal: It is significant that the two sides agreed on a way to establish military trust and reached a compromise for the first time on the NLL issue, a longstanding cause of military tension between the two sides.

2-4. Chapter 3 Inter-Korean Exchange and Cooperation (Articles 15 to 23)

-Article 15: Agreement on balanced development of the national economy, joint development of resources for improvement of people's welfare and internal trade between the two peoples.

-Article 16: Exchange and cooperation in diverse areas including science, technology education, literature, arts, health, sports, environment, newspaper, radio, television, publications, publishing and media reports, etc.

-Article 17: Free visits to and contact between the two sides.

-Article 18: Free exchange of letters and visits between dispersed families/relatives; development of ways to resolve humanitarian issues.

-Article 19: Connection of roads and railroads, opening of a sea route.

-Article 20: Installation of facilities for the exchange of mail and communication between the two sides; keeping each other's secrets confidential.

-Article 21: Mutual cooperation at the international stage

-Article 22: Operation of the Inter-Korean Commission for Economic Exchange and Cooperation to implement the economic and cultural matters stated in the Agreement.

-Article 23: Formation of the Inter-Korea Exchange and Cooperation Subcommittee within one month of effectuation of the Agreement to discuss economic and cultural exchanges.

* Appraisal: "Balanced national economy and internal trade among people" carries considerable significance in the pursuit of reconciliation and cooperation between the two sides.

2-5. Chapter 4 Amendment and Effectuation (Articles 24 and 25)

-Article 24: The Agreement may be amended or supplemented through mutual consultation.

-Article 25: The Agreement shall enter into force on the day the two sides exchange the signed text signed after the effectuation procedure.

- The signatories of the IKBA are as follows: ROK Prime Minister Jeong Wonsik serving as the Chief Representative of the South's

Delegation of Inter-Korean High-Level Talks, and DPRK Government Council Prime Minister Yeon Hyeongmuk serving as the Chief Representative of the North's Delegation for Inter-Korean High-Level Talks. In the Agreement, the two sides used each others' official names and the Agreement was signed by the responsible parties entrusted by those authorized to sign a treaty.

* Appraisal: The following positive aspects of the Agreement enhanced its legal normativity: inclusion of a clause related to its amendment and effectuation, and the use of each country's official name.

3. Legal nature of the IKBA

First of all, the IKBA has binding legal effect. The IKBA is quite different from other political statements and other inter-Korean agreements, which were merely "gentlemen's" agreements, being the first one to have legal binding force signed by the two sides and to fully meet the formal legal requirements (or legal normativity). The IKBA is not merely a policy statement, but a legal norm that binds the parties legally. A policy statement requires neither an effectuation clause (as stated in Chapter 4 of the IKBA) nor a preamble. It can be unclear whether an agreement made by legal entities is a policy statement that has no legal biding force or is one intended to create a legal norm (i.e. rights and obligations) that has legal binding force. In such a case, if the parties have the intention of concluding a contract (animus contrahendi), it is recognized as a treaty, i.e. a legal norm. More specifically, in reality it is not easy to ascertain whether the parties have such an intention. The IKBA can be viewed as a "legal norm" for the following reasons[1]:

1) Generally, a policy statement does not include a clause related to its own effectuation, whereas an agreement that has legal binding

force does. Article 25 of the IKBA contains a clause about its effectuation

2) A policy statement takes the form of "1, 2, 3..," rather than "Article 1, Article 2 Article 3..." The Basic Agreement is composed of a Preamble and 25 clauses.

3) Generally, a policy statement uses the expression "declare," while an agreement that has binding force uses "agree."

4) Generally, a policy statement does not include a clause about its own amendment or supplementation, whereas an agreement that has binding force does, as does the IKBA (Article 24).

The foregoing four factors make it clear that, in signing the IKBA, the two Koreas as the parties, expressly intended to conclude it as one that has legal binding force.[2]

Second, the IKBA is the basic legal norm that regulates the reconciliation and cooperation stage as the first step toward the Korean National Community Unification Formula (1984), the two other steps being the "Inter-Korea Unity" stage (Inter-Korea Unity Charter) and the "One Nation, One Country (Unified Constitution)" stage.

Third, the IKBA defines inter-Korean relations as special relations. The legal nature of inter-Korean relations stated in the Preamble of the IKBA, i.e. "tentatively special relations formed in the process of moving toward reunification, not inter-country relations" is very important, and therefore the two Koreas need to develop and manage the relationship effectively. The IKBA defines the legal relations of a country divided into two as "special" ones that have "tentativeness" and "duality" at the same time. "Duality" refers to the special situation wherein a country is divided into independent states to which international law applies at the international level like the UN, but which internally are one nation. Accordingly, transactions "within one nation" are regarded as internal trade, in which no custom duties or taxes are imposed.

The clause in the IKBA that specifies these special relations is

Article 15, which states that transactions between the two Koreas are internal trade and thus not subject to the Foreign Trade Act or the Customs Act of the South.

West and East Germany took a similar approach, agreeing to internal trade through the Berlin Agreement of 1951. When joining the EC and the GATT, West Germany made a point of inserting an additional protocol clause to the effect that its adhesion should not hamper or negatively impact internal trade between the two Germanies,[3] which was already under way. The German Basic Treaty of 1972 used a means of avoiding making the division an established fact by exchanging "Standing Representatives" with each other instead of ambassadors, which was in fact a very useful way for the two halves of a divided country to aim for peaceful reunification and prevent the division from being accepted as an established fact. The theory of tentatively special relations included in the German Basic Treaty of 1972[4] went a long way in assisting the management of the divided Germany, in promoting exchanges and cooperation and, ultimately, in reuniting the country.[5]

Fourth, the IKBA has the nature of a treaty in a special form. An international treaty is an explicit agreement made by subjects of international law. The North, at least internally, qualifies as a party to sign an international treaty as a belligerent body, which is a subject of international law. Some observers state that relations between the two Koreas are not comparable to relations between sovereign states and, therefore, the South cannot sign a treaty-like agreement with the North; and, further, that an agreement with the North is not a treaty between countries subject to the ratification of the National Assembly as stipulated in Article 60 of the South's Constitution. But such a view is incorrect. One condition required of any entity that signs an international agreement or treaty is that it is a subject of international law, and this includes international organizations and belligerent parties (such as the North in the Cold

War Period) as well as sovereign states.

Fifth, the IKBA's period of validity is tentative. It regulates the first stage of the three leading roadmaps for the peaceful unification of the Korean Peninsula. It is legally temporary as an agreement that is only valid during the reconciliation and cooperation stage.

4. The IKBA's role in promoting peace on the Korean Peninsula

4-1. The role of a navigator at the reconciliation and cooperation stage, the first stage of the Korean National Community Unification Formula (1989)

The IKBA is legal norm that serves as the basis for the first stage leading to the intermediate "Korean Commonwealth" stage of the Korean National Community Unification Formula (1989). Its Preamble states that it is a treaty in which "tentativeness" applies to the first stage that regulates the reconciliation and cooperation stage on the road to peaceful unification. Compared to the July 4 North-South Joint Communiqué of 1972, which was agreed upon by secret envoys, the IKBA meets all the requirements of a treaty under international law in all respects, including in form and substance, with open participation the signatures of the responsible persons of the governments of both sides. Those authorized to act as the treaty signatories promised to observe the agreements on reconciliation and cooperation between the two sides of the Korean nation.

4-2. The role of a basic law that regulates inter-Korean relations in general

A large number of complex agreements on inter-Korean relations have already been signed, and even more will doubtless be signed in the future. However, a basic law is urgently required concerning how to establish basic legal relations in each area of inter-Korean relations. The Inter-Korean Basic Agreement of 1991 could play such a role. The IKBA arranges the basic legal principles that regulate inter-Korean relations in general by dividing them into political reconciliation, non-aggression, and exchange and cooperation. Therefore, the IKBA should be adopted as the basic law for implementing the aforementioned functions.

For the IKBA to be adopted as a basic law, however, it should definitely have internal legal effective, and each side should promptly follow its internal procedure under its own Constitution. It is deeply regrettable that the National Assembly has not yet ratified the IKBA. The Ministry of Unification should have it submitted to a Cabinet meeting and then asked the National Assembly to guarantee the efficacy of the IKBA through ratification. As for the North, its Prime Minister Yeon Hyeongmuk made a report on the IKBA at the 19th Workers Party Central Committee Meeting held in December 1991, and it was approved by the Central Peoples' Committee and the Supreme People's Assembly Presidium in the same month. President Kim Ilsung ratified it right before its effectuation, thus completing the required procedure for ratification of the treaty. Both the South Korean government and the National Assembly should have proceeded with its ratification as soon as possible to display their commitment to putting the IKBA into practice and make it the legally binding document it was intended to be.

4-3. IKBA, a stepping stone in establishing a regime of peace on the Korean Peninsula

Where the roadmap for the peaceful unification of the Korean Peninsula is divided into four stages (Reconciliation/Cooperation;

Establishment of a regime of Peace; Inter-Korea Unity; One Nation, One Country), the IKBA could play the role of managing the reconciliation and cooperation stage in general and serve as a stepping stone to the establishment of a regime of peace on the Korean Peninsula.

4-4. The role of a basic norm in overhauling the laws enacted during the Cold War period

The two Koreas should promptly launch the Inter-Korean Working-level Legal Meeting as stated in the notes to Chapter 1 Inter-Korea Reconciliation Ancillary Agreement (dated September 17, 1992) of the Inter-Korean Basic Agreement of 1991 with regard to the need to overhaul the laws enacted during the Cold War period both in and out of Korea. The notes to Chapter 1 Ancillary Agreement on the Execution and Observation of Inter-Korean Exchange and Cooperation (dated September 17, 1992) of the IKBA state: "The two sides shall discuss the issue of revising or scrapping treaties and agreements made with other countries that run counter to national unity and interests at the Working-level Legal Council and resolve the issue." However, the council has not yet been formed, necessitating the two sides' prompt action to that end.

The two sides should now start overhauling the laws enacted during the Cold War Period in accordance with the spirit of the IKBA and its legal normativity. In particular, the National Security Act of the South, which is designed to antagonize the North, should be now abolished as per the legal normativity of the IKBA. It is also necessary to overhaul the North's Workers' Party Regulations, which are designed to stir anti-regime revolutions in the South and antagonize the South, as well as clauses in the North's Criminal Act which allow analogical interpretation. It is worth noting that the North deleted considerable parts of the analogical interpretation clauses and partially adopted the principle of legality in 2004. Furthermore, at the 8th Congress of the Workers' Party held in January 2021, the North disclosed the Workers' Party Regulations and deleted the part about the need for "anti-regime revolutions in the South" in the Preamble to the Regulations. The said Regulations replaced the wording about the need for nationwide "democratic revolutions for national liberation" with the need for "society's independent and democratic development" in the Party's present purpose.[6]

No amendment has yet been made to the crime of praising or inciting activities of an anti-governmental organization stipulated in Article 7(1) and (5) of the National Security Act of the South since the Constitutional Court's limited constitutionality ruling of their limited constitutionality in April 1990. The said Act has been left completely untouched since May 1991, when the new phrase "with knowledge of the fact that it may endanger the existence and security of the State or democratic fundamental order" was newly inserted into it.

4-5. Acceleration of the Reconciliation/Cooperation Stage through the operation of Inter-Korean subcommittees and joint commissions

The two sides' agreement on the formation and composition of inter-Korean (political, military, and exchanges/cooperation) subcommittees as consultative bodies and of the joint commission as a body for putting ideas into practice is expected to enhance the enforceability of the IKBA. To mark the 32rd anniversary of the signing of the IKBA, the two sides should take prompt steps to form and operate the said bodies so as accelerate the Reconciliation/Cooperation Stage.

5. Conclusion

Following the promise made by the United States and the Soviet Union to put an end to the Cold War through the Malta Declaration of 1989, the two Koreas recognized the need to cope with the situation proactively and signed the IKBA in an effort to secure peaceful coexistence on the Korean Peninsula.

Legally, the IKBA meets all the requirements of an international treaty in terms of its form and substance. In this respect, it is much more detailed and addresses more fundamental issues than the German Basic Treaty of 1972. It adopted the "tentatively special relations" theory for the first time in a bid to manage the complex problems of a divided country. Upon the South's ratification of the IKBA, the Constitutional Court will have to reconsider the stance it displayed in its limited constitutionality ruling that it handed down in April 1990. The Constitutional Court should judge matters concerning inter-Korean exchanges and cooperation based on the IKBA rather than on the National Security Act. The government of the South should consult with the North on the composition of the Inter-Korean Working-Level Legal Council to discuss amendment or abolition of the laws enacted during the Cold War period.

Although the prevailing situation in Korea is not the same as in Germany, it is necessary to review studies on the German Basic Treaty of 1972, which provided the legal groundwork for Willy Brandt's Eastern Policy. The core elements of the German Basic Treaty of 1972 were the development of normal friendly relations based on equal rights, the One Nation, Two Countries principle, the waiver of the right to single-handed representation, recognition of each other's borders, respect for treaties previously signed, and the establishment of standing representatives. In 1972, the conservative local government of Freistaat Bayern, West Germany filed a constitutional petition, arguing that the Basic Treaty of 1972 did not comply with the constitution. The West German Constitutional Court dismissed the petition in July 1973.[7]

At present, the relations between the two Koreas are stalled. As such, they should go back to the spirit of the IKBA and the April 27 (2018) Panmunjeom Declaration, which went into more detail based on the IKBA. It is expected that by February 2024, which marks the 33rd anniversary of the IKBA, the winds of reconciliation and cooperation will start blowing again on the Korean Peninsula.

The government of South Korea should make a proposal to the North to jointly host a special event to commemorate IKBA's anniversary on February 19th, 2024. NGOs should also strive to foster a favorable atmosphere by holding international seminars and special events for peace-related education and by publicizing the core contents of the IKBA. The government should not let the anniversary pass by uneventfully, particularly considering the importance of the IKBA and the fact that the Reconciliation/Cooperation Stage could be completed as the first roadmap for the country's peaceful unification with the complete implementation of the IKBA.

Notes

1. Myung-Ki Kim, *The Treaties on Basic Agreement between The South and The North*, The Institute for International Affairs, Seoul,1992, pp.31-53.

2. Jang-Hie Lee,"The Inter-Korea Basic Agreement of 1991, Its Legal Nature & Its Enforcement", *The Korean Journal of International Law*, Vol. 43, No. 1, June 1998, pp.230-233.

3. Jang-Hie Lee etc., "Intra German Trade and Its Legal Implications for Intra-Korean Commerce", *The Korean Journal of International Law*, Vol. 38, No. 2, December 1993, pp. 110-118.

4. Jochen A. Frowein,"Federal Republic of Germany", *The Effect of Treaties in Domestic Law*, United Kingdom National Committee of Comparative Law, London Sweet & Maxwell 1987, pp. 64-74.

5. Jang-Hie Lee, "Legal and Institutional Aspects of the Transition to German Unification (1949-1989)", *International Relation Law in Transition Period*, Beommunsa Publishing House. Seoul, Korea. 1992, pp. 116-118.

6. "New Party Rules Show North Korean Leader Breaking Away from Predecessors", The Korea Times, 2021-06-03; https://www.koreatimes.co.kr/www/nation/2023/02/103_309879.html#

7. Jang-Hie Lee, "International Legal Anyalysis of German Unification", Young Huh (ed.) *A Legal Approach to German Unification*, Bak-Young-Sa, Seoul, Korea, 1994, pp. 64-78.

Industrial Security Laws in the Republic of Law: Comparison with their Japanese Counterparts

Lee Gyooho
Professor
Chung—Ang University School of Law, Seoul, Korea

I. Introduction

Prior to the enactment of the Act on Special Measures to Strengthen and Protect Competitiveness of National High-tech Strategic Industries (hereinafter "National High-tech Strategic Industries Act")[1], industrial security had been guaranteed by several laws such as the Patent Act including non-disclosure of patent application based on national defense, Act on the Prevention of Unfair Competition and Protection of Trade Secret, Act on Prevention of Divulgence and Protection of Industrial Technology, Act on Support for Protection of Technology of Small and Medium Businesses, and Price Stabilization Act. Under this decentralized system of individual statutes, South Korea had difficulty establishing a centralized control tower for stabilizing supply and demand chains of important items and technologies, jeopardizing national industrial security. Hence, the National High-tech Strategic Industries Act was enacted. In this regard, the enactment of Japanese industrial security laws will have some implications for our industries because some high-tech industries such as semiconductors and storage batteries overlap in both countries.

II. Laws related to industrial security in the Republic of Korea

1. Purpose of the National High-tech Strategic Industries Act

The National High-tech Strategic Industries Act was enacted in 2022 and revised in 2023.[2] The National High-tech Strategic Industries Act purports to contribute to national and industrial security and the development of the national economy by establishing a foundation for sustainable growth of the industry through the creation of an innovative ecosystem for national high-tech strategic industries and the strengthening of technological capabilities.[3]

2. Structure of the National High-tech Strategic Industries Act

The National High-tech Strategic Industries Act consists of (i) general provisions, (ii) framework plans to foster and protect strategic industries etc., (iii) designation and management of technologies for national high-tech strategic industries, (iv) designation of strategic industrial complexes and special cases, etc., (v) support for innovative development of strategic industries, etc., and establishment of their infrastructures, (vi) cultivation of professional manpower in strategic industries, etc., (vii) promotion of solidarity and cooperation in the industrial ecosystem, and (viii) supplementary provisions, etc.. The following explanation focuses on (i), (ii) and (iii) of II. 2. mentioned above.

2.1. General provisions

"National high-tech strategic technology" (hereinafter referred to as "strategic technology") refers to technologies designated under Article 11 of the National Strategic Industries Act as ones that have a significant impact on the national economy, such as stabilization of the supply chain, etc., have a great national economic effect on the areas such as exports and employment, and have a significant ripple effect on related industries.[4] The National High-tech Strategic Industries Act takes precedence over other Acts concerning the promotion of strategic industries, etc. However, if the application of other laws is advantageous to business operators engaged in strategic industries, etc., those laws shall be applied.[5] With regard to the protection measures for strategic technologies, the Act on Prevention of Divulgence and Protection of Industrial Technology shall be applied, except for cases where there are special provisions in the National High-tech Strategic Industries Act.[6]

2.2. Framework plans to foster and protect strategic industries etc.

The Korean government shall establish a basic plan to foster and protect strategic industries, etc. (hereinafter "Framework Plan") every five years for systematic and continuous fostering and protection of strategic industries, etc..[7] The Framework Plan shall include the following matters: (i) Basic directions for fostering and protecting strategic industries, etc.; (ii) Matters concerning the trends and development prospects of strategic industries, etc.; (iii) Matters concerning the establishment and maintenance of systems for fostering and protecting strategic industries, etc.; (iv) Matters concerning the creation of an innovation foundation and ecosystem for fostering and protecting strategic industries, etc.; (v) Matters concerning the improvement of technological power in strategic industries, the designation plan for specialized complexes, the training and protection of professional human resources, etc.; (vi) Matters concerning the procurement and operation of necessary financial resources; and (vii) Other matters related to fostering and protecting strategic industries, etc., as prescribed by Presidential Decree.[8]

The Framework Plan shall be established by the Minister of Trade, Industry, and Energy by integrating sectoral plans for each relevant central administrative agency, and finalized through deliberation by the National High-tech Strategic Industries Committee. The same shall also apply to cases where the framework plan is changed, exclusive of changes in minor matters prescribed by Presidential Decree.[9]

The National High-tech Strategic Industries Committee is established under the Prime Minister's control to deliberate and decide on the following matters concerning major policies and plans related to the promotion and protection of strategic industries, etc.: (i) Matters concerning the establishment and implementation of master plans and action plans, and inspection and evaluation of implementation outcomes; (ii) Matters concerning recommendations for improvement of relevant laws and regulations necessary for fostering and protecting strategic industries, etc.; (iii) Matters concerning the designation, change, and cancellation of strategic technology; (iv) Matters concerning the creation, designation, cancellation, and support of specialized complexes for strategic industries; (v) Matters concerning special cases related to fostering and protection of strategic industries, etc. of related central administrative agencies and local governments; (vi) Matters concerning grievance handling related to fostering and protecting strategic industries, etc.; (vii) Matters concerning the selection and support of solidarity and cooperation models among strategic industry-related companies, institution, or groups; (viii) Matters concerning adjustment for stabilizing supply and demand of items related to strategic technology in emergency situations; (ix) Matters concerning the designation of strategic technology-related experts, etc.; (x) Matters concerning support for persons with strategic technology (hereinafter "strategic technology holder"), and (xi) Other matters deemed necessary by the chairperson in relation to the promotion and protection of strategic industries, etc..[10]

The National High-tech Strategic Industries Committee, whose chairperson is the Prime Minister, consists of 20 persons or less.[11] In cases where the stable supply and demand of strategic technology-related items and the smooth functioning of the industrial supply chain are likely to be hindered due to natural disasters of sudden changes in international trade conditions, and national economic activities are likely to be significantly impeded, the Korean government can make an adjustment for stabilization of supply and demand the items related to the relevant strategic technology within a period of up to six months as prescribed by a Presidential Decree in connection with business operators, consumers, exporters, importers, transporters, or storage businesses of items related to the relevant strategic technology-related items, or public institutions under Article 4 of the Act on the Management of Public Institutions.[12]

2.3. Designation and management of the technologies for national high-tech strategic industries

The Minister of Trade, Industry and Energy may designate strategic technologies through deliberation by the Coordination Committee for high-tech strategic technologies[13] and deliberation and resolution by the National High-tech Strategic Industries Committee. In this case, the following factors shall be taken into account: (i) The impact of the technology on the industrial supply chain and national and industrial security; (ii) The potential for growth and the technical difficulty of a technology; (iii) Ripple effect of the technology on other industries; (iv) Industrial importance of the technology; (v) Impact of the relevant technology on the national economy, such as export and employment; and (vi) Other matters prescribed by Presidential Decree.[14]

The "other matters prescribed by the Executive Decree of

National High-tech Strategic Industries Act" refer to the following matters: (i) Domestic level and industrialization stage of the technology; (ii) Trade scale and international market trends of the technology; and (iii) other matters deemed necessary by the Minister of Trade, Industry and Energy for the protection and development of national high-tech strategic technology.[15] The Minister of Trade, Industry and Energy shall disclose the outcome of its designation of the national high-tech strategic technologies when they are designated. However, he/she may not disclose them when their disclosure is highly likely to cause their divulgence.[16]

The 1st National High-tech Strategic Industries Committee selected the following 15 technologies under three industries as the national high-tech strategic industries.[17] They are as the following Table 2.3.1:

[Table 2.3.1]

Classification		15 national high-tech strategic technologies
Semiconductor (8)	Memory semiconductor	Technology related to design, process, or device applicable to DRAM, and technology related to stack formation
		Stack assembly technology or inspection technology applicable to DRAM
		Technology on design, process, or device applicable to NAND flash
		Stack assembly technology or inspection technology applicable to NAND flash
	System semiconductor	Technology on design, process, or device for image sensors
		Technology on the design of chips for driving display panels
		Technology related to processes, devices, or layered formation applicable to foundries
	Packaging	Technology related to process, assembly, or inspection corresponding to package for system semiconductors

Display (4)	OLED	Technology related to design, production, process, or driving of AMOLED panels
	DP for next generation	Technology for design, manufacturing, process, or driving of panels for which eco-friendly QD materials are applied.
		Technology to design, manufacture, process or drive micro LED display panels
		Technology to design, manufacture, process or drive Nano LED display panels
Rechargeable battery (or secondary cell)		Technology to design, process, manufacture, or drive rechargeable lithium batteries with high energy density
		Technology to design, manufacture, or process high-capacity cathode materials for rechargeable lithium batteries
		Technology to design, process, manufacture, or evaluate rechargeable lithium batteries for next-generation

If a holder of strategic technology intends to export (hereinafter "export of strategic technology") by selling or transferring the relevant strategic technology to a foreign company, etc., it must obtain approval from the Minister of Trade, Industry and Energy.[18] Where a strategic technology holder intends to carry out foreign investment (hereinafter "overseas acquisition, merger, etc."), such as overseas mergers and acquisitions and joint ventures, as prescribed by Presidential Decree, he/she shall obtain prior approval from the Minister of Trade, Industry and Energy.[19] A holder of strategic technology the following measures to prevent the divulgence of strategic technologies: (i) Establishment of protection area, permission to enter, or inspection of belongings upon entry; (ii) Entering in a contract for managing turnover of personnel handling strategic technology and maintaining confidentiality; and (iii) Other matters prescribed by Presidential Decree to prevent leakage of strategic technology.[20]

No one shall commit an act falling under any of the following:

(i) Acts of acquiring strategic technology of a target institution by theft, deceit, threat, or other illegal means, or using or disclosing such acquired strategic technology[21];

(ii) An act of leaking strategic technology, using or disclosing the leaked strategic technology, or allowing a third party to use it, for the purpose of obtaining illicit profits or causing damages, by a person who is obliged to keep the strategic technology secret In accordance with contracts with strategic technology holders under Article 14 of the National High-tech Strategic Industries Act or Article 34 of the "Act on the Prevention of Divulgence of Industrial Technology, etc."[22];

(iii) An act acquiring, using or disclosing the strategic technology while knowing that the act falling under Article 15 subparagraph 1 or 2 of the National High-tech Strategic Industries Act was involved, or an act using or disclosing the strategic technology while knowing that an act falling under Article 15 subparagraph 1 or 2 of the National High-tech Strategic Industries Act after acquiring the strategic technology[23];

(iv) An act acquiring, using or disclosing the strategic technology without knowing that the act falling under Article 15 subparagraph 1 or 2 of the National High-tech Strategic Industries Act was involved with gross negligence, or an act using or disclosing the strategic technology without knowing that an act falling under Article 15 subparagraph 1 or 2 of the National High-tech Strategic Industries Act with gross negligence after acquiring the strategic technology[24];

(v) An act exporting strategic technology without obtaining approval under Article 12 (1) of the National High-tech Strategic Industries Act or obtaining approval through fraudulent means[25];

(vi) An act conducting overseas acquisitions, mergers, etc. without obtaining approval pursuant to Article 13 (1) of the National High-tech Strategic Industries Act or obtaining approval by deceitful or other fraudulent means for the purpose of using or having strategic technology used abroad[26];

(vii) As the right to possess or use the strategic technology expires, the contract with the holder of the strategic technology pursuant to Article 14 of the National High-tech Strategic Industries Act or with the person who is obliged to keep the strategic technology confidential pursuant to Article 34 of the "Act on the Prevention of Divulgence and Protection of Industrial Technology," etc., an act rejecting or avoiding a request for the return of special media records, such as documents, drawings, electronic records, etc., or for deletion of strategic technology from the holder of the strategic technology, for the purpose of obtaining unfair profits or inflicting damage on the holder or possessing a copy thereof[27]; or

(viii) An act using or disclosing the information for a purpose other than the one for which the information was provided by a person who has been provided with information containing strategic technology through lawful channels prescribed by Presidential Decree, such as litigation related to strategic technology[28].

A person who commits an act falling under any of subparagraphs 1 through 3 of Article 15 for the purpose of using or having strategic technology used abroad shall be punished by imprisonment for a term of 5 years or more. In this case, a fine of not more than 2 billion Korean won shall be imposed concurrently.[29] A person who commits an act falling under any of subparagraphs 5 through 8 of Article 15 for the purpose of using or having strategic technology used abroad shall be punished by imprisonment for not more than 20 years or by a fine not exceeding 2 billion Korean won.[30] A person

who commits an act falling under any of the subparagraphs of
Article 15 excluding subparagraphs 4, 6, and 8 shall be punished by
imprisonment for not more than 15 years or by a fine not exceeding
1.5 billion Korean won.[31] A person who commits an act falling
under subparagraph 4 or 8 of Article 15 shall be punished by
imprisonment for not more than five years or by a fine not
exceeding 500 million Korean won.[32] A person who commits an act
falling under any of the subparagraphs of Article 10 (5) shall be
punished by imprisonment for not more than one year or by a fine
of not more than 10 million Korean won.[33]

III. Japan's Economic Security Promotion Act

1. Purpose of the Act

Japan enacted a comprehensive industrial security law in May
11, 2022.[34] The Act states that the Japanese government shall be
responsible for preventing economic activities which harm Japan's
security, taking into account the growing complexity of the global
landscape and changes in the world's socio-economic structure, and
the increasing need to bar such economic activities.

2. Key features of the Act

On May 11, 2022, the Economic Security Promotion Act
(hereinafter "Japanese Promotion Act") was enacted. This law is
based on four pillars: (i) Ensuring stable supply of important goods;
(ii) Ensuring stable provision of basic infrastructure services; (iii)
Supporting development of advanced important technologies, and (iv)
Non-disclosure of patent applications.

The executive decree of the Japanese Promotion Act designates the following materials as specified important materials: (i) Pharma-ceutical formulation of antibacterial substance; (ii) Fertilizer; (iii) Permanent magnet; (iv) Machine tools and industrial robots; (v) Aircraft parts limited to aircraft motors and those that make up the aircraft body; (vi) Semiconductor devices and integrated circuits; (vii) Storage battery; (viii) Programs used in systems that use computers inclusive of input/output devices for information processing by others through the Internet or other advanced information and communica-tion networks; (ix) Combustible natural gas; (x) Metal minerals (manganese, nickel, chromium, tungsten, molybdenum, cobalt, niobium, tantalum, antimony, lithium, boron, titanium, vanadium, strontium, rare earth metals, platinum group, beryllium, gallium, germanium, selenium, rubidium, zirconium, indium, tellurium, indium, tellurium, cesium, barium, hafnium, rhenium, thallium, bismuth, graphite, fluorine, magnesium, silicon and phosphorus); and (xi) Ship parts limited to marine engines, navigation equipment and propellers.[35]

Pursuant to the "basic guidelines for promoting research and development of specified important technologies and appropriate utilization of their results", 20 technologies were selected as the specified important ones in 2022: (i) Biotechnology; (ii) Medical and public health technology including genomics; (iii) Artificial intelligence or machine learning technology; (iv) Advanced computing technology; (v) Microprocessor or semiconductor technology; (vi) Data science/analysis/accumulation/operation technology; (vii) Advanced engineering and manufacturing technology; (viii) Robotics; (ix) Quantum informa-tion science; (x) Advanced monitoring/positioning/sensor technology; (xi) Brain-computer interface technology; (xii) Advanced energy/energy storage technology; (xiv) Cyber security technology; (xv) Space-related technology; (xvi) Marine-related technology; (xvii) Transportation technology; (xviii) Hypersonic; (xix) Chemical/bio-logical/radioactive materials and nucleus; and (xi) Advanced materials science.[36]

Non-disclosure of a patent application refers to a situation in which the safety of Japan and Japanese is largely likely to be harmed by an act performed from outside by proper or other disclosure of information related to the invention described in the specification, etc., which means the specification, scope of patent claims, or drawings of a patent application. It is a measure to prevent the leakage of information on invention that have a high risk of divulgence.[37]

IV. Conclusion

In northeast Asia, the high-tech industries in the Republic of Korea and Japan are overlapping, complementary, and interactive. The Korean government needs to take into account the Japanese situation carefully in this regard. Also, the former needs to delve into how the scope of non-disclosure of a patent application can be extended for the protection of industrial security under the Japanese Promotion Act.

Notes

1. Act No. 18813, enacted on February 3, 2022 and effective since August 4, 2022.
2. Act No. 19205, revised on December 31, 2022 and effective since July 1, 2023.
3. Article 1 of the National High-tech Strategic Industries.
4. Article 2, subparagraph 1 of the National High-tech Strategic Industries Act.
5. Article 4 (1) of the National High-tech Strategic Industries Act.
6. Article 4 (2) of the National High-tech Strategic Industries Act.
7. Article 5 (1) of the National High-tech Strategic Industries Act.
8. Article 5 (2) of the National High-tech Strategic Industries Act.
9. Article 5 (3) of the National High-tech Strategic Industries Act.
10. Article 9 (1) of the National High-tech Strategic Industries Act.
11. Article 9 (2) of the National High-tech Strategic Industries Act.
12. Article 10 (1) of the National High-tech Strategic Industries Act.
13. It is established in the National High-tech Strategic Industries Committee to review and coordinate in advance the designation, change, and cancellation of strategic technologies among the matters deliberated and resolved by the National High-tech Strategic Industries Committee. The chairperson of the Coordination Committee of High-tech Strategic Technologies is the head of the Science and Technology Innovation Division of the Ministry of Science and ICT. See Article 9 (4) of the National High-tech Strategic Industries Act.
14. Article 11 (1) of the National High-tech Strategic Industries Act.
15. Article 14 (5) of the Executive Decree of the National High-tech Strategic Industries Act. See Presidential Decree No. 33004, revised in accordance with the revision of another law and effective since December 1, 2022.
16. Article 14 (4) of the Executive Decree of the National High-tech Strategic Industries Act.
17. Young-bae Kim, The first designation of national high-tech strategic technologies: 15 ones for 3 industries including semiconductors, Hangyeorye Newspaper, November 4, 2022, available at https://www.hani.co.kr/arti/economy/economy_general/1065813.html (accessed on April 4, 2023).
18. Article 12 (1) of the National High-tech Strategic Industries Act.
19. Article 13 (1) of the National High-tech Strategic Industries Act.
20. Article 14 (1) of the National High-tech Strategic Industries Act.
21. Article 15, subparagraph 1 of the National High-tech Strategic Industries Act.
22. Article 15, subparagraph 2 of the National High-tech Strategic Industries Act.
23. Article 15 subparagraph 3 of the National High-tech Strategic Industries Act.
24. Article 15 subparagraph 4 of the National High-tech Strategic Industries Act.
25. Article 15 subparagraph 5 of the National High-tech Strategic Industries Act.
26. Article 15 subparagraph 6 of the National High-tech Strategic Industries Act.

27. Article 15 subparagraph 7 of the National High-tech Strategic Industries Act.

28. Article 15 subparagraph 8 of the National High-tech Strategic Industries Act.

29. Article 50 (1) of the National High-tech Strategic Industries Act.

30. Article 50 (2) of the National High-tech Strategic Industries Act.

31. Article 50 (3) of the National High-tech Strategic Industries Act.

32. Article 50 (4) of the National High-tech Strategic Industries Act.

33. Article 50 (5) of the National High-tech Strategic Industries Act.

34. Japan's Act for the Promotion of Ensuring National Security through Integrated Implementation of Economic Measures (Act No. 43)(2022).

35. Article 7 of the Japanese Promotion Act; Article 1 of the Executive Decree of the Japanese Promotion Act (Cabinet Decree No. 394 (2022)).

36. https://www.cas.go.jp/jp/seisaku/keizai_anzen_hosyohousei/r4_dai1/siryou4. pdf (accessed on April 4, 2023).

37. Article 65 (1) of the Japanese Promotion Act.

KYIL

Normalization of Korea–Japan Relations in the Yoon Suk–Yeol Administration: The Comfort Women Agreement and Judicial Decisions on Compensation for Forced Labor

HONG Sungkee
Professor
Inha University Law School, Incheon, Korea

Key Words

comfort women agreement, forced labor, Property and Claims Settlement Agreement, Korea-Japan Basic Relations Treaty, Reconciliation and Healing Foundation, Hague Peace Conference, Cairo Declaration, San Francisco Peace Treaty, Korean Empire, statue of comfort women

I. Introduction

Paragraph 4 of the US-Japan Joint Statement signed by Japanese Prime Minister Eisaku Sato and US President Richard Nixon in 1969 is the so-called Korean clause. The United States and Japan "highly appreciated the efforts made by the United Nations to maintain peace on the Korean Peninsula" and declared that "Korea's security is essential to Japan's own security."

Korea-Japan relations, which were the cornerstone for peace in Northeast Asia, have changed significantly in half a century. While

South Korea's interest was focused on relations with North Korea and it assumed the role of a mediator in North Korea-U.S. negotiations, relations with Japan deteriorated. The Abe administration's distrust of the Moon Jae-in government peaked during the 2018 Pyeongchang Winter Olympics. Direct negotiations between North Korea and the United States were pursued, and such relations continued as the leaders of South Korea, North Korea, and the United States met at Panmunjom, the military demarcation line on the Korean Peninsula, on June 30, 2019, right after the G20 summit was held in Osaka.[1]

Relations between Korea and Japan have changed dramatically due to an issue that has nothing to do with North Korea relations. The Moon Jae-in administration's handling of the 2015 comfort women agreement, which resulted in significant concessions from Japan, and the administration's lack of sober realism after the 2018 ruling on compensation for forced labor were criticized as benig inconsistent with the status of the Republic of Korea in the international community. Regarding these issues directly related to former Japanese Prime Minister Shinzo Abe, there are many claims calling for "sophisticated and meticulous responses" now that he has left office.[2]

The Korean government, as the party that caused the discord, must take responsibility and initiative for resolving the issues and the simpler the solution, the better. Below, I address the history of the 2015 comfort women agreement and the 2018 Supreme Court ruling on compensation for forced labor, and propose practical measures to improve relations between Korea and Japan.

II. 2015 Comfort Women Agreement

1. Scope of the 1965 Property and Claims Settlement Agreement

In 2005 the Roh Moo-hyun administration disclosed diplomatic documents related to Korea-Japan diplomatic negotiations. After the Seoul Administrative Court's ruling on document disclosure, the government preemptively decided to disclose the documents before the appeal court's decision. Around that time, a "Public-Private Joint Committee on Measures to Disclose Documents from the Korea-Japan Talks" was organized. Lawyer Lee Yong-hoon, who later became Chief Justice, and Prime Minister Lee Hae-chan chaired the public-private joint committee. Moon Jae-in, senior secretary for civil affairs to the President, was also included. On August 26, 2005, the Public-Private Joint Committee announced the issue was the scope of the effect of the 1965 Korea-Japan Property and Claims Settlement Agreement. It argued that the comfort women issue "cannot be seen as resolved by the Property and Claims Settlement Agreement, and the Japanese government remains legally responsible."

In the second Korea-Japan talks held starting in April 1953, the South Korean side demanded compensation for forced labor to conclude the Korea-Japan Basic Relations Treaty, and also demanded the solution of the "comfort women" issue from the viewpoint of "receivables." The fact was omitted from the minutes of the meeting on the Korean side, but it exists in the records on the Japanese side. In other words, Jang Ki-young, representative of the Korean side, told the Claims Committee on May 19, 1953, "there were cases where Korean women went to the South East Asian countries such as Singapore under the jurisdiction of the Navy as 'comfort women' during the war and returned home leaving money or property behind" that asked for a refund. Jang Ki-young said, "comfort women are asking us to do something while presenting receipts issued by the military."[3]

The mobilization of comfort women during the Japanese colonial era was a known fact. The soldiers at the time, including Koreans, came into contact with comfort women. Since the comfort women were an underprivileged class, the discussion may not have been focused in earnest, and since it was an uncomfortable topic to discuss, it may have been implicitly understood and passed on. Regardless of the circumstances, I do not agree with the conclusion of the public-private joint committee that the comfort women issue cannot be seen as resolved by the Property and Claims Settlement Agreement. Since the Property and Claims Agreement is a lump-sum agreement, it should be understood that the comfort women issue has been naturally resolved by the provision "completely and finally settled"[4] in relation to "all claims of one State Party and its nationals against the other State party and its nationals".[5]

Meanwhile, regardless of whether or not the Property and Claims Settlement Agreement includes the comfort women issue, that issue appears to be a typical sovereign immunity case. On January 8, 2021, the Seoul Central District Court recognized damages of 100 million won each for claims made by former comfort women for the Japanese military against Japan,[6] on April 21, 2021, however, a decision was made to dismiss the claims of other comfort women on the grounds of state immunity.[7] Even if sovereign immunity is excluded and a decision is made in favor of a plaintiff against a defendant state it is virtually impossible to enforce,[8] so there is no need for the judiciary to trigger discord with neighboring countries with an unnecessary judgment.[9]

2. Process of the Agreement

a. Background

The "Comfort Women Agreement" in December 2015 was a difficult achievement. The comfort women activists centered on Jeongdaehyeop, which means the Council for Solutions to the Comfort Women Issue, persistently demanded Japan's state respon-sibility, that is, compensation for damages by the state, which Japan accepted. The Japanese government, which has consistently maintained that the issue had already been settled by the 1965 Korea-Japan Claims Settlement Agreement, made a difficult decision. The comfort women agreement was a result of the Korean government's tenacity, Japanese Prime Minister Shinzo Abe's political power, the Obama administration's persuasion, and even Xi Jinping's rear support. The two governments agreed that the issue had been "finally and irreversibly" resolved. Japanese Prime Minister Shinzo Abe announced, "I offer my heartfelt apology and remorse to all those who experienced countless suffering as comfort women and suffered incurable physical and mental wounds."

However, NGO and activists in South Korea criticized this as a "hashed agreement against the will of the victim," and the media reluctantly agreed with this claim. President Park Geun-hye was impeached and the government has changed. On January 9, 2018, Foreign Minister Kang Kyung-wha of the Moon Jae-in government announced that the Japanese government would finance the equivalent of 1 billion yen from the Korean government's budget by the statement of "government's position on the direction of handling the comfort women agreement". On January 21, 2019, the Ministry of Gender Equality and Family revoked the permission to establish the "Reconciliation and Healing Foundation," an executive body for the "2015 Korea-Japan comfort women agreement." President Moon Jae-in, who had made "renegotiation of the comfort women agreement" a presidential campaign promise, disbanded the "Reconciliation and Healing Foundation."[10]

However, at a New Year's press conference on January 18, 2021, President Moon Jae-in suddenly changed his position and confirmed that the 2015 agreement on comfort women between the governments of Korea and Japan was "an official agreement between the two governments." On January 22, 2021, Kang Chang-il, the new ambassador to Japan, made an excuse at Narita Airport that the dissolution of the Reconciliation and Healing Foundation was caused by the resignation of the chairman and directors and not because of government pressure.[11]

b. Progress

On August 30, 2011, the Constitutional Court of Korea ruled that the government's position was unconstitutional due to omission.[12] The Constitutional Court determined that the comfort women's right to claim compensation against Japan had not been extinguished by the relevant provisions of the 1965 Claims Settlement Agreement. According to the interpretation of the Claims Settlement Agreement, the Minister of Foreign Affairs should have diplomatic negotiations with Japan to resolve the comfort women issue, but the Court judged that the Minister had not made such an effort.[13] In December 2011, Jeongdaehyeop stimulated anti-Japanese public opinion by erecting a statue of comfort women in front of the Japanese embassy. President Lee Myung-bak announced at a bilateral summit meeting with Prime Minister Yoshihiko Noda on December 18, 2011 that "unless Japan shows sincerity regarding the comfort women issue, new comfort women statues will continue to be erected." On August 10, he visited Dokdo and declared that Dokdo is Korean territory.[14]

In December 2012, the Liberal Democratic Party won a landslide victory in the general election, and the second Abe administration was launched. In February 2013, President Park Geun-hye was inaugurated, and conservative governments took power consecutively. President Park Geun-hye was adamant that she would not hold a meeting with Prime Minister Abe unless the comfort women issue was resolved. After taking office, President Park Geun-hye broke the custom of visiting the United States and Japan in that order, and visited China first. In 2015, despite opposition from the United States, President Park Geun-hye, who took part in China's 70th anniversary parade of the military victory over Japan, stood side by side with Xi Jinping and Vladimir Putin in a blow to Japan. She suggested to President Xi Jinping that a three-country summit be held in Seoul.[15] Emeritus Professor of Tokyo University Haruki Wada's evaluation is that she tried to pressure Prime Minister Abe with the support of the US and China by holding a Korea-Japan summit along with a trilateral summit. A trilateral summit was held on November 1, 2015, where President Xi Jinping also stressed the importance of historical issues to put pressure on Prime Minister Abe.[16]

The contents of the comfort women agreement between the governments of Korea and Japan on December 28, 2015 acknowledged the Japanese military's involvement in the recruitment of comfort women according to the Kono Statement, supplemented the deficiencies of the Asian Women's Peace Fund in 1995, and would restore the comfort women's honor and dignity and heal their wounds through a foundation established by the Korean government. On the premise that these measures would be ongoing on a consistent basis, it is confirmed that the comfort women issue has been "finally and irreversibly resolved" and that the two countries would each refrain from accusing the other party on the comfort women issue. Afterwards, the Japanese government remitted 1 billion yen to the foundation, and the foundation paid 100 million won each to 35 out of 47 surviving grandmothers and 20 million won each to 64 families of 199 deceased comfort women.

c. Victim-Centred Approach

The 2015 comfort women agreement was criticized for being contrary to a victim-centred approach. On November 29, 1985, the UN General Assembly adopted the Declaration of Basic Principles of Justice for Victims of Crime and Abuse of Power.[17] Since then, the

Principle of Protection of Victims' Rights has been developed into principles of international human rights law, and on December 16, 2005, The Basic Principles and Guidelines on the Right to a Remedy and Reparation for Victims of Gross Violations of International Human Rights Law and Serious Violations of International Humanitarian Law was adopted as major principle in the UN.[18] After the Ministry of Foreign Affairs decided to initiate director-general- level consultations for the comfort women agreement, it met with victims' groups and private experts across the country, and it is said that it contacted victims and related groups more than 15 times in 2015 alone.[19] This was confirmed on May 26, 2022 as a result of a lawsuit filed against the Ministry of Foreign Affairs by the Lawyers for Human Rights and Peace on the Korean Peninsula.[20]

On October 17, 1990, in the early days of the comfort women movement, six conditions were presented to Japanese Prime Minister Toshiki Kaifu and President Roh Tae-woo including acknowledgment of the fact of forced mobilization, official apology, apology to survivors and bereaved families, and compensation for damages etc. by eight women's groups. These six protests were unilaterally organized by women activists without any discussion with the victims.[21] In particular, there are complaints from comfort women that the publication and sale of Comfort Women's Testimonies were carried out arbitrarily by the Jeongdaehyeop without considering the position of comfort women.[22] If so, the Ministry of Foreign Affairs has adhered to the principle of victim-centered approach, and there is no ground for Jeongdaehyeop or a third party to criticize the 2015 comfort women agreement under the guise of victim-centered approach.

Even after the establishment of the Reconciliation and Healing Foundation, the foundation sent an official letter of cooperation to meet the comfort women living together in the House of Sharing, but was rejected. The House of Sharing sent an official letter saying, "the grandmothers are against the Agreement and Reconciliation

Healing Foundation and cannot cooperate because they do not want to meet the officials."[23]

d. Retrospection of Haruki Wada

On June 13, 1995, on the 50th anniversary of the end of the war, Japan announced the launch of the Asian Peace and Friendship Fund for Women (hereinafter referred to as the "Asian Women's Fund"). The contents of the project were to raise funds for national atonement from the private sector, and to provide medical welfare and other projects with government funds. The government intended to express its candid remorse and apology to the comfort women and organize historical materials on the comfort women to serve as a lesson in history. In a joint statement on June 14, the following day, 22 Korean organizations, including Jeongdaehyup, demanded that "the Asian Women's Fund plan be abandoned, and the victims receive an apology and legal compensation through a resolution of the National Assembly." Asian Women's Fund executive director Haruki Wada, professor at the University of Tokyo, said that when he met Jungok Yoon, Eunhee Ji, and Jinseong Jeong, co-representatives of Jeongdaehyeop, on August 11 to explain the details of the project, they did not agree with the purpose of the project.[24]

On January 11, 1997, the Japanese government launched a project with a plan to provide an apology letter from the Prime Minister, 2 million yen in compensation and 3 million yen in medical welfare subsidy to each of the 7 comfort women who expressed their intention to receive funds in Korea despite the opposition of Jeongdaehyeop. Jeongdaehyeop, which demanded recognition of Japan's state responsibility and state compensation, accused the Japanese government of bribe operation through private funds.[25] Yoon Mee-hyang said, "If you receive sympathy money that does not admit guilt, the victim will become a 'volunteer public prostitute' as Japanese politicians and right-wingers have said so far.[26] This will result in Japan receiving an indulgence." Haruki Wada recorded that Jungok Yoon also made the same remarks, and expressed his thoughts, saying, "My respect for Jungok Yoon has not changed then and now, but I think this was something she shouldn't have said."[27] Comfort woman Seok Bok-soon (pseudonym) also testified that Jeongdaehyeop "only made harsh noises in her ears," saying that she was a "horrible bitch when she received donations." The comfort women issue was treated as a national issue, and Korean comfort women were classified as victims who were taken by force.

The Civic Solidarity of Korean activists independently raised money and paid consolation money, excluding 7 people who received the Asian Women's Fund from eligibility for payment. The new government of President Kim Dae-jung, who was elected in the December 1997 election, changed the position of the Kim Young-sam government that it would no longer make any demands on the Japanese government on the comfort women issue. In other words, the government decided to pay 35 million won uniformly to the comfort women who chose not to receive the Asian Women's Fund.[28] In October 1998, President Kim Dae-jung visited Japan and announced the "Joint Declaration of New Korea-Japan Partnership in the 21st Century" with Prime Minister Obuchi. In July 1999, the Korean Red Cross replied that it could not be in charge of the medical welfare support program of the 'Asian Women's Fund' project, causing turmoil. The Asian Women's Fund project ended in 2002, with 61 Korean recipients agreeing to receive the consolation money from the Asian Women's Fund and 60 actual recipients.[29]

III. Judicial Decision on Compensation for Forced Labor

1. Claims of Forced Labor

The claims of forced labor are clearly included in the Property and Claims Settlement Agreement. Item 5 of the "Eight Guidelines for Korea's Claims to Japan" revealed in the Agreed Minutes (1) of the Property and Claims Settlement Agreement stipulates "reimbursement of uncollected money, compensation, and other claims by the Korean forced labors." However, the Supreme Court judged that the eight guidelines presented by the South Korean side were basically about the financial and civil debt relationship between Korea and Japan, and that there was no provision premised on the illegality of Japanese colonial rule anywhere else in the eight guidelines. Paragraph 5 also does not presuppose an illegal act on the part of Japan, and therefore, the claim for compensation for forced labor was not found to be included in the "claim for reimbursement of uncollected money, compensation and other claims of the Korean forced laborers."[30]

This is because the Park Chung-hee government recognizes the funds for claims as the "price of the blood of our nation," and the principle governing the use and management of funds is to warn descendants not to repeat the shame of the past and to create large-scale projects that will make a national impact. The assertion that the idea of "national blood tax" was frequently invoked for the sake of individual victims is contrary to historical fact.[31]

2. Background

On October 30, 2018, just before the Reconciliation and Healing Foundation was dissolved, the Supreme Court rejected Nippon Steel's second and final appeal.[32] This was a ruling that directly contradicted

Japan's position that the scope of the 1965 Property and Claims Settlement Agreement included individual claims. With the number of victims of forced labor recognized by the Korean government reaching 220,000 and more than 70 cases of forced labor lawsuits filed against Japanese companies, the ruling has emerged as the biggest point of contention between Korea and Japan. The Supreme Court's ruling in 2018 is based on the its reversal of two High Court rulings in May 2012 that dismissed the claims of conscripted workers, stating as grounds for reversal that "Japan's ruling presupposes the recognition that colonial rule is legal, and therefore runs counter to the values of the Constitution."[33] Regarding the Supreme Court ruling in May 2012, it should be noted that most of the post-war responsibility after World War II was handled as a lump sum compensation agreement concluded through state-to-state negotiations and individual rights extinguished through it. According to the Supreme Court's judgment, even after a diplomatic agreement between countries, individuals who are not satisfied with the result can still file a lawsuit, prompting criticism that the other country may not respond to diplomatic negotiations in the first place.[34]

Later, the High Court of appeal recognized damages on remand, and Nippon Steel appealed again to the Supreme Court. The Japanese government protested that it would bring the case before the International Court of Justice (ICJ) if the Korean judiciary acknowledged Nippon Steel's responsibility for damages.[35] Realizing the seriousness of the problem, the Supreme Court seems to have even considered a way to remand the case. With a change in administration and the start of an investigation into judicial manipulation, a chief judge who worked as a research judge at the time posted the case on Facebook as if the review of the reversal and remand were a corruption scandal, and the media also followed suit.[36] According to a related article the Office of National Court Administration drafted documents titled "Concerning the judgment on forced labors – relations with the

Ministry of Foreign Affairs (confidential)" in 2013 and 2014 to the effect that it should on two occasions follow the opinion of the Ministry of Foreign Affairs in relation to the Mitsubishi case, and this consideration was given to reversing the case. The presiding judge ordered the research judge to review the Mitsubishi case again in the direction of reversal and remand, as it is an incident that could trouble diplomatic relations between Korea and Japan. There was a risk that the case would be brought before the International Court of Justice.[37]

An adjudication on remand is bound by the factual findings and legal judgments that the appeal court used as the reason for the reversal.[38] The judge in the re-appeal case would have tried to review the plan to remand the reversed case on the ground that "several issues were not reviewed" by the court. If the Supreme Court had assigned the second appeal case to the Court en banc from the beginning and reviewed international law issues that had not been judged before, the burden of reversal and remand could have been lessened. In August 2013, the case was assigned to a chamber of the Supreme Court, not to the Court en banc, and a change in administration took place in May 2017 during review. In September 2017, the Chief Justice of the Supreme Court was replaced by Myung-Soo Kim, and as suspicions of trial transactions were reported, the case was referred to the Court en banc on July 27, 2018.[39] On October 30, 2018, the entire Supreme Court dismissed Nippon Steel's re-appeal, and the relationship between Korea and Japan took a turn for the worse.

3. Separation of Powers and International Law

Immediately after the Supreme Court ruling in 2018, President Moon Jae-in consistently put forward the separation of powers as the rationale for the forced mobilization issue. On the other hand, since the Japanese government held that the Korean government should resolve individual claims according to the Property and Claims Settlement Agreement, a dispute arose between Korea and Japan over the interpretation of the Agreement. From the Japanese point of view, the Supreme Court ruling that colonial rule was illegal under the Korean constitution would be an unacceptable logic as it went beyond the Claims Agreement and ignored the Treaty on Basic Relations between Korea and Japan.[40] In January 2019, the Japanese government requested diplomatic negotiations pursuant to Article 3 (1) of the Property and Claims Settlement Agreement, followed by an arbitration committee pursuant to Article 3(2) and (3) of the Agreement by setting a deadline for response on May 20, 2019. However, the Korean government did not respond at all.[41]

The separation of powers, a constitutional principle of national governance, cannot be presented as a justification for a domestic judgment that violates international law. Neither party to a treaty shall interpret the treaty in its favor to the exclusion of the other party.[42] The preamble to the Vienna Convention on the Law of Treaties, which reflects customary international law, provides that states should not violate their treaty obligations under the guise of their own constitutions.[43] Japan's protest is not a request for the Korean government to ignore the separation of powers and intervene in the final judgment, but rather a request for appropriate measures to prevent the judgment from affecting Japanese companies.

4. Settlement

On June 7, 2021, the Seoul Central District Court dismissed a claim for damages against 16 Japanese companies, including Nippon Steel, Nissan Chemical, and Mitsubishi Heavy Industries, by 85 conscripted workers and surviving families. The court issued a ruling in conclusion consistent with the minority opinion of the Supreme

Court decision in 2018, stating that "the individual right of a Korean citizen to make a claim against Japan or Japanese nationals cannot be said to have been extinguished or waived by the Korea-Japan Property and Claims Settlement Agreement, but that right cannot be exercised through a lawsuit."[44]

IV. Illegal Occupation

1. Interpretation of "Already Null and Void"

Article 2 of the 1965 Treaty on Basic Relations between the Republic of Korea and Japan (Korea-Japan Basic Relations Treaty) states, "it is confirmed that all treaties or agreements concluded between the Empire of Korea and the Empire of Japan on or before August 22, 1910 are already null and void." The "already null and void" part of this regulation corresponds to an "agreement to disagree" that South Korea and Japan are expected to interpret differently. Korea interpreted it as null and void at the time of signing the Annexation Treaty in 1910, while Japan thought it was valid until August 15, 1945, and interpreted it as "already invalid" at the time of signing the Basic Relations Treaty in 1965. In other words, it is a provision that is expected to be understood domestically in the way each country wants, assuming that both Korea and Japan have completely different positions on the illegality of colonial rule.

Even at the time of the conclusion of the annexation treaty, Korea as a country did not have enough experience in concluding international treaties. In 1882, when the Korea-US Treaty of Amity and Commerce, which can be called Korea's first modern treaty, was signed, the text of the treaty was made between Commodore Robert W. Shufeldt of the United States and Lee Hong-jang of China. The draft of the treaty was the work of Ma Geon-chung who studied in France. On May 14, 1882, Shin Heon and Kim Hong-jip boarded the Chinese warship of Jeong Yeo-chang and Ma Geon-chung, which arrived from Tianjin, and headed for Beijing to conduct the Samgwe-gugodurye(三跪九叩頭禮), accepting Lee Hong-jang and Shufeldt's drafts almost as they were.[45] On June 6, 1882, the Treaty of Amity and Commerce between Korea and the UK was concluded through the mediation of Ma Geon-chung. The content and format were exactly the same as the Korea-US Treaty of Amity and Commerce.[46] In Korea, it was said that there were many procedural and formal defects, such as the absence of Emperor Sunjong's signature on the ratification of the Treaty on the Annexation of Korea, and it was popular to argue that the treaty failed at original establishment due to the defects. There is also a general perception that Japan's coloniza-tion of Korea was an illegal occupation by military force.[47]

Meanwhile, on November 11, 1905, six days before the conclusion of the Eulsa Protectorate Treaty, Konsuke Hayashi, the Japanese minister to Korea, carried out a secret payment of 100,000 won according to Secret No. 119 of the Ministry of Foreign Affairs of Japan. A confidential document from the Japanese Ministry of Foreign Affairs retrieved from the Korean History Database of the National Institute of Korean History confirms the record that 20,000 won was paid into the Emperor's hands, the rest was divided among Lee Ha-yeong (Minister of Justice) and Lee Wan-yong, and the remaining balance of 39,000 won was returned.[48] While the monarchs of countries degraded to imperialist colonies changed their status to commoners and their property was confiscated, the royal family of the Korean Empire was renamed the Lee Wangga, and Sunjong's direct lineage became the royal family of Japanese emperor, and his brothers became aristocrats. The old imperial family received salaries from the budget of the Joseon Government-General. 2% of the colonial expenditure went to the former ruling class, which was less than 1/100,000 of the Korean people.[49] Considering these circumstances, even if the annexation treaty is interpreted as invalid, it does not change the fact that Korea, which failed in modernization, lost its sovereignty due to the incompetence and corruption of the ruling class.

2. Illegality of Colonial Rule

Since the 19th century, imperialism has emerged as a universal phenomenon.[50] The illegality of colonial rule must be judged according to the international law of the time of imperialism. Current domestic norms should not be used as a tool for interpreting colonial illegality.

The imperialist powers, including China and Russia, which were competing with Japan, did not pay attention to the Korean Empire's claim that the 1905 Eulsa Protectorate Treaty and the 1910 Annexation Treaty were invalid. The United States, Britain, France, etc., which signed treaties with Joseon, did not raise objections to Japan's measures to suspend the validity of each treaty. After the Eulsa Protectorate Treaty in 1905, Russia received the consul general's credentials from the Japanese government, blocked the Korean Empire's access to the Hague Peace Conference at Japan's request, and handled the Korean Empire-related affairs through the Japanese Residency-General.[51] The background of the Allied Powers discussing Korea's independence at the Cairo Declaration in November 1943 and the Potsdam Conference in July 1945 was only to separate part of the territory in order to hold Japan accountable for the defeat, but it was not based on the premise of the illegality of colonial rule. In the 1951 San Francisco Peace Treaty, even former colonies of the Allied Powers, such as the Philippines, Laos, and Vietnam, received war reparations as members of the Allied Powers, but the reason why Korea was unable to participate in the

Peace Treaty was probably because the Korean Empire was deemed to have disappeared with the 1910 Annexation Treaty.[52]

On the other hand, the fact that Japan gave up considerable property located on the Korean Peninsula after defeat in the war and separated Korea should also be considered. As of August 1945, 5.25 billion dollars (24% of the total amount) of Japan's total foreign assets of 21.88 billion dollars were located in Korea. The Allied Forces Supreme Command (GHQ) estimated that Japanese assets in South Korea were $2.28 billion and Japanese assets in North Korea were $3 billion.[53] The U.S. Military Government, which had jurisdiction over South Korea, reverted Japanese property in Korea to the U.S. Military Government, regardless of state or private ownership, according to the Military Government Ordinance No. 33 promulgated on December 6, 1945. It was transferred to the Government of the Republic of Korea according to the 「Initial Agreement on Finance and Property between the Government of the Republic of Korea and the Government of the United States」 that took effect on September 20, 1945. The Korea-Japan Basic Relations Treaty and the Property and Claims settlement Agreement were established in this context.

V. Conclusion

Article 38 (1) of the Statute of the International Court of Justice recognizes "the general principles of law recognized by civilized nations" as a source of international law. The principle that "a contract must be kept" (pacta sunt servanda) corresponds to the "principle of law recognized by civilized nations." The Moon Jae-in administration showed an inconsistent attitude, contradicting itself over time even after effectively breaking the comfort women agreement of 2015, and showed the same attitude after the 2018 ruling on compensation for forced labor. Promises between countries must be kept despite changes in administration, and if a problem arises between the two countries due to a misunderstanding of international norms by the judiciary, the problem should first be resolved in accordance with the dispute resolution procedure of diplomatic consultation and arbitration stipulated in the Property and Claims Settlement Agreement. If there was an extraordinary reason not to go through such a procedure, Korea should have reached an understanding with Japan and pledged to take measures to ensure that Japanese companies would not be affected by the execution of the ruling.

The deterioration of bilateral relations between Korea and Japan was solely attributable to the Korean government's avoidance of appropriate measures. Korea, a party to the Property and Claims Settlement Agreement, should not unilaterally interpret or change the relevant treaty, excluding Japan, the other party. Nonetheless, the Korean courts used the preamble of the Korean Constitution and the provisions of the Special Investigation Committee on Anti-National Acts of the Constituent Assembly to interpret the Property and Claims Settlement Agreement. Given the nature of the Property and Claims Settlement Agreement, which is a lump sum compensation treaty, it is appropriate to interpret that "all claims related to colonial rule" fall within its scope, excluding the "exceptions" in Article 2 (2). However, the Korean government arbitrarily excluded by interpretation the comfort women issue from the scope of application of the Property and Claims Settlement Agreement, and the Korean Supreme Court distorted the meaning of the "claims of the forced labor," which the Property and Claims Settlement Agreement clearly covered.

Under these circumstances, the measures the Yoon Suk-yeol government should take are simple. It is necessary to express regret about the Moon Jae-in administration's attitude toward the 2015 comfort women agreement and restore the Reconciliation and Healing Foundation to implement the Comfort Women Agreement. Necessary measures must be taken to ensure that the ruling on compensation for forced labor does not adversely affect Japanese companies. The sooner this is done the better, as these are measures former President Moon Jae-in should have taken right after the Supreme Court ruling in 2018.

In a similar follow-up judgment, it is appropriate to change the precedent of the compensation case for the forced labor, but the government should without waiting for such change prevent compulsory execution including, if necessary, by taking over the amount of the judgment. It is better not to bring up the Moon Hee-sang's idea that Korean and Japanese companies would participate in the fund-raising together. A proposal that Japan cannot accept will only result in resentment.

In addition, the statue of comfort women in front of the Japanese embassy should also be moved. Since 2011, Jeongdaehyeop has illegally occupied the public road in front of the Japanese embassy by installing a comfort woman statue without permission. And with the sudden intervention of the Ministry of Gender Equality and Family, Jongno-gu even revised the ordinance, and on September 21, 2017, the statue was finally registered as a public sculpture. Above all, this is a sculpture that violates international law, let alone the process is also lamentable. The Vienna Convention on Diplomatic Relations obliges the receiving State to take all appropriate measures to protect the security of the foreign mission.[54]

Notes

1. Kang Sang-joong, translated by Roh Su-gyeong, 『The Future of the Korean Peninsula and Japan』, Four Seasons, 2021, p. 122
2. Chosun Ilbo, 2022. 7. 16. Kang Cheon-seok column "It can be more difficult to deal with Japan without Abe", Seoul Shinmun, July 13, 2022, Kimiya Tadashi "The death of former Prime Minister Abe and Korea-Japan relations", Segye Ilbo, 2022 July 13, 2013, Choi Eun-mi, "Where will Korea-Japan relations go after Abe's death?"
3. Lee Dong-Jun, An Uncomfortable Retrospective on 70 Years of Korea-Japan Relations from Diplomatic Historical Records, Samin, 2016, pp.79~80
4. Article 2 (3)
5. Article 2 (1)
6. Seoul Central District Court 2021. January 8 Decision 2016 Gahap 506092
7. Seoul Central District Court 2021. April 21. Decision 2016 Gahap 580239
8. Vienna Convention on Diplomatic Relations
   Article 22.
   3. The premises of the mission, their furnishings and other property thereon and the means of transport of the mission shall be immune from search, requisition, attachment or execution.
9. Seoul Shinmun, January 23, 2021, Japanese Foreign Minister, "Extremely Regrettable . . . Korea Must Rectify" at the Finalization of the Comfort Women Compensation Judgment
10. Kang Sang-jung(translated by No Su-kyung), Korean Peninsula and Japan's Future, Four Seasons, 2021, pp.111~112
11. Donga Ilbo 2021.01.22.; Chosun Ilbo 2021.01.23.
12. Constitutional Court 2011. 8. 30. 2006HeonMa788Decision
13. Claims Agreement Articles 2 and 3
14. Kang Sang-jung(translated by No Su-kyung), Korean Peninsula and Japan's Future, Four Seasons, 2021, pp.108~109
15. Ibid., p.110
16. Haruki Wada(tranlated by Jung Jae-jung), For the Settlement of the Comfort Women Issues by Japanese Soldiers, History Space, 2016, pp.238~243
17. <https://www.un.org/en/ga/search/view_doc.asp?symbol=A/RES/40/34> (Accessed August 20, 2021)
18. Basic Principles and Guidelines on the Right to a Remedy and Reparation for Victims of Gross Violations of International Human Rights Law and Serious Violations of International Humanitarian Law <https://undocs.org/A/RES/60/147> (Accessed August 20, 2021).
19. Shim Gyu-sun, Comfort Women Movement, from Sanctuary to Plaza, Nanam, 2021, p.297

20. Yonhap News, May 26, 2022, Ministry of Foreign Affairs Document on "Comfort Women" Agreement states "Bureau Director Met with Yoon Mee-hyang to Explain" (General)

21. Shim Gyu-sun, Comfort Women Movement, from Sanctuary to Plaza, Nanam, 2021, p.297

22. Korea Economic Daily, May 25, 2020, Jeonguiyeon (Justice and Memory Solidarity) "Grandmother Lee Yong-su Heartbroken at Conference," No Specific Position Declared

23. Shim Gyu-sun, Comfort Women Movement, from Sanctuary to Plaza, Nanam, 2021, p.307

24. Haruki Wada (tranlated by Jung Jae-jung), For the Settlement of the Comfort Women Issues by Japanese Soldiers, History Space, 2016, pp.137~138

25. The Dong-a Ilbo ran a positive article on January 13, 1997, "Surprise 'Fund' Payment; Compensation Farther Away than Ever," to the effect that it was "a project that provided practical help" to elderly comfort women.

26. "Process and Prospects of the Resolution Movement", Sharing Newsletter, 1998.3

27. Haruki Wada(tranlated by Jung Jae-jung), For the Settlement of the Comfort Women Issues by Japanese Soldiers, History Space, 2016, p.167

28. Chung Eui-yeon's Position on the Press Conference of Lee Yong-soo, 2020.5.8

29. Haruki Wada(tranlated by Jung Jae-jung), For the Settlement of the Comfort Women Issues by Japanese Soldiers, History Space, 2016, p.191

30. Supreme Court 2018. 10. 30. Decision 2013da61381

31. Jung Jae-jung, 『The History of Korea-Japan Relations in the 20th Century Reading by Topics and Issues』, History and Criticism, 2014, pp.224~225

32. Supreme Court 2018. 10. 30. Decision 2013 da61381. The original judgment was made by the Seoul High Court on July 10, 2013. Sentence 2012 Na44947 judgment. Nippon Steel merged with Sumitomo Metals in October 2012 and changed its name to Nippon Steel & Sumitomo Metal.

33. Supreme Court 2012. 5. 24. Decision 2009 da68620.

34. Jung In-sup, International Law, Parkyoungsa, 2018, p.454

35. Seoul Economic Daily, November 25, 2013, Japan Will "Bring Suit Before International Court of Justice" if Korean Supreme Court Renders Judgment to Compensate Conscription Victims

36. The Dong-a Ilbo, July 27, 2018, Supreme Ct. Internally Directed Second Reversal and Remand for Japanese Conscription Compensation Suit

37. The Dong-a Ilbo, July 27, 2018, Supreme Ct. Internally Directed Second Reversal and Remand for Japanese Conscription Compensation Suit; Seoul Economic Daily, July 27, 2018, Supreme Court, Spooked by Whistleblowing on Trial Horse Trading, Starts Hearing on Forced Conscription After Five Years

38. Article 436 (2) of the Civil Procedure Act

39. Joo Jin-yeol, "A Study on International Law Issues in the 1965 Korea-Japan Claims Settlement Agreement and the Individual Claims Case – Focusing on the

Supreme Court's 2013 Da 61381 Decision on October 30, 2018", Seoul International Law Review, Vol.25(2), December 2018, p.175

40. Treaty on Basic Relations between Korea and Japan.

41. Kim Chnag-jun, "The Nature and Solution of the Controversy over the Korea-Japan Claims Settlement Agreement", Law Times 2019.10.14.

42. Joo Jin-yeol, "A Study on International Law Issues in the 1965 Korea-Japan Claims Settlement Agreement and the Individual Claims Case – Focusing on the Supreme Court's 2013Da61381 Decision on October 30, 2018", Seoul International Law Review, Vol.25(2), December 2018, pp.178~179

43. Recognizing the ever-increasing importance of treaties as a source of inter-national law and as a means of developing peaceful co-operation among nations, whatever their constitutional and social systems,
Noting that the principles of free consent and of good faith and the pacta sunt servanda rule are universally recognized, ...

44. Aju Business Daily, June 8, 2021, Court Strikes Down Japanese Forced Conscription Compensation of Unprecedented Proportions; "Would Damage Relations with Japan"

45. Ham Jae-bong, Makin Korean People Ⅱ, Asanseowon, 2018, pp.347~348

46. Key-hiuk Kim, The Last Phase of the East Asian World Order: Kore, Japan,and the Chinese Empire, 1860-1882 (Berkerly: University of California Press, 1980), p.307, Ham Jae-bong, Makin Korean People Ⅱ, Asanseowon, 2018, p.350

47. Jung Jae-jung, Korean-Japanese History Seen in Kyoto, Hyohyung Publishing, 2010, p.273

48. https://db.history.go.kr/item/level.do?sort=levelId&dir=ASC&start=1&limit=20&page=1&pre_page=1&setId=-1&totalCount=0&prevPag

49. Park Jong-in, Betrayer Gojong, Wise Map, 2020, pp.346~347

50. Hae-dong Yun, Colonial State and Symmetrical State, Somyung Publishing, 2022, p.4

51. Choi Deok-kyu, "Russia's policy toward Korea and Japan's annexation of Korea (1905-1901)", Siberian and Far East Research Vol.5, 2009, pp.119~121

52. Joo Jin-yeol, "A Study on International Law Issues in the 1965 Korea-Japan Claims Settlement Agreement and the Individual Claims Case – Focusing on the Supreme Court's 2013Da 1381 Decision on October 30, 2018", Seoul International Law Review, Vol.25(2), December 2018, p.189

53. Jung Jae-jung, The History of Korea-Japan Relations in the 20th Century Reading by Topics and Issues, History and Criticism, 2014, p.67

54. Article 22 (2) of the Property and Claims Settlement Agreement.

International Legal Review of the Invasion of Dokdo and the Korea-Japan Treaty in 1905 resumed by the San Francisco Peace Treaty in 1951

DOH See-Hwan
Senior Research Fellow
Northeast Asian History Foundation, Seoul, Korea

Key Words

International Law, Korea's sovereignty over Dokdo, *Terra nullius*, San Francisco peace treaty, 1905 Korea-Japan Treaty, Invasion of Dokdo, SCAPIN 677, William J. Sebald, Rusk letter, Japanese colonialism, extreme nationalism, historical reflection, international legal Justice, violence and greed, East Asian peace community

1. INTRODUCTION

This year marks the 70th anniversary of the entry into force of the San Francisco Peace Treaty. Forty-eight allied powers, including the United States, the victor of World War II, and Japan, the defeated country, signed the treaty in 1951 to clear up responsibility for the Asia-Pacific War and establish a peace regime in East Asia.[1]

At the time of the signing of the treaty, it was intended to settle Japan's war responsibilities; on the other hand, it was also criticized as a contradictory evaluation as a treaty to build a Cold War regime in East Asia.[2]

This is because Japan, which is paradoxically the biggest benefi-ciary even though it is a perpetrator, is causing territorial conflicts that run counter to the East Asian peace community, presupposing the San Francisco Peace Treaty, which is evaluated as an unpre-cedented "generous peace treaty" as its stance has shifted from a punitive treaty to an anti-communist treaty due to the rise of the Cold War regime.

On that premise, it is worth noting that the Japanese government and Japanese society of international law are re-summoning the doctrine of terra nullius through the San Francisco Peace Treaty, because it was impossible to establish Japan's historical title to Dokdo, over which Korea's sovereignty had been recognized by the Edo Shogunate's 1696 prohibition of crossing and the Dajokan directive of state in 1877 after the Ulleung Island dispute that began after the capture of An Yong-bok in 1693.[3]

2. KOREA'S SOVEREIGNTY OVER DOKDO AND SAN FRANCISCO PEACE TREATY

It is important to identify the essential problem of legal distortion inherent in the research work of the Japanese Society of International Law which has been building the policy basis of the Japanese government's claim to Dokdo, as the essence of violence and greed declared in the Cairo Declaration in the process of establishing the San Francisco Peace Treaty.

The most important decisions in the territorial policy toward Japan implemented by the Allied powers in wartime were the Cairo Declaration of 1943 and the Potsdam Declaration of 1945. The Cairo Declaration is a document of basic principle in the territorial policy of the Allied Powers and has been cited in the provisions of Article

8 of the Potsdam Declaration, thus establishing itself as the official territorial policy of the Allied Powers. The declaration consisted of withdrawal from all areas that Japan had taken by violence and greed, and liberation and independence of Korea at the appropriate time.

The Potsdam Declaration specified the territory of postwar Japan through the succession of the Cairo Declaration, and it became the basic principle of the Allies' agreement at the end of the war by determining the demand for surrender to Japan and the principle for the treatment of postwar Japan. Article 8, which defines the implementation of the Cairo Declaration and the territory of Japan, was specific that Japanese sovereignty shall be limited to the islands of Honshu, Hokkaido, Kyushu, Shikoku and such minor islands determined by the Allies.

Under the policy of separating Dokdo from Japan after World War II until the San Francisco Peace Treaty entered into force, the Allied Powers General Headquarters defined Dokdo as an area excluded from Japan's rule throughout the allied occupation of Japan through the Supreme Commander for the Allied Powers Instruction Notes (SCAPIN) 677 (Jan. 29, 1946) and SCAPIN 1033 (June 22, 1946).

As a continuation of such exclusion, Dokdo was specified as Korean territory until the fifth draft of the San Francisco Peace Treaty. Dokdo was, incidentally, changed over to Japanese territory in the sixth draft due to lobbying through a telegram (Nov. 14, 1949) and written opinion (Nov. 19, 1949) of William J. Sebald, a political adviser to Japan. However, in the final draft after the seventh draft, Dokdo was omitted from the text of the treaty without being mentioned specifically.[4]

The 1951 Rusk letter, based on Japan's false information that Dokdo is under the jurisdiction of the Oki Islands Branch Office of Shimane Prefecture of Japan since 1905,[5] was published in 1978 as a US foreign relations document. Since then, the Japanese Society of International Law, which has denied the effect of the SCAPIN, insists that the San Francisco Peace Treaty recognized Dokdo as part of Japanese territory through the Rusk letter.

3. A REVIEW ON THE INVASION OF DOKDO AND THE KOREA-JAPAN TREATY IN 1905 RESUMED BY SAN FRANCISCO PEACE TREATY

3-1. Japan's "Takeshima Day" proclaimed on the 100th anniversary of the Korea-Japan Treaty in 1905

The Japanese Society of International Law claims the invasion of Dokdo and the Japan-Korea Treaty of 1905 are fully legal and legitimate under international law, which was resumed through the San Francisco Treaty and the Rusk Letter in 1951.

This is an attempt on Japan's part to legalize the previous invasion of Dokdo through the legalization of the 1905 Korea-Japan Agreement, which is an invalid treaty under international law due to coercion of the national representative. In other words, it is attempting to legalize the invasion of Dokdo on the premise of 'legitimate theory of colonial rule' under international law.

This year marks the 117th anniversary of the Japan-Korea Treaty of 1905, the substantive starting point of Japan's colonial rule, which was the essential cause of the historical conflict between Korea and Japan, and the attempted distortion of legalizing Japan's colonial rule under international law at the time.

In 2005, 100 years after the signing of the Japan-Korea Treaty of 1905, Japan declared "Takeshima Day" through Shimane Prefecture, commemorating the annexation of Korea's easternmost Dokdo island in 1905.

It was not only an indication that efforts for historical reconciliation between Korea and Japan would drift apart in the future, but ironically, that finding the essential causes of the historical conflict between Korea and Japan and looking for ways to overcome it would become a historical task and a calling for justice.

Since the end of the 19th century, Japan has been striving to secure international legal grounds as a device to glorify and legalize its imperialist methods of annexation, which are the basis of Japan's colonial rule.

This legal basis was embodied in a series of treaties forced by Japan to gain sovereignty over Korea in the process of forced annexation, and it went through five steps: the Korea-Japan Protocol, the First Korea-Japan Agreement, the Second Korea-Japan Agreement (Japan-Korea Treaty of 1905), the Third Korea-Japan Agreement (Japan-Korea Treaty of 1907) and the Korea-Japan Annexation Treaty (Japan-Korea Treaty of 1910).[6]

3-2. Japan's denial of responsibility for illegal colonialism on the premise of the Korea-Japan Treaty in 1905

The reason we discuss the international legal effect of the Japan-Korea Treaty of 1905 as an important legal issue lies in the Japanese government's denial of its responsibility for its illegal colonial rule on the premise that the 1910 forced Annexation Treaty was legal under international law based on the 1905 treaty.

Therefore, it is essential and important to prove the illegality and invalidity of the Japan-Korea Treaty of 1905 as the starting point for debunking the legitimacy of the forced annexation of Korea as claimed by the Japanese government.

It is worth noting that when anti-colonial fighter Ahn Jung-geun assassinated Ito Hirobumi, who was in charge of Japan's colonial rule in Korea in 1909, he pointed out 15 crimes that prompted the act and charged that the most serious of the crimes were Japanese militarism and imperialist aggression. Nevertheless, Ahn was sentenced to death after a trial by the Japanese imperial government based on the Japanese Penal Code in 1910, which is based on Article 1 of the 1905 Treaty.[7]

Moreover, in February 1992, the UN Human Rights Commission asked about the Japanese government's legal responsibility for forcibly mobilizing women on the Korean Peninsula into sex slavery, as victims of Japan's colonial rule caused by the Japan-Korea Treaty of 1905.[8]

The Japanese Territorial Sovereignty Exhibition Hall, which reopened in 2020, still claimed that both the incorporation of Dokdo in 1905 and the Japan-Korea Treaty of 1905 are valid under international law.

3-3. International legal review on the legitimate theory of 1905 Korea-Japan Treaty by Japanese scholars as a prerequisite for the a community of peace in East Asia

The deep-rooted Japanese colonialist invasion of Korea's sovereignty, human rights, and territory is still ongoing, and the Japan-Korea Treaty of 1905 is positioned as the common denominator and as a prerequisite for an East Asian community of peace.

In addition to the deficiency of ratification as a requirement for the international legal establishment of the 1905 Treaty and the deficiency of the validity requirements resulting from coercion of the national representative, the Japanese government argues that it was legal under international law at the time of the signing of the Korea-Japan Treaty of 1905.

However, even though it tried to establish international legal requirements in order to conceal the coercion on the national representative, a treaty that did not include the commission of full powers and the ratification of the head of state was invalid under international law at that time.

It is worth noting that the Japanese international law community, which is building the basis for the Japanese government's claim to the legalization of colonial rule, is silent about international legal norms based on the national representative's free will and the equality of sovereign states.[9] This is nothing more than an illegal basis for the implementation of Japanese legal positivism as extreme nationalism associated with invasive state practice.

Moreover, when Harvard Law School presented representative cases of treaties invalid for the coercion of the national representative at the time of the League of Nations in 1935, the Forced Protectorate Treaty in 1905 was among the three cases mentioned alongside the Treaty of Partition through the Siege of the Polish Parliament by the Russian Army in 1773 and the Protectorate Treaty through the Siege of Haiti by the US Army in 1915. The invalidity of these treaties was reaffirmed in the process of legalization of the Treaty Law Convention of the United Nations International Law Commission in 1963.

4. A REVIEW ON INTERNATIONAL LEGAL TITLES ON THE SAN FRANCISCO PEACE TREATY ARGUED BY THE JAPANESE SOCIETY OF INTERNATIONAL LAW

Regarding the research of the treaty-based title of the Japanese society of international law on the San Francisco Peace Treaty, I reviewed the problems of distortions on the legal principles of international law as follows:

First, in relation to SCAPIN 677 paragraph 6, which stipulates that it is not the ultimate determination of the minor islands, Japanese international law scholars argue for the nullification of

SCAPIN by the San Francisco Peace Treaty.[10] However, paragraph 6, the exclusion clause, should be interpreted in connection with paragraph 5 as an exemplary provision. Paragraph 5 stipulates that unless the territory of Japan is specified separately in all orders to be issued by the headquarters, the territorial scope of Japan shall continue to be effective.[11]

Second, Sebald's proposal through lobbying was as follows: "In view of security, establishing a weather and radar base on Dokdo is a matter of interest to the United States," he said. In accordance with the interests of Japan and the United States, in the sixth draft, Dokdo was designated temporarily as Japanese territory.[12] In the end, the Dokdo notation itself disappeared. Sebald's lobby also ended in failure. It is worth noting that Dokdo was marked as Korean territory in "the reference map of the Japanese territory" of the Japan National Maritime Security Agency in August 1951, which was produced based on this premise.[13]

Third, regarding the Rusk letter, which was not released to Japan in 1951, it is necessary to pay attention to re-summoning the doctrine of terra nullius on Dokdo in 1905 based on false information provided by Japan,[14] in addition to its utilization of the changes in the international situation caused by the rise of the Cold War,[15] as can be seen from the temporary change in U.S. policy due to Sebald's lobby.

Fourth, in relation to the claim that Dokdo became Japanese territory before Japan's forced annexation of Korea, it is worth noting that the invasion of Dokdo and the coercion of the treaty by Japan, which and null and void for illegality under international law,[16] started with the occupation of Jinhae Bay and Masan City on Feb. 6, 1904, an invasion against the Korean Empire, which declared wartime neutrality on Jan. 21, 1904.[17]

5. CONCLUSION

The Japanese government's frame of historical distortion that puts international law at the fore under the policy stance of breaking away from the post-war regime for revising Japan's peace constitution, and on historical revisionism for the distortion of past history, which undercuts the establishment of the foundation for a community of peace in East Asia. Moreover, Japan's claim to Dokdo, lacking legality and legitimacy under international law contrary to Japan's claims, is the essence of violence and greed of ongoing Japanese colonialism and a serious violation of Korea's territorial sovereignty.

Thus, the claims made by the Japanese government, such as the legitimate theory of 1910 colonization, the completion theory of the 1965 Korea-Japan agreement, and the incorporation theory of Dokdo of 1905, are nothing but the structured and repeated violence of Japanese colonialism based on the Korea-Japan Treaty of 1905.

Under such a premise, the Joint Statement by 1,139 Korean-Japanese intellectuals who declared the original invalidation of the Korea-Japan Annexation Treaty in 1910 was an East Asian version of the Durban Declaration of 2001, which marks the historical end of colonialism, and it is here that we must seek true historical reconciliation on the basis of true history.

There can be no rectification of history unless it is realized by the implementation of international legal justice on the sovereignty, human rights and territory of Korea infringed by Japanese colonialism. This is an ongoing task for communities of historical justice and peace.

It is therefore our task today as we pass the 70th anniversary of the San Francisco Peace Treaty and the 117th year of the Korea-Japan Treaty of 1905, to build a basis for a true East Asian community of peace through historical reflection and international legal justice, in addition to the basic peace under international law that calls for apology and compensation for Japan's colonial rule and wars of aggression.

Notes

1. See-hwan Doh, "Korea's Dokdo sovereignty and San Francisco Peace Treaty," Korea Times, Dec. 20, 2022, p. 13.
2. Yutaka Yoshida, The Japanese Views of War, Iwanami Shoten, 1995, p. 70.
3. See-hwan Doh, "A review on Korea's sovereignty over Dokdo and Japan's claim of treaty-based title from the Perspective of International Law," The Journal of Dokdo, No. 31, Dec. 2022, pp. 109~154.
4. See-hwan Doh, "International Legal Implications of the San Francisco Peace Treaty and Dokdo's Sovereignty," Korean Yearbook of International Law, Vol. 4, 2016, pp. 58~63.
5. NARA, RG59, Lot54 D423, Japanese Peace Treaty Files of John Foster Dulles, Box 8, Korea; Foreign Relations of the United States 1951, Vol. 6, p. 1203, f.n.3.
6. See-hwan Doh, "Considerations of the Korea-Japan Annexation Treaty from the Viewpoint of Historical Truth and International Law," Korean Journal of International Law, Vol. 55, No. 4, Dec. 12, pp. 17~18.
7. See-hwan Doh, "Revisiting the Protectorate Treaty of 1905 from the Perspective of International Law," Korean Journal of International Law, Vol. 60, No. 4, Dec. 12, p. 126.
8. Etsuro Totsuka, "Japan's forced annexation of Korea, 1965 Korea-Japan agreement, incomplete Japanese colonial responsibility and liquidation," Revisiting the fifty years of the agreement between South Korea and Japan V, Northeast Asian History Foundation, 2016, pp. 129~133.
9. Nagao Ariga, Theory of a protected state, Waseda University Press, 1906, pp. 205~208; Fukuju Unno, Studies on the history of the annexation of Korea, Iwanami Shoten, 2000, pp. 184~237; Shigeki Sakamoto, "Effect of the Japan-Korea Protection Treaty: From the Viewpoint of the Treaty by Coercion," The Law Review, Kansai University, Vol. 44, No. 4~5, p. 350.
10. Sung-whoan LEE, "Rusk Letter and Legal Title to Territorial Sovereignty over Dokdo Island in the San Francisco Peace Treaty," Dokdo's Territorial Sovereignty and International Legal Title Ⅱ, Northeast Asian History Foundation, 2021, p. 285.
11. Hyun-jin Park, A Study on Dokdo's Territorial Sovereignty, Kyungin Publishing, 2017, pp. 376~378.
12. Takashi Tsukamoto, "The Peace Treaty and Takeshima(Re-discussion)," Reference 44(3), National Library of Congress, pp. 43~44.
13. Tae-man Chung, "The perception and its change of Korea and neighboring countries on Dokdo after 17th century," Ph. D. dissertation, Dankook University, p. 169.
14. See-hwan Doh, supra note 3, pp. 139~141.
15. Kimie Hara, Blind Spots in the San Francisco Peace Treaty: The Cold War in

the Asia-Pacific Region and Unresolved Postwar Issues, Keisuisha, p. 50; Alexis Dudden, "Disputed Legacies of the San Francisco Treaty," Territory and Seas, Vol. 22, 2021, p. 31.

16. See-hwan Doh, supra note 7, pp. 128.

17. Haruki Wada, "Russian-Japanese War and Japan's Annexation of Korea-Thinking of the Russian Factor," One Hundred Years After Japan's Forced Annexation of Korea: History and Tasks, Northeast Asian History Foundation. 2013, pp. 76-77.

RECENT DEVELOPMENTS

Military Activities in Other States' Exclusive Economic Zones

Lee Seok-Yong
Emeritus Professor
Hannam University, Daejeon, Korea

I. Introduction

The conflicts and tensions between the law of the sea and naval operations became more evident as the law of the sea regulations underwent codification since mid 19th century. Along with the codification of international law of the sea, the international law of armed conflict has passed a codification process leading to the conclusions of the Conventions adopted at the Hague Peace Conferences in 1899 and 1907, the four Geneva Conventions in 1949, and the two Additional Protocols in 1977. However, as new warships such as submarines and aircraft carriers appeared and new electronic weapon systems were developed, the ocean became more and more subject to diverse forms of regulation. At the same time, the freedom of navigation has been on the verge of decline.[1]

The Exclusive Economic Zone (EEZ), which was recognized as a maritime jurisdiction through customary development in the mid-1970s and finally codified by the 1982 United Nations Convention on the Law of the Sea (the "Law of the Sea Convention" or "LOS Convention"), is perceived to be a maritime zone with the characteristics of both the territorial sea and the high seas. The argument that

197

freedom of the high seas should be applied to the EEZ except for economic jurisdiction seems logical and persuasive, but the argument that the rights of coastal states in the EEZ should be respected get support from developing coastal states. Diverse conflicts have occurred between maritime powers and coastal states because of the ambiguity surrounding the legal nature of the EEZ. Foremost among them involve military activities in EEZ. Controversy rages between states and scholars who defend the position of maritime states to extend the freedoms of the high seas to EEZ and other states and scholars who support the position of developing coastal states trying to limit military activities by foreign ships in their EEZs. In particular, the United States, the largest maritime power, differentiated the international waters comprising the high seas and EEZs from waters under national sovereignty to insist on the freedom of navigation, overflight and various military activities there. On the other hand, China supported stronger jurisdiction of coastal state over their EEZs. As a consequence, the two sides have been involved in disputes relating to the conflicts such as collision of the US EP-3 reconnaissance aircraft and the Chinese F-8 fighter jet in 2001, military surveys by the USS Bowditch in the Yellow Sea in 2001 and the US Impeccable in the South China Sea in 2009, and Aircraft Carrier Washington's entry into the Yellow Sea after the artillery shelling on Yeonpyeong Island by North Korea in 2010.[2] In addition, the widespread use of drones in the Ukrainian-Russian war that began in 2022 and reconnaissance activities around the Seoul area by North Korea using drones in 2022 show the need for review of military activities using drones.

The Law of the Sea Convention does not completely prohibit the military use of the sea. However, the presence of foreign warships, military exercises, military survey, and the development and movement of weapons of mass destruction in EEZs have posed significant threats to the security of the coastal states. Moreover, concerns are rising over terrorism at sea, unlawful offenses, military survey, and marine scientific research.[3] This issue is becoming more and more important to Asia-Pacific region. Large areas of this region are semi-enclosed seas, and there are conflicting claims to maritime jurisdiction. The naval capabilities of the states in this region are seeing rapid improvement, and intelligence collection and marine research attract attention to support naval operations. They also strive to reorganize weapons systems to enhance cyber power and to expand information power and data.[4]

In spite of the importance of the relevant issues, the Law of the Sea Convention does not include specific provisions dealing with military activities in EEZs of other states. Therefore, questions remain unresolved, such as whether the military activities constitute freedom of navigation or another lawful uses in EEZ, whether due regard in exercising rights and duties could be used as a standard in deciding the limit of military activities, whether peaceful purposes could be a limitation on the freedom of navigation, and how to decide the lawfulness of various maritime activities related to marine scientific research.[5]

II. The United Nations and Military Activities at Sea

As the seas have been used for trade between states and functioned as an expressway for ships including warships, military uses of the seas have been closely associated with naval power. However, the connection between the law of the sea and naval power became evident in 17th century, when the history of the international law of the sea had just begun with academic confrontation. Hugo Grotius asserted the principle of the "Free Sea" for virtually unfettered access to the oceans for trade and fishery, but Selden's "Closed Sea" allowed wide national jurisdiction for national safety.

The victory of the Grotian view meant the establishment of the freedom of the sea as a fundamental principle of the law of the sea and the recognition of the maritime powers' influence even in peacetime. As Professors Rothwell and Stephens put it, the 17th century perspective on Law of the Sea and naval power prevails today, because most naval powers still aim to maintain the freedom of the seas as the most valuable principle in law of the sea.[6]

The law of naval war developed initially in customary law, and was gradually codified through international conferences. In 1899 and 1907, the Hague Conferences adopted the Hague Convention which specified the status of enemy merchant ships at the outbreak of hostilities, the conversion of merchant ships into warships, the laying of automatic submarine mines, naval bombardment in time of war, and the right of capture. The Convention dealt with distinctions between belligerents and neutral states and sought to maintain certain freedoms of trade by merchant ships.[7]

After the end of WW II, the development of the law of naval armed conflict was delayed. While the 1928 Briand-Kellog Pact (The Pact of Paris) had some limited effect on outlawing the war, the United Nations Charter prohibited the threat and use of force against the territorial integrity and political independence of a state. In spite of these provisions, it is not clear whether international law can now recognize a state of war to invite the application of the Law of War in traditional way. However, this question had little importance in reality, because laws applicable to armed conflicts between combatants could be applied not only to all declared war but also to any other armed conflict by the Geneva Convention concluded in 1949.[8]

As the UN Charter bans use of force, including war, and adopts a collective security system, the possibility of legal neutrality on this issue seems to have almost disappeared. Questions were therefore raised whether the traditional laws of war and neutrality laws can be applied were raised. There have been armed conflicts between countries in recent years, and the parties to the armed conflict, either direct or indirect, seek to protect their own interests by using the traditional laws of war and neutrality.[9]

International humanitarian law aims to protect the wounded, the sick and civilians and to restrict the means and methods of warfare. Major parts of international humanitarian law are contained in the four Geneva Conventions concluded in 1949. The Conventions have been expanded and supplemented by the two Additional Protocols of 1977 for the protection of victims of armed conflicts. These multilateral agreements provide specific rules to safeguard combatants, the wounded and the sick or shipwrecked, prisoners of war, and civilians.

The Hague Conventions focusing on regulating the conduct of armed conflict and the Geneva Conventions focusing on protecting the persons affected by armed conflict are now recognized as important sources to limit military activities on the sea.[10]

Military activities in the sea can be lawfully conducted when the Security Council decides to impose sanction against a specific country in accordance with the UN Charter. The United Nations Charter prohibits not only war but also the use and threat of force generally. However, the UN allowed the use of force in accordance with the resolution of the Security Council against threats to or breaches of peace, and also allowed the use of force for self-defense. If relevant resolutions are adopted by the Security Council, military activities could be deemed to be legitimate. The UN Security Council has adopted several resolutions to suppress production and trade in weapons of mass destruction such as nuclear weapons.

Article 39 of the UN Charter provides that the Security Council determines the existence of a threat to peace, breach of the peace or an act of aggression, and decides what action to take for the maintenance and restoration of international peace and security. The "threat to peace" referred to here is not limited to armed conflict

between states. It has been recognized when human rights or the
right to self-determination were violated. The UN Security Council
considered Rhodesia's unilateral declaration of independence and
South Africa's racial discrimination to be threats to peace. In a
resolution of December 16, 1966, the Security Council decided that
the situation in Rhodesia was a threat to international peace, and
requested member states to suspend trade with the state.[11] Examples
of breaches of peace recognized by the Council include North
Korea's invasion into South Korea in 1950, Argentina's conduct
during the Falkland conflict in 1980, the Iran-Iraq war in 1987, and
the Iraqi invasion into Kuwait in 1990. According to Article 40 of
the Charter, the Security Council may take provisional measures such
as ceasefire, cessation of hostilities, and withdrawal of troops to
prevent deterioration of the situation before making any recommendations or decisions. Subsequently, the Security Council may take
non-military or military measures for the restoration of peace, but
non-military measures shall be taken first. In accordance with Article
41 of the UN Charter, the Security Council may take measures that
do not involve the use of military force. Limitations on economic
relations, means of transportation (railway, navigation, and aviation),
communication (mail and radio communications) and on diplomatic
relations may be imposed. The Security Council requested member
states to suspend trade with Iraq following the Iraqi invasion into
Kuwait. Exports of goods to Rhodesia were banned because of the
Security Council's sanctions against the white minority government
of Ian Smith.[12]

If non-military measures fail, the Security Council may resort to
military sanctions mobilizing armed forces. Article 42 of the UN
Charter provides that the Security Council may, if non-military
measures are insufficient, take such action by air, sea, or land forces
as may be necessary to maintain or restore international peace and
security. The measures may include demonstrations, blockades and

other operations by the military forces of the member states. In a resolution adopted during the Korean War in 1950, the Security Council recommended military aid and dispatch of troops to South Korea. When Iraq invaded Kuwait in 1991, the Council adopted Resolution 678 to give coalition forces the power to use "all necessary means" to defeat Iraqi forces.[13]

The United Nations allows the use of force for self-defense in Article 51 of the Charter. It provides that nothing in this Charter prejudices the right to individual or collective self-defense in the event of an armed attack against a member state. In particular, the use of force in the sea has often been carried out as an exercise of the right to self-defense rather than collective action by the United Nations.[14] The right to self-defense is the right of a state to use force to escape the situation when its territory, aircraft or ships are under the armed attack by another state. In order to exercise the right of self-defense, an armed attack must have already occurred or is imminent. Furthermore, there should be no realistic alternative other than the use of force. The exercise of this right is permitted only to the extent necessary to stop or prevent infringements.[15]

Armed conflict between Russia and Ukraine began with Russia's invasion into Ukraine in February 2022. Since Russia invaded Ukraine by mobilizing its army, navy, and air force, the UN Security Council could decide to impose economic or military sanctions to Russia, but it is unlikely that such measures will be taken as Russia is a Permanent Member of the Council. Ukraine can invoke the Russian invasion as a cause of use of force for self-defense. In the Sino-Taiwan conflict triggered by the US House Speaker Nancy Pelosi's visit to Taiwan in 2022, China fired cannons and missiles and launched fighter jets into the waters surrounding Taiwan, which constitutes a threat to peace prohibited by the UN Charter. Although China claims Taiwan as a part of its territory, Taiwan may claim its right to self-defense. However, given the reality of international society, inappropriate measures taken by great powers often go unchecked, whereas military measures strongly opposed by the great powers are not easily implemented.[16]

As international society takes measures to regulate military activities in international waters due to growing concerns about security, the freedom of navigation in the high seas has been under pressure. Three cases will be reviewed here: First, the UN Security Council has restricted the freedom of navigation through resolutions adopted according to the Chapter 7 of UN Charter to suppress the proliferation of nuclear materials. The UN Security Council has adopted resolutions to suppress North Korea's nuclear program. Resolution No. 1874, adopted in 2009, allowed the member states to stop and inspect ships suspected of transporting prohibited nuclear materials. In Resolution No. 1540, adopted in 2004, the Council established general measures to be taken by member states to combat the proliferation of nuclear and biochemical weapons such as blocking illegal trade of WMD. This resolution became the potential basis for the Proliferation Security Initiative (PSI), which was formed to prohibit the proliferation of WMD.[17]

Second, the PSI is an US-led multilateral cooperation initiative to deter the proliferation of WMDs. PSI was formed on the basis of the shared international realization that the traditional international legal system for deterring transportation of WMDs was flawed, as seen in the case of the North Korean ship *The Seosan* in 2002. PSI, joined by more than 100 states, allowed member states to stop, detain, or arrest weapon-transporting ships from or to states or terrorist groups suspected of potential WMD proliferation. The geographical scope of PSI practices includes internal waters, territorial sea, EEZ, and the high sea. PSI allows member states to stop and inspect suspected ships and seize the confirmed freight, but this was criticized for infringing the established international legal order of the sea, particularly the freedom of navigation on the high seas.

Third, after terrorists attacked the cruise ship Achille Lauro in the Mediterranean, the International Maritime Organization (IMO) led the adoption of the Convention for the Suppression of Unlawful Acts Against the Safety of Maritime Navigation (SUA Convention) in 1988. This Convention specified a series of unlawful acts relating to terrorism on the sea and allowed states to seize the ships with the agreement of the flag state. The Convention was revised in 2005 to expand the relevant rights so that states other than the flag state may interdict a ship in the high seas with the agreement of the flag state if the ship is suspected of transporting WMD or relevant materials.[18]

III. EEZ : Freedom of Navigation and Residual Rights

1. EEZ: Freedom of Navigation v. Rights of Coastal States

The Convention on the Law of the Sea does not have clear provisions on the legal status of the Exclusive Economic Zone (EEZ). EEZ is explained to be a special (*sui generis*) zone with its own characteristic system that mixes the characteristics of the territorial sea and high seas. Unlike the territorial sea, EEZ is not an area in which coastal states have unlimited sovereignty and legal rights, and unlike the high seas, it is not an area in which other countries enjoy unlimited freedom. In other words, EEZ is an amalgam or a multi-functional zone, in which coastal states have sovereign rights over economic resources and jurisdiction over other matters. It was not easy to imagine emergence of a maritime zone called EEZ which is intermediate between the free ocean (*mare liberum*) and the closed ocean (*mare clausum*).[19]

As coastal states expand and strengthen their jurisdiction over the EEZ, different positions over the legal character of the EEZ loom large. Maritime powers such as the United States claim that EEZ is a part of the high seas subject to the special rights of the coastal state, but developing coastal states argue that, although freedom of navigation and overflight is partly granted to third states, EEZ is basically a part of the ocean space where the jurisdiction of the coastal state applies.[20] Although Article 55 of the Law of the Sea Convention states that EEZ is subject to special legal system so that the rights and jurisdiction of coastal states and the rights and freedoms of other states are governed by the relevant provisions of the Convention, the issue surrounding legal nature of this zone could not be solved.

Maritime powers have stressed that introduction of EEZ was a result of a package deal made at the Third United Nations Conference on the Law of the Sea (UNCLOSIII). The agreement made there was that while the coastal states would gain recognition of their resource-related rights in their EEZs, other states retain most freedoms of the high seas. Article 58(1) of the Law of the Sea Convention provides that in the EEZ all States, subject to the relevant provisions of this Convention, enjoy the freedoms referred to in Article 87 such as freedoms of navigation, overflight, laying of submarine cables and pipelines, and other internationally lawful uses of the sea related to these freedoms. Exceptionally, the freedom of fisheries does not apply in EEZs.[21] According to the maritime powers, this means that in the EEZ of any state, ships and aircraft of other states enjoy the freedom of navigation and overflight similar to the freedom of the high seas. Furthermore, activities such as military surveys and reconnaissance are not MSR, and these activities are covered by the freedom of the high seas.[22] Pete Pedrozo of the US Naval War College enumerates the military activities which can be undertaken in EEZ as the following; intelligence, surveillance, and reconnaissance (ISR) operations; military marine data collection and naval oceanographic surveys; war games and military exercises;

bunkering and underway replenishment; testing and use of weapons; aircraft carrier flight operations and submarine operations; acoustic and sonar operations; naval control and protection of shipping; establishment and maintenance of military-related artificial islands; ballistic missile defense operations and ballistic missile test support; maritime interdiction operations (e.g. board, search and seizure); conventional and ballistic missile testing; belligerent rights in naval warfare (e.g. the right of visit and search); strategic arms control verification; maritime security operations (e.g., counter-terrorism and counter-proliferation); and sea control.[23] States may also conduct non-resource-related maritime law enforcement activities in foreign EEZs without notice to the coastal state or its consent pursuant to Article 58(2) of the Convention. These activities include actions to counter slave trade (Article 99), to repress piracy (Articles 100-107), to suppress unauthorized broadcasting (Article 109) and narcotics trafficking (Article 108). The right of approach and visit (Article 110) and the right to hot pursuit (Article 111) are also included.[24]

According to the "territorialist" stance supported by many developing countries, EEZ is an area where the jurisdiction of a coastal state extends and, with some exceptions, a coastal state exercises sovereign rights there.[25] They contend that the Convention has never allowed a state to conduct military exercises and military operations in EEZ of another state without the permission of that state. Bangladesh, in ratifying the Convention, declared that the Government of Bangladesh understood the Convention as not permitting other states to conduct military exercises and operations in EEZ without the consent of the coastal states. Brazil, Cape Verde, India, Malaysia, Pakistan, Uruguay, etc. made similar declarations upon ratifying the Convention, and Iran took a similar position in its domestic law. China and North Korea also agreed to this position.[26]

Zhang Haiwen of China stressed that the Law of the Sea Convention unequivocally excluded the EEZ from the high seas to incorporate it into the national jurisdiction of the coastal state. This proves that the demand of developing countries to expand the national jurisdiction of coastal states was broadly acknowledged by the international community. A coastal state therefore exercises sovereign rights for the purpose of exploring, exploiting, conserving and managing natural resources of the EEZ and other activities for the economic uses of the EEZ and have jurisdiction with regard to matters including environmental protection and MSR. According to her, this shows the essential difference of EEZ and high seas.[27] Zhang said that she fully agrees with the position of Western scholars safeguarding the freedoms of navigation and overflight in/over foreign EEZs, but safeguarding these freedoms does not mean allowing some states to conduct military surveys, reconnaissance, and other military activities in the EEZ of other coastal states.[28] However, according to the US, these arguments do not conform with the Law of the Sea Convention and state practice.[29]

Some coastal states have strengthened and expanded their jurisdictions in their EEZs requiring their consent to conduct military activities there. China in particular has tried to strengthen its control over military survey, surveillance, and reconnaissance in EEZ and to expand its jurisdiction. The developed states Britain, Germany, and Italy opposed these claims by developing countries. The United States asserts that military operations, military exercises and military activities have always been considered lawful maritime uses under international law, and all states have the right to conduct such activities in EEZ of another state.[30]

This conflict of opinions gave rise to disputes between the United States and China in instances such as the Bowditch incident in March 2001, the Impeccable incident in 2009, and the EP-3 reconnaissance plane incident in 2001. The US also clashed with North Korea in the 1968 Pueblo incident.[31]

2. Residual Rights

"Military activities" generally means the operation of military vessels and aircraft, and devices for military exercises and training, weapons practices, and intelligence collection.[32] The rights that other states have in another state's EEZ, especially the freedom of military activities in EEZ, are closely related to the freedom of navigation in the high seas. The 1958 Convention on the High Seas states that freedoms of the high seas include freedom of navigation, freedom of fishing, freedom of laying submarine cables and pipelines, freedom of overflight, and other freedoms recognized under the principles of general international law. Article 87(1) of the 1982 Law of the Sea Convention enumerates six freedoms by adding the "freedom to construct artificial islands and other facilities" and the "freedom to conduct scientific research" to the traditional four freedoms on the high seas stipulated by the 1958 Convention. However, the same Article provides that the "freedom on the high seas includes, in particular (*inter alia*), the following freedoms," indicating that the six freedoms listed are not exhaustive and only exemplify some of the freedoms on the high seas.[33] There may be disagreements among states over the other freedoms on the high seas. There are activities on the high seas that some states may consider to be part of the freedom of the high seas, while others do not, giving rise to the issue of so-called "residual rights."

If there are activities over which the Law of the Sea Convention does not clearly confer any rights or jurisdiction to the coastal states within their EEZs and it is not clear whether third states have any rights or duties over such activities, it is necessary to determine whom such rights or jurisdiction belong to. Generally, coastal states claim that the remaining rights belong to the coastal states, while maritime states claim that those rights belong to the international community. In this regard, Article 59 of the Convention provides that if the right or jurisdiction in the EEZ does not belong to a coastal state or any other state under this Convention, and conflict arises between them over their interests, the conflict will be resolved in light of all relevant circumstances on the basis of equity, taking into account the importance of the parties' interests and the interests of the international community as a whole. The Law of the Sea Convention requires states parties to resolve the residual rights issue on a case-by-case basis and on the basis of equity considering all the relevant circumstances. To utilize this mechanism, more study and consideration of other abstract concepts such as equity and relevant circumstances are needed. The Convention leaves open the possibility that disputes regarding residual rights over military activities in EEZs may not be clearly resolved until the practice of states converges or a new agreement emerges.[34]

IV. Due Regard

As the high seas have seen heavier use, conflicts arising out of the use of the high seas and EEZ have increased. Conflicts between military activities and other uses such as navigation, fishery, and environment protection could take place. All ships and aircraft including warships and military airplanes used to have freedom of navigation and overflight including military exercises, surveillance, intelligence gathering on the high seas and in EEZ, but these activities are supposed to be conducted with due regard for the rights and duties of other states.

Residual rights issues should be viewed against the background of there being no central authority granting rights to states in international law, limited access to international justice, and no specific provision dealing with the extent of the rights of third states in the EEZs of coastal states. The legal status of peacetime military activities by third states in a coastal state's EEZ remains highly uncertain as a result.[35]

Articles 56(2) and 58(3) of the Law of the Sea Convention introduce brief provisions on "due regard" with respect to military activities in the EEZs of other states. Article 56(2) provides that in exercising its rights and performing its duties under the Convention in the EEZ, the coastal state shall have due regard to the rights and duties of other states and shall act in a manner compatible with the provisions of the Convention. Article 58(3) provides that, in exercising their rights and performing their duties under the Convention in the EEZ, states shall have due regard to the rights and duties of the coastal state and shall comply with the laws and regulations adopted by the coastal state in accordance with the provisions of the Convention and other rules of international law. The Convention thus tries to maintain the balance of interests and rights of the coastal states and other states in the EEZ.[36]

The Convention gives no clear guidance to the meaning of the concept "due regard." However, the early proposals by developing states tried to restrict the other states' rights and freedoms in the EEZ, and China's proposal included the duty of other states to observe the laws and regulations of the coastal state. At the third session (1975), the Evenson Group produced the text introducing the term "due regard" to the rights and duties of the coastal states. This history demonstrates that the term due regard was mainly understood as non-infringement of the coastal state's rights. However, there is no agreed specific criterion for states to apply in deciding whether their activities have fulfilled the due regard standard. The important criteria applicable to cases are the activities related to the rights and interests of the coastal state and the activities related to environmental protection.[37] China maintains the security interest of the coastal state is an issue of inherent, primal importance and must be given paramount consideration.[38]

It has been argued that due regard should be used as the general standard for resolving conflicts of legal interest, in particular between the rights of coastal states and the freedom of navigation including military action. Coastal states have stressed the importance of national security to regulate foreign ships' passage and aircraft overflight in their EEZs. The move to enhance jurisdiction over foreign ships and aircraft for national security is prevalent in EEZ. On April 1, 2001, a Chinese F-8 fighter collided with a US Navy reconnaissance aircraft EP-3 over the Chinese EEZ about 70 nautical miles southeast of Hainan Island. The Chinese fighter pilot was killed, and after the US Navy EP-3 made an emergency landing on the Hainan military base the American pilot was detained by the Chinese authorities. China asserted that the US took undue advantage of the right of overflight in EEZ and neglected the duty of "due regard" to the rights of the coastal state, as specified in Article 58(3) of the Law of the Sea Convention. China claimed the right to intervene in overflights by foreign aircraft in its EEZ, if there is a threat to security.[39] The Convention does not provide explicitly whether foreign countries can engage in military activities in the EEZ of another state. The only criterion the Convention establishes is the provision that a foreign state should have due regard to the rights and duties of the coastal state.[40] In general, states tend to restrict foreign ships' passage and aircraft overflight in their EEZs more stringently for national security as ascertained in the case of non-proliferation of WMD.[41]

Environmental limitations imposed on military activities in the EEZ are not specifically mentioned in the Law of the Sea Convention, and the status of any right to conduct military activities in the EEZ is still uncertain. Here, it is important to confirm whether some rights and interests are superior to the others. Considering the advisory opinion regarding the *Responsibility of Contracting States for the Activities conducted in the Area,* the obligations related to the conservation of the environment in the high seas arguably have an *erga omnes* character. However, the Law of the Sea Convention is silent on how to solve and prevent such conflicts.

States have strengthened their authority, based on the environmental jurisdiction in the EEZ, to regulate the passage of foreign ships carrying highly hazardous materials such as nuclear materials, reprocessing facilities, and nuclear waste repositories. Some states have asserted that they have the right to require prior notification of the passage of ships carrying such freight and to refuse such ships' passage in their EEZ.[42] The 1989 Basel Convention on the Control of Transboundary Movements of Hazardous Wastes and Their Disposal provided for the notification and consent system that require consent from all transit states for the export of hazardous wastes.[43] From the 1990s onward, passages of ships carrying nuclear materials between Europe and Japan have raised significant controversies. Argentina, Chile, Colombia, Dominica Republic, New Zealand, South Africa, and Mauritius claimed the right to regulate these ships in their EEZs and territorial seas. France, Portugal, and Spain introduced new regulations after the wreck of the oil tanker Prestige in November 2002 off the coast of Spain. Oil tankers were required to obtain prior notification before passage in their EEZs, and single-hull tankers older than 15 years to accept inspection.[44]

V. Peaceful Use and Peaceful Purpose

As professors Rothwell and Stephens put it, given that UNCLOS III began at the height of the Cold War, and that the security implications of the law of the sea has become sensitive due to the emergence of a new maritime zone (EEZ) and changes in the scope of maritime jurisdictions, the successful conclusion of the Law of the Sea Convention was surprising. As negotiations progressed at the

UNCLOS Ⅲ, it became clear that the Convention would inevitably affect maritime security, but would have limited impact on military activities. The Conference focused on the peaceful uses of the sea regarding the military activities in EEZs.[45]

Article 301(Peaceful Uses of the Sea) of the Law of the Sea Convention provides, "In exercising their rights and performing their duties under this Convention, States Parties shall refrain from any threat or use of force against the territorial integrity or political independence of any State, or in any other manner inconsistent with the principles of international law embodied in the Charter of the United Nations." This provision could be understood to reflect the positions established at the Conference. The Convention states that the high seas must be used for peaceful purposes, that the use of the deep seabed must be for peaceful purposes only, and that MSR must also be exclusively for peaceful purposes.[46]

The foundation on which military operations rest is the freedom of navigation that originally belongs to the freedom of the high seas. Article 87 of the Law of the Sea Convention provides that the high seas are open to all States and that the freedoms of the high seas "shall be exercised by all States with due regard for the interests of other States in their exercise of the freedom of the high seas, and also with due regard for the rights under this Convention with respect to activities in the Area." Article 58 recognizes that all States enjoy within EEZs the freedoms referred to in Article 87 including freedoms of navigation and overflight and of the laying submarine cables and pipelines, and other internationally lawful uses of the sea related to these freedoms. Article 86 of the Convention confirms the broad interpretation of Article 58. Hence, both the EEZ (including the contiguous zone) and the high seas beyond the EEZ are often referred to as "international water" or "high seas" for the purposes of navigation and overflight rights. Article 301 require States to refrain from any threat or use of force against the territorial integrity or political independence of any State, or in any other manner inconsistent with the principles of international law embodied in the Charter of the United Nations.

The freedom of the high seas means freedom of activity on the high seas, and the types and ranges of activities that states can engage in on the high seas continue to expand due to the development of science and technology. As the high seas do not fall under the jurisdiction of any state, no state could control the activities of other states on the high seas, and states could enjoy almost unlimited freedom to use the oceans as they want. As new maritime science and technologies were developed, the freedom of the high seas enjoyed by states became more and more diverse.

Under these circumstances, the argument that the obligation to use the sea peacefully as an important criterion to distinguish between permitted activities and prohibited activities among military activities has gained validity and persuasiveness. The Law of the Sea Convention mentions "peaceful uses" and "peaceful purposes" many times. The preamble of the Convention mentions the peaceful use of the sea as one of the purposes of the legal order established by it, while Articles 88 and 58(2) mention peaceful purposes in relation to the high seas and EEZ. Articles 141, 143(1), 147(2)(d) and 155(2) mention these terms relating to the reservation of the Deep Seabed. Article 240(a) and paragraph 3 refer to peaceful uses and peaceful purposes in relation to the purposes of marine scientific research and consent to research by third countries. In particular, Article 301 provides, "In exercising their rights and performing their duties under this Convention, States Parties shall refrain from any threat or use of force against the territorial integrity or political independence of any State, or in any other manner inconsistent with the principles of international law embodied in the Charter of the United Nations." Although the Convention uses the terms "peaceful use" and "peaceful purpose" numerous times, it does not provide the definitions of these terms. The term was used in a number of multilateral treaties even before the conclusion of the Convention, some of which meant complete demilitarization, while others banned some military activities. Thus, as Boczek argued, since there is no unified understanding of peaceful purposes, the implications and roles of peaceful use and peaceful purposes of the Convention must be deduced from the context and circumstances of the particular instruments in which it is used.[47]

During the 4th session of the UNCLOS III, three groups of states participated in the debate on the question of peaceful uses of ocean space. Many states including developing states interpreted the clause as prohibiting all military activities, while other states considered it as prohibiting military activities for aggressive purposes. Many states were of the opinion that the test of whether an activity is peaceful depends on whether it is consistent with the UN Charter and other obligations under international law. The United States, a strong supporter of this position, stressed that the conduct of military activities for peaceful purposes is in full accord with the Charter, and that limitation on military activities would require more detailed negotiation.[48] As explained before, there was continued controversy over whether the peaceful uses/purposes clause has been focused on whether it entails prohibition or limitation of all military activities, but the US and the USSR at UNCLOS III were determined to protect the broadest possible freedom to conduct military activities at sea.[49] International law scholars generally agree that, based on various provisions of the Law of the Sea Convention relating to the freedom of military vessels to navigate, the privileged status granted to military vessels, and the optional exclusion from compulsory judicial settlement of disputes concerning military activities, it is logical and realistic to interpret the peaceful uses and peaceful purposes clauses as prohibiting only those activities which are inconsistent with the United Nations Charter.[50]

In summary, it is reasonable to interpret Article 301 of the Convention as prohibiting military activities that harm the territorial integrity or political independence of other states or that are contrary to the purposes of the UN Charter in the exercise of rights and obligations of states parties. In reality, states rarely restricted their military activities as long as their use of the high seas did not violate norms such as the Nuclear Test Ban Treaty and the Undersea Denuclearization Treaty. Of course, since EEZs are not high seas, the same criteria cannot be applied, but the room for coastal states to intervene will be greatly reduced than they have expected.[51] Although military activities in the EEZ can not be allowed almost without limit as the United States and American scholars argue, the scope of situation requiring permission from the coastal state for military activities in the EEZ will not be so wide as claimed by some coastal states.

China has not been satisfied with the US's argument that it has signed bilateral agreements with many countries including Soviet Union to maintain the freedom to conduct military activities at sea. China raised the question, as the US maintained that military intelligence activities are not a threat to other states nor are aggressive, should China allow the US to collect and take away marine data, especially seabed data, from the EEZ of China? Furthermore, as Professor Sam Bateman pointed out, some military hydrographic surveys by states may not be for peaceful purposes.[52] In summery, even criteria such as "peaceful uses" and "peaceful purposes" could be used to restrict military activities in EEZs of other states.

VI. Marine Scientific Research and Military Activities

1. Marine Scientific Research

Marine Scientific Research (MSR) activities have contributed to human welfare through the increase of scientific knowledge about the ocean. However, as MSR activities were diversified and the results of the research were used for military and commercial purposes, the international community has tried to regulate MSR activities. MSR was on the agenda at the UNCLOS III, and the issue of military activities in the EEZ has been treated as an important one. The Conference introduced relevant provisions on MSR into the Law of the Sea Convention. However, the Convention contains no specific provisions dealing with the issue of military activities in the EEZ. This does not mean that the Convention is completely silent on the issue: what is important is to find a compromise position considering the words, context, and drafting history.[53]

Article 245 of the Law of the Sea Convention provides that "Coastal States, in the exercise of their sovereignty, have the exclusive right to regulate, authorize and conduct MSR in their territorial sea" and adds, "MSR therein shall be conducted only with the express consent of and under the conditions set forth by the coastal State." This means that coastal states have the exclusive rights to regulate, authorize and conduct MSR in their territorial sea, and the research state should obtain express consent to conduct MSR in the territorial sea of another state. Similar rules are applicable to the internal waters and archipelagic waters where the coastal state's sovereignty applies.[54] Article 19(2) of the Convention provides in relation to innocent passage that the passage of a foreign ship shall be considered to be prejudicial to the peace, good order or security of the coastal state if in the territorial sea it engages in not only (a) any threat of peace or use of force against the sovereignty, territorial integrity, or political independence of the coastal state, (b) any exercise or practice with weapons of any kind, (e)(f)launching, landing of any aircraft and military device, but also (j) conducting research or survey activities. In the international straits or archipelagic sea lanes, foreign ships including ships for MSR and hydrographic survey cannot conduct any investigation or survey during transit passage or archipelagic sea lanes passage without prior consent of the coastal or archipelagic state.[55]

At the UNCLOS I held in 1958, there were conflicts of opinion over whether the consent of coastal state should be necessary for MSR on continental shelves. According to the Continental Shelf Convention adopted at the Conference, research states or international organizations should obtain the coastal state's consent for MSR on the continental shelf, but the coastal state should consent if the request was for pure scientific research on the physical or biological properties of the continental shelf. Article 246(1) and (2) of the Law of the Sea Convention provide that coastal state have the right to regulate, authorize, and conduct MSR in its EEZ and on the continental shelf, and that MSR therein shall be conducted with the consent of the coastal state. In other words, the Convention prescribed the coastal state's consent as a necessary condition for MSR in the EEZ and on the continental shelf of another state. On the other hand, Article 246(3) provides that coastal states shall, in normal circumstance, grant their consent for MSR projects by other states or competent international organizations in their EEZ or on their continental shelf, on the condition that the project is planned for peaceful purposes and to increase scientific knowledge of the marine environment for the benefit of all mankind. The Convention allows not only express consent but also implied consent for MSR in EEZ and continental shelf. The Convention provides also that states and international organizations may proceed with a MSR project six months after the date on which the information required pursuant to

Article 248 was provided to the coastal state. However, Article 245 (5) of the Convention specifies cases in which coastal states may refuse their consent.

Article 87 of the Convention specified the freedom of scientific research as one of the freedoms of the high seas enjoyed by all states. Regarding marine scientific research (MSR) in the high seas, Article 257 of the Convention states that all states and competent international organizations have the right to conduct MSR in the water column beyond the limits of the EEZ. However, the freedom of the high seas is not enjoyed by only one state. Hence, the freedom of MSR should not interfere with other nations' use of the high seas. In relation to MSR in the Area, Article 256 of the Convention provides that all states and the competent international organizations have the right to conduct MSR in the Area in conformity with the provisions of Part 11. Furthermore, Article 143(1) of the Convention provides that MSR in the Area shall be carried out exclusively for peaceful purposes and the benefit of mankind as a whole.

2. Hydrographic Surveys, Military Surveys, and Underwater Drones

The Law of the Sea Convention does not have detailed definition on MSR. As a result, the definitions of related concepts such as hydrographic survey, military survey, and operational oceanography and clarifying the relationship between these concepts and MSR remain unclear. The relationship between these ambiguous concepts and the MSR influences the scope of military activities permitted in the sea. The legal status and scope of use of underwater drones, which are being used for military purposes today, became controversial issues. In the case of hydrographic surveys, whether the activities belong to MSR or not is important. Review is necessary on whether or not military surveys and underwater drones belong to MSR and the scope of permitted activities.

According to the International Hydrographic Organization (IHO), a hydrographic survey aims to measure the physical properties of the ground surface and the passage area, and to perform investigations for vessel safety. Survey results are mainly used for making maritime charts and other documents.[56] The position that hydrographic surveys are different from MSR and free from coastal states' control is based on several grounds" First, there are differences in purposes of hydrographic survey and MSR. Hydrographic surveys aim to investigate the depth of the sea, topography, tides, and tidal height for the safety of ships and collect data for marine charts, while MSR aims to enhance the knowledge of the marine environment. Second, differences are found in provisions of the Law of the Sea Convention. The Convention has regulations applied equivalently to MSR and hydrographic survey in Article 19(j), Article 21(1)(g), Article 40, and Article 54, but Part 13 on MSR did not comment on hydrographic surveys.[57] On the other hand, opinions that regard hydrographic surveys as a part of MSR faced criticism because of practices using the materials developed by hydrographic surveys for economic or military ends.[58] To differentiate these two concepts, the purpose of the activities should be considered together with the contents and methods, but it is not easy in reality.

In summary, it has been the established position of the international society to divide hydrographic survey from MSR and to allow it to be performed in EEZ and continental shelf without the consent of coastal states. However, according to a Chinese scholar, the Law of the Sea Convention provided different rules for marine data collection at different locations while failing to provide rules for each kind of marine data collection activity. She wrote that it is impossible to draw a sharp distinction between MSR and similar marine activities, and technological developments of marine research equipments have made the distinction even more difficult.[59]

Military surveys are activities undertaken in the ocean for military purposes. A military survey collects data from the sea for military purposes such as maritime operation and anti-submarine warfare. Military surveys can include oceanographic, geological, geophysical, chemical, biological data. The equipment and methods used in military surveys may sometimes be the same as that used in MSR, but the information and data from such activities is intended for military uses.[60] Military surveys are different from hydrographic surveys in that they are performed secretly for strategic or tactical purposes. The United States and other maritime powers contend that military surveys are not MSR, and constitute legitimate activity related to the freedom of navigation in EEZ. United States presented this position in 2001 when the USNS Bowditch conducted a military survey 26 nautical miles away from the west coast of South Korea. The Korean government raised objections to the MSR carried out in its EEZ without prior authorization. The US then admitted to the military survey by USNS Bowditch, but it argued that the activities correspond to international customary law codified in the Convention.[61]

On the other hand, many coastal states require prior consent by them for military activities in their EEZs. Brazil, Cape Verde, India, and Malaysia stated in their interpretative declarations of the Convention that the Convention prohibited military drills and the installation of military devices in their EEZs without their consent. China in its 2022 legislation required the consent of the government for any survey or cartographic activity in its EEZ.[62] When the USS Impeccable was blocked by 5 Chinese ships while performing marine reconnaissance 75 nautical miles south of Hainan Island in March 2009, China asserted that it could regulate passage, MSR, and reconnaissance activities in its EEZ.[63]

It is not easy to find clear criteria to divide military survey and MSR and to decide whether military survey activities are allowed or not in EEZ of a coastal state. However, given the reality that more than a few states want to regulate the military activities by other states in their EEZs, more or less strict criteria could be applied to the surveys carried out for military purposes. Some scholars proposed guidelines regarding military activities in maritime zones. According to the guidelines, military activities including military exercises and intelligence gathering as well as hydrographic surveys should not be carried out within 12 miles of the territorial sea. Military vessels or aircraft navigating or flying over the EEZ of other states also should not disturb or threaten the sovereignty, territorial integrity, or independence of the coastal states.[64]

Recently, unmanned instruments such as self-floating floats, underwater drones, and ocean gliders have attracted attention. As these instruments widen the scope of use from scientific research to new fields, especially military uses, questions have been raised whether the activities using the instruments are part of MSR or not and what kind of regulations can be applied to them. A float is an autonomous equipment used for collecting oceanographic data. It stays in the water, floating repeatedly to a designated surface by artificial satellite technology, and transmits the collected oceanographic data such as water temperature, salinity, and ocean current to a data processing center through the satellite. Currently thousands of floats are deployed over the world's oceans to measure wave height, water temperature, salinity, and tides. In particular, the Argo Project operates more than 3,300 Argo floats and transmits real-time data collected by the floats to artificial satellites.[65] Recently, autonomous underwater vehicles such as underwater drones or marine gliders designed to move to the desired position according to the programmed software or remote control from the land, are widely used to collect data from a range of depths and a vast area of ocean. Drones are already widely used for military purposes as well. They are proving their performance and effectiveness in the armed conflict between Russia and Ukraine as means of reconnaissance and weapons against military and non-military targets. As drone technology proves its applicability for military purposes, countries worldwide are trying to develop high-performance underwater drones.[66]

Part 13, Section 4 of the Law of the Sea Convention stipulates the legal status of installations and equipment for MSR. Article 258 of the Convention provides that the deployment and use of scientific research installations or equipment in the marine environment shall be subject to the same conditions as are prescribed in the Convention for the conduct of MSR in any area. This means that the use of all types of scientific research installations or equipment in a certain area shall follow the regulations and conditions of the Convention on MSR in the corresponding maritime zone. If the floats and drones are considered scientific research installations or equipment as provided in the Convention, states and international organizations that intend to deploy and use them in the territorial sea and archipelagic waters must obtain "express consent" from the coastal state. Coastal state consent is also required for deploying the floats and drones in the EEZ or on the continental shelf.

Regarding the legal status of MSR installations and equipment, a distinction could be made between scientific equipment that is not fixed to the seabed, e.g. floating buoys, artificial islands, and installations that are fixed to the ocean floor. If the scientific research proposed involves the construction or use of artificial islands and installations, the coastal state may withhold its consent regardless of the purpose and nature of the research by virtue of Article 246(5)(c) of the Convention. On the other hand, the state should consent to the deployment and use of scientific installations and equipment for the purpose of pure research that are not fixed to the ocean floor. Coastal states have the discretion not to give their consent for the deployment of floating scientific installations and equipment for the purposes of applied research.[67] In summary, coastal states can not refuse consent to the deployment and use of equipment for pure research, but applied research focused on resources requires the consent of the coastal state.

It is not clear how the activities of these instruments or autonomous underwater vehicles such as floats, underwater drones, and marine gliders are to be classified under the law of the sea. Should the activities be regarded as MSR, hydrographic survey, or operational oceanography?[68] Should these devices be treated as new weapons of war which are not related to MSR?

The operation of floats, underwater drones, and marine gliders are not classified as hyrographic surveys since these devices are not deployed to make maritime charts or to enhance maritime safety. Given the fact that the activities aiming at the collection of meteorological data had already been recognized as routine observation and data collection to be considered as activities not covered by MSR, the operation of instruments or autonomous underwater vehicles such as floats, underwater drones, and marine gliders could be considered operational oceanography.[69] However, states have divergent opinions on whether maritime activities using floats and underwater drones belong to MSR or operational oceanography, and whether operational oceanography constitutes MSR. The US maintains the position that operational oceanography is not MSR. The US Senate Foreign Relations Committee once commented that marine activities includes such activities as operational oceanography. This would mean that operational oceanography is not be regarded as MSR. At a discussion hosted by the International Oceanography Committee (IOC) Executive Council, the UK presented a similar position to that of America.[70] On the other hand, France pointed out that the Convention had no special provisions on the Argo floats or operational oceanography, and said that such activities should be regarded as MSR stipulated in Part 13 of the Convention. Japan supported this position, and developing countries such as Peru and Argentina expressed similar opinions. At the IOC Experts Advisory Board, Peru argued that oceanographic data collection is MSR and requires the consent of coastal states. Argentina was of the opinion that the collection of scientific data through equipment deployed in jurisdictional waters of a coastal state should follow the provisions of Part 13 of the Convention.[71]

In summary, many developing states believe that it is reasonable to apply the MSR rules to the marine activities of floats, underwater drones, and ocean gliders. They are, in other words, of the opinion that operational oceanographic activity belongs to MSR. Nevertheless, the view of major maritime powers that operational oceanography and MSR are different concepts is influential. There are floats and drones that are unlikely to meet the conditions required by the Convention for MSR on technical points. The MSR regime of the Convention is based on the premise that MSR is conducted at a specified area of the sea within a limited time according to a plan. Research by self-floating floats or underwater drones do not fulfill these conditions. In particular, Article 248 of the Convention prescribes that states intending to perform MSR in the EEZ or on the continental shelf of a coastal state shall provide the state at least six months in advance of the expected starting date of the MSR project with the full description of the manual of scientific equipment, the precise geographical areas in which the project is to be conducted, and the expected dates of deployment of the equipment and its removal. Strict application of the provisions of Part 13 of the Convention to floats, gliders, and drones raises practical difficulties.[72] Moreover, as seen in the Russia-Ukraine armed conflict, drones go beyond reconnaissance and are used as defensive as well as offensive weapons. Therefore, it seems reasonable to regard it as a new weapon of war beyond the realm of marine scientific research.

Above all, the most important factor in deciding whether marine activities using floats and underwater drones constitute MSR is the purpose of the states or international organizations operating the instruments or equipment. However, in practice it is not easy to verify the operators' purpose.

VII. Observations

The most urgent reason for holding the UNCLOS III was to establish a deep-sea resource development regime, but the achievement that had the greatest impact on the international maritime order was the establishment of the EEZ. EEZ is explained to be a *sui generis* zone with its own characteristic system that mixes the characteristics of the territorial sea and high seas. EEZ is an amalgam or a multi-functional zone. This ambiguity surrounding the legal nature of the EEZ has given rise to diverse conflicts have occurred between maritime powers and coastal states. Foremost among them involve military activities in EEZ. The argument that freedom of the high seas should be applied to the EEZ except for economic jurisdiction seems logical and persuasive, but the argument that the rights of coastal states in the EEZ should be respected get support from developing coastal states.

The United Nations Charter prohibits not only war but also the use and threat of force generally. However, the UN allowed the use of force in accordance with the resolution of the Security Council against threats to or breaches of peace, and also allowed the use of force for self-defense. If relevant resolutions are adopted by the Security Council, military activities could be deemed to be legitimate. The UN Security Council has adopted several resolutions to suppress production and trade in weapons of mass destruction such as nuclear weapons.

The Law of the Sea Convention does not have specific provisions dealing with military activities in EEZs of other states.

Various questions remain unresolved as a result. This article analyzed the debate between the maritime states and coastal states on whether the military activities in other state's EEZ are justified as freedom of navigation or another lawful uses in the zone. As Articles 56(2) and 58(3) of the Law of the Sea Convention introduce brief provisions on "due regard" with respect to activities in the EEZs of other states, this article analyzed whether due regard could be used as a standard in deciding the limit of military activities. This article also confirmed "peaceful uses" and "peaceful purposes" could be used as criteria to restrict military activities in EEZs of other states.

Today, countries conduct various marine scientific research activities and utilize an array of instruments, facilities, and structures not only for pure marine scientific research but also for military and economic uses of the ocean. As the Law of the Sea Convention does not have detailed definition on MSR, this article clarified the definitions of related concepts such as hydrographic survey, military survey, and operational oceanography and clarified the relationship between these concepts and MSR. The relationship between these concepts and the MSR influences the scope of military activities permitted in the sea. However, more review is required for new marine research equipment such as underwater drones.

Notes

1. Donald R. Rothwell and Tim Stephens, *The International Law of the Sea*, 2nd edition, Bloomsbury, 2016, p. 278.

2. Chang-Wee Lee (이창위), "Conflicts over Military Activities in the Exclusive Economic Zone between the Maritime Powers and the Coastal States (배타적경제수역에서의 군사활동에 대한 해양강대국과 연안국의 대립)," Journal of the International Korea Society of International Law (국제법학회논총), Vol. 59 No. 1, 2014, pp. 120-121.

3. Yoshifumi Tanaka, *The International Law of the Sea*, 2nd edition, Cambridge University Press, 2015, p. 378.

4. Sam Bateman, "Prospective Guidelines for Navigation and Overflight in the Exclusive Economic Zone," *Maritime Studies September-October 2005*, University of Wollongong, 2005, pp. 17, 20.

5. Sienho Yee, "Agora : Military Activities in the EEZ", *Chinese Journal of International Law*, 2010, pp. 2-3.

6. Rothwell and Stephens, *op. cit.*, p. 279.

7. *Ibid.*, pp. 280-281.

8. R. R. Churchill and A. V. Lowe, *The Law of the Sea*, Manchester University Press, 1999, p. 422.

9. The majority argue that the use of force is justified only when the UN Security Council or the General Assembly(according to the Uniting for Peace Resolution) permit, and in accordance with the right to self-defense as stipulated in Article 51 of the UN Charter. All measures previously referred to in the law of war or in the law of neutrality must now be justified in accordance with these provisions of the UN Charter. However, during the Iran-Iraq War, which began in 1980 and continued until 1988, the United States cited traditional warfare and neutrality laws to explain the rights and obligations of the participating and neutral states, but Britain did not use such terms in the United Nations Charter. *Ibid.*, pp. 422-423.

10. Rothwell and Stephens, *op. cit.*, p. 281.

11. Ray August, *Public International Law*, Prentice Hall, 1995, p. 513.

12. *Ibid.*, p. 516.

13. Churchill and Lowe, *op. cit.*, p. 423.

14. *Ibid.*, p. 424.

15. Robert Jennings and Arthur Watts (eds), *Oppenheim's International Law*, Longman, 1992, p. 422.

16. *Ibid.*, pp. 425-426.

17. Rothwell and Stephens, *op. cit.*, p. 241.

18. *Ibid.*, pp. 241-242.

19. *Ibid.*, pp. 87-88.

20. Louis B. Sohn, John E. Noyes, Erik Francks, and Kristen G. Juras, *Cases and Materials in the Law of the Sea*, 2nd ed., Brill/Nijhoff, 2014, p. 494.

21. Following the provision in Article 79(3) of the Convention that the delineation of the course for the laying of pipelines is subject to the consent of the coastal state, activities except for the laying pipelines may be undertaken without notice to or consent of coastal states.

22. Zhang Haiwen, "Is It Safeguarding the Freedom of Navigation or Maritime Hegemony of the United States? Comments on Raul (Pete) Pedrozo's Article on Military Activities in the EEZ," *Chinese Journal of International Law*, vol. 9, 2010, p. 32.

23. Pete Pedrozo, "Maintaining Freedom of Navigation and Overflight in the Exclusive Economic Zone and on the High Seas," *Indonesian Journal of International Law*, vol. 17, no. 4, 2020, pp. 479-480.

24. *Ibid.*, p. 480.

25. Bateman, *op. cit.*, pp. 17-18.

26. *Ibid.*, p. 18; Tanaka, *op. cit.*, pp. 395-396.

27. Zhang, *op. cit.*, pp. 33-34.

28. *Ibid.*, p. 32.

29. Raul Pedrozo, "Preserving Navigational Rights and Freedoms: The Right to Conduct Military Activities in China's Exclusive Economic Zone", *Chinese Journal of International Law*, vol. 9, 2010, pp. 9-10.

30. *Ibid.*, p. 18; Tanaka, *op. cit.*, pp. 395-396.

31. *Ibid.*, pp. 12-13.

32. Bateman, *op. cit.*, p. 25.

33. Churchill and Lowe, *op. cit.*, pp. 205-206; Sohn, Noyes, Francks, and Juras, *op. cit.*, pp. 61-62. According to Churchill and Lowe, although not listed in the Conventions as a freedoms of the high seas, the freedom to launch satellites and to engage in military activities could be considered as part of the freedom of the high seas.

34. Moritaka Hayashi, "Military and Intelligence Gathering Activities in the EEZ: Definition of Key Terms," *Marine Policy*, vol. 29, 2005, pp. 127-128; Sienho Yee, *op. cit.*, p. 3.

35. Ioannis Prezas, "Foreign Military Activities in the Exclusive Economic zone: Remarks on the Applicability and Scope of the Reciprocal Due Regard Duties of Coastal and Third states," *The International Journal of Marine and Coastal law*, vol. 34, 2019, pp. 98-99.

36. *Ibid.*, p. 99; Hayashi, *op. cit.*, p. 132.

37. *Ibid*(Hayashi)., pp. 132-133.

38. Yee, *op. cit.*, p. 4.

39. Eric Donnelly, "The United States – China EP-3 Incident: Legality and Realpolitik", *Journal of Conflict of Security Law*, 2004, pp. 25, 30.

40. Rothwell and Stephens, *op. cit.*, p. 95.

41. Natalie Klein, "Legal Implications of Australia's Maritime Identification", International and Comparative Law Quarterly, vol. 55, 2006, p. 337. The Australian Maritime Identification System of 2004 is a good example. According to this system, Australia was able to collect information on all ships, except leisure boats, navigating to Australian ports or entering its EEZ from the Maritime Identification Zone extending to 1,000 miles from its coast.

42. Rothwell and Stephens, op. cit., p. 94.

43. Ashley Roach and Robert W. Smith, United States Responses to Excessive Maritime Claims, 2nd edition, Martinus Nijhoff, 1996, pp. 421-422. America, Germany, UK, and Italy asserted that the Basel Convention provided no ground for coastal states to require prior notification and consent from the ships exercising the freedom of navigation, while Colombia, Ecuador, Mexico, Uruguay, and Venezuela declared that the Convention adequately protected their rights as coastal states.

44. Rothwell and Stephens, op. cit., p. 94

45. Ibid., p. 286.

46. Law of the Sea Convention, Arts., 88, 141, 120.

47. Hayashi, op. cit., pp. 123-124: B. Boczek,"Peaceful Purposes Provisions of the United Nations Convention on the Law of the Sea", Ocean Development and International Law, vol. 20, 1989, p. 363.

48. Ibid(Hayashi), p. 124.

49. Ibid., p. 125.

50. Ibid.

51. Ibid., p. 123.

52. Zhang, op. cit., pp. 44-45.

53. Yee, op. cit., p. 2.

54. Tanaka, op. cit., p. 339 ; Churchill and Lowe, op. cit., pp. 404-405.

55. United Nations Division for Ocean Affairs and the Law of the Sea(UN DOALOS), Marine Scientific Research : A Revised Guide to the Implementation of the Relevant Provisions of the United Nations Convention on the Law of the Sea, United Nations, 2010, p. 9.

56. Tobias Hofmann and Alexander Proelss, "The Operation of Gliders Under the International Law of the Sea," Ocean Development and International Law, vol. 46, 2015, pp. 169-170.

57. Rothwell and Stephens, op. cit., pp. 357-358.

58. Ibid., p. 338.

59. Zhang, op. cit., pp. 42-43.

60. Bateman, op. cit., pp. 19-20 ; Roach and Smith, op. cit., p. 248.

61. Sohn and Noyes, Cases and Materials in the Law of the Sea, Transnational Publishers, 2004, pp. 579-580.

62. Rothwell and Stephens, op. cit., p. 369.

63. Ibid., p. 369-370.

64. Hasjim Djalal, Alexander Yankof, and Anthony Bergin, "Draft Guidelines for Military and Intelligence Gathering Activities in the EEZ and Their Means and

Manner of Implementation", *Marine Policy*, vol. 29, 2005, p. 176.

65. The Argo Project is a global scale sea measurement program, operated jointly by IOC and the World Meteorological Organization (WMO), which deploys a large number of floats over the oceans worldwide for observation. The Argo floats usually drift around 2,000 m in depth. About every 10 days, they float to the surface to transmit the data to an artificial satellite and then submerge underwater. Deployment of the Argo floats began in 2000 and ended in 2007. About 3,000 floats were deployed in an average distance of about 3,000km providing data on the marine environment.

66. Hofmann and Proelss, *op. cit.*, pp. 167-168.

67. Rothwell and Stephens, *op. cit.*, p. 367; Tanaka, op, cit., p. 343; Churchill and Lowe, *op. cit.*, pp. 413-414.

68. Hofmann and Proelss, *op. cit.*, p. 168.

69. *Ibid*, pp. 172-173.

70. *Ibid*, p. 173.

71. *Ibid*, pp. 172-173.

72. Tanaka, *op. cit.*, pp. 343-344 ; Rothwell and Stephens, *op. cit.*, pp. 367-368.

Resolutions Relating to International Law Adopted by the 21st National Assembly in 2022

CHUNG Min Jung
Legislative Research Officer
National Assembly Legislative Research Service

The National Assembly of the Republic of Korea (hereinafter "Korea") gathers and expresses its positions regarding the government's foreign policy in the form of resolutions. Such resolutions commonly urge the Korean government, foreign governments, or the international community to implement specific measures related to Korea. To facilitate international cooperation, the resolutions use commonly accepted international communication channels (international agreements, charters, etc.). Resolutions can be viewed as an effective tool by which the constitutional authority of the National Assembly can be protected while also guaranteeing a democratic process domestically. Given the growing importance of public diplomacy, the role of the National Assembly as a flexible form of diplomacy is also growing, and greater weight is expected to be placed on the National Assembly's resolutions.

As of December 31, 2022, there were a total of five resolutions related to international law adopted at the plenary session by the 21st National Assembly in 2022 (Table 1). In general, resolutions related to international law are adopted by the Foreign Affairs and Unification Committee. However, in 2022, the Foreign Affairs and

Unification Committee only made two of the five resolutions, whereas the National Defense Committee made two. This shows that South Korea's foreign policy in 2022 was geared toward preparations for a potential security crisis on the Korean Peninsula through the efficient operation of the Korea-U.S. alliance by comprehensively and strategically strengthening the Korea-U.S. alliance.

One of the characteristics of the 2022 National Assembly resolutions related to international law is a significant decrease in quantity. In 2022 there were only five resolutions, compared to eight in 2021. In addition to this quantitative decrease, in 2022, there was a qualitative change from 2021 in that the proportion of human rights resolutions decreased (from five out of eight cases in 2021 to one out of five cases in 2022), while in 2021 there were more resolutions declaring the will to realize justice by applying human rights, a universal value of international law, equally to all countries. In 2022, two out of five resolutions called for further strengthening the Korean-U.S. alliance in the economic and trade sectors, as well as in defense and security, while in the past there were many condemning Korea's historic antagonist Japan or condemning North Korea's military provocations. In 2023, it is expected that the Korean National Assembly will identify a number of agendas that reflect the universal perspective of international law (promotion of international peace, global environment, global economic order, and democracy) and adopt resolutions on them.

Table 1. Resolutions Related to International Law Adopted by the 21ˢᵗ National Assembly in 2022

(As of December 31, 2022)

Bill Number	Bill Name	Committee responsible	Date of Adoption at the Plenary Session
2118696	Resolution condemning the violent suppression of Iran's women's rights protests and calling for a peaceful settlement	Foreign Affairs and Unification Committee	December 8, 2022
2118120	Resolution condemning the provocative ballistic missile launches by North Korea and calling for a stop to them	National Defense Committee	November 10, 2022
2117250	Resolution commemorating the establishment of the Wall of Remembrance in Washington and calling for the continued growth of Korea-U.S. relations	National Defense Committee	September 27, 2022
2117083	Resolution calling for U.S. tax support for Korean-made electric vehicles based on the Korea-U.S. free trade agreement (FTA)	Foreign Affairs and Unification Committee	September 1, 2022
2114734	Resolution calling for the Japanese government to withdraw its campaign for the Sado Gold Mine World Heritage listing	Culture, Sports and Tourism Committee	February 14, 2022

Source: National Assembly Bill Information System (last accessed on January 18, 2023), http://likms.assembly.go.kr/bill/BillSearchResult.do.

1. Resolution condemning the violent suppression of Iran's women's rights protests and calling for a peaceful settlement

Mahsa Amini, an Iranian woman, was arrested on September16, 2022 for alleged failure to properly wear a hijab, and she died under suspicious circumstances after being arrested. Iranians were outraged by the incident and protested against wearing the hijab, which turned into anti-government demonstrations. A massive anti-government demonstration near Tehran was violently suppressed by the Iranian authorities, who fired guns and wielded weapons. Many protesters were arrested, killed, or injured as a result.

As a member of the United Nations, Iran must abide by the UN Charter and its related resolutions. According to the United Nations Charter, basic human rights, human dignity, and the belief in equality between men and women must be reaffirmed, and all human rights and basic freedoms must be respected. Nevertheless, Iran has restricted freedom of assembly since 2019, suppressing protests for human rights improvements and economic solutions with military force, and has also limited freedom of expression by controlling access to the Internet. Moreover, since the Islamic Revolution, Iran has instituted a dress code for women, punishing those who fail to adhere to it. The Third Committee of the United Nations General Assembly expressed serious concerns on November 16, 2022 that the Iranian government is violating the human rights of Iranian women by enforcing dress codes against them. This has led to the UN adopting a resolution calling on the Iranian government to eliminate all forms of organizational discrimination against Iranian women, including dress codes.

The Korean National Assembly adopted a resolution on December 8, 2022 calling upon the Iranian government to come up with a democratic and peaceful solution to the issue of women's rights and to cease the violent and ruthless oppression of anti-government protests triggered by the anti-hijab movement in Iran. This resolution demanded that the South Korean government cooperate with the international community and nongovernmental organizations in investigating Iranian human rights violations through international organizations, and, if necessary, to make diplomatic efforts to disqualify Iran from membership on the UN Commission on the Status of Women. Lastly, the Korean National Assembly expressed deep concern about the threat to the lives and freedoms of

Korean nationals living in Iran during the Iranian government's hardline oppression of anti-hijab protests, and urged the Iranian and South Korean governments to protect their safety.

2. Resolution condemning the provocative ballistic missile launches by North Korea and calling for a stop to them

As of November 4, 2022, North Korea had launched 81 missiles as part of 34 ballistic missile provocations. In accordance with the *Agreement on the Implementation of the Historic Panmunjom Declaration in the Military Domain* (dated September 19, 2018; hereinafter referred to as the "September 19 Military Agreement"), gunfire and maritime maneuvers are to be suspended in waters between the coasts of Sokcho of South Korea and Tongcheon of North Korea in the East Sea, and from the north of Deokjeokdo Island to the south of Chodo Island in the West Sea. North Korea, however, fired more than 1,100 artillery rounds into the waters in October 2022, directly violating the September 19 Military Agreement. On November 2, 2022, it escalated its provocation by launching a ballistic missile 26 km south of the East Sea Northern Limit Line (NLL) and 57 km east of Sokcho for the first time since partition.

At the same time, the North Korean government was preparing for a seventh nuclear test. South Korea had been promised practical measures and denuclearization efforts by North Korea through the 1992 Joint Declaration of the Denuclearization of the Korean Peninsula, the 2005 Denuclearization Agreement, and the 2018 Commitment to Denuclearization. Despite this, the Supreme People's Assembly of North Korea enacted nuclear force policies on September 8, 2022. Regarding the purpose of such legislation, Kim Jong-un said, "North Korea will not give up its nuclear power and is seeking to maintain its mobilization behavior so that it can deploy nuclear weapons in any conditions and circumstances."

In a resolution adopted by the Korean National Assembly on November 10, 2022, North Korea's offensive nuclear strategy and artillery firing within the no-hostile activity zone, which continue to pose a threat to international peace and safety, are characterized as illegal acts that violate both the September 19 Military Agreement and UN Security Council resolutions, and are strongly condemned. Meanwhile, the resolution urged North Korea to immediately stop reckless provocations and resume denuclearization negotiations. Furthermore, the resolution called on the South Korean government to establish a strong security posture as soon as possible to protect the nation and the people against North Korea's nuclear and missile threats, as well as to make all practical and effective diplomatic efforts aimed at achieving North Korea's denuclearization in a peaceful manner.

3. Resolution commemorating the establishment of the Wall of Remembrance in Washington and calling for the continued growth of Korea-U.S. relations

The freedom and prosperity enjoyed by the Korean people today are owing to the dedication and sacrifices of the 22 countries (the 16 countries that participated in fighting were the United States, Britain, Canada, Turkey, Australia, the Philippines, Thailand, the Netherlands, Colombia, Greece, New Zealand, Ethiopia, Belgium, France, South Africa, and Luxembourg; the 6 countries that provided medical care were India, Norway, Denmark, Sweden, Italy, and Germany) and the 1.95 million veterans who fought in the 1950 Korean War to protect the freedom and peace of Korea. In particular, with 1,789,000 Americans participating and 36,634 American deaths, the United States played a major role in the defense of the Republic of Korea.

This marked the beginning of the Korea-US alliance, known as the blood alliance.

Currently, the Korean War Veterans Memorial stands in Washington, D.C., honoring veterans who fought for peace during the Korean War. A ceremony was held on July 27, 2022 to mark the completion of the Wall of Remembrance, which bears the names of 43,808 veterans, including 36,634 U.S. soldiers and 7,174 Korean military KATUSA sacrificed in the Korean War.

The Korean War Veterans Memorial Wall of Remembrance Act of 2016, H.R. 1475, was passed unanimously by the U.S. Congress in 2016, giving the Korean War Veterans Memorial Foundation (KWVMF) authority to build a wall of remembrance, and entered into force on October 7, 2016. Likewise, the Korean National Assembly passed the Resolution Calling for Support for the Construction of the Wall of Remembrance on November 17, 2016. Accordingly, a sum of 26.6 billion won was donated from the government budget toward the construction of the Wall of Remembrance.

The Korean National Assembly also adopted a resolution celebrating the construction of the Wall of Remembrance, which was unveiled on July 27, 2022, in the Korean War Veterans Memorial in Washington, D.C., USA, to honor the noble sacrifices and dedication of Korean War veterans. Moreover, the Korean National Assembly hoped to strengthen its alliance with the United States, the allied nation that had suffered the most casualties in the war on the Korean peninsula. The Korean National Assembly believes that the alliance must develop into a comprehensive strategic alliance covering economic, social, cultural, and military aspects, along with defense and security, in order to promote peace and prosperity for the world, including the Korean Peninsula and Northeast Asia.

4. Resolution calling for U.S. tax support for Korean-made electric vehicles based on the Korea-U.S. free trade agreement (FTA)

The Inflation Reduction Act (IRA) was passed by the U.S. Congress on August 12, 2022, and signed by President Joe Biden on August 16. Its purpose was to reduce the price burden on the American people while promoting the use of electric vehicles powered by eco-friendly energy to combat climate change. However, only all-electric vehicles, hydrogen electric vehicles, and plug-in hybrid cars whose final assembly takes place in North America qualify for government subsidies. Consequently, domestic electric vehicles exported to the United States will not be eligible for subsidies of up to $7,500 per unit, a decision with devastating effects on Korea's electric vehicle sales and car exports in the United States.

With the Korea-U.S. Free Trade Agreement (FTA), the two countries have reduced and eliminated barriers to trade and invest-ment, and have faithfully adhered to global trade norms such as those of the World Trade Organization (WTO). The IRA of the U.S., however, contradicts the principles of the Korea-U.S. FTA and the WTO agreement, including the principle of national treatment. Korea participates in global supply chain partnerships, such as the Indo-Pacific Economic Framework (IPEF) led by the United States. Moreover, South Korean automakers have invested more than $13 billion in the U.S. market and created more than 100,000 jobs in the past 30 years, contributing to economic growth and job creation in the U.S. In 2022, South Korean automakers even announced plans to invest massively in the United States. In any case, the implement-ation of the U.S. IRA is contrary to the direction of economic and trade cooperation between the two countries, and is undesirable for a mutually beneficial relationship.

Accordingly, on September 1, 2022, the Korean National Assembly passed a resolution addressing the following two matters in the hope that Korean electric vehicles and related companies would be included in the provisions of the IRA, thereby protecting them from losing their competitive edge in the U.S. market. First, Korea's National Assembly emphasized the importance of the IRA of the United States operating in a manner that respects international trade norms. At the same time, the Korean National Assembly lauded the U.S. government's commitment to carbon neutrality by promoting eco-friendly cars, including electric cars, and added a diplomatic statement saying Korea would also play an important role as an ally of the United States in fighting climate change. Second, the Korean National Assemblya urged the South Korean government to negotiate with the U.S. government to ensure that Korean companies are treated fairly when exporting electric vehicles to the U.S. and can compete in fair conditions. Internally, it has called for analyses of the overall impact of the U.S. IRA on each industry sector and for developing and implementing countermeasures for those industries.

5. Resolution calling for the Japanese government to withdraw its campaign for the Sado Gold Mine's World Heritage listing

After deciding to promote Sadoshima No Kinzan (hereinafter referred to as the "Sado Gold Mine") in Sado City, Niigata Prefecture, as a World Heritage Site, the Japanese government filed a registration application with the United Nations Educational, Scientific and Cultural Organization (UNESCO) on February 1, 2022. In response to the application, the International Council on Monuments and Sites (ICOMOS), a UNESCO advisory body, will examine whether to list the Sado Gold Mine on the World Heritage List.

The Korean National Assembly is arguing against Japan's application to list Meiji-era modern industrial facilities like the Sado Gold Mine as a world heritage site, as it is obvious that the site's history of human violations are clearly too severe for its consideration as a world heritage site to further pride in Japanese culture. Japanese companies and governments mobilized hundreds of thousands of South Koreans, soldiers from the Allied Forces, including U.S. and British troops, and Chinese and Southeast Asian civilians in forced labor during World War II in gross violation of international law. The UNESCO World Heritage Committee had already advised Japan on this matter in 2015 when it decided to list other Meiji-era modern industrial facilities in Japan as World Heritage sites, which were also sites of severe forced labor by Koreans during the Japanese colonial period. Japan promised at the time to take follow-up measures, but has not implemented them effectively to date.

UNESCO's 39th World Heritage Committee announced in July 2015 that 23 sites of Japan's Meiji Industrial Revolution were to be designated as World Heritage Sites, including 7 facilities of the Hashima Coal Mine, Miike Coal Mine, Takashima Coal Mine, and Yahata Steel Works, and 3 facilities at the Mitsubishi Shipyard that mobilized tens of thousands of Koreans for forced labor during World War II. At that time, Japan was advised to prepare an interpretation strategy to allow for the understanding of the full history of each site. According to Sato Kuni, the ambassador of Japan to UNESCO, UNESCO's recommendation will be implemented by setting up an information center so visitors can learn that in the 1940s many Koreans were brought to the sites and forced to work under harsh conditions against their will, as well as by taking appropriate measures to honor these victims. A formal document on the UNESCO World Heritage Committee's decision (WHC Decision 39 COM 8B.14) included this remark by the Japanese representative.

However, the progress report submitted by the Japanese government later omitted details of the appropriate measures to make certain that visitors know the mobilization of forced labor and to honor the victims. The exhibition at the Japan Industrial Heritage Information Center in Tokyo, which opened on June 15, 2020, did not implement any measures to honor victims of forced labor, but rather included testimonies and materials denying Koreans' forced labor. In July 2021, the 44th World Heritage Committee expressed deep regret over the failure of Japan to implement the committee's decision regarding Meiji-era modern industrial facilities that had used the forced labor of Koreans and allied prisoners and adopted a resolution to urge faithful implementation.

In the meantime, Japan is seeking to have the Sado Gold Mine, another site that saw forced labor by Koreans under Japanese occupation, listed as a World Heritage Site. An official document drafted by the Niigata Labor Standards Bureau records that at least 1,140 Koreans had been pressed into forced labor at the Sado Mine. Moreover, the Korea Foundation for Victims of Forced Mobilization by Imperial Japan published data in 2019 verifying that up to 1,200 Koreans were forcibly mobilized during wartime.

Under the San Francisco Peace Treaty, Japan declared after its defeat on September 8, 1951 that it would acknowledge the principles of the United Nations Charter and work to fulfill the Universal Declaration of Human Rights. The Allied Powers severely punished Nazi Germany and Japan after World War II for forced labor during the war. It is directly against universal human rights norms, such as the UN Charter, ILO Convention, and international criminal law that punishes war crimes and crimes against humanity, that Japan is attempting to register Meiji-era modern industrial facilities as World Heritage Sites, concealing the fact that many of them were sites of forced labor.

The Korean National Assembly therefore appealed to international law, universal values, and human conscience on February 14, 2022 to address the following three issues: First, the Korean National

Assembly urged the Japanese government to faithfully implement UNESCO's recommendations and to take follow-up measures that it had voluntarily committed to as a condition for the designation of Meiji-era modern industrial facilities as World Heritage sites. According to this resolution, the Japanese government should take measures to honor the victims by reflecting on their labor and suffering at the exhibition of Industrial Heritage Information Center testimony, presenting the evidence that forced labor was carried out under harsh conditions against the will of Korean victims. The Japanese government was called on to withdraw its application to list the Sado Gold Mine as a World Heritage site until such time.

Second, the Korean National Assembly expressed regret that Japan failed to engage Korea in meaningful dialogue before applying for the World Heritage designation for the Sado Gold Mine. In addition, it urged the Japanese government to maintain contact with the Korean government and the international community to comply with "Operational Guidelines for Implementation of the World Heritage Convention" (revised in July 2021), which suggests that dialogue should take place between interested parties before a World Heritage listing application is submitted. Finally, the Korean National Assembly requested that UNESCO reconsider the decision to list the Sado Gold Mine as a tentative World Heritage Site in light of the Japanese government's repeated failure (in 2015 and 2021) to implement the recommendations of the UNESCO World Heritage Committee.

ICSID Arbitration Tribunal Award on *Lone Star Holdings v. Republic of Korea* and Its ISDS Implications

WON Jae-Chun
Professor
Handong Global University, Faculty of Law / International Law School, Pohang, Korea

1. The Arbitration Tribunal's Decision on *Lone Star Holdings v. Republic of Korea*[1]

A. Important Facts of *Lone Star v. Republic of Korea*

An ICSID arbitration tribunal handed down an award in 2022 dealing with the hedge fund Lone Star's investment in South Korea. The Lone Star case brought the following three main issues to light: First, whether there was unequal treatment by the Korean government of foreign investors in unduly delaying the administration process procedure in the banking and financial industry; second, whether Lone Star's financial crime impacted consequential government measures and also caused damage to other shareholders' and stakeholders' interests. Third, whether there are ethical or legal implications of using a paper company in a third country for ISDS[2] purposes.

The case centered on Dallas-based Lone Star Capital Investment (hereinafter Lone Star)'s claim that its attempted sale of an ownership stake in the now-defunct Korea Exchange Bank (hereinafter KEB) had been unduly delayed by the Korean government's legal and regulatory measures. The Korean government denied all allegations and stated that it acted prudently without discriminating against foreign investors.[3]

The Korean economy was hit hard following the Asian financial crisis. In 1997 South Korea received a $55 billion bailout from the International Monetary Fund (IMF), its largest-ever rescue package at the time. Then, in 2003, Lone Star acquired a controlling stake in a troubled KEB for around $1.2 billion, and later sold its KEB share to Hana Financial Group Inc.(hereinafter "Hana") for around $3.5 billion at the time, making a profit of $2.3 billion.[4]

In 2008, one of the former heads of Lone Star's Korea unit was found guilty of stock-price manipulation relating to KEB's credit-card unit, prompting strict review by Korea's regulatory agencies of Lone Star's business sector thereafter.

Lone Star argued before the tribunal that it had been pressured by the Korean government to lower the 2012 selling price to Hana by around $433 million. Lone Star also challenged Korea's capital gains tax on the sale, referring to an investment treaty between Korea and Belgium[5] where Lone Star was also registered.

The tribunal held that while Korean government regulatory action resulted in delaying Lone Star's buy-out was not justified, the tax orders were proper and the treaty between Korea and Belgium did not apply to the case.

2. Historical Context of Investments and Disputes in Korea: Fair and Equitable Treatment

A. Characteristics of the Banking and Financial Industry as a Private and Quasi-Public Domain

In the United States, the financial industry has been closely regulated and appropriate government interventions were practiced. For instance, the government bailed out the financial industry to protect consumers during the Great Depression and the Global Financial Crisis in 2008. Responding to each crisis, the United States Congress enacted laws such as the Homeowners' Loan Act, Sarbanes Oxley Act, and Dodd-Frank Act to restructure the financial industry and bail it out using taxpayers' money, a benefit accompanied by heightened regulation. The US government used public money to bail out the damages arising out of mortgage-backed securities practices, thus showing that the financial industry comes under the public interest domain. Accordingly, the banking and financial industry has the dual characteristic of a private industry as well as a function of a quasi-public industry as evidenced in the Great Depression and subsequent financial crises. Regulatory agencies have a duty to protect consumers and guard against any deceitful or questionable practices of financial companies while fostering a free market economy.

a) The "IMF Crisis" and the Creation of the Korean Financial Services Commission

In the US in the 1930s, the Great Depression resulted in the collapse of the American economy as industrial production and unemployment soared, followed by banking panics resulting in bank failures. The US government began imposing various federal regulations by establishing the Securities Exchange Commission (hereinafter "SEC") to protect investors in 1934 and to set the norms for trading. Eventually, the SEC became a global financial regulation standard.[6]

Likewise, in Korea, before and during the IMF crisis, many small investors suffered tremendous losses to hedge funds and irregular paper companies manipulating the financial industry, which was subject to only minimal regulation at that time.

During a foreign exchange crisis, Korea signed a memorandum

of understanding with the IMF on December 3, 1997. As a condition of its loan, the IMF demanded the introduction of policies such as fiscal and financial austerity, high interest rates, the dissolution of chaebols (large family-owned business conglomerate), a flexible labour market, and floating exchange rates as conditions for bailouts. To prevent the country from going bankrupt, Korea accepted those conditions. It was during this time that Korea established the Korean Financial Supervisory Service (FSS) in 1999. Later in 2008 it launched the Financial Services Commission (FSC), which is the equivalent of the US SEC, and brought about necessary reforms and established norms for protecting investors and regulating the financial industry.

The government then implemented the IMF Program-Structural reform in four major sectors, namely finance, corporate, public sector, and labor. In the corporate sector, the government required transparency in management and accounting. Also, the government strengthened the responsibility of controlling shareholders and management of corporations as well as introducing provisions for independent corporate directors and corporate audit committees.[7]

Accordingly, Korea was able to graduate from the IMF crisis and created a much more secure and predictable financial industry.[8] The role of the FSC was to protect financial consumers, such as depositors and investors, by establishing sound credit order and fair financial transaction practices.[9]

b) Lone Star's Role as a Hedge Fund Company and its Regulatory Compliance

In 2011, Lone Star was found guilty of a financial crime in Korea for stock-price manipulation relating to KEB's credit card unit. Considering this was during the Korean financial crisis, the criminal conviction caused the government regulatory agency to apply strict scrutiny for the company concerned, and heightened due diligence was performed in reviewing an application for sale—something that is consistent with Korean regulatory practices.

Another key issue was whether Lone Star as a "paper company" set up in Belgium has standing in ISDS purpose according to the Belgium-Luxembourg-Korea Investment Treaty of 2011. There is also an issue of retroactive application of tax benefits under the Treaty. The tribunal recognized that Lone Star had a legal standing, yet despite Lone Star's demonstration of its extreme sophistication in its tax strategies,[10] the treaty should not be applied retroactively as various tribunals have consistently emphasized the principle of non-retroactivity.[11]

c) Due Process, Ethics, and Compliance in the Korean Financial Industry

Although the ICSID tribunal did not accept Korea's position in delaying the approval of the KEB sale by FSC, in the historical context of its financial industry Korea had exercised due diligence in addressing necessary issues and achieved the transformation of the financial industry. Moreover, the Korean criminal prosecution of any illegal financial activities, including Lone Star's case, is independently administered by FSC. The conviction caused alarm to FSC authorities when reviewing Lone Star's financial engagement including selling out of its interest. All in all, a multi-layered check and balanced system in administrative, judicial, and legislative measures had functioned adequately in Korea and brought integrity and confidence back to the Korean banking and financial industry.

3. Rectification Proceedings for Arbitration Awards of the Lone Star Case

A. New Evidence Requirement

Generally, parties to international arbitration proceedings assume that decisions are final and binding and that tribunals will not revisit decisions once made. However, limited rectification, revision, or annulment may arise in the following cases: First, where new evidence is discovered, and second, where the information provided to the tribunal had been misleading or the tribunal was in error, and third, whether the tribunal omitted the issue or had overstepped its authority.[12]

The ICSID Rules of Procedure for Arbitration Proceedings and the ICSID Convention provide for several remedies where a party considers a final award to be unsatisfactory in some respect. A party can apply for the interpretation of an award where it argues there is a lack of clarity.[13] A party may also request to rectify an award if there is an error.[14] If a party later discovers some facts that were not known to the petitioning party or the tribunal at the time the award was rendered, despite due diligence, and the fact would have "decisively" affected the award, the party can apply to have the award amended through a process known as revision.[15] A party also has the right to apply for annulment of an award on procedural grounds.[16]

However, neither the ICSID Rules nor the ICSID Convention specifically addresses whether a tribunal has the power to revisit its own decisions made in the course of an arbitration. Absent a specific provision, a tribunal is competent to review its own decision, and the absence of a separate appeal panel or ad hoc Committee seemed to undermine the acceptability of the final award and validity of the arbitral tribunal from the complaining party's perspective.

The following two decisions shed light on the jurisprudence of post-award remedies.[17]

a) *Perenco v. Ecuador*

In *Perenco v. Ecuador*, Ecuador gave a notice that it intended to submit a motion for reconsideration of a Decision on Remaining Issues of Jurisdiction and Liability by the tribunal. The tribunal permitted the motion to proceed, but emphasized "that only in exceptional circumstances would it be open for the Tribunal to reconsider its prior reasoned decisions" and directed Ecuador "to focus its Motion on the existence of those exceptional circumstances which would justify the reconsideration of the Tribunal's Decision." The tribunal's directions were notable because they appeared to accept that a tribunal would have jurisdiction to reconsider its own decisions, in at least some circumstances. Ecuador argued that the tribunal had repeatedly omitted to determine issues put to it, violating fundamental rules of procedure, manifestly exceeding its powers, and failing to state the reasons on which the decision at issue was based. Ecuador argued that these errors would be grounds for annulment, but that in any event, a lower standard of review applied pre-award.[18]

The tribunal found that in the circumstances of the case, it was not open to reconsidering its prior decision. It held that a decision that contains no reversible errors should stand against the annulment. Furthermore, it would generally be undesirable (and not in accordance with the scheme of the ICSID Convention) for an arbitral panel to simultaneously act as a tribunal and an annulment committee. The tribunal also emphasized that the power to revise an award only existed in one very specific instance – where new evidence is discovered. As a result, the tribunal concluded that once a tribunal decides with finality any of the factual or legal questions put to it by the parties, such a decision becomes res judicata.[19]

b) *Standard Chartered Bank Limited v. Tanzania Electric Supply Company Limited*

In *Standard Chartered Bank Limited v. Tanzania Electric Supply Company Limited*, the respondent requested the annulment of the tribunal's decision on the payment of costs, in which the tribunal decided the losing party, the respondent, should bear all or part of the costs of the proceedings, including those of the prevailing party. The tribunal found that it did have competence to reconsider a prior decision concerning jurisdiction. The circumstances of that case were unique because the tribunal concluded that not only had new evidence come to light but also that information provided to the tribunal by the respondent had been misleading.[20] Still, the ad hoc Committee which was set up to review the Annulment Application by the respondent dismissed the Annulment Application in its entirety, not accepting the respondent's argument and ordering the respondent to pay the costs of the Annulment Proceeding as well.

B. New Evidence and the Business Judgment Rule in Government Actions

The business judgment rule in the United States provides a director and executive of a corporation immunity from liability when a plaintiff sues on the ground that the director violated the duty of care to the corporation, so long as the board director or corporate officer's actions fall within the parameters of the rule.

Under the Business Judgment Rule, a court will uphold the decisions of a director as long as they are made with all three of the following elements: (1) in good faith, (2) with the level of care that a reasonably prudent person would exercise, and (3) with the reasonable belief that the director is acting in the best interests of the corporation.[21]

In the Lone Star case, applying the business judgment rule, *Korean government action could be justified as long as the regulatory action was in good faith, reasonably prudent, and constituted proper measures in the best interests of the financial industry without being discriminatory to any particular domestic or foreign company or investors.*

Moreover, the tribunal should have been familiar with the extraordinary context of the Korean financial crisis and government action, especially considering the conviction of Lone Star's stock manipulation. Moreover, the issue is not whether there was a delay or not, but whether a such thorough regulatory review was necessary and justified in light of the breach of the company's fiduciary duty by committing investment crime and causing reasonable suspicion and heightened scrutiny of Lone Star's financial engagement. Accordingly, considering this context and anticipation of the new evidence from the apprehension of the CEO of Lone Star Korea in 2023[22] to further collaborate with the FSC action, together with the application of the business judgment rule to government regulatory practice, would be sufficient cause for the ISCID tribunal to rule its award to be justified.

4. Conclusion

The Arbitration tribunal may not have fully understood the Korean banking, its financial industry, and its regulatory measures. The tribunal appeared to overlook the particular context that existed within the Korean economy which required necessarily strict regulatory scrutiny of the financial industry by the Korean government. Legal doctrines such as the "government judgment rule" and new evidence should be further considered in the rectification proceeding especially when the financial crisis spurred the recognition of the financial industry's public interest domain. Korea's action could be duly

justified if the FSC's strict scrutiny was equally applied to all
investors domestic and foreign, as fair and equitable while meeting
the ethical standards of International Investment.

Notes

1. LSF-KEB Holdings SCA and others v. Republic of Korea (ICSID case no. ARB/12/37)

2. Martin Valasek et al. *Frequently asked questions about investor-state dispute settlement,* Norton Rose Fullbright, 2017.

   Investor-state dispute settlement (ISDS) is a mechanism utilized by foreign investors to resolve disputes with the government of the country where their investment was made (host state) through international arbitration. ISDS agreements are most commonly found in international treaties between states but may also be found in domestic legislation and contracts. These instruments typically set out the substantive protections or obligations that foreign investors are entitled to, the breach of which gives rise to a right to bring a claim directly against the host state.

   ISDS provides a remedy to foreign investors in the face of arbitrary or other unfair treatment by a host state. Historically, foreign investors could only seek to resolve disputes with host states before the state's local courts. However, obtaining full – or indeed any – recovery was difficult. Obstacles included an absence of protections under the local law, domestic sovereign or crown immunity rules, or a lack of judicial independence. Diplomatic intervention on behalf of the foreign investor, to the extent available, was inconsistent and not always appropriate to resolve the dispute. State-to-state dispute resolution mechanisms would politicize otherwise private disputes. ISDS emerged in part from a desire to depoliticize disputes by removing them from the realm of diplomacy and interstate relations.

   Anecdotal evidence suggests that voluntary compliance with awards is not unusual. However, where an award is not voluntarily complied with, there are two main regimes for enforcement. If the award is an ICSID award, it may be enforced under the Convention on the Settlement of Investment Disputes between States and Nationals of Other States (ICSID Convention). That convention provides that ICSID awards are to be treated as final court judgments of Contracting States. There are 153 Contracting States to the ICSID Convention. In the case of non-ICSID arbitrations, the award may be enforced under the New York Convention on the Recognition and enforcement of Foreign Arbitral Awards 1958 (New York Convention). There are [more than 160] Contracting States to the New York Convention. The New York Convention facilitates award compliance by constraining the grounds on which a court may refuse to recognize or enforce a foreign award.

3. *South Korea Must Pay Lone Star Funds More Than $216 Million in Decadelong Case,* Wall Street Journal (Aug. 31, 2022), https://www.wsj.com/articles/south-korea-must-pay-lone-star-funds-more-than-216-million-in-decadelong-case-11661945324.

4. *Id.*

5. LEU (Belgium-Luxembourg Economic Union) - Korea, Republic of BIT (1974)

6. Great Depression, Encyclopedia Britannica, https://www.britannica.com/event/ Great-Depression

7. O. Yul Kwon, *The Korean financial crisis: Diagnosis, remedies and prospects, Journal of the Asia Pacific Economy,* 347, 3(3) (1998).

8. International Monetary Fund, *The Korean Financial Crisis of 1997 – A Strategy of Financial Sector Reform* (Mar. 1, 1999), https://www.imf.org/en/Publications/WP/Issues/2016/12/30/The-Korean-Financial-Crisis-of-1997-A-Strategy-of-Financial-Sector-Reform-2903.

9. <Act On The Establishment, Etc. of Financial Services Commission> [금융위원 회의 설치 등에 관한 법률] Art. 1 (Purpose)
    "The purpose of this Act is to contribute to the growth of the national economy by promoting the advancement of the financial industry and the stability of financial markets, by establishing sound credit order and fair financial transaction practices, by protecting financial consumers, such as depositors and investors, by the establishment of the Financial Services Commission and the Financial Supervisory Service."

10. *LSF-KEB Holdings SCA and others v. the Republic of Korea,* ICSID Case No. ARB/12/37, para. 909.

11. *See The Renco Group, Inc. v. The Republic of Peru (II),* PCA Case No. 2019-46, Decision on Expedited Preliminary Objections, 30 June 2020; *Ping An Life Insurance Company of China, Limited, and Ping An Insurance (Group) Company of China, Limited v. Kingdom of Belgium,* ICSID Case No. ARB/12/29, 30 April 2015; *OOO Manolium Processing v. The Republic of Belarus,* PCA Case No. 2018-06, 22 June 2021; *Aaron C. Berkowitz, Brett E. Berkowitz and Trevor B. Berkowitz v. Republic of Costa Rica,* ICSID Case No. UNCT/13/2, 25 October 2016.

12. Paul Stothard et al., *Requests for reconsideration in ICSID and UNCITRAL arbitrations,* Norton Rose Fullbright, 2017.

13. Interpretation: ICSID Article 50 and Rule 50, 51, 53-54.

14. Rectification: ICSID Article 49(2) and Rule 49

15. Revision: ICSID Article 52 and Rule 50, 52, 53 & 54

16. Annulment: ICSID Article 52 and Rule 50, 52-55

17. *Supra no. 11.*

18. *Perenco v Ecuador,* ICSID Case No. ARB/08/6, April 10, 2015 (Perenco).

19. *Id.*

20. *Standard Chartered Bank (Hong Kong) Limited v Tanzania Electric Supply Company Limited (Tanesco),* ICSID Case No. ARB/10/20, September 12, 2016 (Standard Chartered).

21. *Business Judgment Rule,* Cornell Law School Legal Information Institute, https://www.law.cornell.edu/wex/business_judgment_rule

22. In March 2023, The CEO of Lone Star Korea has been apprehended in the USA and is in the process of extradition to Korea. Stephen Lee was suspected of playing a key role in the purchase of KEB by manipulating financial records and collaborating with Korean government officials and financial heavyweights.

CONTEMPORARY PRACTICE AND JUDICIAL DECISIONS

Judicial Decisions in Pubic International Law (2022)

HONG Eungi
Judge
Seoul Central District Court, Seoul, Korea

Supreme Court Decision No. 2021DO17103
Rendered on 28 April 2022

Main Issue

1. Whether the arrest of a foreign national is illegal when the investigative agency failed to notify the right to Consular notification without delay
2. The admissibility of evidence collected in the arrest process

Facts

1. The police officer arrested the defendant, a foreigner of Indonesian nationality, on the criminal charge of violating the Immigration Act and seized urine and hair samples voluntarily submitted by the defendant.
2. The urine screen test yielded a positive result for MDMA ("ecstasy"), a psychotropic drug, and the defendant confessed to all the violations of the Immigration Act and Narcotics

Control Act in the police interrogation. The police officer asked if the defendant had an objection to an arrest notice to the defendant's employer - and the defendant stated there was no objection.

3. During the investigation, when the prosecutor asked the defendant if he had informed the Indonesian consulate of his arrest, he replied that he did not notify and that there was no particular reason for not doing so. The defendant did not request the prosecutor to notify the pertinent consular office.

Reasoning

1. Applicable Provisions and the legality of the arrest

Article 36(1)(b) of the Vienna Convention on Consular Relations (hereinafter referred to as the "Vienna Convention") provides that "If he so requests, the competent authorities of the receiving State shall, without delay, inform the consular post of the sending State if, within its consular district, a national of that State is arrested or committed to prison or to custody pending trial or is detained in any other manner" and that "The said authorities shall inform the person concerned without delay of his rights under this subparagraph."

Accordingly, Article 91(2), (3) of Police Investigation Rules (Ordinance of the Ministry of Administration and Security) stipulates that "When the police arrests a foreigner, the officer should inform that they can freely communicate with consular officials to the extent that they do not violate domestic laws and regulations, and ask the consular agency to notify them of the arrest. A police officer shall, when a foreigner requests such notification, prepare a written notification in the attached form and notify the relevant consular agency of the arrest without delay".

The above regulations are intended to help foreigners' home

countries take proper measures to protect their citizens as needed. Therefore, if the investigative agency did not notify the right to Consular notification without delay when an arrest is made, the arrest procedure is illegal as it violates the Vienna Convention§36(1)(b), which has the same effect as domestic law.

In this case, there is no evidence that the police officer notified the right to Consular notification even though he was aware that the defendant was an Indonesian national when the arrest was made. Therefore, the arrest of this case is illegal in violation of the above provisions of the Vienna Convention.

2. Admissibility of the evidence

No evidence obtained in violation of due process shall be admissible (Criminal Procedure Act §308-2). However, where procedural violations of the law enforcement agency do not constitute infringement on the substantive component of the due process, but rather, where denying the admissibility of evidence obtained from such procedural violations result in an outcome that contradicts the intentions of criminal procedure under the Constitution[of the Republic of Korea] and the Criminal Procedure Act, the court may use that evidence as incriminating evidence.

In this case, the defendant did not request Consular notification even after he learned about the right during the investigation that he could notify the Indonesian consulate of his arrest. Furthermore, at the time of the arrest, the defendant was notified in the Indonesian language of the reason for the arrest and the right to appoint a lawyer, and confessed the crime with objective evidence presented during the investigation process with the help of an interpreter. Before the Court, he did not claim the illegality of the investigation procedure, but rather confessed with the help of a public defender as well as an interpreter.

Although it was unlawful to violate the Vienna Convention in the process of arrest, the contents and severity of the procedural violations are neither grave nor considered to have fundamentally undermined the rights and legal interest of the defendant that the procedural provisions afford protection to. Therefore, the evidence obtained after the arrest and evidence based thereon may be used as incriminating evidence in this case.

Conclusion

The arrest procedure was unlawful as the police officer failed to notify without delay the defendant of the right to consular notification in violation of §36(1)(b) of the Vienna Convention.

Evidence collected during the illegal arrest process is inadmissible, but this case qualifies as an exception where the evidence is admissible considering the content and severity of the procedural violations and the interests of the defendant to be protected by the law.

Seoul Administrative Court No.2021GUHAB78282
Rendered on 18 August 2022

Main Issue

Whether the deportation order of a refugee is illegal against the principle of non-refoulement in case where the order does not specify the repatriation country

Facts

1. The plaintiff, a foreigner of Ugandan nationality, was recog-

nized as a refugee because he was found to have a well-founded fear of being tortured if he returns to Uganda. During his stay in Korea, he committed more than 20 crimes such as assault, injury, and indecent act by compulsion. He was punished with a fine 10 times, but afterwards, he was sentenced to 8 months in prison for committing a crime again during the probation period, and served the sentence.

2. The defendant, the head of a regional immigration service, ordered the plaintiff to be deported on the grounds that he falls under §59 of Immigration Control Act (which provides that the head of a regional immigration service may make a deportation order when a suspect was released after having been sentenced to imprisonment or deemed highly likely to engage in any conduct harming the interest, public safety, social order or good morals). In the deportation order (hereinafter "the order"), the country of repatriation was not specified.

Reasoning

1. Arguments of the plaintiff and the defendant

The plaintiff seeks the revocation of the order for the following reasons. The plaintiff is at risk of being repatriated or bound to be sent to Uganda, where he will be highly likely tortured. Therefore, the above order is illegal in violation of the principle of non-refoulement.

The defendant argues that the disposition of the order is legitimate under the following grounds. The Immigration Control Act provides separately for a deportation order and its enforcement, and thus the repatriation country is not determined at the stage of issuing the deportation order. Also, the above order did not specify a repatriation country to take account the plaintiff's wish at the execution stage. Lastly, at this point, the plaintiff's repatriation country has not been determined to be Uganda, so the principle of non-refoulement cannot be applied in this case.

2. Reasoning

a. Whether it is necessary to examine the principle of non-refoulement when ordering the deportation of refugees

1) Artical 3 of the Refugee Act stipulates that no recognized refugee nor refugee applicant shall be repatriated compulsorily against one's will under Article 33 of the Convention relating to the Status of Refugees (hereinafter the "Refugee Convention") and Article 3 of the Convention against Torture and Other Cruel, Inhuman or Degrading Treatment (hereinafter the "Convention against Torture").

Article 33(1) of the Refugee Convention prescribes the principle of non-refoulement for refugees, while Article 33(2) provides an exception for a refugee - who cannot claim the benefit when he constitutes a danger to the community of that country by having been convicted by a final judgment of a particularly serious crime. Meanwhile, Article 3(1) of the Convention against Torture declares without exception that no state party shall expel a person to another state where there are substantial grounds for believing that he would be in danger of being subjected to torture.

Considering the abovementioned provisions, the court interprets that even refugees who fall under the exception of the principle of non-refoulement under the Refugee Convention are still prohibited from being repatriated to a country in which they are at risk of torture under the Convention against Torture.

2) According to Articles 46 and 59 of the Immigration Act and

Article 83 of the Enforcement Rule of the Immigration Act, the head
of a regional immigration office may issue a deportation order for a
foreigner who engaged in any conduct harming the public interest or
disturbing social order, and the deportation order must specify the
country of repatriation along with the applicable laws and reasons for
deportation.

In ordinary cases involving foreigners it is relatively easy to
determine whether they are subject to a deportation order for
committing crimes. However, in refugee cases the authority should
also ensure the deportation order for the refugee does not violate the
ban on compulsory repatriation stipulated by Article 3 of the Refugee
Act. Hence, there is considerable need to examine whether the
destination in the deportation order is deemed to be the area
prohibited from repatriation.

3) The defendant argues that in practice, it evaluates the reasons
of deportation when rendering the deportation order and the
destination of repatriation is determined later at the enforcement
stage.

However, Article 63 of the Immigration Act stipulates that the
agency should repatriate the foreigner to the destination country
"without delay" when executing a deportation order, which makes it
very difficult for refugees with language barriers to seek judicial
relief once the order is rendered. The court finds that the defendant's
practice, when applied to refugees, contravenes the procedural
protections provided by the Refugee Convention, the Convention
against Torture, and the Refugee Act because the refugees' opportunity to challenge the deportation order in judicial proceedings is
substantially infringed upon.

b. Legality of the deportation order

The court decides that the deportation order of the defendant was illegal in violation of the principle of non-refoulement under Article 3 of the Refugee Act for the following reasons:

1) The defendant did not conduct a review even though it was obligated to investigate the country of repatriation for the plaintiff, a recognized refugee, and evaluate whether it violated Article 3 of the Refugee Act before issuing a deportation order.

2) According to Articles 47, 52, and 64 of the Immigration Act, the defendant can detain the foreigner for up to 20 days to examine whether such foreigner is subject to deportation while investigating the country of repatriation. In this case, the defendant detained the plaintiff for 20 days, but did not even ask his opinion on the country of repatriation.

3) The plaintiff still has a well-founded fear that he is at imminent risk of torture if repatriated to Uganda. However, the defendant did not state that Uganda was excluded from the country of repatriation of the deportation order, rather the relevant evidence indicated that the defendant seemed to have given the order on the premise that the plaintiff may be repatriated to Uganda.

Conclusion

The defendant should have examined whether the country of repatriation listed in the deportation order for the plaintiff would violate the principle of non-refoulement under Article 3 of the Immigration Act, but failed to conduct a review or specify the repatriation country. The deportation order should therefore be revoked.

Supreme Court of Korea (En Banc Order) No.2020SEU616 Rendered on 24 November 2022

Main Issue

Whether legal gender change can be recognized for a transgender person who is not married and has minor children, and what would be the criteria for such a recognition

Facts

1. The applicant was born as a male but had a sense of being a woman since childhood. She (back then, "he") married with her gender identity hidden and had two children. After 5 years of marriage, she divorced and underwent gender affirmation surgery.

2. The applicant applied for recognition of a change in legal gender from male to female. Seoul Family Court rejected the request on the grounds that her gender change could bring negative impact on her minor children's welfare. The appellate court confirmed the lower court's decision.

Reasoning
[The majority opinion]

1. Issue

The Supreme Court of Korea handed down a 2011 en banc decision (2009SEU117) that a person is not allowed to change legal gender when the applicant is married or has minor children. The issue in this case concerns the latter element, and whether it is reasonable to consider minor children as a negative requirement in recognizing legal gender change for a transgender person.

2. Whether to allow legal gender change

Considering Articles 10 and 11 (1) of the Constitution of the Republic of Korea, transgender people have the right to pursue happiness and are entitled to a life worthy of human beings as equal members of society. When the court determines whether to allow a legal gender change for a transgender person, the abovementioned fundamental rights should be the guiding principles of the decision.

The Court cannot assume that the legal gender change of a transgender person will pose a substantial threat to the welfare of the children in all cases. In many cases, request for legal gender change is a means to correct one's gender on the public record for those who actually have changed their physical and social gender. Hence the change of legal gender itself does not necessarily bring psychological and mental shock to minor children. Especially when there is already an emotional bond between a transgender person and their minor children based on their gender identity, it may even be desirable to allow the change of gender to best serve the welfare of the minor children.

Considering Article 2 of the Universal Declaration of Human Rights and the resolution of the United Nations Human Rights Council (A/HRC/RES/32/2, adopted on July 15, 2016) which Korea voted in favour of, all humans enjoy the freedom and rights prescribed by the Universal Declaration of Human Rights and the Council deplores acts of violence and discrimination committed against individuals because of their sexual orientation and gender identity. In addition, countries such as Germany, France, the United Kingdom, the Netherlands, Sweden and the United States allow gender change for transgender people. None of those countries other than Japan treats the fact that transgender people have minor children as a factor for disallowing gender change. Therefore, denying the requests of transgender people solely because they have minor children is against international human rights instruments and inconsistent with the policies of countries around the world.

3. The criteria for legal gender change

The court should examine as a whole fundamental constitutional rights, such as the transgender people's own dignity and worth as human beings, the right to pursue happiness, and the welfare of the minor children. To be specific, the impact of the gender change on children's welfare needs to be carefully evaluated on a case-by-case basis, considering the age of the children, their physical and mental status, their consent or understanding of gender change, types of care and parenting, the family bond formed by the transgender person with other family members, and other elements of the family environment.

4. Conclusion

The lower court's decision to deny the applicant's request on the grounds that the applicant has minor children is contrary to Articles 10 and 11 of the Constitution which prescribe the fundamental rights that all humans have in their dignity and value, the right to pursue happiness, and the equality of all citizens before the law. The judgment of the lower court is reversed and remanded.

[The dissenting opinion of Justice LEE Dongwon]

In 2006, the Supreme Court of Korea decided en banc (2004 SEU42) on the principle that in order to allow a legal gender change of a transgender person, it should be acceptable in our society without causing significant changes in relationship status or negatively affecting society. The second en banc decision (2009SEU117) clarified that if a transgender person has a minor child, the case is inconsistent with the said principle, and does not set a new requirement for legal gender change.

The second en banc decision should remain as it is because it accords with our legal system, the welfare of minor children, and prevailing social norms. I cannot agree with the majority opinion to depart from the decision.

Taking into account as a whole Article 36 of the Constitution and Chapter 4 of the Civil Act , it is clear that our legal system presupposes a man for a father and a woman for a mother. A father who is a woman or a mother who is a man cannot be allowed under the current legal system. Permitting legal gender change for a transgender parent with children therefore creates a parental relationship that is not allowed under the Korean legal system.

The majority opinion brings significant changes to the system of family law that has long been established as the basis of Korean society. Since the issue deals with core social values relating to ethics, philosophy, and religion, it is not desirable to solve it by expanding the jurisprudence on the change of legal gender. Rather, it has to be resolved with legal basis promulgated by the National Assembly through careful discussion and deliberation by collecting opinions from the general public.

According to Articles 909, 912, and 913 of the Civil Act a parent shall exercise parental authority for the welfare of their child, and in some cases shall bear the restriction on the basic rights of one's own for the welfare of their child. This interpretation is also consistent with the United Nations Convention on the Rights of Children, which declared that the best interests of the child shall be a primary consideration in all activities concerning children. Even when the Court decides whether to allow gender change for a transgender person, it is in accordance with the provisions of the Convention on the Rights of Children and the Civil Act to interpret and apply the law in a way that does not negatively affect the welfare of the child.

[The concurring opinion to the majority opinion by Justice PARK Junghwa, RHO Junghee, LEE Heungkoo]

The dissenting opinion is unacceptable in depriving the essence of fundamental rights of transgender people and could be contrary to the welfare of minor children.

Limiting the right of a transgender person to change their legal gender infringes on an essential part of their dignity and worth as a human being and the right to pursue happiness; what is more, the degree of such limitation is intense. Therefore, it should be clear that such limitation is required to protect and realize another's interests or rights, and that there is no alternative means to achieve this purpose other than the contested limitation. In other words, such limitation can be justified only where the right to gender change of transgender parents should be adjusted to guarantee their dignity as much as possible in relationship with their minor children. However, according to the second en banc decision, a court must deny gender change solely because the applicant has minor children without examining the content of the welfare of the minor children at issue, the effect which the gender change might bring, and the degree of such effect. This conclusion leads to a situation in which a court infringes on the rights both of transgender parents and their children despite its obligation to protect and harmonize such rights.

According to Article 29 of the Convention on the Rights of Children, the children's best interests can be achieved through education without social prejudice and discrimination, and the state should make efforts to ensure that all children practice tolerance and consideration for marginalized groups or social minorities. In the cases of minor children of transgender parents, it is in their best interests to create an environment where the children can understand and accept their parents' gender change through constant dialogue and interaction within their families.

Unlike the legislature and the executive dominated by majority rule, the judiciary serves as the last bastion to protect minorities and guarantee the fundamental rights of the people free from political, religious and social interests of the majority. It is the duty and responsibility of the Court, whose mission is to protect minority rights and guarantee human rights, to empower transgender people to pursue their own lives as equal members of society with their true gender identity legally recognized. The Court needs to exercise its discretion in this case to draw the most reasonable and desirable conclusion by considering the given circumstances of individual cases.

QUARANTINE ACT

Korea Legislation Research Institute

Wholly Amended by Act No. 9846, Dec. 29, 2009
Amended by Act No. 9932, Jan. 18, 2010
Act No. 11972, Jul. 30, 2013
Act No. 12445, Mar. 18, 2014
Act No. 13980, Feb. 3, 2016
Act No. 14839, Jul. 26, 2017
Act No. 15266, Dec. 19, 2017
Act No. 17068, Mar. 4, 2020
Act No. 17472, Aug. 11, 2020
Act No. 18604, Dec. 21, 2021

CHAPTER I GENERAL PROVISIONS

Article 1 (Purpose)

The purpose of this Act is to prevent the spread of infectious diseases within the Republic of Korea and overseas by providing for matters concerning the procedures for quarantining persons, all means of transportation and cargo, which enter or depart from the Republic of Korea and measures for preventing infectious diseases, thereby contributing to the maintenance and protection of the public health. *<Amended on Mar. 4, 2020>*

Article 2 (Definitions)

The terms used in this Act are defined as follows: <*Amended on Jan. 18, 2010; Feb. 3, 2016; Dec. 19, 2017; Mar. 4, 2020; Aug. 11, 2020*>

  1. The term "quarantinable infectious disease" means any of the following diseases:
    (a) Cholera;
    (b) Pest;
    (c) Yellow fever;
    (d) Severe Acute Respiratory Syndrome (SARS);
    (e) Animal influenza infection in humans;
    (f) Novel influenza;
    (g) Middle East Respiratory Syndrome (MERS);
    (h) Ebola virus disease;
    (i) Infectious diseases deemed as requiring emergency quarantine measures and publicly notified by the Commissioner of the Korea Disease Control and Prevention Agency, because they occurred in foreign countries and are likely to spread into the Republic of Korea or occurred in the Republic of Korea and are likely to spread into other countries, except as otherwise prescribed in items (a) through (h);
  2. The term "means of transportation" means any ship, aircraft, train or motor vehicle;
  2-2. The term "the head of a means of transportation" means a person who operates or runs a means of transportation, a person responsible for operating or running a means of transportation, or an owner of a means of transportation;
  3. The term "patient of a quarantinable infectious disease" means a person infected with the pathogen of a quarantinable infectious disease to show symptoms and confirmed by a physician, a dentist, or an oriental medical doctor through diagnosis and laboratory test;

4. The term "probable patient of a quarantinable infectious disease" means a person suspected of being infected with the pathogen of a quarantinable infectious disease and in the stage prior to being confirmed;

5. The term "contact of a quarantinable infectious disease, etc." means a person who has, or is suspected of having, contact with a patient or probable patient of a quarantinable infectious disease or with a pathogen carrier (hereinafter referred to as "patient of a quarantinable infectious disease, etc.");

6. The term "vector of infectious diseases" means a rodent or vermin prescribed by Ordinance of Ministry of Health and Welfare that can transmit infectious pathogens harmful to public health;

7. The term "quarantine inspection required area" means any area designated under Article 5 because a quarantinable infectious disease is, or is likely to be, epidemic in such area and is likely to be introduced into the Republic of Korea;

8. The term "strict quarantine inspection required area" means any area designated under Article 5 from among quarantine inspection required areas because strict quarantine is required due to the fatality and high infectivity of a quarantinable infectious disease that is, or is likely to be, epidemic in such area.

Article 3 (Responsibilities of the State)

(1) The State shall protect human rights during which quarantine services are provided.

(2) The State shall establish countermeasures to promptly cope with the spread of quarantinable infectious diseases in the Republic of Korea and overseas.

(3) Deleted. <*Feb. 4, 2020*>

[*Title Amended on Mar. 24, 2020*]

Article 3-2 (Rights and Obligations of Citizens)

(1) Citizens have the right to know information about the outbreaks, prevention and control of quarantinable infectious diseases and how to deal with, the quarantinable infectious diseases.

(2) Citizens, if quarantined or isolated due to quarantinable infectious diseases, can be compensated for any damage caused by such quarantine or isolation.

(3) Citizens shall fully cooperate with the State or a local government in its policies to prevent the spread of quarantinable infectious diseases in the Republic of Korea and overseas.

[This Article Newly Inserted on Mar. 4, 2020]

Article 4 (Relationship to Other Statutes)

This Act shall apply to quarantine-related duties except as otherwise provided for in other Acts.

Article 4-2 (Establishment and Implementation of Quarantine Control Master Plans)

(1) The Commissioner of the Korea Disease Control and Prevention Agency shall establish and implement a quarantine control master plan (hereinafter referred to as "master plan") every five years following deliberation by the quarantine advisory committee (referring to the advisory committee in the field of quarantine established under the Infectious Disease Control Committee pursuant to Articles 9 and 10 (3) of the Infectious Disease Control and Prevention Act; hereinafter the same shall apply). *<Amended on Aug. 11, 2020>*

(2) A master plan shall include the following:

1. Basic objectives of quarantine and directions for accomplishing such objectives;

2. Quarantine project plans and methods for promoting such plans;

3. A scheme to manage statistics and information on quarantine;

4. A scheme to train, and strengthen the capabilities of, public officials in charge of quarantine under Article 30;

5. Other matters necessary for quarantine control.

(3) The director of every quarantine station shall establish and implement an annual action plan under his or her jurisdiction in accordance with the master plan established under paragraph (1).

(4) The Commissioner of the Korea Disease Control and Prevention Agency and the director of a quarantine station may request relevant administrative agencies or organizations to provide materials necessary to establish and implement the master plans and action plans. *<Amended on Aug. 11, 2020>*

(5) Upon receipt of a request under paragraph (4), the heads of relevant administrative agencies or organizations shall comply with the request unless good cause exists.

[This Article Newly Inserted on Mar. 4, 2020]

Article 5 (Designation and Cancellation of Quarantine Inspection Required Area or Similar Area)

(1) The Commissioner of the Korea Disease Control and Prevention Agency may designate or cancel the designation of a quarantine inspection required area or a strict quarantine inspection required area (hereinafter referred to as "quarantine inspection required area or similar area") following deliberation by the quarantine advisory committee. *<Amended on Jan. 18, 2010; Mar. 4, 2020; Aug. 11, 2020>*

(2) The standards and procedure for designating and cancelling the designation of quarantine inspection required areas or

similar areas under paragraph (1) and other necessary matters shall be prescribed by Ordinance of the Ministry of Health and Welfare. <*Amended on Jan. 18, 2010; Mar. 4, 2020*>

[*Title Amended on Mar. 24, 2020*]

Article 5-2 Deleted. 〈*Mar. 4, 2020*〉

CHAPTER II QUARANTINE INSPECTION

Article 6 (Subject Matters of Quarantine Inspection)

(1) Any of the following persons, means of transportation and cargo (including containers, furnished supplies, consumable goods, and personal belongings carried by a means of transportation; hereinafter the same shall apply) shall undergo quarantine inspections under Article 12: <*Amended on Jan. 18, 2010; Mar. 4, 2020; Aug. 11, 2020*>

1. All persons, including passengers and crew members, (hereinafter referred to as "persons entering or departing from the Republic of Korea"), the means of transportation, and cargo prescribed by Ordinance of Ministry of Health and Welfare that enter or depart from the Republic of Korea;

2. Persons, means of transportation and cargo that have had contact with the means of transportation provided for in subparagraph 1 on the grounds prescribed by Presidential Decree while conducting duties to prevent or investigate crimes or arrest suspects.

(2) means of transportation, persons, and cargo that have not undergone a quarantine inspection provided for in paragraph (1) shall not enter or depart from the Republic of Korea before the quarantine procedure is completed.

(3) Notwithstanding paragraphs (1) and (2), all or part of a quarantine inspection may be omitted for any of the following means of transportation without any patients of a quarantinable infectious disease, etc. or deceased case, as prescribed by Presidential Decree: <*Amended on Jan. 18, 2010; Mar. 4, 2020; Aug. 11, 2020*>

1. A means of transportation (including persons and cargo) departing from the Republic of Korea, which is deemed by the Commissioner of the Korea Disease Control and Prevention Agency as not likely to spread a quarantinable infectious disease that occurred within the Republic of Korea to overseas:

2. A means of transportation prescribed by Ordinance of Ministry of Health and Welfare among those that temporarily stay in the Republic of Korea to be supplied with fuel, materials, necessities, etc.;

3. A means of military transport, the head of which notifies that there is no patient of a quarantinable infectious disease, etc and vector of any infectious disease therein;

4. A means of transportation requested by the Minister of Unification under Article 23 (2) of the Inter-Korean Exchange and Cooperation Act (In such cases, the quarantine inspection or some of quarantine inspection procedures can be omitted.);

5. A means of transportation deemed by the Commissioner of the Korea Disease Control and Prevention Agency, for which the head of the relevant central administrative agency requests the omission of a quarantine inspection.

[*Title Amended on Mar. 24, 2020*]

Article 7 Deleted. <*Mar. 4, 2020*>

Article 8 Deleted. *<Mar. 4, 2020>*

Article 9 (Notification of Quarantine)

(1) Where a means of transportation subject to quarantine inspection under Article 6 approaches a place for quarantine, the head of the means of transportation shall notify the director of the quarantine station having jurisdiction over the place for quarantine of the matters prescribed by Ordinance of the Ministry of Health and Welfare, including whether there is a patient of a quarantinable infectious disease, etc. and the sanitary state, as prescribed by Ordinance of the Ministry of Health and Welfare: Provided, That where a means of transportation inevitably arrives at any place other than a place for quarantine in order to escape imminent danger, the head of the means of transportation shall notify the director of the quarantine station having jurisdiction over the quarantine location nearest to the place of arrival of such matters. *<Amended on Jan. 18, 2010; Mar. 4, 2020>*

(2) The director of the quarantine station being notified under the proviso of paragraph (1) may give the head of a means of transportation instructions to take necessary measures, such as measures for a patient of a quarantinable infectious disease, etc. and the head of the means of transportation given the instructions shall follow such instructions. *<Newly Inserted on Mar. 4, 2020>*

(3) Notwithstanding paragraph (1), if a means of transportation approaches for such reasons as seizure, surrender or distress, the head of an investigation agency may give notification to the director of the competent quarantine station. *<Newly Inserted on Mar. 4, 2020>*

(4) If there is any change to the matters notified under paragraph (1) or (3), the head of the means of transportation or the head

of the investigation agency shall immediately notify the head of the quarantine station of such change. <*Newly Inserted on Mar. 4, 2020*>

(5) Methods and procedures for notification under paragraphs (1) through (4) and other necessary matters shall be prescribed by Ordinance of Ministry of Health and Welfare. <*Newly Inserted on Mar. 4, 2020*>

Article 10 (Place for Quarantine)

(1) The Commissioner of the Korea Disease Control and Prevention Agency shall designate a place for quarantine in consultation with the head of the relevant central administrative agency. <*Amended on Jan. 18, 2010; Aug. 11, 2020*>

(2) Any person or means of transportation entering or departing from the Republic of Korea that intends to be quarantined shall undergo a quarantine inspection after arriving at the place for quarantine: Provided, That if the person or the means of transportation has difficulty in undergoing, or cannot complete, a quarantine inspection at the place for quarantine, the person or the means of transportation may undergo a quarantine inspection at any quarantine area prescribed by Ordinance of the Ministry of Health and Welfare. <*Amended on Mar. 4, 2020*>

(3) Notwithstanding paragraph (2), a quarantine inspection can be conducted at a place for quarantine designated by the director of the quarantine station in any of the following cases: <*Amended on Mar. 4, 2020*>

1. If it is unavoidable for such reasons as seizure, surrender, distress or an emergency patient;

2. In cases prescribed by Ordinance of the Ministry of Health and Welfare due to weather conditions or other unavoidable causes.

(4) Deleted. <*Mar. 4, 2020*>

Article 11 (Quarantine Time)

(1) Deleted. <*Mar. 4, 2020*>

(2) The director of the quarantine station shall conduct a quarantine inspection immediately after a person or means of transportation subject to quarantine inspection under Article 6 arrives at a place for quarantine: Provided, That if unavoidable causes prescribed by Ordinance of the Ministry of Health and Welfare make an immediate quarantine inspection impossible, the director of the quarantine station may permit passengers and crew members to get off and cargo to be unloaded on condition that they wait or are quarantined in a specified place for quarantine. <*Amended on Mar. 4, 2020*>

(3) The head of a means of transportation departing from the Republic of Korea shall notify the director of the quarantine station of a scheduled departure time.

(4) The director of the quarantine station shall complete a quarantine inspection before a scheduled departure time notified pursuant to paragraph (3).

Article 12 (Quarantine Inspection)

(1) The director of the quarantine station shall conduct a quarantine inspection on the following matters: Provided, That in cases of a motor vehicle, the matters, other than those provided for in subparagraph 2, may be omitted: <*Amended on Mar. 4, 2020*>

1. Progress and current status of health and sanitary conditions of a means of transportation and cargo;
2. Whether persons entering or departing from the Republic of Korea are infected with any quarantinable infectious disease

and have any risk factors of quarantinable infectious diseases, and prevention and control thereof;

3. The storage status of food in a means of transportation;
4. Whether vectors for infectious diseases inhabit and the state of their breeding.

(2) Persons entering or departing from the Republic of Korea through land routes shall undergo a quarantine inspection at a quarantine area or a place designated by Ordinance of the Ministry of Health and Welfare before entering or departing from the Republic of Korea. <*Amended on Jan. 18, 2010; Jul. 30, 2013; Mar. 4, 2020*>

(3) In order to conduct a quarantine inspection under paragraph (1), the director of the quarantine station may request persons and the heads of a means of transportation entering or departing from the Republic of Korea to submit or present necessary documents and may ask necessary questions to, or inspect or investigate, them. <*Amended on Mar. 4, 2020*>

(4) The directors of quarantine stations may utilize such equipment as IT devices, image processing devices and electronic-sensing devices in order to perform quarantine duties promptly and accurately. <*Newly Inserted on Mar. 4, 2020*>

(5) Necessary matters concerning methods of and procedures for a quarantine inspection referred to in paragraphs (1) through (4) shall be prescribed by Ordinance of the Ministry of Health and Welfare. <*Amended on Jan. 18, 2010; Mar. 4, 2020*>

Article 12-2 (Duty to Report and Measures)

(1) Any of the following persons shall report his or her health conditions and other relevant matters to the director of the quarantine station, as prescribed by Ordinance of the Ministry of Health and Welfare, if the maximum incubation period for a quarantinable infectious disease under Article 17 (3) has not

expired since his or her departure from a quarantine inspection required area or strict quarantine inspection required area:

1. A person who has any suspected symptom of a quarantinable infectious disease among those who enter the
   Republic of Korea after staying in or via the quarantine
   inspection required area;
2. A person who enters the Republic of Korea after staying in
   or via the strict quarantine inspection required area.

(2) The Commissioner of the Korea Disease Control and Prevention Agency shall establish an overseas infectious disease
report center at the places prescribed by Ordinance of the
Ministry of Health and Welfare, such as arrivals halls at the
airports, ports, and land routes, so that persons falling under
any of the subparagraphs of paragraph (1) can report his or
her health conditions, etc. <*Amended on Aug. 11, 2020; Dec. 21, 2021*>

(3) If the director of the quarantine station determines that a
quarantinable infectious disease is likely to spread, the
director may take the following measures in relation to a
person who reports under paragraph (1):

1. Requesting information about the area and duration of his
   or her travel;
2. Requesting information about his or her health conditions
   in relation to the quarantinable infectious disease;
3. Requesting a document certifying that he or she is
   vaccinated;
4. Testing and examining the person to check if he or she is
   infected with the quarantinable infectious disease;
5. Other measures prescribed by Ordinance of the Ministry of
   Health and Welfare as necessary to prevent the spread of
   the quarantinable infectious disease.

(4) If a quarantinable infectious disease that has broken out in
the Republic of Korea is likely to spread overseas, a person

having a suspected symptom of the quarantinable infectious disease among those who go abroad shall report his or her health conditions and other relevant matters to the overseas infectious disease reporting center established under paragraph (2). In such cases, the director of the quarantine station may take the measures provided in paragraph (3) in relation to the person who reports his or her health conditions and other relevant matters.

(5) Procedures and methods for reporting under paragraphs (1) and (4), the establishment and operations of the overseas infectious disease reporting centers under paragraph (2), and other necessary matters shall be prescribed by Ordinance of the Ministry of Health and Welfare.

[This Article Newly Inserted on Mar. 4, 2020]

Article 12-3 (Aircraft Quarantine Inspection)

(1) The head of a means of transportation who intends to under-go an aircraft quarantine inspection shall submit documents necessary for such quarantine inspection to the director of the quarantine station, as prescribed by Ordinance of the Ministry of Health and Welfare.

(2) If the director of the quarantine station determines that a quarantinable infectious disease is unlikely to spread in the Republic of Korea by reviewing the documents submitted under paragraph (1), the director may conduct a quarantine inspection through document review: Provided, That the director shall conduct a quarantine inspection onboard the aircraft if there is a high risk of the spread of a quarantinable infectious disease or in cases prescribed by Ordinance of the Ministry of Health and Welfare.

(3) Submittal of documents under paragraph (1) and quarantine inspections through document review under the main clause of

paragraph (2) may be done using an electronic system.

(4) If any information contained in the documents submitted under paragraph (1) is found to be false, necessary measures including re-quarantine shall be taken, as prescribed by Ordinance of the Ministry of Health and Welfare.

[This Article Newly Inserted on Mar. 4, 2020]

Article 12-4 (Ship Quarantine Inspection)

(1) The head of a means of transportation who intends to undergo a ship quarantine inspection shall submit documents necessary for such quarantine inspection to the director of the quarantine station, as prescribed by Ordinance of the Ministry of Health and Welfare. In such cases, the head of the means of transportation shall fly a yellow flag or turn on a yellow headlight to indicate a state of quarantine after arriving at the place for quarantine.

(2) In requesting the head of a means of transportation to submit documents under Article 12 (3), the director of the quarantine station may require the representative of a shipping agency registered under Article 33 of the Marine Transportation Act to submit or present the relevant documents before the arrival of the means of transportation.

(3) If the director of the quarantine station determines that a quarantinable infectious disease is unlikely to spread in the Republic of Korea by reviewing the documents submitted under paragraph (1), the director may conduct a quarantine inspection through document review: Provided, That the director shall conduct a quarantine inspection onboard the ship if there is a high risk of the spread of a quarantinable infectious disease or in cases prescribed by Ordinance of the Ministry of Health and Welfare.

(4) Submittal of documents under paragraph (1) and quarantine

inspections through document review under the main clause of paragraph (3) may be done using an electronic system.

(5) The director of the quarantine station may select a ship and conduct a health and sanitation inspection after a quarantine inspection, as prescribed by Ordinance of the Ministry of Health and Welfare, in order to verify whether the information contained in the documents submitted under paragraph (1) is accurate and for health and sanitation control.

(6) If any information contained in the documents submitted under paragraph (1) is found to be false, necessary measures including re-quarantine shall be taken, as prescribed by Ordinance of the Ministry of Health and Welfare.

[This Article Newly Inserted on Mar. 4, 2020]

Article 12-5 (Quarantine Inspection for Land Route)

(1) Persons and means of transportation entering or departing from the Republic of Korea through land routes shall undergo a quarantine inspection, as prescribed by Ordinance of the Ministry of Health and Welfare.

(2) If the Minister of Unification requests a consultation about persons and means of transportation using land routes to enter or depart from the Republic of Korea under the proviso of Article 23 (2) of the Inter-Korean Exchange and Cooperation Act, the Commissioner of Korea Disease Control and Prevention Agency may omit part of the procedures for quarantine notification under Article 9 (1), as prescribed by Ordinance of the Ministry of Health and Welfare. *<Amended on Aug. 11, 2020>*

[This Article Newly Inserted on Mar. 4, 2020]

Article 13 (Boarding Prior to Quarantine)

(1) Anyone, other than public officials in charge of quarantine

under Article 30, shall be prohibited from boarding a means of transportation subject to a quarantine inspection before a quarantine certificate is issued after completion of the quarantine inspection: Provided, That this shall not apply to persons permitted by the director of the quarantine station as prescribed by Ordinance of the Ministry of Health and Welfare. *<Amended on Jan. 18, 2010; Mar. 4, 2020>*

(2) Anyone who has boarded a means of transportation without any permission from the director of the quarantine station shall undergo a quarantine inspection and, if a person onboard a ship or aircraft with permission of the director of the quarantine station under the proviso of paragraph (1) has any symptom of a quarantinable infectious disease or has contact with a patient of a quarantinable infectious disease, etc., the person shall immediately report to the director of the quarantine station. *<Amended on Mar. 4, 2020>*

(3) Upon receipt of reporting under paragraph (2), the director of the quarantine station shall immediately conduct a quarantine inspection on the relevant person. *<Newly Inserted on Mar. 4, 2020>*

(4) Methods for quarantine inspections under paragraph (3) shall be prescribed by Ordinance of the Ministry of Health and Welfare. *<Newly Inserted on Mar. 4, 2020>*

Article 14 Deleted. *<Mar. 4, 2020>*

Article 15 (Quarantine Measures)

(1) In order to block the introduction and spread of quarantinable infectious diseases, the Commissioner of the Korea Disease Control and Prevention Agency may take all or part of the following measures for a confirmed or suspected case of a quarantinable infectious disease, or a means of transportation or cargo contaminated or suspected of being contaminated

with the pathogen of a quarantinable infectious disease or suspected of being inhabited by vectors of a quarantinable infectious disease: <*Amended on Feb. 3, 2016; Mar. 4, 2020; Aug. 11, 2020*>

1. Monitoring or isolating a patient of a quarantinable infectious disease, etc.;

2. Monitoring or quarantining a contact of a quarantinable infectious disease or a person exposed to a risk factor of a quarantinable infectious disease prescribed by Ordinance of Ministry of Health and Welfare (hereinafter referred to as "person exposed to a risk factor of a quarantinable infectious disease");

3. Disinfecting, destructing, or prohibiting the transfer of cargo contaminated with or suspected of being contaminated with the pathogen of a quarantinable infectious disease;

4. Disinfecting any place contaminated or suspected of being contaminated with the pathogen of a quarantinable infectious disease, and prohibiting or restricting the use of such place;

4-2. Inspecting a means of transportation or cargo, if it is deemed necessary to confirm whether such means of transportation or cargo is contaminated with the pathogen of a quarantinable infectious disease;

5. Deleted; <*Mar. 4, 2020*>

6. Ordering the head of a means of transportation or the owner or manager of cargo to disinfect the means of transportation or the cargo in which vectors of a quarantinable infectious disease live or are suspected of living, and to eradicate the vectors of a quarantinable infectious disease;

7. Medically examining or testing persons if it is deemed necessary to confirm whether they are infected with a quarantinable infectious disease;

8. Vaccinating persons for the prevention of a quarantinable

infectious disease.

(2) Deleted. <*Mar. 4, 2020*>

(3) The head of a means of transportation or the owner or manager of cargo who has received an order referred to in paragraph (1) 6 shall outsource disinfection, etc. to any other person qualified as prescribed by Ordinance of the Ministry of Health and Welfare and shall submit the results of such disinfection to the director of the quarantine station for confirmation. <*Amended on Jan. 18, 2010; Mar. 4, 2020*>

(4) Where the Commissioner of Korea Disease Control and Prevention Agency cannot take proper measures pursuant to paragraph (1), the Commissioner may notify the head of a means of transportation of the grounds therefor and give instructions to return or move to a place designated by the Commissioner. In such cases, the head of the relevant means of transportation shall comply with such instruction. <*Amended on Mar. 4, 2020; Dec. 21, 2021*>

(5) If necessary to take quarantine measures pursuant to paragraph (1), the Commissioner of the Korea Disease Control and Prevention Agency may request cooperation from the relevant agency as prescribed by Presidential Decree, and the head of the relevant agency in receipt of the request shall comply with such request unless there is a compelling reason not to do so. <*Amended on Mar. 4, 2020; Aug. 11, 2020*>

Article 16 (Isolation of Patients of Quarantinable Infectious Disease)

(1) The Commissioner of the Korea Disease Control and Prevention Agency shall isolate patients of a quarantinable infectious disease, etc. in any of the following facilities pursuant to Article 15 (1) 1: Provided, That the Commissioner of the Korea Disease Control and Prevention Agency may

exclude such patients, etc. from isolation, if the possibility of person-to-person transmission is low or in cases prescribed by the Commissioner of Korea Disease Control and Prevention Agency: <Amended on Jan. 18, 2010; Dec. 19, 2017; Mar. 4, 2020; Aug. 11, 2020; Dec. 21, 2021>

1. Isolation facilities managed by a quarantine station and designated by the Commissioner of the Korea Disease Control and Prevention Agency;
2. Infectious disease control agencies, places of isolation, sanatoriums or clinics provided for in Article 36 or 37 of the Infectious Disease Control and Prevention Act;
3. At home;
4. Infectious disease specialty hospitals under Article 8-2 of the Infectious Disease Control and Prevention Act;
5. A facility or place designated by the Commissioner of the Korea Disease Control and Prevention Agency if the patients, etc. have no residence in the Republic of Korea.

(2) Where the isolation facilities, infectious disease control agencies, etc. under paragraph (1) are deficient due to the high occurrence of patients of a quarantinable infectious disease, etc., the Commissioner of the Korea Disease Control and Prevention Agency may install and operate temporary isolation facilities, as prescribed by Ordinance of the Ministry of Health and Welfare. <Amended on Jan. 18, 2010; Mar. 4, 2020; Aug. 11, 2020>

(3) Where it is deemed necessary for taking isolation measures (including transfer) referred to in paragraph (1), the Commissioner of the Korea Disease Control and Prevention Agency may request cooperation from the Special Metropolitan City Mayor, a Metropolitan City Mayor, a Special Self-Governing City Mayor, a Do Governor, or a Special Self-Governing Province Governor (hereinafter referred to as "Mayor/Do

Governor"), or the head of a Si/Gun/Gu (the head of a Gu refers to the head of an autonomous Gu; hereinafter the same shall apply). In such cases, the Mayor/Do Governor or the head of a Si/Gun/Gu shall cooperate with such request unless there is a compelling reason not to do so. <Amended on Mar. 4, 2020; Aug. 11, 2020>

(4) The isolation period of a patient of a quarantinable infectious disease, etc. shall be until the time such patient, etc. is completely free from infectivity, and such patient, etc. shall be released from isolation immediately upon the expiration of the isolation period. <Amended on Mar. 4, 2020>

(5) Any person isolated during the period referred to in paragraph (4) shall be prohibited from having contact with any other person without permission from the director of the quarantine station.

(6) Where the director of the quarantine station isolates a patient of a quarantinable infectious disease, etc., the director shall notify the isolated person or his or her family member or guardian or a person designated by the isolated person of such fact, as prescribed by Ordinance of the Ministry of Health and Wealth. <Amended on Jan. 18, 2010; Mar. 4, 2020>

Article 17 (Monitoring of Contacts of Patient of Quarantinable Infectious Disease)

(1) The Commissioner of the Korea Disease Control and Prevention Agency may request a Special Self-Governing Province Governor or the head of a Si/Gun/Gu in an area where a contact of a quarantinable infectious disease or a person exposed to a risk factor of a quarantinable infectious disease resides or stays after entering the Republic of Korea to monitor such person's health conditions pursuant to Article 15 (1) 2 or to quarantine such person pursuant to Article 49

(1) of the Infectious Disease Control and Prevention Act. *<Amended on Mar. 4, 2020; Aug. 11, 2020>*

(2) Where a contact of a quarantinable infectious disease or a person exposed to a risk factor of a quarantinable infectious disease is confirmed as a patient of a quarantinable infectious disease, etc. while being monitored under paragraph (1), a Special Self-Governing Province Governor or the head of a Si/Gun/Gu shall take necessary measures, such as isolation, without delay and immediately report the case to the Commissioner of the Korea Disease Control and Prevention Agency. *<Amended on Mar. 4, 2020; Aug. 11, 2020>*

(3) The period of monitoring or quarantine under paragraph (1) shall not exceed the maximum incubation period for each quarantinable infectious disease prescribed by Ordinance of Ministry of Health and Welfare: *<Amended on Feb. 3, 2016; Dec. 19, 2017; Mar. 4, 2020>*

1. Deleted; *<Mar. 4, 2020>*
2. Deleted; *<Mar. 4, 2020>*
3. Deleted; *<Mar. 4, 2020>*
4. Deleted; *<Mar. 4, 2020>*
5. Deleted; *<Mar. 4, 2020>*
6. Deleted. *<Mar. 4, 2020>*

[Title Amended on Mar. 24, 2020]

Article 18 (Prohibition on Removing Goods from Isolation Facility)

No goods used or kept in an isolation facility and temporary isolation facility under Article 16 may be removed therefrom without permission of the director of the quarantine station. *<Amended on Mar. 4, 2020>*

[Title Amended on Mar. 24, 2020]

Article 19 (Prohibition of Transfer of Contaminated Means of Transport)

(1) The Commissioner of the Korea Disease Control and Prevention Agency may take measures, such as prohibition of transfer, with respect to passengers, crew members, and persons having access on foot, who are infected with or suspected of being infected with a quarantinable infectious disease, and the means of transportation and cargo that are contaminated or are suspected of being contaminated with the pathogen of a quarantinable infectious disease (hereafter in this Article referred to as "contaminated means of trans-portation, etc.") as prescribed by Ordinance of the Ministry of Health and Welfare, until the measures such as inspection on whether a confirmed or suspected case occurs, disinfection, and destruction of goods are completed at a place designated by the director of a quarantine station. In such cases, no person shall come in contact with or aboard the contaminated means of transportation, etc. without permission of the director of the quarantine station. <Amended on Jan. 18, 2010; Mar. 4, 2020; Aug. 11, 2020>

(2) The director of the quarantine station shall cancel the measures, such as prohibition of transfer, where it is deemed that a quarantinable infectious disease is unlikely to spread within the Republic of Korea by taking measures in relation to the contaminated means of transportation, etc. In such cases, the criteria for lifting the prohibition of transfer, shall be prescribed by Ordinance of the Ministry of Health and Welfare. <Amended on Jan. 18, 2010>

Article 20 (Preventive Measures against Non-Quarantinable Infectious Diseases)

The director of the quarantine station may take necessary

preventive measures, such as medical examination, testing and disinfection, as prescribed by Ordinance of the Ministry of Health and Welfare, upon finding of any of the following persons while conducting quarantine inspections: <*Amended on Jan. 18, 2010; Mar. 4, 2020*>

1. A patient of a non-quarantinable infectious disease;
2. A probable patient of a non-quarantinable infectious disease;
3. A person who died of a non-quarantinable infectious disease;
4. A means of transportation contaminated or likely to be contaminated with the pathogen of a non-quarantinable infectious disease.

Article 21 (Keeping of Goods Requiring Disinfection)

The director of the quarantine station may request the head of the relevant customs office to isolate goods deemed to require disinfection from other goods in order to keep the former from having contact with the latter among goods on the list of loaded goods.

Article 22 (Quarantine Certificates)

Where the director of the quarantine station determines that a person, a means of transportation or cargo entering or departing from the Republic of Korea poses no risk of spreading any quarantinable infectious disease in Korea or oversea and no problem is found by a quarantine inspection, the director shall, upon request, issue a quarantine certificate to the person or the head of the means of transportation, as prescribed by Ordinance of the Ministry of Health and Welfare. <*Amended on Jan. 18, 2010; Mar. 4, 2020*>

Article 23 (Conditional Quarantine Certificates)

(1) The director of the quarantine station may issue a conditional

quarantine certificate to the head of a means of transportation on condition of quarantine disinfection, etc. as a result of its quarantine inspection. *<Amended on Mar. 4, 2020>*

(2) Where the head of a means of transportation issued a conditional quarantine certificate fulfills the imposed condition, the director of the quarantine station shall issue a quarantine certificate to the head of the means of transportation. In such cases, the head of the means of transportation shall discard the conditional quarantine certificate previously issued. *<Amended on Mar. 4, 2020>*

(3) Where the head of a means of transportation fails to meet the condition imposed in a conditional quarantine certificate referred to in paragraph (1), the director of the quarantine station may take measures, such as the prohibition of transfer.

(4) Where the director of the quarantine station determines that the head of a means of transportation issued a conditional quarantine certificate under paragraph (1) has difficulty fulfilling the condition imposed on the means of transportation, the director may give instructions to move the means of transportation to a place the director designates, stating the reasons therefor, as prescribed by Ordinance of the Ministry of Health and Welfare. In such cases, the head of the means of transportation shall comply with such instructions. *<Amended on Jan. 18, 2010; Mar. 4, 2020>*

Article 24 (Request for Prohibition or Suspension of Entry and Departure)

If the Commissioner of the Korea Disease Control and Prevention Agency deems that the following persons are likely to pose a substantial risk to public health, the Commissioner of the Korea Disease Control and Prevention Agency may request the Minister of Justice to prohibit or suspend the entry and departure of such persons: Provided, That a request for prohibition or suspension of entry shall apply to foreigners alone: *<Amended on Jan. 18, 2010; Feb. 3, 2016; Mar. 4, 2020; Aug. 11, 2020>*

1. A patient of a quarantinable infectious disease, etc.;
2. A contact of a quarantinable infectious disease, etc.;
3. A person exposed to a risk factor of a quarantinable infectious disease;
4. A person entering the Republic of Korea from or via a quarantine inspection required area or similar area.

Article 25 (Bringing-In and Inspection of Dead Body)

(1) Any person who intends to bring a dead body into the Republic of Korea shall submit or present necessary documents as prescribed by Ordinance of the Ministry of Health and Welfare to confirm whether the dead person has been infected with a quarantinable infectious disease. *<Amended on Jan. 18, 2010>*

(2) If the corpse, bones, or remains of a person who died of a quarantinable infectious disease fail to be treated by preservation and sealed in the impenetrable coffin or fail to be cremated, the director of the quarantine station shall not grant a permit to bring them into the Republic of Korea.

(3) Dead bodies during the operation of a means of transportation shall undergo a quarantine inspection, as prescribed by Ordinance of the Ministry of Health and Welfare. *<Amended on Jan. 18, 2010; Mar. 4, 2020>*

(4) If the cause of death of a person is unidentifiable or a dead person is suspected of having been infected with a quarantinable infectious disease as a result of a quarantine inspection conducted under paragraph (1) or (3), the director of a quarantine station may order an autopsy on the dead person for tests and, if necessary, may request cooperation from

relevant agencies. In such cases, Article 20 of the Infectious Disease Control and Prevention Act shall apply mutatis mutandis to methods and procedures for autopsy, and the "Commissioner of the Korea Disease Control and Prevention Agency" shall be construed as the "director of a quarantine station". *<Newly Inserted on Mar. 4, 2020; Aug. 11, 2020>*

(5) If a patient of a quarantinable infectious disease, etc. died or a dead person is confirmed to have had the pathogen of a quarantinable infectious disease, the director of a quarantine station may impose restrictions on the funeral handling methods, etc. of the dead person to the extent necessary to block, and prevent the spread of, the quarantinable infectious disease. In such cases, Article 20-2 of the Infectious Disease Control and Prevention Act shall apply mutatis mutandis to funeral handling methods, procedures, etc., and the "Commissioner of the Korea Disease Control and Prevention Agency" shall be construed as the "director of a quarantine station". *<Newly Inserted on Mar. 4, 2020; Aug. 11, 2020>*

Article 26 Deleted. *<Mar. 4, 2020>*

Article 27 (Issuance of Ship Sanitation Certificates)

(1) Where the captain or owner of a ship requests the issuance of a ship sanitation certificate, the director of the quarantine station shall conduct an investigation as to whether the ship is contaminated with the pathogen of a quarantinable infectious disease or carries vectors of an infectious disease and shall issue a ship sanitation control exemption certificate valid for six months if the ship is found to have not been contaminated with the pathogen of any quarantinable infectious disease and free from vectors of an infectious disease by such investigation. *<Amended on Jan. 18, 2010; Mar. 4, 2020>*

(2) Where the director of the quarantine station determines that a ship is suspected of being contaminated with the pathogen of a quarantinable infectious disease and vectors of an infectious disease inhibit in a ship by an investigation as provided in paragraph (1), the director shall issue a ship sanitation certificate valid for six months after requiring a person who has the qualifications prescribed by Ordinance of Health and Welfare to disinfect the ship or eradicate vectors of an infectious disease. *<Amended on Mar. 4, 2020>*

(3) Where the captain or the owner of a ship disinfects the ship or eradicates vectors of an infectious disease as provided for in Article 15 (3) upon an order referred to in Article 15 (1) 6 requests the issuance of a certificate of compliance of the order, the director of the quarantine station shall issue a ship sanitation certificate valid for six months.

(4) Where a ship returns to the place of shipment or there is a compelling reason for not performing a quarantine inspection and taking quarantine measures under Articles 12 and 15, the director of a quarantine station may extend the term of validity of the ship sanitation control exemption certificate issued under paragraph (1) and the ship sanitation certificate under paragraphs (2) and (3) by up to one month. *<Amended on Mar. 4, 2020; Dec. 21, 2021>*

(5) The director of the quarantine station shall conduct a quarantine inspection referred to in Article 12 for a ship with an expired certificate under paragraphs (1) through (3), a ship without a certificate or a ship with a certificate in which the necessity of reinspection is specified.

(6) Details of investigations under paragraph (1), the procedure for application for and issuance of ship sanitation certificates and ship sanitation control exemption certificates and other necessary matters shall be prescribed by Ordinance of the

Ministry of Health and Wealth. *<Amended Jan. 18, 2010; Mar. 4, 2020>*

[Title Amended on Mar. 24, 2020]

Article 28 (Issuance of Other Certificates)

(1) Upon request of the head of a means of transportation, the director of the quarantine station shall issue a certificate of deratting and disinsection after verifying whether the head of the means of transportation has eradicated vectors of infectious diseases therein, as prescribed by Ordinance of the Ministry of Health and Welfare. *<Amended on Jan. 18, 2010; Mar. 4, 2020>*

(2) Upon request of a person who intends to export goods, the director of the quarantine station shall issue a certificate falling under any of the following after taking preventive measures against quarantinable infectious diseases or verifying whether the person has taken such preventive measures, as prescribed by Ordinance of the Ministry of Health and Welfare: *<Amended on Jan. 18, 2010; Mar. 4, 2020>*

  1. A certificate of disinfection of the goods: Inspection on whether the goods are infected with quarantinable infectious diseases, disinfection and eradication of vectors of infectious diseases;

  2. A certificate of bacteriological test on the goods: Bacteriological tests on whether the goods carry pathogens of quarantinable infectious diseases.

(3) Upon request of a person who intends to travel overseas, such as a passenger or crew member, the director of the quarantine station shall issue a pathogen test certificate after conducting a test to check whether the person is infected with any quarantinable infectious disease and has pathogens of quarantinable infectious diseases as prescribed by Ordinance

of the Ministry of Health and Welfare: *<Amended on Jan. 18, 2010; Mar. 4, 2020>*

    1. Deleted; *<Mar. 4, 2020>*

    2. Deleted. *<Mar. 4, 2020>*

(4) Necessary matters concerning the issuance of a certificate, other than certificates referred to in paragraphs (1) through (3), the details of preventative measures and the procedure for issuance of certificates shall be prescribed by Ordinance of the Ministry of Health and Welfare. *<Amended on Jan. 18, 2010>*

(5) Disinfection and eradication of vectors of infectious diseases as required under paragraphs (1) and (2) shall be conducted by a person qualified as prescribed by Ordinance of the Ministry of Health and Welfare. *<Amended on Jan. 18, 2010>*

Article 28-2 (Internationally Certified Vaccinations)

(1) Upon request by a person who intends to travel overseas, the Commissioner of the Korea Disease Control and Prevention Agency shall provide vaccinations against quarantinable infectious diseases and issue an international certificate of vaccinations to such person. *<Amended on Aug. 11, 2020>*

(2) The Commissioner of the Korea Disease Control and Prevention Agency shall be furnished with first aid kits in preparation for adverse reactions to vaccinations against quarantinable infectious diseases. *<Amended on Aug. 11, 2020>*

(3) Upon vaccinating a person against a quarantinable infectious disease, the head of an internationally certified vaccination center designated under Article 28-3 shall issue a vaccination certificate to the person, and the director of the quarantine station shall issue an international certificate of vaccination to the person after verifying the information stated in the vaccination certificate.

(4) Procedures for issuing international certificates of vaccination

under paragraphs (1) and (3), control of adverse reactions under paragraph (2) and other necessary matters shall be prescribed by Ordinance of the Ministry of Health and Welfare.

[This Article Newly Inserted on Mar. 4, 2020]

[Previous Article 28-2 moved to Article 28-3 <*Mar. 4, 2020*>]

Article 28-3 (Designation of Internationally Certified Vaccination Center)

(1) The Commissioner of the Korea Disease Control and Prevention Agency may designate an institution that can administer internationally certified vaccinations (hereinafter referred to as "internationally certified vaccination center") from among the following institutions. In such cases, the Commissioner of the Korea Disease Control and Prevention Agency shall publicly announce such designation: <*Amended on Mar. 4, 2020; Aug. 11, 2020*>

1. Medical institutions under Article 3 of the Medical Service Act;

2. National institutions, local governmental institutions and public institutions established under the Act on the Management of Public Institutions which have dispensaries with full-time physicians.

(2) The Commissioner of the Korea Disease Control and Prevention Agency may revoke the designation of an internationally certified vaccination center, if it falls under any of the following cases: <*Amended on Aug. 11, 2020*>

1. Where it has no record of vaccinations against quarantinable infectious diseases during the last three years;

2. Where it violates this Act or medical services-related statutes in connection with vaccinations against quarantinable infectious diseases.

(3) Except as provided in paragraphs (1) and (2), the standards and procedures for designating internationally certified vaccination centers, and revocation of the designation and other necessary matters shall be prescribed by Ordinance of the Ministry of Health and Welfare.

[This Article Newly Inserted on Mar. 18, 2014]

[Moved from Article 28-2 *<Mar. 4, 2020>*]

Article 29 (Management of Health and Sanitation in Quarantine Areas)

(1) If the Commissioner of the Korea Disease Control and Prevention Agency deems that a quarantinable infectious disease or a non-quarantinable infectious disease is, or is likely to be, epidemic, the Commissioner may take any of the following measures necessary for public health and sanitation control with respect to any means of transportation, facilities, buildings, and goods within the quarantine area and other places and related persons, or may give necessary instructions thereto, as prescribed by Ordinance of the Ministry of Health and Welfare: *<Amended on Jan. 18, 2010; Feb. 3, 2016; Mar. 4, 2020; Aug. 11, 2020>*

1. Epidemiological investigation of the quarantinable infectious disease or non-quarantinable infectious disease;

2. Disinfection to kill insects and germs and eradicate vectors of the infectious disease;

3. Inspection to find germ carriers and vaccination against the quarantinable infectious disease or non-quarantinable infectious disease;

4. Inspection of food materials, food and portable water loaded into means of transportation;

5. Sanitary guidance, education, and public relations for persons who handle fish and shellfish as well as foodstuff;

6. Survey of distribution of vectors of the infectious disease in the quarantine area;

7. Inspection of ballast water within a ship;

8. Other matters deemed by the Commissioner of the Korea Disease Control and Prevention Agency as necessary for the prevention of quarantinable infectious diseases and non-quarantinable infectious diseases.

(2) If necessary for taking measures or giving instructions under paragraph (1), the Commissioner of the Korea Disease Control and Prevention Agency may request cooperation from relevant agencies or persons, and the heads of the relevant agencies or relevant persons in receipt of the request shall comply with such request unless there is a compelling reason not to do so. *<Amended on Mar. 4, 2020; Dec. 21, 2021>*

Article 29-2 (Establishment and Operation of Quarantine Information System)

(1) The Commissioner of the Korea Disease Control and Prevention Agency may establish and operate a quarantine information system to electronically process information on persons, etc. subject to quarantine, in order to efficiently perform quarantine work, including early detection of persons who are infected with or suspected of being infected with a quarantinable infectious disease and means of transportation suspected of being contaminated. *<Amended on Mar. 4, 2020; Aug. 11, 2020>*

(2) In order to perform quarantine work, the Commissioner of the Korea Disease Control and Prevention Agency may request quarantine-related information from the heads of relevant agencies via the following information systems. In such cases, the heads of the relevant agencies shall comply with such request unless there is good cause: *<Newly Inserted on*

Mar. 4, 2020; Aug. 11, 2020>

1. The information system for safe use of drugs (DUR, Drug Utilization Review) established under Article 23-3 (1) of the Pharmaceutical Affairs Act;
2. The Passport Information Comprehensive Administration System established under Article 8 (2) of the Passport Act;
3. The information system processing immigration information under the Immigration Act;
4. The Comprehensive Customs Duties Information Network of Korea (UNI-PASS) established under Article 327 of the Customs Act;
5. Other information systems prescribed by Ordinance of the Ministry of Health and Welfare.

(3) The Commissioner of the Korea Disease Control and Prevention Agency shall not use the information processed through the systems under paragraph (1) for other purposes than the efficient conduct of quarantine work, and shall carefully manage such information to not infringe on privacy. *<Amended on Mar. 4, 2020; Aug. 11, 2020>*

(4) Except as provided in this Act, the protection and management of information under paragraphs (1) and (2) shall be governed by the provisions of the Personal Information Protection Act. *<Newly Inserted on Mar. 4, 2020>*

(5) The establishment and operation of systems under paragraphs (1) and (2) and other necessary matters shall be prescribed by Ordinance of the Ministry of Health and Welfare. *<Amended on Mar. 4, 2020>*

[This Article Newly Inserted on Feb. 3, 2016]

CHAPTER II-2 REQUESTS FOR SUBMISSION OF DATA

Article 29-3 Deleted. <*Mar. 4, 2020*>

Article 29-4 (Requests for Passenger Reservation Data)

(1) The Commissioner of the Korea Disease Control and Prevention Agency may request the head of a means of transportation to give access to passenger reservation data held by the head of the means of transportation for perusal via the information and communications network or to submit such passenger reservation data in writing (or in electronic form) without delay, if deemed necessary to perform the following work: <*Amended on Mar. 4, 2020; Aug. 11, 2020*>

1. To provide quarantine services for a person who enters, or is suspected of entering, the Republic of Korea, from or via, a country where a quarantinable infectious disease has broken out;

2. To provide quarantine services for a confirmed or suspected patient when the patient enters or departs from the Republic of Korea;

3. To conduct a quarantine inspection under Article 12;

4. To take measures under Article 12-2 (3).

(2) The head of a means of transportation in receipt of a request under paragraph (1) shall comply with the request unless good cause exists. <*Amended on Mar. 4, 2020*>

(3) The scope of data that can be accessed or submitted under paragraph (1) shall be limited to the following:

1. Name, nationality, date of birth, passport number, and booking reference;

2. Address and telephone number;

3. Number of the means of transportation and time of arrival;

4. Time of reservation and time of check-in;

5. Boarding pass number, seat number, date of issue, and place of issue;
6. Travel route and travel agency;
7. Details about accompanying passengers, such as family or tourist group, their seat numbers;
8. Data about luggage.

(4) Methods for retaining passenger reservation data submitted under paragraph (1), the retention period, destruction of such data and other necessary matters shall be prescribed by Presidential Decree.

[This Article Newly Inserted on Feb. 3, 2016]

Article 29-5 (Cooperation from Relevant Agencies)

In order to prevent and control a quarantinable infectious disease, the Commissioner of the Korea Disease Control and Prevention Agency may request the resident registration number, immigration records, baggage declaration, and financial information about a confirmed or suspected patient of a quarantinable infectious disease, etc., and other urgently necessary data and information prescribed by Presidential Decree, from any of the following heads of the relevant central administrative agencies (including the heads of their affiliated agencies and responsible administrative agencies; hereafter in this Article the same shall apply). In such cases, the head of the relevant central administrative agency in receipt of the request shall comply with such request unless there is good cause: *<Amended on Jul. 26, 2017; Mar. 4, 2020; Aug. 11, 2020>*

1. The Minister of Foreign Affairs;
2. The Minister of Justice;
3. The Minister of the Interior and Safety;
4. The Minister of Land, Infrastructure and Transport;
5. The Chairperson of the Financial Services Commission;

6. The Commissioner of the Korea Customs Service;
7. The head of a central administrative agency prescribed by
   Presidential Decree.

[This Article Newly Inserted on Feb. 3, 2016]

Article 29-6 (Notification and Education)

(1) The manager of a facility, such as an airport defined under
subparagraph 3 of Article 2 of the Airport Facilities Act or a
harbor defined under subparagraph 1 of Article 2 of the
Harbor Act, shall notify the users of the facility about the
locations of a quarantine inspection required area or similar
area, the type of the quarantinable infectious disease that has
broken out in the contaminated area and the preventive
measures, measures to be taken when a confirmed or
suspected case occurs and other matters, as prescribed by
Ordinance of the Ministry of Health and Welfare. *<Amended on
Dec. 19, 2017; Mar. 4, 2020>*

(2) If necessary to notify a quarantine inspection required area or
similar area and provide education for the prevention of a
quarantinable infectious disease, the director of the quarantine
station shall request the head of a means of transportation to
notify or educate persons entering or departing from the
Republic of Korea about the following matters. In such cases,
the director of the quarantine station shall provide the head of
a means of transportation with contents of notification and
education in the form of videos and other visual media, and
the head of a means of transportation in receipt of the request
shall comply with such request unless good cause exists:
<Amended on Dec. 19, 2017; Mar. 4, 2020>

1. The location of the quarantine inspection required area or
   similar area;
2. Type, dangerousness and preventive measures of the quaran-

tinable infectious disease that has broken out in the quarantine inspection required area or similar area;

3. Measures to be taken if a confirmed or suspected case occurs;
4. How to report health conditions and fever checking;
5. Procedures and methods for reporting under Article 12-2;
6. Other matters notification and education on which is requested by the director of the quarantine station as the director deems to be necessary.

[This Article Newly Inserted on Feb. 3, 2016]

Article 29-7 (Establishment of Quarantine Stations)

(1) National quarantine stations (hereinafter referred to as "quarantine stations") shall be established and operated at airports, ports, railway stations and land-border crossings in order to prevent the spread of quarantinable infectious diseases in the Republic of Korea and overseas and to safely protect the health of citizens.

(2) The Commissioner of the Korea Disease Control and Prevention Agency may operate regional key quarantine stations according to the standards prescribed by Presidential Decree.

<Amended on Aug. 11, 2020>

[This Article Newly Inserted on Mar. 4, 2020]

Article 29-8 (Functions and Duties of Quarantine Stations)

The quarantine stations shall carry out the following functions and duties:

1. To provide quarantine services for the prevention of introduction of quarantinable infectious diseases to the Republic of Korea and the spread thereof overseas;
2. To conduct epidemiological investigations of arriving passengers who have symptoms of quarantinable infectious diseases;

3. To have a patient of a quarantinable infectious disease, etc. or a contact of a quarantinable infectious disease isolated or quarantined and to conduct diagnostic tests;

4. To provide health and sanitation control in quarantine areas;

5. To provide preventive education and campaign about quarantinable infectious diseases;

6. Other duties prescribed by Ordinance of Ministry of Health and Welfare in relation to quarantine.

[This Article Newly Inserted on Mar. 4, 2020]

Article 29-9 (Facilities and Equipment in Quarantine Stations)

The quarantine stations shall be furnished with facilities, equipment, etc. that comply with the standards prescribed by Ordinance of the Ministry of Health and Welfare.

[This Article Newly Inserted on Mar. 4, 2020]

CHAPTER III PUBLIC OFFICIALS IN CHARGE OF QUARANTINE

Article 30 (Public Officials in Charge of Quarantine)

(1) Every quarantine station shall have a director, quarantine officers and other public officials (hereinafter referred to as "public officials in charge of quarantine") to perform duties provided in this Act. *<Amended on Mar. 4, 2020>*

(2) The Commissioner of the Korea Disease Control and Prevention Agency shall regularly provide public officials in charge of quarantine with education and training about the performance of their duties. *<Newly Inserted Mar. 4, 2020; Aug. 11, 2020>*

(3) Necessary matters concerning qualifications of public officials in charge of quarantine shall be prescribed by Ordinance of the Ministry of Health and Welfare. *<Amended on Jan. 18, 2010; Mar. 4, 2020>*

Article 31 (Authority of Public Officials in Charge of Quarantine)

(1) Public officials in charge of quarantine may enter the means of transportation subject to quarantine and other necessary places in order to perform duties provided in this Act and may inspect and investigate documents, facilities, equipment, etc. related to the operation of the means of transportation. *<Amended on Mar. 4, 2020>*

(2) Public officials in charge of quarantine may ask question to persons and the heads of means of transportation entering or departing from the Republic of Korea or may request them to submit or present other necessary materials for quarantine inspections. *<Newly Inserted on Mar. 4, 2020>*

Article 32 (Operation of Quarantine Ship)

(1) The director of the quarantine station may operate a quarantine ship, quarantine vehicle, etc. to perform quarantine-related duties and necessary detailed matters shall be prescribed by Ordinance of the Ministry of Health and Welfare. *<Amended on Jan. 18, 2010>*

(2) Where it is necessary to take emergency quarantine measures, such as occurrence of patients, the director of the quarantine station may request the head of the relevant agency to provide a quarantine ship, etc. required for the performance of quarantine-related duties and the head of the relevant agency in receipt of the request shall comply with such request unless any good cause exists.

Article 33 (Uniforms of Public Officials in Charge of Quarantine)

(1) Public officials in charge of quarantine shall wear their uniforms when performing the duties provided for in this Act and carry their certificates indicating their authority and present them to the persons concerned at their request.

(2) Matters concerning uniforms and certificates of public officials in charge of quarantine referred to in paragraph (1) shall be prescribed by Ordinance of the Ministry of Health and Welfare. <*Amended on Jan. 18, 2010; Mar. 4, 2020*>

CHAPTER IV SUPPLEMENTARY PROVISIONS

Article 34 (Collection of Fees)

The Commissioner of the Korea Disease Control and Prevention Agency may collect fees from the heads of the means of transportation, owners or managers of cargo, passengers, crew members, etc., as prescribed by Ordinance of the Ministry of Health and Welfare, where he or she takes the following measures: <*Amended on Jan. 18, 2010; Mar. 4, 2020; Aug. 11, 2020; Dec. 21, 2021*>

1. Where the Commissioner takes measures provided for in Article 15 (1) 3, 4, 4-2, 7, and 8;
1-2. Where the Commissioner takes measure provided for in Article 25 (4);
2. Where the Commissioner takes measures provided for in Articles 27, 28 and 28-2 or issues a certificate with regard thereto.

Article 34-2 (Hearings)

If the Commissioner of the Korea Disease Control and Prevention Agency intends to revoke the designation of an internationally certified vaccination center pursuant to Article 28-3, he or she shall hold a hearing. <*Amended on Mar. 4, 2020; Aug. 11, 2020*>
[This Article Newly Inserted on Mar. 18, 2014]

Article 35 (Bearing of Expenses)

Expenses incurred in isolation or quarantine and monitoring

provided for in Articles 16 and 17 shall be borne by the State.

Article 36 (Establishment and Operation of Disease-Control Organization)

The Commissioner of the Korea Disease Control and Prevention Agency may establish and operate a disease-control organization to entrust quarantine work and other administrative affairs prescribed by other statutes, as prescribed by Presidential Decree, notwithstanding Articles 3 and 4 of the Government Organization Act. <*Amended on Jan. 18, 2010; Aug. 11, 2020*>

Article 37 (Delegation of Authority)

Part of the authority of the Commissioner of the Korea Disease Control and Prevention Agency under this Act may be delegated to the head of an agency affiliated with the Korea Disease Control and Prevention Agency, as prescribed by Presidential Decree.

Article 38 (Duty to Maintain Confidentiality)

No person who has performed or performs the duties related to quarantine, such as quarantine inspections, shall divulge to another person any confidential information that he or she becomes aware of in the course of performing the duties, such as conducting quarantine inspections under Article 12, taking the measures under Article 12-2, conducting aircraft quarantine inspections, ship quarantine inspections and quarantine inspections for persons entering or departing from the Republic of Korea through land routes under Articles 12-3, 12-4 and 12-5, establishing and operating the quarantine information system under Article 29-2, requesting access to passenger reservation data under Article 29-4 or requesting cooperation from related agencies under Article 29-5. <*Amended on Feb. 3, 2016; Mar. 4, 2020*>

CHAPTER V PENALTY PROVISIONS

Article 39 (Penalty Provisions)

(1) Any of the following persons shall be punished by imprisonment with labor for not more than one year or by a fine not exceeding 10 million won: *<Amended on Mar. 4, 2020; Aug. 11, 2020>*

1. A person, the head of a means of transportation, or the owner or manager of cargo which enters or departs from the Republic of Korea without undergoing a quarantine inspection under Article 6 (1);

2. A person who refuses, obstructs, and evades a request for documents provided for in Article 12 (3) or submits or presents any falsified document;

3. A person who fails to comply with measures taken by the Commissioner of the Korea Disease Control and Prevention Agency under Article 15 (1);

4. A person who fails to comply with the measure taken to isolate or quarantine him or her under Articles 16 (1) and 17 (1);

5. A person who divulges to another person any confidential information that he or she has learned in the course of performing business, in violation of Article 38.

(2) Any of the following persons shall be punished by a fine not exceeding five million won: *<Amended on Mar. 4, 2020>*

1. A person who fails to comply with an order for disinfection, etc., in violation of Article 15 (3) or who fails to be confirmed by the director of the quarantine station regarding the results of performance;

2. The head of a means of transportation who refuses to follow the instruction to move pursuant to Article 15 (4) or 23 (4);

3. A person who removes goods used or kept from an isolation facility or temporary isolation facility without approval of the director of the quarantine station, in violation of Article 18;

4. A person who fails to follow any of the measures, such as the prohibition of transfer pursuant to Article 19 (1).

Article 40 (Joint Penalty Provisions)

If the representative of a juristic person, or an agent, employee, or any other employed person of a juristic person or individual violates Article 39 in connection with the business affairs of the juristic person or individual, such juristic person or individual shall be punished, and the juristic person or the individual shall also be punished by a fine under the relevant provisions: Provided, That the same shall not apply where the juristic person or individual is not negligent in paying due attention to or providing supervision of the relevant duties in order to prevent such violation.

Article 41 (Administrative Fines)

(1) Any of the following persons shall be subject to an administrative fine not exceeding 10 million won: <Newly Inserted on Feb. 3, 2016; Mar. 4, 2020>

1. A person who fails to report in violation of Article 12-2 (1) or a person who falsely reports;

2. A person who fails to comply with a request for passenger reservation data made under Article 29-4 or a person who submits false passenger reservation data.

(2) Any of the following persons shall be subject to an administrative fine not exceeding five million won: <Amended on Feb. 3, 2016; Mar. 4, 2020>

1. Deleted; <Mar. 4, 2020>

2. The head of a means of transportation who fails to notify as provided in Article 9 or who notifies false information;

2-2. A person who fails to follow the measures taken under Article 12-2 (3);

3. A person who boards a ship or plane before undergoing a quarantine inspection, in violation of Article 13;

4. A person in isolation who has contact with any other person during the isolation period, in violation of Article 16 (5);

5. Deleted; <*Mar. 4, 2020*>

6. A person who fails to follow any of the measures taken or instructions given under Article 29 (1);

7. A person who fails to comply with a request without good cause, in violation of Article 29-6 (2).

(3) Administrative fines referred to in paragraphs (1) and (2) shall be imposed and collected by the director of the quarantine station, as prescribed by Presidential Decree. <*Amended on Feb. 3, 2016*>

ADDENDA <*Act No. 9846, Dec. 29, 2009*>

Article 1 (Enforcement Date)

This Act shall enter into force one year after the date of its promulgation.

Article 2 (Transitional Measure concerning Disposition, etc.)

Any act performed by an administrative agency and any act performed in relation to an administrative agency pursuant to the previous provisions as at the time this Act enters into force shall be deemed any act performed by an administrative agency and any act performed in relation to an administrative agency pursuant to this Act.

Article 3 (Transitional Measures concerning Penalty Provisions and Administrative Fines)

The application of the penalty provisions or administrative fines to any act committed before this Act enters into force shall be governed by the previous provisions.

Article 4 Omitted.

Article 5 (Relationship to Other Statutes)

Where the previous Quarantine Act or its provisions are cited by other statutes as at the time this Act enters into force, the corresponding provisions of this Act, if any, shall be deemed to have been cited in lieu of the previous Quarantine Act or its provisions.

ADDENDA <*Act No. 9932, Jan. 18, 2010*>

Article 1 (Enforcement Date)

This Act shall enter into force two months after the date of its promulgation: Provided, That Article 4 (24) of the Addenda shall enter into force on April 2, 2010, Article 4 (11) and (107) of the Addenda shall enter into force on December 30, 2010, and Article 40 (26) and (31) of the Addenda shall enter into force on January 1, 2011, respectively.

Articles 2 through 5 Omitted.

ADDENDUM <*Act No. 11972, Jul. 30, 2013*>

This Act shall enter into force three months after the date of its promulgation.

ADDENDA <*Act No. 12445, Mar. 18, 2014*>

Article 1 (Enforcement Date)

This Act shall enter into force six months after the date of its promulgation.

Article 2 (Transitional Measures concerning Institutions Designated for Internationally Certified Vaccinations)

Institutions designated as an internationally certified vaccination center under the Ordinance of the Ministry of Health and Welfare as at the time this Act enters into force shall be deemed designated as an internationally certified vaccination center under the amended provisions of Article 28-2.

ADDENDUM <Act No. 13980, Feb. 3, 2016>

This Act shall enter into force six months after the date of its promulgation.

ADDENDA <Act No. 14839, Jul. 26, 2017>

Article 1 (Enforcement Date)

This Act shall enter into force on the date of its promulgation: Provided, That the amendments to the Acts which were promulgated before this Act enters into force but the enforcement dates of which have not yet arrived, among the Acts amended by Article 5 of the Addenda, shall enter into force on the enforcement dates of the respective Acts.

Articles 2 through 6 Omitted.

ADDENDUM <Act No. 15266, Dec. 19, 2017>

This Act shall enter into force on the date of its promulgation.

ADDENDA <Act No. 17068, Mar. 4, 2020>

Article 1 (Enforcement Date)

This Act shall enter into force one year after the date of its promulgation: Provided, That amended provisions of subparagraphs 7 and 8 of Article 2 and Articles 5 and 24 shall enter into force on the date of its promulgation.

Article 2 (Transitional Measures concerning Quarantine Inspection Required Areas or Similar Areas)

Contaminated areas or adjacent areas to contaminated areas designated under the previous provisions as at the time this Act enters into force shall be deemed to be quarantine inspection required areas or strict quarantine inspection required areas designated under Article 5 (1).

Article 3 (Transitional Measures)

(1) Notwithstanding the amended provisions of Article 5 entering into force under the proviso of Article 1 of the Addenda, "a contaminated area and adjacent areas to the contaminated area" under Article 5-2 and Article 29-6 (which are in force before a partial amendment to the Quarantine Act by Act No. 17068) shall be deemed to be a quarantine inspection required area or similar area under the amended provisions of Article 5 until before the enforcement date of this Act.

(2) Notwithstanding the amended provisions of Article 5 entering into force under the proviso of Article 1 of the Addenda, "a contaminated area" under Article 29-3 shall be deemed to be "a contaminated area" under Article 5 (which is in force before a partial amendment to the Quarantine Act by Act No. 17068) until before the enforcement date of this Act.

(3) Notwithstanding the amended provisions of Article 5 entering into force under the proviso of Article 1 of the Addenda, "a contact of a patient of a quarantinable infectious disease, etc."

under the amended provisions of subparagraph 2 of Article 24 shall be deemed to be "a person suspected of contracting a quarantinable infectious disease" as defined in subparagraph 5 of Article 2 (which is in force before a partial amendment to the Quarantine Act by Act No. 17068) until before the enforcement date of this Act.

Article 4 Omitted.

ADDENDA <Act No. 17472, Aug. 11, 2020>

Article 1 (Enforcement Date)
This Act shall enter into force one year after the date of its promulgation: Provided, That ...

Articles 2 through 5 Omitted.

ADDENDA <Act No. 18604, Dec. 21, 2021>
Article 1 (Enforcement Date)
This Act shall enter into force six months after the date of its promulgation.
Article 2 (Applicability to Collection of Fees)
The amended provisions of subparagraph 1 of Article 34 shall begin to apply to cases where the means of transportation and cargo are inspected pursuant to Article 15 (1) 4-2 after this Act enters into force.

Last updated : 2022-12-27

FRAMEWORK ACT ON CARBON NEUTRALITY AND GREEN GROWTH FOR COPING WITH CLIMATE CRISIS

Korea Legislation Research Institute

Act No. 18469, Sep. 24, 2021

CHAPTER I GENERAL PROVISIONS

Article 1 (Purpose)

The purpose of this Act is to strengthen policy measures to reduce greenhouse gases and adapt to climate change for preventing serious impacts of climate crisis, to resolve economic, environmental, and social disparity that may arise in the course of transition to a carbon neutral society, and to foster, promote, and revitalize green technology and green industry for a harmonious development of the economy and environment, thereby improving the quality of life of present and future generations, protecting the ecosystem and climate system, and contributing to the sustainable development of the international community.

Article 2 (Definitions)

The terms used in this Act are defined as follows:

1. The term "climate change" means a change in the climate

system caused by increased concentrations of greenhouse gases as a consequence of human activities, which occurs in addition to natural climate change that has been observed during a considerable period of time;

2. The term "climate crisis" means a state in need of a radical reduction of greenhouse gases because climate change is posing an irreversible risk to human civilization, including water deficiency, food shortage, ocean oxidization, sea level rise, ecosystem collapse as well as extreme weather conditions;

3. The term "carbon neutrality" means a state where greenhouse gas emissions emitted, released, or leaked out into the atmosphere become net-zero as they are offset by greenhouse gas absorption elsewhere;

4. The term "carbon neutral society" means a society in which people lower or eliminate dependence on fossil fuels and lay the foundation for finance, technology, system, etc. for adaptation to climate crisis and just transition to smoothly achieve carbon neutrality and prevent and minimize damage and adverse effects that may arise in the process;

5. The term "greenhouse gas" means any gaseous matter in the atmosphere which absorbs or re-emits radiant heat to cause greenhouse effects, including carbon dioxide (CO_2), methane (CH_4), nitrous oxide (N_2O), hydrofluorocarbon (HFCs), perfluorocarbon (PFCs), sulfur hexafluoride (SF_6), and other substances specified by Presidential Decree;

6. The term "greenhouse gas emission" means direct emission of greenhouse gases, which are emitted, released, or leaked out in the course of human activities, as well as indirect emission of greenhouse gases, which are induced by using electricity or heat (limited to heat using fuels or electricity as a heat source) supplied from other persons;

7. The term "greenhouse gas reduction" means all kinds of

activities to reduce or absorb greenhouse gas emissions to alleviate or delay climate change;

8. The term "greenhouse gas absorption" means that greenhouse gases are removed from the atmosphere by means of land utilization, changes in land utilization, forestry activities, etc.;

9. The term "new and renewable energy" means new and renewable energy defined in subparagraphs 1 and 2 of Article 2 of the Act on the Promotion of the Development, Use and Diffusion of New and Renewable Energy;

10. The term "energy conversion" means converting the entire system of producing, transferring, and consuming energy to cope with climate crisis (referring to a series of activities to address climate crisis, such as reduction of greenhouse gases, adaptation to climate change, and establishment of related infrastructure; hereinafter the same shall apply) and to pursue environmental protection, safety, energy security, and sustainability;

11. The term "adaptation to climate crisis" means all kinds of activities to reduce the vulnerability to climate crisis and enhance adaptability and resilience to health damage and natural disasters caused by climate crisis, to minimize the current or foreseeable ripple effects and impacts of the climate crisis or to turn them into opportunities to take advantage of the climate crisis;

12. The term "climate justice" means to acknowledge that each social group has different share of responsibility for greenhouse gas emissions causing climate change, and to ensure that all interested parties equally and substantially participate in the decision-making process to overcome the climate crisis and fairly distribute the burden of transition to a carbon neutral society and benefits of green growth according to their disproportionate share of responsibility for climate change,

thereby ensuring equality between different socio-economic groups and generations;

13. The term "just transition" means a policy direction-setting for protecting workers, farmers, small and medium entrepreneurs, etc. in regions or industries that could suffer direct or indirect damage in the course of transition to a carbon neutral society, to make the society share the burden caused in the transition process and minimize damage to the vulnerable social groups;

14. The term "green growth" means an economic growth in harmony with the environment, which can be achieved by saving and efficiently using energy and resources to mitigate climate change and environmental damage, and securing new growth engines and creating job opportunities through research and development of clean energy and green technology;

15. The term "green economy" means an economy where the use of fossil fuels is phased out and green technology and green industry are fostered to strengthen the national competitiveness and pursue sustainable development;

16. The term "green technology" means a technology to achieve carbon neutrality and promote green growth by replacing the use of fossil fuels and using energy and resources more efficiently throughout the entire process of social and economic activities, which includes a technology to cope with climate change (referring to technology for coping with climate change defined in subparagraph 6 of Article 2 of the Act on the Promotion of Technological Development for Climate Change), technology for efficient use of energy, clean production technology, technology for new and renewable energy, technology for resources circulation (referring to resources circulation defined in subparagraph 1 of Article 2 of the Framework Act on Resources Circulation; hereafter the same shall apply), and eco-friendly technology (including

related convergence technologies);

17. The term "green industry" means all kinds of industries for realizing carbon neutrality and facilitating green growth by replacing the use of fossil fuels generating greenhouse gas emissions, enhancing the efficient use of energy and resources, and producing goods and providing services to improve the environment.

Article 3 (Basic Principles)

The transition to a carbon neutral society and green growth shall be promoted based on the following basic principles:

1. It shall be based on the principle of intergenerational equality that the current generation is responsible for ensuring the survival of future generations and the principle of sustainable development;

2. It shall promote the transition to a carbon neutral society and green growth as a comprehensive crisis response strategy, based on rational recognition of the severity of global climate crisis and changes in the international economic environment corresponding thereto;

3. It shall formulate policies to reduce greenhouse gases and adapt to climate crisis, based on the scientific prediction and analysis of climate change and in comprehensive consideration of every field and sector that affect or are affected by climate crisis;

4. It shall promote climate justice to ensure proportionate distribution of the responsibility for and benefits from climate crisis throughout the society, with the aim of overcoming the climate crisis and social disparity at once, thereby realizing a just transition to protect the vulnerable social groups, sectors, and regions susceptible to damage that may occur in the course of transition to a carbon neutral society;

5. It shall endeavor to realize the polluter pays principle by reorganizing the taxation, financial systems, etc. to ensure that the economic costs of environmental pollution or greenhouse gas emission are reasonably reflected in the market price of goods or services;

6. It shall overcome climate crisis through transition to a carbon neutral society, and at the same time, turn it into an opportunity to expand national growth engines, strengthen national competitiveness in the international arena, and create jobs, by boosting investment in and support for green technology and green industries with high growth potential and competitiveness;

7. It shall ensure every citizen's democratic participation in the process of transition to a carbon neutral society and promotion of green growth;

8. It shall aggressively participate in the efforts of the international community to hold the rise in the global average temperature to below 1.5 degrees Celsius above pre-industrial levels, not undermine the environment and social justice of developing countries, and strengthen cooperation for support for climate crisis response, based on the recognition that the climate crisis is a common challenge for humanity.

Article 4 (Responsibilities of the State and Local Governments)

(1) The State and local governments shall endeavor to ensure that the basic principles prescribed in Article 3 are reflected in all sectors, including economy, society, education, and culture, and shall create various conditions, such as improvement of relevant statutes or regulations, increase of financial investment, and establishment of related facilities and systems.

(2) The State and local governments shall comprehensively consider the impacts on climate crisis, harmonious development

of economy and environment, etc. in the process of formulating various plans and implementing projects.

(3) A local government shall take into consideration local characteristics, conditions, etc. of the local government when it formulates and implements measures for the transition to a carbon neutral society and promotion of green growth.

(4) The State and local governments shall evaluate the implementation results through a regular inspection of policies for coping with climate change, and analyze international negotiation trends and policies of major countries and local governments to prepare thorough measures.

(5) The State and local governments shall devise measures necessary to help public institutions under Article 4 of the Act on the Management of Public Institutions (hereinafter referred to as "public institution"), business entities, and citizens to efficiently reduce greenhouse gases and to strengthen the ability to adapt to climate crisis.

(6) The State and local governments shall protect the safety and property of citizens from climate crisis in accordance with the principles of climate justice and just transition.

(7) The State and local governments shall promote scientific research, impact forecast, etc. on climate change, provide citizens and business entities with relevant information transparently, and guarantee them an opportunity to actively participate and cooperate in the decision-making process.

(8) The State and local governments shall aggressively participate in international efforts to implement the transition to a carbon neutral society and promote green growth, and actively promote international cooperation for coping with climate crisis, such as providing support in terms of policy, technology, and finance to developing countries.

(9) The State and local governments shall endeavor to foster

professional human resources necessary for coping with climate crisis, such as the transition to a carbon neutral society and promotion of green growth.

Article 5 (Responsibilities of Public Institutions, Business Entities, and Citizens)

(1) Public institutions shall actively cooperate in policy measures taken by the State and local governments for the transition to a carbon neutral society, induce investment and job creation in green technology and green industries through preferential purchase, etc. of green products prescribed in Article 66 (4), and shall endeavor to minimize impacts on the climate crisis in all kinds of activities, including the formulation and execution of budget, and selection and implementation of projects.

(2) Business entities shall endeavor to minimize greenhouse gas emissions generated in the course of business activities through green management under Article 55 and to boost investment and employment in research and development of green technology and in green industries, and shall participate and cooperate in policy measures of the State and local governments.

(3) Citizens shall actively practice a green life campaign under Article 67 (1) at home, schools, places of business, etc. and participate and cooperate in policy measures of the State and local governments.

Article 6 (Relationship to Other Statutes)

Except as otherwise provided in other statutes, this Act shall govern the transition to a carbon neutral society and promotion of green growth.

CHAPTER II NATIONAL VISION AND GREENHOUSE GAS REDUCTION TARGETS

Article 7 (National Vision and Strategy)

(1) The Government shall establish a national vision for transition to a carbon neutral society and promotion of harmonious development of economy and environment, with the aim of achieving carbon neutrality by 2050.

(2) In order to achieve the national vision under paragraph (1) (hereinafter referred to as "national vision"), the Government shall formulate a national strategy for carbon neutrality and green growth (hereinafter referred to as "national strategy"), including the following matters:

1. Matters regarding the policy objectives, including the national vision;

2. Sectoral strategies and key tasks to achieve the national vision;

3. Matters regarding linkage with related policies, such as policies on the environment, energy, national land, and ocean;

4. Other matters deemed necessary for the transition to a carbon neutral society, such as financing, taxation, finance, training of human resources, education, and public relations activities.

(3) If the Government intends to formulate or modify a national strategy, it shall endeavor to hear opinions of relevant experts, local governments, interested parties, etc. through public hearings, etc. and reflect such opinions in the strategy-setting.

(4) If the Government formulates or modifies the national strategy, it shall submit it to the State Council for deliberation, after going through deliberation by the 2050 Carbon Neutral Green Growth Committee under Article 15 (1)

(hereinafter referred to as the "Committee"): Provided, That deliberation by the Committee and the State Council may be omitted where minor matters prescribed by Presidential Decree are modified.

(5) The Government shall re-examine the national strategy every five years in consideration of technical conditions and prospects, social conditions, etc. and modify it if necessary.

(6) Matters necessary for the details of the national strategy under paragraphs (2) through (5), procedures for formulating and modifying the national strategy, etc. shall be prescribed by Presidential Decree.

Article 8 (National Midand Long-Term Greenhouse Gas Reduction Targets)

(1) The Government shall set a national mediumand long-term greenhouse gas emission reduction target (hereinafter referred to as "mid-to long-term reduction target") to reduce national greenhouse gas emissions by a ratio prescribed by Presidential Decree to the extent of not less than 35 percent from the 2018 levels by 2030.

(2) The Government shall set a greenhouse reduction target for each sector, including industries, buildings, transportation, power generation, and wastes (hereinafter referred to as "sectoral reduction target"), to achieve the midto long-term reduction targets.

(3) The Government shall set annual greenhouse gas emission reduction targets for the entire nation and each sector (hereinafter referred to as "annual reduction target") to achieve the midto long-term reduction targets and the sectoral reduction targets.

(4) The Government shall re-examine midto long-term reduction targets, sectoral reduction targets, and annual reduction targets

(hereinafter referred to as "midto long-term reduction target, etc.") every five years in consideration of domestic and international conditions, such as the Paris Agreement (hereinafter referred to as the "Agreement"), and shall modify or reset such targets in accordance with the principle of progression under Article 4 of the Agreement, if necessary: Provided, That if it is necessary due to changes, etc. in social and technical conditions, the targets may be modified or reset before five years elapse.

(5) When the Government sets or modifies the midto long-term reduction targets, etc., it shall take into account the following matters:
1. Medand long-term outlook for the national greenhouse gas emission and absorption;
2. National visions and strategies;
3. Attainability of the midto long-term reduction targets, etc.;
4. Sectoral contributions to greenhouse gas emissions and reductions;
5. Impacts on national energy policies;
6. Impacts on the domestic industry, especially on the industry type and region highly dependent on fossil fuels;
7. Impacts on the national finance;
8. Prospect of related technologies for reducing greenhouse gases, etc.;
9. Trend of the international community in coping with climate crisis.

(6) If the Government sets or modifies the midto long-term reduction targets, etc., it shall endeavor to hear the opinions of relevant experts, interested parties, etc. and reflect their opinions, through the holding of public hearings, etc.

(7) Matters necessary for setting, modification, etc. of the midto long-term reduction targets, etc. under paragraphs (1) through

(6) shall be prescribed by Presidential Decree.

Article 9 (Inspection of Current Status of Implementation)

(1) The chairperson of the Committee (hereinafter referred to as the "chairperson") shall inspect the current status of implementation of the annual reduction targets each year to achieve the midto long-term reduction targets and sectoral reduction targets, and shall prepare and disclose a report on the inspection results.

(2) A report on the results under paragraph (1) shall include whether the amount of greenhouse gas emissions meets the annual reduction targets, matters having poor performance and requiring improvement found as a result of the inspection under paragraph (1), and other matters prescribed by Presidential Decree.

(3) If greenhouse gas emissions are found to fall short of the annual reduction targets as a result of the inspection under paragraph (1), the head of an administrative agency in charge of affairs relating to the relevant sector shall prepare a plan for reducing greenhouse gases and submit it to the Committee.

(4) If any matters have poor performance or require improvement under paragraph (2), the head of a central administrative agency, the heads of local governments, and the heads of public institutions shall reflect such matters in policies, etc. of the relevant agencies.

(5) Matters necessary for methods of inspecting the current status of implementation and procedures for disclosing a report on the inspection results under paragraph (1), methods of submitting a plan for reducing greenhouse gases under paragraph (3), etc. shall be prescribed by Presidential Decree.

CHAPTER III FORMULATION OF NATIONAL FRAMEWORK PLAN FOR CARBON NEUTRALITY AND GREEN GROWTH

Article 10 (Formulation and Implementation of National Framework Plan for Carbon Neutrality and Green Growth)

(1) The Government shall formulate and implement a 20-year national framework plan for carbon neutrality and green growth (hereinafter referred to as "national framework plan") every five years to achieve the national vision and the midto long-term reduction targets, etc. in line with the basic principles under Article 3.

(2) A national framework plan shall include the following matters:

1. Matters regarding the national vision and greenhouse gas emission reduction targets;

2. Domestic and international trends and future prospects of climate change and changes in concentration of greenhouse gases in the atmosphere;

3. Current status of and outlook for the greenhouse gas emission and absorption;

4. Sectoral and annual measures to attain the midto long-term reduction targets, etc.;

5. Matters regarding adaptive measures, including monitoring and prediction of climate change, assessment of impacts of and vulnerability to climate change, and prevention of disasters;

6. Matters regarding just transition;

7. Matters regarding policy measures for green growth, including fostering of green technology and green industries, and revitalization of green finance;

8. Matters regarding international negotiation and cooperation related to coping with climate crisis;

9. Matters regarding cooperation between the State and local governments in coping with climate crisis;

10. The scale of and procurement methods of financial resources required for the transition to a carbon neutral society and promotion of green growth;

11. Other matters prescribed by Presidential Decree as necessary for the transition to a carbon neutral society and promotion of green growth.

(3) Where a national framework plan is formulated or modified, it shall be deliberated by the State Council, following deliberation by the Committee: Provided, That deliberation by the Committee or the State Council may be omitted where minor matters prescribed by Presidential Decree are modified.

(4) The Minister of Environment shall assist with affairs related to the formulation, implementation, etc. of the national framework plan, and the head of the relevant central administrative agency shall spare no efforts to cooperate therewith, such as providing data requested by the Minister of Environment.

(5) Matters necessary for the methods, procedures, etc. for formulating and modifying the national framework plan under paragraphs (1) through (3) shall be prescribed by Presidential Decree.

Article 11 (Formulation of City/Do Plans)

(1) The Special Metropolitan City Mayor, a Metropolitan City Mayor, a Special Self-Governing City Mayor, a Do Governor, and a Special Self-Governing Province Governor (hereinafter referred to as "Mayor/Do Governor") shall formulate and implement a 10-year City/Do master plan for carbon neutrality and green growth (hereinafter referred to as "City/Do plan") every five years, taking into account the national framework plan and the regional characteristics of the region under

jurisdiction.

(2) A City/Do plan shall include each of the following matters:

1. Regional current status of and outlook for the greenhouse gas emission and absorption;

2. Regional midand long-term greenhouse gas emission reduction targets and sectoral and annual implementation measures;

3. Matters regarding regional adaptive measures including monitoring and prediction of climate change, assessment of impacts of and vulnerability to climate change, and prevention of disasters;

4. Impacts of climate crisis on public property defined in subparagraph 1 of Article 2 of the Public Property and Commodity Management Act and countermeasures therefor;

5. Matters regarding international cooperation in each region to cope with climate crisis;

6. Matters regarding cooperation among local governments to cope with climate crisis;

7. Matters regarding education and publicity for the transition to a carbon neutral society and promotion of green growth;

8. Matters regarding promotion of green growth, including the fostering of green technology and green industries;

9. Other matters that the Mayor/Do Governor deems necessary for the transition to a carbon neutral society and promotion of green growth.

(3) Where a Mayor/Do Governor intends to formulate or modify a City/Do plan, he or she shall submit it for deliberation to the 2050 Local Carbon Neutrality and Green Growth Committee established under Article 22 (1) (hereinafter referred to as the "Local Committee"): Provided, That the deliberation may be omitted where minor matters prescribed by Presidential Decree are modified.

(4) Where a City/Do plan is formulated or modified, a Mayor/ Do Governor shall submit it to the Minister of Environment, and the Minister of Environment shall compile the City/Do plans submitted and report them to the Committee.

(5) The Government may devise support measures necessary to facilitate the implementation of a City/Do plan.

(6) Matters necessary for the formulation, implementation, and modification of City/Do plans, submission and reporting thereof, devising of support measures, etc. under paragraphs (1) through (5) shall be prescribed by Presidential Decree.

Article 12 (Formulation of Si/Gun/Gu Plans)

(1) The head of a Si/Gun/Gu (a Gu refers to an autonomous Gu; hereinafter the same shall apply) shall formulate and implement a 10-year Si/Gun/Gu master plan for carbon neutrality and green growth (hereinafter referred to as "Si/Gun/Gu plan") every five years, taking into consideration the national framework plan, City/Do plans, regional characteristics of the competent region, etc.

(2) Article 11 (2) and (3) shall apply mutatis mutandis to the formulation and modification of a Si/Gun/Gu plan. In such cases, "Mayor/Do Governor" shall be construed as "head of a Si/Gun/Gu."

(3) Where a Si/Gun/Gu plan is formulated or modified, the head of a Si/Gun/Gu shall submit it to the Minister of Environment and the competent Mayor/Do Governor, and the Minister of Environment shall compile the Si/Gun/Gu plans received and report them to the Committee.

(4) The Government may devise support measures necessary to facilitate the implementation of Si/Gun/Gu plans.

(5) Matters necessary for the formulation, implementation, and modification of Si/Gun/Gu plans, devising of support measures,

etc. under paragraphs (1) through (4) shall be prescribed by Presidential Decree.

Article 13 (Inspection of Implementation Progress of National Framework Plan)

(1) The chairperson of the Committee shall qualitatively and quantitatively inspect the implementation progress and major achievements of the national framework plan every year, and prepare and disclose a report on the inspection results.

(2) A Mayor/Do Governor and the head of a Si/Gun/Gu shall qualitatively and quantitatively inspect the implementation progress and major achievements of City/Do plans and Si/Gun/Gu plans every year, prepare a report on the inspection results, and after deliberation by the Local Committee, submit the reports on Ci/Do plans to the Minister of Environment and the reports on Si/Gun/Gu plans to the Minister of Environment and the competent Mayor/Do Governor, respectively, and the Minister of Environment shall compile the reports submitted and report them to the Committee.

(3) The chairperson may suggest the opinion on improvement to the head of the relevant central administrative agency, a Mayor/Do Governor, or the head of a Si/Gun/Gu on matters that are found to be in need of improvement in the inspection results under paragraphs (1) and (2). In such cases, the head of the relevant central administrative agency, a Mayor/Do Governor, or the head of a Si/Gun/Gu shall reflect such opinion in policies, etc. of the relevant agencies, unless there is a compelling reason not to do so.

(4) Matters necessary for the inspection methods, procedures for disclosure, etc. under paragraphs (1) and (2) shall be prescribed by Presidential Decree.

Article 14 (Notification of Enactment and Amendment of Statutes or Regulations)

(1) Where the head of a central administrative agency intends to enact, amend, or repeal any statutes or regulations that contain details affecting the national vision or to formulate or modify a midand long-term administrative plan related to the national framework plan, he or she shall notify the Committee of the details thereof.

(2) Where the head of a local government intends to enact, amend, or repeal any municipal ordinance that contains details affecting the national vision or to formulate or modify an administrative plan related to a City/Do plan or a Si/Gun/Gu plan, he or she shall notify the Committee and a Local Committee of the details thereof.

(3) The Committee or a Local Committee shall review the details of the statutes and regulations, municipal ordinances, or administrative plans notified pursuant to paragraph (1) or (2) and notify the results of the review to the head of the relevant central administrative agency or the head of a relevant local government (hereafter in this Article referred to as "head of the relevant agency").

(4) If deemed necessary for review under paragraph (3), the Committee or a Local Committee may request the head of the relevant agency to submit relevant data. In such cases, the head of the relevant agency shall comply with the request unless there is a compelling reason not to do so.

(5) In receipt of notification of the results of review under paragraph (3), the head of the relevant agency shall properly reflect the details of review in enactment, amendment, or repeal of the relevant statutes and regulations or municipal ordinances, or in formulation or modification of administrative plans.

(6) Matters necessary for the subject matters, methods, notification procedures, etc. of review under paragraphs (1) through (4) shall be prescribed by Presidential Decree.

CHAPTER IV 2050 CARBON NEUTRALITY AND GREEN GROWTH COMMITTEE

Article 15 (Establishment of 2050 Carbon Neutrality and Green Growth Committee)

(1) The 2050 Carbon Neutrality and Green Growth Committee shall be established under the jurisdiction of the President to deliberate and decide on the Government's key policies, plans, and implementation thereof for the transition to a carbon neutral society and promotion of green growth.

(2) The Committee shall be comprised of at least 50 but not exceeding 100 members, including two chairpersons.

(3) The Prime Minister shall serve as one of the chairpersons of the Committee, and the other shall be appointed by the President from among the committee members prescribed in paragraph (4) 2.

(4) The members of the Committee shall be each of the following persons:

1. The Minister of Economy and Finance, the Minister of Science and ICT, the Minister of Trade, Industry and Energy, the Minister of Environment, the Minister of Land, Infrastructure and Transport, the Minister of the Office for Government Coordination, and other public officials pre-scribed by Presidential Decree;

2. Persons commissioned by the President from among those who have extensive knowledge of and experience in the fields of climate science, reduction of greenhouse gas

emissions, prevention of and adaptation to climate change, energy and resources, green technology and green industry, just transition, etc.

(5) In commissioning committee members pursuant to paragraph (4) 2, the President shall receive recommendations of candidates and hear the opinion of various social groups including youths, women, workers, farmers and fishermen, small and medium entrepreneurs, and civic groups, to ensure that the representativeness of each social group is reflected.

(6) The Committee shall have one administrative secretary to deal with administrative affairs, and the Minister of the Office for Government Coordination shall serve as the administrative secretary.

(7) When a chairperson is unable to perform his or her duties due to any unavoidable reason, a committee member designated in advance by a chairperson who is the Prime Minister shall act on his or her behalf.

(8) The committee members referred to in paragraph (4) 2 shall hold office for a term of two years, and may be appointed consecutively for only one further term.

(9) Matters necessary for the composition, operation, etc. of the Committee under paragraphs (1) through (8) shall be prescribed by Presidential Decree.

Article 16 (Functions of the Committee)

(1) The Committee shall deliberate and decide on the following matters:

   1. Matters regarding the basic direction-setting of policies for the transition to a carbon neutral society and promotion of green growth;

   2. Matters regarding setting of the national vision, the midto long-term reduction targets, etc.;

3. Matters regarding formulation and modification of the national strategy;

4. Matters regarding inspection of the implementation progress under Article 9;

5. Matters regarding formulation and modification of the national framework plan;

6. Matters regarding disclosure of the inspection results of the national framework plan, City/Do plans, and Si/Gun/Gu plans and suggestion of the opinion on improvement under Article 13;

7. Matters regarding formulation, modification, and inspection of national adaptive measures for climate crisis under Articles 38 and 39;

8. Matters regarding laws and systems related to the transition to a carbon neutral society and green growth;

9. Matters regarding the direction-setting of distribution of financial resources and efficient use of such resources for the transition to a carbon neutral society and promotion of green growth;

10. Matters regarding research and development, training of human resources, and fostering of industries related to the transition to a carbon neutral society and green growth;

11. Matters regarding enhancement of public understanding, and publicity and communication related to the transition to a carbon neutral society and green growth;

12. Matters regarding international cooperation for the transition to a carbon neutral society and green growth;

13. Matters subject to deliberation by the Committee under any other statutes;

14. Other matters deemed by the chairperson as necessary for reduction of greenhouse gas emissions, adaptation to climate crisis, just transition, and green growth.

Article 17 (Meetings)

(1) The chairperson shall convene and preside over the meetings of the Committee.

(2) A majority of the Committee members shall constitute a quorum, and any decision thereof shall require the concurring vote of a majority of the members present: Provided, That the Committee may deliberate and decide in writing in cases prescribed by Presidential Decree.

Article 18 (Disqualification of, Challenge to, or Recusal of, Committee Members)

(1) A Committee member falling under any of the following subparagraphs shall be disqualified from deliberation and decision by the Committee:

1. Where a committee member or his or her current or former spouse becomes a party to the relevant case or is or was a joint right holder or a joint obligor to the case;

2. Where a committee member is or was a relative of a party to the case;

3. Where a committee member gives or gave any testimony, appraisal, or legal advice on the case;

4. Where a committee member engages or engaged as the agent of a party to the case.

(2) If any circumstances indicate that it would be impractical to expect an impartial deliberation or decision from a committee member, a party to the case may file an application with the Committee for a challenge to the member, and the Committee shall decide on the challenge by resolution. In such cases, the member subject to challenge shall not participate in the resolution.

(3) If a committee member falls under the grounds for disqualification referred to in any of the subparagraphs of paragraph

(1), he or she shall voluntarily refrain from deliberation of the relevant agenda item.

Article 19 (Establishment of Subcommittees)

(1) The Committee may have subcommittees or special committees within the Committee as prescribed by Presidential Decree to perform its duties efficiently.

(2) A subcommittee shall be comprised of the committee members, and the chairperson of each subcommittee shall be elected by and from among members of the subcommittee.

(3) Matters delegated by the Committee and deliberated and decided upon by a subcommittee or a special committee shall be deemed to have been deliberated and decided upon by the Committee.

(4) Each subcommittee may have specialized committees to review agenda items for deliberation and resolution in advance and handle matters delegated by the Committee.

(5) Matters necessary for the composition and operation of the subcommittees, special committees, and specialized committees under paragraphs (1) through (4) shall be determined by the chairperson following resolution by the Committee.

Article 20 (Investigation and Hearing of Opinions)

(1) If necessary for operation of the Committee, subcommittees, and special committees, the Committee may make a request or conduct an investigation as follows:

1. A request for submission of data, documents, etc. to the head of the relevant central administrative agency;

2. A request for the attendance and statement of opinion by interested parties, expert witnesses, or relevant public officials;

3. On-site inspections by relevant administrative agencies, etc.

(2) The head of the relevant central administrative agency may require public officials under his or her control or related experts to attend the Committee and state their opinions or submit necessary data, in relation to the transition to a carbon neutral society and green growth.

Article 21 (Secretariat)

(1) The secretariat shall be established under the jurisdiction of the Committee to handle administrative affairs.

(2) The secretariat shall have one secretary general and necessary employees, and a public official in political service shall be the secretary general.

(3) Other matters necessary for the organization, operation, etc. of the secretariat shall be prescribed by Presidential Decree.

Article 22 (Composition and Operation of 2050 Local Carbon Neutrality and Green Growth Committee)

(1) A local government may have a 2050 Local Carbon Neutrality and Green Growth Committee to deliberate and decide on its key policies, plans, and implementation thereof for the transition to a carbon neutral society and promotion of green growth.

(2) A local committee may have a secretariat to assist with the operation and affairs of the local committee in consultation with the head of the competent local government.

(3) Matters necessary for the composition, operation, functions, etc. of a local committee shall be prescribed by Presidential Decree.

(4) If no local committee has been established, a Mayor/Do Governor or the head of a Si/Gun/Gu may omit the deliberation or notification under Article 11 (3) (including cases applied mutatis mutandis pursuant to Article 12 (2)), 13 (2), 14 (2), and 40 (2) and (4).

CHAPTER V GREENHOUSE GAS REDUCTION POLICY MEASURES

Article 23 (Climate Change Impact Assessment)

(1) Where the head of the relevant administrative agency or a business entity who formulates or implements a plan for a project subject to environmental impact assessment under the Environmental Impact Assessment Act conducts a strategic environmental impact assessment or an environmental impact assessment with regard to a plan or development project prescribed by Presidential Decree, such as a project emitting a massive amount of greenhouse gases, which is subject to a strategic environmental impact assessment or environmental impact assessment under Articles 9 and 22 of that Act, he or she shall include an analysis and assessment on the impacts the policies or development projects under his or her jurisdiction may have on climate change or the impacts the climate change may have on the policies or development projects (hereinafter referred to as "climate change impact assessment"), in the strategic environmental impact assessment or environmental impact assessment.

(2) Where the head of the relevant administrative agency or a business entity requests the Minister of Environment to have consultation on a statement of a strategic environmental impact assessment or an environmental impact assessment report under Articles 16 and 27 of the Environmental Impact Assessment Act with regard to the plans or development projects for which a climate change impact assessment is conducted pursuant to paragraph (1), he or she shall also request the consultation on the review of climate impact assessment.

(3) Upon receipt of a request for consultation under paragraph

(2), the Minister of Environment shall review the results of climate impact assessment and may take measures, such as collecting necessary information or requesting such information from a business entity.

(4) Matters necessary for the methods of conducting a climate change impact assessment under paragraph (1), the methods of review under paragraph (3), etc. shall be prescribed by Presidential Decree.

[Enforcement Date: Sep. 25, 2022] Article 23

Article 24 (Greenhouse Gas Reduction Cognitive Budget System)

(1) The State and local governments shall initiate a greenhouse gas reduction responsive budget system, in which they analyze the impacts of budget and fund have on climate change and reflect the analysis results in the financial operation of the State and local governments, as prescribed by relevant statutes.

Article 25 (Greenhouse Gas Emissions Trading System)

(1) The Government shall operate a system for trading greenhouse gas emission permits by setting a cap on greenhouse gas emissions and taking advantage of market functions (hereinafter referred to as "emissions trading system") to achieve the national vision, midto long-term reduction targets, etc. more efficiently.

(2) The Act on the Allocation and Trading of Greenhouse-Gas Emission Permits shall apply to the method of allocating a permitted amount of greenhouse gas emissions, method of registration and management, establishment and operation of an exchange, etc. for the implementation of the emissions trading system.

Article 26 (Greenhouse Gas Target Control in Public Sector)

(1) In order to achieve the national vision and the midto long-term reduction targets, the Government may require institutions prescribed by Presidential Decree, such as the relevant central administrative agencies, local governments, City/Do offices of education, and public institutions (hereafter in this Article referred to as "public institutions, etc."), to set their own greenhouse gas emissions reduction targets, and may provide guidance and supervision on the progress thereof.

(2) Public institutions, etc. shall comply with the targets set under paragraph (1) and submit annual performance records to the Government and disclose them.

(3) The Government shall prepare a registry of performance records submitted under paragraph (2) and manage it in a systematic manner.

(4) If the performance records of public institutions, etc. fall short of the targets under paragraph (1), the Government may order the public institutions, etc. to make improvements necessary for accomplishing the targets. In such cases, the public institutions, etc. shall set up a plan for improvement in compliance with the improvement order and implement the plan faithfully.

(5) The National Assembly, the Court, the Constitutional Court, and the election commissions (hereafter in this Article referred to as "constitutional institutions, etc.") shall voluntarily set and implement their respective greenhouse gas emission reduction targets each year, and shall notify the Government of their performance results and disclose them. In such cases, the Government shall record the performance results notified in a registry and manage it in a systematic manner.

(6) If it is necessary to enable public institutions, etc. to achieve the targets set under paragraph (1) and to implement the

improvement plan under paragraph (4) smoothly, the Government may provide financial, taxation, management, and technical support, conduct fact-finding surveys and diagnosis, provide data and information, and establish a related information system, etc., and if it is necessary to enable the constitutional institutions, etc. to voluntarily set and implement the targets under paragraph (5), the Government may provide financial and technical support, data and information, etc.

(7) Matters necessary for setting the greenhouse gas emission reduction targets under paragraph (1), fulfilling the targets and submitting and disclosing performance records thereof under paragraph (2), preparing and managing a registry under paragraph (3), issuing and implementing improvement orders under paragraph (4), setting the greenhouse gas emission reduction targets, notifying and disclosing performance results, and preparing and managing a registry under paragraph (5), etc. shall be prescribed by Presidential Decree.

Article 27 (Greenhouse Gas Target Control of Controlled Emitter)

(1) The Government shall designate an entity that emits greenhouse gases in excess of the standard amount prescribed by Presidential Decree (hereinafter referred to as "controlled emitter"), and set and control a greenhouse gas reduction target to be attained within a commitment period prescribed by Presidential Decree, in consultation with the controlled emitter.

(2) In order to designate a controlled emitter, the Government may request a controlled emitter and an entity expected to be a controlled emitter (hereafter in this Article referred to as "preliminary controlled emitter") to submit data for calculating the volume of greenhouse gas emissions for the recent three

years. In such cases, a controlled emitter or a preliminary controlled emitter in receipt of a request for providing data shall comply with such request unless there is a compelling reason not to do so.

(3) A controlled emitter shall comply with the targets under paragraph (1), and submit a detailed statement of greenhouse gas emissions (hereinafter referred to as "statement") to the Government after it has been verified by an external institution specialized in verification under Article 24-2 (1) of the Act on the Allocation and Trading of Greenhouse-Gas Emission Permits (hereinafter referred to as "verification institution"). In such cases, if the Government finds in an review of the statement submitted any matters requiring a revision or supplementation, the Government may request the controlled emitter to revise or supplement it, and the controlled emitter shall comply with such request unless there is a compelling reason not to do so.

(4) The Government shall prepare a registry based on the statements submitted under paragraph (3) and manage it systematically, and may disclose the quantity of greenhouse gas emissions from each controlled emitter, whether it has achieved its targets, etc. In such cases, a controlled emitter may request non-disclosure, if it has any special reason to believe that such disclosure may seriously infringe on its rights or trade secrets.

(5) Upon receiving a request for non-disclosure of information from a controlled emitter under the latter part of paragraph (4), the Government shall organize an examination committee to decide on whether to disclose such information, and shall notify the controlled emitter of the results within 30 days from receipt of the request for non-disclosure.

(6) Where the performance of reducing greenhouse gas emissions

by a controlled emitter falls short of the targets set under paragraph (1), the Government may issue an order for improvement for a specified period not exceeding one year. In such cases, the controlled emitter shall prepare and implement an improvement plan in accordance with the improvement order.

(7) If necessary for a controlled emitter to achieve the targets set under paragraph (1) and implement an improvement plan under paragraph (6) without obstacles, the Government may provide it with financial, taxation, management, and technical support, conduct a fact-finding survey and diagnosis, provide data and information, and build a related information system.

(8) Matters necessary for the designation of controlled entities and setting of greenhouse gas emission reduction targets under paragraph (1), observance of the targets, and submission, revision, and supplementation of statements under paragraph (3), management of a registry, scope and method of disclosure of information, and methods of requesting non-disclosure under paragraph (4), composition and operation of the examination committee and decision on disclosure of information under paragraph (5), improvement orders and implementation thereof under paragraph (6), etc. shall be prescribed by Presidential Decree.

Article 28 (Succession to Rights and Obligations of Controlled Emitters)

(1) Where a controlled emitter is merged or divided, or transfers or leases the relevant place of business or facilities, a corporation established after a merger or division, or to a transferee or lessee shall succeed to the rights and obligations of the controlled emitter prescribed in this Act, at the time of transfer of the place of business or facilities that belong to the competent controlled emitter: Provided, That the same shall

not apply where an entity that is obliged to succeed to such rights and obligations due to merge, division, acquisition by transfer, lease, etc. does not fall under the criteria for designation of a controlled emitter under paragraph 27 (1) in spite of succeeding to the rights and obligations.

(2) A controlled emitter that has transferred its rights and obligations pursuant to paragraph (1) shall report such transfer to the Government within 15 days from the date of concluding a contract on the merge, division, acquisition by transfer, and lease, which led to the transfer: Provided, That if a controlled emitter which has transferred its rights and obligations no longer exists, a report shall be filed by the succeeding entity.

(3) Matters necessary for the succession to the rights and obligations under paragraph (1), reporting under paragraph (2), etc. shall be prescribed by Presidential Decree.

Article 29 (Designation of Carbon Neutral Cities)

(1) The State and local governments shall formulate and implement policies to create a city that embodies carbon neutrality in a spatial manner (hereinafter referred to as "carbon neutral city") by fully utilizing plans and technologies related to carbon neutrality.

(2) The Government may designate a city which intends to implement the following projects as a carbon neutral city, directly or at the request of the head of a local government:

1. Projects for reducing greenhouse gases and enhancing energy self-sufficiency in cities;

2. Projects for preparing, expanding, and improving carbon sinks, etc. under Article 33 (1) in cities;

3. Conservation of the ecological network and restoration of the ecosystem in cities;

4. Creation of a resource-circulating city for coping with

climate crisis;

5. Other projects necessary for coping with climate crisis, transition to a carbon neutral society, and improvement of the environmental quality in cities.

(3) The head of a local government having jurisdiction over the carbon neutral city designated under paragraph (2) shall formulate and implement a carbon neutral city development project plan.

(4) The Government may fully or partially subsidize expenses incurred in implementing a carbon neutral city development project.

(5) The Government may designate an institution prescribed by Presidential Decree from among public institutions as a support organization, in order to formulate and implement a project plan under paragraph (3), inspect the progress of the project, conduct surveys and research therefor, etc.

(6) Where a carbon neutral city designated under paragraph (2) no longer complies with the standards for designation pre-scribed by Presidential Decree, the Government may revoke its designation.

(7) Matters necessary for the designation of a carbon neutral city, revocation of such designation, formulation and imple-mentation of a carbon neutral city development project plan, designation of supporting organizations, revocation of such designation, etc. under paragraphs (2) through (6) shall be prescribed by Presidential Decree.

Article 30 (Support for Local Energy Conversion)

(1) In order to cope with climate crisis, the Government shall formulate and implement policies to support energy conversion by local governments, such as devising measures to distribute and expand new and renewable energy in each region in

accordance with the basic principles prescribed in Article 3.

(2) The Government may fully or partially subsidize local governments, within the budget, for expenses incurred in implementing the policies to support energy conversion under paragraph (1).

Article 31 (Expansion of Green Buildings)

(1) The Government shall formulate and implement policies to increase the number of buildings with high efficiency in energy use, high percentage of using new and renewable energy, and minimum greenhouse gas emissions (hereinafter referred to as "green buildings").

(2) The Government shall set and manage a midand long-term target and a periodic target for the buildings not below the criteria prescribed by Presidential Decree in order to reduce energy consumption and greenhouse gas emissions by the buildings.

(3) The Government shall formulate and implement measures and standards for each stage of design, construction, maintenance, dismantling, etc. of buildings, such as enhancing design standards and construction permission and review, in order to minimize the consumption of energy and resources and reduce greenhouse gas emissions throughout the entire process of design, construction, maintenance, dismantling, etc. of buildings.

(4) The Government shall continue to implement projects for reducing greenhouse gas emissions through energy diagnosis, energy saving projects under Article 25 of the Energy Use Rationalization Act, and green remodeling projects under Article 27 of the Green Buildings Construction Support Act, to help convert existing buildings into green buildings.

(5) The Government may require newly constructed or renovated

buildings to install and manage smart meters that can control and reduce energy consumption including power consumption.

(6) The Government shall establish implementation plans to convert the buildings of the central administrative agencies, local governments, and public institutions, educational institutions, etc. prescribed by Presidential Decree into green buildings, and apply policy measures under paragraphs (1) through (5) to inspect and manage the implementation progress.

(7) The Government shall proactively distribute green buildings in cases of developing a new city or re-developing cities in excess of a certain scale, as prescribed by Presidential Decree.

(8) If necessary for expanding the number of green buildings, the Government may provide financial support as prescribed by Presidential Decree.

Article 32 (Revitalization of Green Transport)

(1) The Government shall set and control greenhouse gas emissions reduction targets, etc. and formulate and implement a policy for phasing out the sale and operation of internal combustion engine vehicles as prescribed by Presidential Decree, in order to revitalize green transport which is a transport system boosting the efficient use of energy and minimizing greenhouse gas emissions.

(2) The Government shall set the efficiency standards for average energy consumption for motor vehicles and the permissible levels of greenhouse gas emissions from motor vehicles, respectively, in order to promote energy conservation by improving the efficiency of average energy consumption for motor vehicles and to help maintain a pleasant and appropriate atmospheric environment by reducing greenhouse gases among motor vehicle exhaust gases. In such cases, a motor vehicle manufacturer referred to in Article 46 (1) of the

Clean Air Conservation Act shall choose to comply with one of the efficiency standards for average energy consumption for motor vehicles and the permissible levels of greenhouse gas emissions from motor vehicles.

(3) The Government shall set the annual distribution targets, etc. to promote the distribution of electric vehicles, solar-powered vehicles, and hydrogen electric vehicles defined in subparagraphs 3, 4, and 6 of Article 2 of the Act on Promotion of Development and Distribution of Environment-Friendly Motor Vehicles, and electric propulsion ships and fuel cell propulsion ships defined in subparagraph 3 (c) and (e) of Article 2 of the Act on Promotion of Development and Distribution of Environment-Friendly Ships, and shall report on the implementation progress to the Committee.

(4) In order to facilitate the distribution of electric vehicles, etc. under paragraph (3), the Government may devise measures to adopt and expand related systems, such as financial and taxation support, research and development, mandating the purchase of electric vehicles, and setting a target for distributing low-pollution vehicles.

(5) The Government shall continuously expand investment in railway to help it become the backbone of the national core transport network, expand means of public transportation, such as bus, subway, and light rail, and set and manage the midand long-term targets and phased targets for the modal share of railway transport and the modal share of public transportation.

(6) In order to minimize greenhouse gases and air pollution, drastically reduce social costs incurred by traffic congestion, and fundamentally resolve traffic congestion in large cities, the Seoul metropolitan area, etc., the Government shall devise measures to control traffic demand including each of the following matters, as prescribed by Presidential Decree:

1. Improvement of the systems for traffic congestion charges and traffic inducement charges;
2. Expansion of exclusive lanes for buses and low-pollution vehicles and no-entry zones for passenger cars;
3. Expansion and establishment of a smart traffic information system that can disperse traffic efficiently;
4. Measures to introduce various means of transportation, such as the use of bicycles and facilitation of coastal shipping.

Article 33 (Expansion of Carbon Sinks)

(1) The Government shall formulate and implement policy measures for creating or expanding carbon sinks, other biomass, etc. (hereinafter referred to as "carbon sinks, etc.") under subparagraph 10 of Article 2 of the Act on the Management and Improvement of Carbon Sink, which absorb and store greenhouse gases (referring to the isolating of greenhouse gases absorbed from the atmosphere permanently or semi-permanently) in forest, farmland, wetlands, marsh, permanent abode, marine forest defined in subparagraph 6 of Article 2 of the Fishery Resources Management Act, and others or for improving the capacity of carbon sinks, etc. to absorb greenhouse gases.

(2) The policy measures for creating and expanding carbon sinks, etc. and improving the capacity of absorbing greenhouse gases under paragraph (1) shall include the following matters:

1. Objectives and basic direction-setting for creating and expanding carbon sinks, etc. and improving the capacity of absorbing greenhouse gases;
2. Measures for evaluation and inspection of the current status of creating and expanding carbon sinks, etc. and the progress on improvement of the capacity of absorbing greenhouse gases;

3. Measures for protecting and conserving the health of the ecosystem, including biodiversity, when conducting projects for creating and expanding carbon sinks, etc. and improving the capacity of absorbing greenhouse gases;

4. Matters regarding compilation of information and statistics on greenhouse gas absorption;

5. Other matters necessary for creating and expanding carbon sinks, etc. and improving the capacity of absorbing greenhouse gases, such as research and development, training of professional human resources, financing, education, and publicity.

(3) The Government may provide administrative, financial, and technical support necessary for a business entity to voluntarily create and expand carbon sinks, etc.

Article 34 (Fostering of Technology for Carbon Capture, Use, and Storage)

(1) The Government shall formulate policy measures to support the development and growth of technology to capture and use or store carbon dioxide in the emission phase (hereinafter referred to as "technology for carbon capture, use, and storage") to contribute to achieving the national vision and the midto long-term reduction targets, etc.

(2) Special cases for regulation, etc. for demonstration of technology for carbon capture, use, and storage shall be separately prescribed by other statutes.

Article 35 (Implementation of International Mitigation Projects)

(1) Any person who intends to conduct a project for technology support, investment, purchase, etc. to attain the mitigation outcomes of greenhouse gas emissions pursuant to Article 6 of the Agreement (hereinafter referred to as "international

mitigation project") shall submit to the Government a project plan containing the details of the project, estimated greenhouse gas reductions, etc., and obtain prior approval thereof, as prescribed by Presidential Decree.

(2) A person who has obtained prior approval under paragraph (1) (hereafter in this Article referred to as "project implementer") shall conduct monitoring to objectively prove the amount of greenhouse gas emission reductions attained from the relevant project, and shall prepare a monitoring report in a measurable, reportable, and verifiable manner, obtain verification from a verification institution, and report it to the Government.

(3) A project implementer who has attained greenhouse gas reductions, which are deemed appropriate in light of the measurement, reporting, and verification manner under Article 6 of the Agreement (hereinafter referred to as "international mitigation outcomes"), through an international mitigation project shall report it to the Government without delay, and the Government shall register the reported international mitigation outcomes in the international mitigation register and manage it systematically: Provided, That if the details of report fail to comply with the standards of the Agreement, the Government may request supplementation thereto.

(4) A project implementer may trade the registered international mitigation outcomes by transactions or other means, and when the mitigation outcomes are traded or extinguished, he or she shall report such fact to the Government: Provided, That a person who intends to transfer the international mitigation outcomes to abroad or into the Republic of Korea shall obtain prior approval from the Government.

(5) The Government may utilize the registered international mitigation outcomes to achieve the midto long-term reduction

targets, etc.

(6) The Government may conduct an international mitigation project jointly with a foreign government, and may establish an international consultative body on mitigation projects in consultation with a foreign government implementing the joint project for deliberation on the following matters:

1. Approval of the implement method of projects;
2. Registration of international mitigation projects;
3. Transfer of international mitigation outcomes.

(7) Matters necessary for the standards, methods, and procedures for prior approval under paragraph (1), preparation methods and verification procedures of monitoring reports under paragraph (2), reporting methods under paragraph (3), reporting methods and standards and procedures for prior approval under paragraph (4), etc. shall be prescribed by Presidential Decree.

Article 36 (Establishment of National Greenhouse Management System)

(1) The Government shall establish and operate a National Greenhouse Management System for developing, analyzing, verifying, preparing, and managing various information and statistics related to greenhouse gases, such as the amount of greenhouse gas emission and absorption, and emission and absorption coefficient by country and region, and shall establish the Greenhouse Gas Inventory and Research Center (hereinafter referred to as the "GIR") within the Ministry of Environment.

(2) The head of the relevant central administrative agency shall fully cooperate in ensuring that the National Greenhouse Management System under paragraph (1) is operated smoothly, by compiling ever year the data and statistics in the com-

petent sector, such as energy, industrial process, agriculture, wastes, oceans and fisheries, and forestry, and submit them to the GIR.

(3) A Mayor/Do Governor and the head of a Si/Gun/Gu shall fully cooperate in ensuring that the National Greenhouse Management System under paragraph (1) is operated smoothly, by compiling and submitting each year the relevant data and statistics for the calculation, analysis, etc. of regional statistics on greenhouse gas emissions, and the Government shall secure coherence between the national greenhouse gas emissions and the regional greenhouse gas emissions.

(4) The Government shall spare no efforts to comply with the standards under the Agreement in developing, analyzing, verifying, compiling, and managing various data and statistics or establishing the National Greenhouse Management System under paragraph (1) to improve transparency, accuracy, completeness, consistency, and comparability.

(5) The Government shall analyze and verify various data and statistics under paragraph (1), including national, sectoral, and regional greenhouse gas emissions and their estimated figures, and disclose the results thereof every year.

(6) Matters necessary for the establishment of the National Greenhouse Management System, operation of the GIR, the scope of information and statistics subject to submission by the heads of the relevant central administrative agencies, Mayors/Do Governors, and the heads of Sis/Guns/Gus, and the development, analysis, verification, compilation, and management of the information and statistics, as well as the timing, methods, etc. for disclosure of various information and statistics under paragraphs (1) through (5), shall be prescribed by Presidential Decree.

CHAPTER VI CLIMATE CRISIS ADAPTATION POLICY MEASURES

Article 37 (Monitoring and Prediction of Climate Crisis)

(1) The Government shall establish and operate a meteorological data management system to constantly measure and survey changes in concentration of greenhouse gases in the atmosphere, improve the capability to observe, forecast, provide information on, and utilize meteorological phenomena, and increase the accuracy of monitoring and predicting climate crisis, as prescribed by Presidential Decree.

(2) The Government shall establish and operate a climate crisis adaptation data management system to investigate and assess the impacts of climate crisis on the ecosystem, biodiversity, atmosphere, water environments, public health, agriculture and food, forest, oceans and fisheries, industries, prevention of disasters, etc. and their vulnerability to climate crisis, risks, and social and economic ripple effects.

(3) The Government may promote policy measures for surveys and research, technological development, support for specialized institutions, establishment of domestic and international cooperative systems, etc. for the establishment and operation of the meteorological data management system under paragraph (1) and the climate crisis adaptation data management system under paragraph (2).

(4) Matters necessary for the establishment and operation of the meteorological data management system under paragraph (1) and the climate crisis adaptation data management system under paragraph (2), the promotion of policy measures under paragraph (3), etc. shall be prescribed by Presidential Decree.

Article 38 (Formulation and Implementation of National Climate Crisis Adaptation Measures)

(1) The Government shall establish and implement national climate crisis adaptation measures (hereinafter referred to as "climate crisis adaptation measures") every five years.

(2) Each climate crisis adaptation measure shall include the following matters:

1. Matters regarding enhancement of the capability to monitor, forecast, provide information on, and utilize climate crisis;

2. Matters regarding the sectoral and regional impacts on climate crisis and assessment of sectoral and regional vulnerability to climate crisis;

3. Matters regarding sectoral and regional climate crisis adaptation measures;

4. Matters regarding the prevention of disasters for vulnerable social groups, regions, etc. caused by climate crisis;

5. Matters regarding international agreements, etc. for adaptation to climate crisis;

6. Other matters prescribed by Presidential Decree as necessary for adaptation to climate crisis.

(3) Where the climate crisis adaptation measures are established or modified, it shall be subject to deliberation by the Committee: Provided, That the same shall not apply where minor matters prescribed by Presidential Decree are modified.

(4) The head of the relevant central administrative agency shall formulate and implement detailed action plans to perform the duties under his or her jurisdiction of climate crisis adaptation measures (hereinafter referred to as "detailed action plan for adaptation measures") more efficiently and systematically.

(5) The Government may provide technical, administrative, and financial support necessary to ensure that the relevant central administrative agencies, local governments, public institutions,

business entities, etc. strengthen their capabilities to adapt to climate crisis in line with the climate crisis adaptation measures.

(6) Matters necessary for the formulation, implementation, modification, etc. of climate crisis adaptation measures and detailed action plans for adaptation measures under paragraphs (1) through (4) shall be prescribed by Presidential Decree.

Article 39 (Inspection of Implementation Progress of Climate Crisis Adaptation Measures)

(1) The Government shall annually inspect the implementation progress of climate crisis adaptation measures and detailed action plans for climate crisis adaptation measures each year, and shall prepare a report on the inspection results and disclose it after deliberation by the Committee.

(2) A report on the results under paragraph (1) shall include sectoral major adaptation measures and their performance records, major excellent cases on adaptation measures, and matters having poor performance and requiring improvement found in the inspection results under paragraph (1).

(3) If deemed necessary for preparing a report on the results under paragraph (1), the Government may request the head of the relevant central administrative agency to submit related information or data, and the head of the relevant central administrative agency shall comply with such request, unless there is a compelling reason not to do so.

(4) Where any matters have poor performance or require improvement under paragraph (2), the head of the relevant central administrative agency shall reflect such details in policies, etc. of the relevant agency.

(5) Matters necessary for the methods, procedures, etc. for inspection under paragraph (1) shall be prescribed by Presidential Decree.

Article 40 (Formulation and Implementation of Regional Adaptation Measures for Climate Crisis)

(1) A Mayor/Do Governor and the head of a Si/Gun/Gu shall formulate and implement measures to adapt to climate crisis in districts under their respective jurisdictions (hereinafter referred to as "regional adaptation measures for climate crisis") every five years, in consideration of the climate crisis adaptation measures, regional characteristics, etc.

(2) In order to formulate or modify regional adaptation measures for climate crisis, a Mayor/Do Governor and the head of a Si/Gun/Gu shall submit them to the Local Committee for deliberation: Provided, That the deliberation may be omitted where minor matters prescribed by Presidential Decree are modified.

(3) Where regional adaptation measures for climate crisis are formulated or modified, a Mayors/Do shall submit them to the Minister of Environment, the head of a Si/Gun/Gu shall submit them to the Minister of Environment and the competent Mayors/Do Governors, respectively, and the Minister of Environment shall compile the submitted regional adaptation measures for climate crisis and report it to the Committee.

(4) A Mayor/Do Governor and the head of a Si/Gun/Gu shall inspect the implementation progress of regional adaptation measures for climate crisis, prepare a report on the inspection results, and submit it for deliberation by the Local Committee; and the Mayor/Do governor shall submit it to the Minister of Environment, the head of a Si/Gun/Gu shall submit it to the Minister of Environment and the competent Mayor/Do Governor, respectively, and the Minister of Environment shall report a compilation of them to the Committee.

(5) Matters necessary for the formulation, implementation, modification, inspection, etc. of regional adaptation measures

for climate crisis under paragraphs (1) through (4) shall be prescribed by Presidential Decree.

Article 41 (Public Institutions' Adaptation Measures for Climate Crisis)

(1) An institution prescribed by Presidential Decree, such as public institutions that have and manage the facilities vulnerable to climate crisis (hereinafter referred to as "vulnerable institutions") shall formulate and implement public institutions' measures for adaptation to climate crisis every five years in consideration of the climate crisis adaptation measures, characteristics of the competent facilities, etc. (hereinafter referred to as "public institutions' adaptation measures for climate crisis"), and shall prepare performance records every year.

(2) Where the head of a vulnerable institution has formulated public institutions' adaptation measures for climate crisis or prepared performance records, he or she shall submit the results thereof to the Minister of Environment, the head of the relevant central administrative agency, and the head of the competent local government.

(3) Matters necessary for the formulation and implementation of public institutions' adaptation measures for climate crisis, preparation of performance records thereof, etc. under paragraph (1) shall be prescribed by Presidential Decree.

Article 42 (Implementation of Regional Climate Crisis Response Projects)

(1) The State or local governments may implement regional climate crisis response projects to comprehensively and effectively cope with environmental pollution and damage being aggravated by climate change, and to protect and support vulnerable regions, social groups, etc. having difficulties in

maintaining the existing industries like agriculture due to the changing natural environment, natural disasters, etc. caused by climate crisis.

(2) The Government may fully or partially subsidize expenses incurred in implementing regional climate crisis response projects under paragraph (1).

(3) The Government may designate an institution prescribed by Presidential Decree from among public institutions as a support organization to formulate and implement a plan for a regional climate crisis response project under paragraph (1), inspect the progress of such project, and conduct investigations and research thereon.

(4) Matters necessary for the implementation of regional climate crisis response projects under paragraph (1) and the standards, procedures, etc. for the designation of support organizations and revocation thereof under paragraph (3) shall be prescribed by Presidential Decree.

Article 43 (Water Management for Coping with Climate Crisis)

With the aim of efficiently coping with natural disasters, such as drought, flood, and heat wave, water shortage and water quality deterioration, and changes in the aquatic ecosystem, which are caused by climate crisis, and ensuring that every citizen equally benefits from water, the Government shall formulate and implement policy measures including the following matters:

1. Supply of clean and safe drinkable water and securing of stable water resources in preparation for drought, etc.;

2. Conservation and management of the aquatic ecosystem and improvement of water quality;

3. Demand management including saving water, maintenance of water circulation system such as proactive rainwater management and reuse of sewage, and prevention of flood damage;

4. Eco-friendly conservation and restoration of rivers;

5. Development of technology for prevention and management of water pollution, provision of related services, etc.

Article 44 (Management of Green Homeland)

(1) To conserve and manage the national land in a safe and sustainable manner against climate crisis (hereinafter referred to as "green homeland"), the Government shall reflect the matters regarding coping with climate crisis when formulating and implementing the following plans:

1. Comprehensive national land plans under the Framework Act on the National Land (hereinafter referred to as "comprehensive national land plan");

2. Urban or Gun master plans under the National Land Planning and Utilization Act;

3. Other plans prescribed by Presidential Decree for the conservation and management of national land in a sustainable manner.

(2) The Government shall prepare policy measures including the following matters, to create green homeland:

1. Reduction of greenhouse gas emissions from cities and agricultural and fishing villages, and improvement of the self-sufficiency of energy in each village and city and the cycling of resources;

2. Expansion of forests and green areas, and conservation of the ecological network and restoration of the ecosystem in multi-regional areas;

3. Maintenance and promotion of the ecosystem service in areas subject to development and urban areas;

4. Eco-friendly development, utilization, and conservation of farmland and ocean;

5. Eco-friendly construction of infrastructure facilities, such as

roads, railroads, airports, and ports, and eco-friendly conversion of the existing facilities;

6. Expansion of eco-friendly transportation systems;

7. Minimization of damage to national land caused by natural disasters, such as climate disasters, and improvement of the resilience of national land.

(3) When the Government formulates plans prescribed by Presidential Decree, such as a comprehensive national land plan, and a five-year balanced national development plan under the Special Act on Balanced National Development, it shall hear the opinion of the Committee in advance.

Article 45 (Promotion of Conversion of Agriculture, Forestry, and Fisheries)

(1) The Government shall formulate and implement policy measures for conversion of agriculture, forestry, and fisheries to reduce greenhouse gas emissions generated in the course of producing crops, livestock, etc. and to ensure food security by coping with climate crisis, thereby contributing to the transition to a carbon neutral society.

(2) Policy measures for conversion of agriculture, forestry, and fisheries under paragraph (1) shall include the following matters:

1. Matters regarding the conversion of the structure of agriculture, forestry, and fisheries, such as initiating precision agriculture and organic farming;

2. Matters regarding the development and distribution of technologies, equipment and materials, and facilities for reducing greenhouse gases in the fields of agriculture, forestry, and fisheries;

3. Matters regarding the reduction of usage of fossil fuels in the fields of agriculture, forestry, and fisheries, distribution

of new and renewable energy, circulation of energy, and establishment of a self-reliance system;

4. Matters regarding the prediction of changing conditions of agriculture, forestry, and fisheries caused by climate crisis and enhancement of the food self-sufficiency rate through improvement, etc. of new varieties.

(3) Where the Government formulates and implements a plan to develop agriculture, rural communities, and the food industry under Article 14 of the Framework Act on Agriculture, Rural Community and Food Industry, it shall reflect policy measures that can reduce greenhouse gas emissions and enhance their resilience to climate crisis.

Article 46 (Designation and Evaluation of Korea Adaptation Center for Climate Change)

(1) The Minister of Environment may designate Korea Adaptation Center for Climate Change (hereinafter referred to as "KACCC") to support the formulation and implementation of climate crisis adaptation measures.

(2) The KACCC shall conduct projects related to adaptation to climate crisis prescribed by Presidential Decree, including surveys and research to promote the climate crisis adaptation measures.

(3) The Minister of Environment may evaluate the performance records, etc. of the KACCC.

(4) The Minister of Environment may fully or partially subsidize the expenses incurred in conducting projects by the KACCC within the budget.

(5) Matters necessary for the designation, projects, evaluation, etc. of the KACCC under paragraphs (1) through (3) shall be prescribed by Presidential Decree.

CHAPTER VII JUST TRANSITION

Article 47 (Preparation of Social Safety Network for Climate Crisis)

(1) The Government shall figure out the current status of social groups vulnerable to climate crisis and regions and industries where socio-economic discrimination is being aggravated, such as job losses, impacts on the regional economy, and shall prepare support measures to alleviate such status and measures to strengthen the capability to prepare for disasters.

(2) In order to minimize damage caused by conversion of projects and structural unemployment in the course of the transition to a carbon neutral society, the Government shall conduct a regular survey on the impacts on employment status, such as occurrence of unemployment, as prescribed by Presidential Decree, and shall prepare measures to support re-training, re-employment, change of occupation, etc. or to support living.

Article 48 (Designation of Special District for Just Transition)

(1) The Government may designate any of the following areas as a special district for just transition (hereinafter referred to as "special district") following deliberation by the Committee:

1. An area in which the employment environment has changed or is likely to change significantly due to rapid job losses, regional economic slump, and changing industrial structures in the course of transition to a carbon neutral society;

2. An area meeting the requirements prescribed by Presidential Decree, which is expected to experience or has experienced rapid changes in the socio-economic environment in the course of transition to a carbon neutral society;

3. Any other area which the Committee deems it necessary to

designate as a special district to resolve socio-economic imbalance that is likely to arise in the course of transition to a carbon neutral society.

(2) The Government shall establish and implement measures for areas designated as special districts, including the following support:

1. Employment security, research and development, commercialization, domestic sale, and support for export for enterprises and micro enterprises;

2. Prevention of unemployment, and support for maintaining livelihoods and helping reemployment of unemployed persons;

3. Support for fostering new industries and attracting investment therein;

4. Support for a person who conducts business related to boost of employment;

5. Other administrative or financial support measures necessary to facilitate the conversion of industry and employment, or tax benefits prescribed by the Acts on taxation, such as the Restriction of Special Taxation Act.

(3) If there are any grounds prescribed by Presidential Decree, such as where grounds for designation under paragraph (1) cease to exist, the Government may modify or revoke the designation of a special district, after deliberation by the Committee.

(4) Matters necessary for the designation, modification, revocation of designation of a special district, and details, methods, etc. of support for a special district under paragraphs (1) through (3) shall be prescribed by Presidential Decree.

Article 49 (Support for Business Conversion)

(1) Where a small or medium entrepreneur under Article 2 (1)

of the Framework Act on Small and Medium Enterprises, among the enterprises engaged in the type of business which is prescribed by Presidential Decree as likely to be affected in the course of coping with climate crisis and transition to a carbon neutral society, requests for a conversion to a type of business in the green industry, the Government may provide support therefor.

(2) Matters necessary for eligibility for support for business conversion under paragraph (1), business types falling in the green industry, selection procedures, kinds and scope of support, etc. shall be prescribed by Presidential Decree.

Article 50 (Minimization of Risk of Property Loss)

(1) The Government shall evaluate the impacts of the transition to a carbon neutral society on the operation of an enterprise, whose greenhouse gas emissions meet or exceed the criteria prescribed by Presidential Decree, such as the decline in the value of existing assets, and shall formulate policy measures for support to minimize property loss, such as early business conversion.

(2) The Government shall prepare a system that requires economic entities, such as enterprises, to transparently publish and disclose the risk of property loss due to climate crisis, for the protection of investors, etc.

Article 51 (Support for Guarantee of Citizen Participation)

(1) The Government may provide administrative and financial support necessary under Articles 52 and 53 of the Administrative Procedures Act in order to guarantee citizens' participation in the course of establishing and implementing policies for the transition to a carbon neutral society and to reflect proposed opinions through the platforms for policy proposals

by the State and local governments.

(2) Matters necessary for the scope, methods, etc. of support under paragraph (1) shall be prescribed by Presidential Decree.

Article 52 (Activation of Cooperatives)

(1) The Government may provide administrative, financial, and technical support for the activities of the cooperatives and social cooperatives prescribed in subparagraphs 1 and 3 of Article 2 of the Framework Act on Cooperatives in order to ensure a just and fair sharing of benefits generated in the course of energy conversion, such as distribution and spread of new and renewable energy, and the transition to a carbon neutral society.

(2) Matters necessary for the scope, methods, etc. of support under paragraph (1) shall be prescribed by Presidential Decree.

Article 53 (Establishment of Just Conversion Support Center)

(1) The State and local governments may establish and operate a just transition support center (hereinafter referred to as "transition center"), in consideration of the characteristics of the industries and regions experiencing the aggravation of social and economic inequalities, such as job losses and slump of the local economy, in the course of transition to a carbon neutral society.

(2) The business affairs of the conversion center shall be as follows:

1. Fact-finding surveys on the impacts on jobs and local communities caused by transition to a carbon neutral society;

2. Measures for the conversion of industry, labor, and local economy, and research and support for job conversion model;

3. Education and training for conversion of jobs, including

reemployment and change of careers, and support for employment;

4. Consulting and support for business conversion of enterprises, such as the conversion of business type;

5. Proposal of improvement of relevant statutes, regulations, and systems;

6. Other matters prescribed by Presidential Decree to support vulnerable areas and social groups in the course of transition to a carbon neutral society.

(3) The State or local governments may subsidize budgets for establishment and operation of conversion centers.

(4) Matters necessary for the establishment, operation, etc. of conversion centers under paragraphs (1) through (3) shall be prescribed by Presidential Decree.

[Enforcement Date: Jul. 1, 2022] Article 53

CHAPTER VIII POLICY MEASURES FOR GREEN GROWTH

Article 54 (Fostering of and Support for Green Economy and Green Industries)

In order to enhance the soundness and competitiveness of the national economy by materializing the green economy, and to foster and support a new green industry with high growth potential, the Government shall formulate policy measures, including each of the following matters:

1. Matters regarding economic conditions and prospects home and abroad;⌐

2. Matters regarding a phased conversion of the existing industry to green industry;

3. Matters regarding midand long-term targets and phased targets, and execution strategies to promote green industry;

4. Matters for fostering and supporting green industries as new growth engines;

5. Matters regarding the conversion of existing national infrastructure, including electricity, information and communications, transport into environmentally-friendly facilities;

6. Matters regarding fostering of the counseling service industry for green management under Article 55;

7. Matters regarding training of human resources for green industry and job creation;

8. Other matters for facilitating green economy and green industries.

Article 55 (Facilitation of Green Management of Enterprises)

In order to support and facilitate enterprises to save and use resources and energy efficiently, minimize greenhouse gas emissions and environmental pollution, and take social and ethical responsibilities in their business activities (hereinafter referred to as "green management"), The Government shall formulate and implement policy measures, including the following matters:

1. Technical support for conversion to an environmentally-friendly production system;

2. Disclosure of the amount of greenhouse gas emissions, performance of greenhouse gas reductions, and plans for greenhouse gas reduction of enterprises;

3. Disclosure of enterprises' achievements in green management, including efficient use of energy and resources, creation of forests, conservation of the natural environment, and information on sustainable development;

4. Support for green management of small and medium enterprises and promotion of commercialization of green technology;

5. Support for guidance, transfer, and dispatch of human resources for green technology by large companies to small and medium

enterprises;

6. Support for joint development of green technology by large companies and small and medium enterprises;

7. Training and securing of professional human resources in green technology and green industries and advancement into overseas markets;

8. Other matters regarding facilitation of green technology and green management of enterprises.

Article 56 (Facilitation of Research, Development, and Commercialization of Green Technology)

(1) In order to facilitate research, development, commercialization, etc. of green technology, the Government shall formulate and implement policy measures, including the following:

1. Collection, analysis, and provision of information related to green technology;

2. Development and distribution of evaluation techniques of green technology;

3. Financial support for the facilitation of research, development, commercialization, etc. of green technology;

4. Fostering of professional human resources and international cooperation, etc. for green technology.

(2) The Government shall promptly promote the transition to a knowledge-based green economy by facilitating convergence of green technology with other technology areas, such as information and communications technology, nano-technology, and bio-technology, and by turning green technology into intellectual property.

(3) If any policy measures under paragraph (1) are to be included in the master plan for science and technology under Article 7 of the Framework Act on Science and Technology, the Committee's opinion shall be heard in advance.

Article 57 (Operation of Taxation System)

The Government shall operate the taxation system in the direction of reducing goods and services that generate greenhouse gases and pollutants or have a low efficiency rate in the use of energy and resources and of facilitating environmentand climate-friendly goods and services, in order to effectively cope with climate crisis and depletion of energy and resources.

Article 58 (Financial Support and Revitalization)

(1) The Government shall formulate and implement financial policy measures, including schemes to create financial resources, provide support funds, develop financial instruments, revitalize private investment, strengthen the publication system of information on carbon neutrality, and reinvigorate trade in the carbon market, for the purpose of coping with climate change, such as the transition to a carbon neutral society, and promotion of green growth.

(2) Matters regarding the promotion of finance for coping with climate crisis under paragraph (1) shall be separately prescribed by statutes.

Article 59 (Support for and Special Cases concerning Green Technology and Green Industries)

(1) The State or local governments may provide support, such as subsidies, as may be necessary for green technology and green industries within budgetary limits.

(2) The Korea Credit Guarantee Fund established pursuant to the Credit Guarantee Fund Act and the Korea Technology Finance Corporation established pursuant to the Korea Technology Finance Corporation Act may provide credit guarantees preferentially to green technology and green industries or provide them with preferential conditions for credit guarantee.

(3) The State or local governments may support enterprises related to green technology and green industries by exempting them from income tax, corporate tax, acquisition tax, property tax, registration tax, etc., as prescribed by the Restriction of Special Taxation Act and the Restriction of Special Local Taxation Act.

(4) Where an enterprise related to green technology or green industry invites foreign investment under Article 2 (1) 4 of the Foreign Investment Promotion Act, the State or local governments shall endeavor to assist the enterprise to the fullest extent possible.

(5) The Committee shall survey the grievances of enterprises, research institutes, etc. related to green technology or green industry every year, and where any matters requiring correction, such as unreasonable regulation, are found, it may recommend the relevant institutions to take corrective measures or present its opinions.

(6) Matters necessary for investigation of grievances, recommendation for correction, presentation of opinions, etc. under paragraph (5) shall be prescribed by Presidential Decree.

Article 60 (Standardization and Certification of Green Technology and Green Industries)

(1) The Government may establish a foundation for standardization to ensure that green technology and green industries already developed or being developed within the country comply with the international standards under subparagraph 2 of Article 3 of the Framework Act on National Standards, and may provide support necessary for activities, etc. for the international standardization of green technology and green industries.

(2) In order to promote the development of green technology

and green industries, the Government may grant certification of the conformity to green technology and green products, etc. under Article 66 (4), accredit enterprises with the high ratio of green technology or high sales of green products under Article 66 (4) (hereinafter referred to as "specialized green enterprise"), impose an obligation on public institutions and others prescribed by Presidential Decree to purchase green products, and provide technical guidance on green technology.

(3) The Government shall revoke the certification of conformity or the accreditation of a specialized green enterprise under paragraph (2) in any of the following cases:

1. Where a person obtains the certification or accreditation by fraud or other improper means;

2. Where the certification or accreditation is deemed improper due to a serious defect.

(4) Matters necessary for the standardization, certification and accreditation, revocation thereof, etc. under paragraphs (1) through (3) shall be prescribed by Presidential Decree.

Article 61 (Development of Cluster and Complex of Green Technology and Green Industries)

(1) The Government may develop a cluster or complex for the joint research and development of green technology, common utilization of facilities and equipment, and establishment of networks connecting industrial sectors, academic circles, and research institutes, or may provide support for the development project of such cluster and complex.

(2) Where a project under paragraph (1) is implemented, the following matters shall be taken into consideration:

1. Matters regarding the current status of industrial clustering in each cluster and complex;

2. Matters regarding strengthening of research and development

competence of enterprises, universities, research institutes, etc. and interconnection therefor;

3. Matters regarding expansion of industrial clustering infrastructure and attraction of excellent human resources for green technology and green industries;

4. Business implementation system and plans for raising funds for green technology and green industries;

5. Matters regarding establishment of an efficient energy use system and arrangement of plans for procurement of new and renewable energy to meet the demand for energy in clusters and complex.

(3) The Government may require an institution or organization prescribed by Presidential Decree to develop a cluster or complex for green technology or green industries, with the aim of developing green technology and green industry.

(4) The Government may fully or partially contribute to expenses incurred by an institution or organization under paragraph (3) in performing a project for developing a cluster or complex for green technology or green industries under that paragraph.

Article 62 (Job Creation of Green Technology and Green Industries)

(1) The Government shall create and expand jobs for green technology and green industries so that many citizens can benefit in the course of transition to a carbon neutral society and promotion of green growth.

(2) The Government may provide financial and technical support to enterprises and citizens within the budget, to facilitate efficient mobility and conversion of manpower in each industrial sector in the course of creating jobs for green technology and green industries, to increase opportunities for citizens to learn new technology, and to create job

opportunities related to green technology and green industries.

Article 63 (Policy Measures for Information and Communications Technology and Services)

(1) In order to reduce greenhouse gas emissions, save energy, and improve energy use efficiency by actively utilizing information and communications technology and services, the Government shall formulate and implement policy measures for information and communications technology and services, including the following matters:

1. Expansion of the foundation for information and communications, such as broadcasting and communications networks;
2. Development and distribution of new information and communications services;
3. Promotion of development of green technology for the information and communications industry and the devices, etc. therefor.

(2) The Government shall formulate and implement policy measures for broadcasting and communications to spread the green life under Article 67 (1), such as promoting home working, virtual conference, remote education, and remote medical treatment.

(3) The Government shall develop and upgrade smart electricity networks using the information and communications technology, to provide high quality electricity services, optimize energy use efficiency, and reduce greenhouse gases drastically.

Article 64 (Revitalization of Circular Economy)

The Government shall formulate and implement policy measures which include the following matters, to minimize the input of energy and resources by improving the sustainability of products and establishing the circular networks of abandoned resources, thereby revitalizing an eco-friendly economic system to simultaneously realize the preservation of the ecosystem and mitigation of greenhouse gas emissions (hereafter in this Article referred to as "circular economy"):

1. Matters regarding enhancing the circular performance of materials, fuels, etc. used in the manufacturing process;

2. Matters regarding establishing the foundation for the use of sustainable products and expanding their use;

3. Matters regarding revitalizing the selecting and recycling system of wastes and the re-manufacturing industry;

4. Matters regarding collecting and utilizing biomass, such as timber, plants, and agricultural products used as energy resources;

5. Matters regarding enhancing monitoring of resources, such as establishment of a national management system of statistics on resources.

CHAPTER IX TRANSITION TO CARBON NEUTRAL SOCIETY AND SPREAD OF GREEN GROWTH

Article 65 (Local Governments' Action Alliance for Carbon Neutrality)

(1) In order to promote local governments' voluntary activities to cope with climate crisis and mutual cooperation among them for the transition to a carbon neutral society and promotion of green growth, a local government may organize and operate the Local Governments' Action Alliance for Carbon Neutrality (hereinafter referred to as the "Action Alliance") with the participation of the heads of local governments.

(2) The Action Alliance may designate more than one representative among the heads of local governments participating in the

Action Alliance, for the smooth cooperation and systematic promotion of projects.

(3) The Action Alliance shall endeavor to achieve each of the following matters:

1. Achieving carbon neutrality by 2050;
2. Reaching a social agreement and building a consensus on the transition to a carbon neutral society;
3. Finding and providing support for projects for achieving carbon neutrality;
4. Practicing and disseminating a leading climate-responsive action for facilitating the transition to a carbon neutral society;
5. Mutual communication and joint cooperation for reducing greenhouse gases and adapting to climate crisis;
6. Other matters determined by mutual agreement among the heads of local governments participating in the Action Alliance, which are necessary for coping with climate crisis, such as reduction of greenhouse gas emissions, adaptation to climate crisis, and green growth.

(4) A secretariat shall be established to support the activities of the Action Alliance.

(5) Matters necessary for the organization, operation, etc. of the Action Alliance under paragraph (1), the organization, operation, etc. of a secretariat under paragraph (4), etc. shall be prescribed by Presidential Decree.

Article 66 (Spread of Production and Consumption Cultures for Transition to Carbon Neutral Society and Green Growth)

(1) The Government shall formulate and implement policy measures for the saving and efficient use of energy and resources and the mitigation of greenhouse gas emissions throughout the entire process of production, consumption,

transportation, and disposal (hereinafter referred to as "production, etc.") of goods.

(2) The Government shall ensure that the energy consumption, greenhouse gas emissions, etc. are reasonably linked to and reflected in the price of goods and services and the accurate information thereon is disclosed and delivered to consumers, in order to expand and enhance the consumers' right to choose.

(3) The Government may establish and operate an information management system through which consumption of energy and resources, emissions of greenhouse gases and pollutants, etc. throughout the entire process of production, etc. of goods can be analyzed and evaluated and data on the results of analysis and evaluation can be accumulated and used.

(4) The Government shall formulate and implement policy measures that require producers, sellers, etc. of goods to indicate and disclose the information or grade on the amount of greenhouse gas emissions and pollutants generated in the process, etc. of producing the goods to help consumers easily recognize such information or grade, in order to promote and spread the use and consumption of products that minimize the input of energy and resources and the generation of greenhouse gases and pollutants (hereinafter referred to as "green product").

(5) The Government may establish a cooperative system with enterprises as prescribed by Presidential Decree and provide incentives by utilizing credit cards, etc. under subparagraph 3 of Article 2 of the Specialized Credit Finance Business Act, in order to promote the production and consumption cultures for the transition to a carbon neutral society and promotion of green growth.

Article 67 (Support, Education, and Public Relations for Green Life Campaign)

(1) The Government shall formulate policy measures to support a life of minimizing the generation of greenhouse gases and pollutants through saving of energy and resources and conversion of consumption toward green products in citizens' everyday life from production to consumption to activities, etc. (hereinafter referred to as "green life"), establish a cooperative system aimed at carbon neutrality with local governments, enterprises, private organizations, etc., and reinforce education and public relations, thereby aggressively spreading a national green life campaign.

(2) The Government may provide relevant private organizations, institutions, etc. with necessary financial and administrative support to ensure the green life campaign is spread as a voluntary practice movement driven by the private sector.

(3) The Government may implement the following programs for the spread of a green life:

1. Programs to provide incentives to house or commercial buildings according to the reduction level of usage of electricity, water supply, urban gas, etc.;

2. Programs to provide incentives based on the reduction rate of annual mileage of passenger vehicles and buses for passengers;

3. Other programs prescribed by Presidential Decree as necessary to increase public awareness of the transition to a carbon neutral society and green growth and to support their practice.

(4) The Government shall expand education and public relations for the transition to a carbon neutral society and green growth to encourage business entities, citizens, etc. to voluntarily participate in relevant policies and activities and practice

green life in their everyday life.

(5) The Government shall strengthen school education, such as developing teaching materials including curriculum books and training teachers, reinforce an integrated education linked to general cultural education, vocational education, basic lifelong education courses, etc., and implement a program for training and supporting professional human resources relating to the transition to a carbon neutral society and green growth, in order to ensure that citizens in all generations can practice green life.

(6) The Government shall strengthen education and public relations activities through mass media, including newspapers, broadcasting, and Internet portal, so as to facilitate the settlement and spread of green life.

(7) Public broadcasting shall spare no efforts to produce and broadcast programs for coping with climate crisis and to promote public service announcement related to climate crisis.

Article 68 (Establishment of Carbon Neutrality Support Center)

(1) The head of a local government may establish or designate and operate a carbon neutrality support center in the competent region as prescribed by Presidential Decree, in order to support the transition to a carbon neutral society and promotion of green growth by formulating and implementing regional plans for carbon neutrality and green growth and promoting energy conversion, etc.

(2) The carbon neutrality support center under paragraph (1) shall perform the following affairs:

1. Support for the formulation and implementation of City/Do plans or Si/Gun/Gu plans;

2. Support for the formulation and implementation of regional adaptation measures for climate crisis;

3. Promotion of energy conversion by each local government and development and spread of energy conversion models;
4. Other affairs prescribed by Presidential Decree, which are necessary for the transition to a carbon neutral society and promotion of green growth in the competent region.

(3) If a carbon neutrality support center designated pursuant to paragraph (1) fails to meet the standards for designation prescribed by Presidential Decree, the head of the competent local government may revoke its designation.

(4) The head of the relevant central administrative agency may provide financial support in the competent sector to the carbon neutrality support center under paragraph (1) within the budget.

(5) Matters necessary for designation of a carbon neutrality support center and revocation thereof under paragraphs (1) and (3) shall be prescribed by Presidential Decree.

[Enforcement Date: Jul. 1, 2022] Article 68

CHAPTER X ESTABLISHMENT AND OPERATION OF CLIMATE RESPONSE FUND

Article 69 (Establishment of Climate Response Fund)

(1) The Government shall establish the Climate Response Fund (hereinafter referred to as the "Fund") to secure financial resources necessary to effectively cope with climate crisis and facilitate the transition to a carbon neutral society and promotion of green growth.

(2) The Fund shall consist of the following financial resources:
1. Contributions from the Government;
2. Contributions or donations from any person other than the Government;

3. Money transferred from other accounts and funds;

4. Money transferred from general accounts under Article 71;

5. Loans from financial institutions, other funds, and other financial resources under paragraph (3);

6. Deposits from the Public Capital Management Fund prescribed in the Public Capital Management Fund Act;

7. Revenues generated from the allocation of emission permits at a cost under Article 12 (3) of the Act on the Allocation and Trading of Greenhouse-Gas Emission Permits;

8. Profits earned from the operation of the Fund;

9. Other revenues prescribed by Presidential Decree.

(3) If a shortage of funds occurs or is expected to occur when making expenditures from the Fund, the Government may take out a loan from other financial institutions, other funds, or any other financial resources at the expense of the Fund.

(4) A local government may establish a local climate response fund as prescribed by municipal ordinance, to promote projects for coping with climate crisis according to each regional characteristics.

[Enforcement Date: Jan. 1, 2022] Article 69

Article 70 (Purposes of Fund)

The Fund shall be used for any of the following purposes:

1. Creation and operation of the Government's foundation for reducing greenhouse gases;

2. Support for conversion of industries, labor, and local economy, and greenhouse gas reduction activities of enterprises, for the transition to a carbon neutral society and promotion of green growth;

3. Support for conversion and creation of jobs in the regions with worsening social and economic conditions, or for workers and social groups suffering, in the course of coping with climate

crisis;

4. Research and development, and training of human resources, of green technology for coping with climate crisis;

5. Loan, investment, or other financial support necessary for coping with climate crisis;

6. Education and public relations for coping with climate crisis;

7. International cooperation for coping with climate crisis;

8. Repayment of the principal and interest of loans;

9. Repayment of the principal and interest of deposits from the Public Capital Management Fund prescribed in the Public Capital Management Fund Act;

10. Disbursement of expenses to establish, operate, and manage the Fund;

11. Other purposes prescribed by Presidential Decree for coping with climate crisis.

[Enforcement Date: Jan. 1, 2022] Article 70

Article 71 (Money Transferred from General Accounts)

The Government shall transfer the amount equivalent to 70/1,000 of traffic, energy, and environment taxes under the Traffic, Energy and Environment Tax Act from general accounts to the Fund every fiscal year.

[Enforcement Date: Jan. 1, 2022] Article 71

Article 72 (Operation and Management of Fund)

(1) The Minister of Economy and Finance shall operate and manage the Fund.

(2) The Minister of Economy and Finance may entrust part of the affairs for the operation and management of the Fund to a corporation or organization designated by the Minister of Economy and Finance.

(3) If necessary for the efficient operation and management of

the Fund, the Minister of Economy and Finance may conduct an accounting by establishing a separate account as prescribed by Presidential Decree.

(4) In order to deliberate on comprehensive matters regarding the operation and management of the Fund, a Deliberative Council on Fund Management shall be established under the jurisdiction of the Minister of Economy and Finance pursuant to Article 74 of the National Finance Act.

(5) The Minister of Economy and Finance may report to the Committee important matters prescribed by Presidential Decree concerning the operation and management of the Fund.

(6) Other matters necessary for the operation and management of the Fund shall be prescribed by Presidential Decree.

[Enforcement Date: Jan. 1, 2022] Article 72

Article 73 (Accounting Agency of Fund)

(1) The Minister of Economy and Finance shall appoint fund revenue-collection officials, fund financial officials, fund disbursing officials, and fund accounting officials from among public officials under his or her jurisdiction to assign them the administrative affairs related to the revenue and expenditure of the Fund.

(2) Where the Minister of Economy and Finance entrusts an institution with the administrative affairs regarding the management and operation of the Fund pursuant to Article 72 (2), the Minister shall appoint an executive officer in charge of the fund revenue and an executive officer in charge of encumbrance of the Fund from among the executive officers of the institutions entrusted with such affairs, and a fund disbursement officer and a fund accounting officer from among the employees of the institutions, respectively. In such cases, the executive officer in charge of the fund revenue

shall perform the duties of the fund revenue-collection official, the executive officer in charge of encumbrance of the Fund shall perform the duties of the fund financial official, the fund disbursement officer shall perform the duties of the fund disbursement official, and the fund accounting officer shall perform the duties of the fund accounting official, respectively.

[Enforcement Date: Jan. 1, 2022] Article 73

Article 74 (Disposal of Profits and Losses)

(1) Where any profit accrues upon the settlement of the Fund accounts, all such profits shall be accumulated as a reserve.

(2) Where any loss accrues upon the settlement of the Fund accounts, the loss shall be made up for from the reserve under paragraph (1), and where the reserve is insufficient, the Government may make up for the shortfall from general accounts.

[Enforcement Date: Jan. 1, 2022] Article 74

CHAPTER XI SUPPLEMENTARY PROVISIONS

Article 75 (Strengthening of International Cooperation)

(1) The Government shall formulate various policy measures to strengthen international cooperation with foreign governments and international organizations, such as information exchange, technical cooperation and standardization, and joint survey and research on coping with climate crisis.

(2) The Government shall endeavor to faithfully assume its responsibilities as a member of the international community, by helping developing countries to cope with climate crisis through financial support, etc.

(3) The Government shall devise necessary measures such as providing information and financial support to local governments, civic groups, etc. to facilitate international cooperation activities related to coping with climate crisis.

Article 76 (Response to International Standards)

(1) The Government shall collect, survey, and analyze the international trends and information on the programs and policies for coping with climate crisis that any foreign government or international organization intends to establish or adopt, and shall prepare proper countermeasures, such as improving related programs and policies more reasonably and establishing a supportive program therefor.

(2) The Government shall fully provide enterprises and citizens with matters regarding the trends, information, and countermeasures under paragraph (1), to improve their capabilities to cope with climate crisis.

Article 77 (Preparation of National Reports)

(1) The Government may prepare and update the following reports, in accordance with the United Nations Framework Convention on Climate Change (hereinafter referred to as the "Convention") and the Agreement:

1. National reports under the Convention;
2. Reports on Nationally Determined Contributions (NDC) under the Agreement;
3. Biennial transparency reports under the Agreement;
4. Adaptation reports under the Agreement;
5. Other reports prescribed by Presidential Decree, which are under the Convention or Agreement.

(2) The Government may request the head of the relevant central administrative agency and the head of a local government to

submit data necessary for preparing reports under paragraph (1), and the head of the relevant central administrative agency shall comply with such request, unless there is a compelling reason not to do so.

(3) When the Government intends to submit reports under paragraph (1) to the Conference of the Parties of the Convention, it shall submit the reports to the Committee for deliberation.

(4) Matters necessary for the preparation of reports and submission of data under paragraphs (1) through (3) shall be prescribed by Presidential Decree.

Article 78 (Reporting to the National Assembly)

(1) When the Government formulates or modifies the national framework plan, it shall report it to the National Assembly without delay: Provided, That the same shall not apply where minor matters prescribed by Presidential Decree are modified.

(2) When a Mayor/Do Governor or the head of a Si/Gun/Gu formulates or modifies a City/Do plan or a Si/Gun/Gu plan, he or she shall report it to a local council without delay: Provided, That the same shall not apply where minor matters prescribed by Presidential Decree are modified.

(3) The Committee shall report the inspection results of the implementation progress of the national framework plan under Article 13 (1) to the National Assembly every year, and the Mayor/Do Governor or the head of a Si/Gun/Gu shall report the inspection results of the implementation progress of the City/Do plans or Si/Gun/Gu plans under paragraph (2) of that Article to the local council every year.

(4) Matters necessary for the timing, methods, etc. for reporting to the National Assembly and local councils under paragraphs (1) through (3) shall be prescribed by Presidential Decree.

Article 79 (Designation of Chief Officer of Compliance with Carbon Neutrality)

(1) In order to ensure a smooth transition to a carbon neutral society and promotion of green growth, the head of a central administrative agency, a Mayor/Do Governor, or the head of a Si/Gun/Gu shall designate a chief officer of compliance with carbon neutrality from among public officials under his or her jurisdiction.

(2) Matters necessary for the requirements for designation, duties, etc. of a chief officer of compliance with carbon neutrality under paragraph (1) shall be prescribed by Presidential Decree.

Article 80 (Hearings)

Where the Government intends to take any of the following dispositions, it shall hold a hearing:

1. Revocation of designation under Article 29 (6);
2. Revocation of designation of a supporting organization under Article 29 (7);
3. Revocation of designation under Article 42 (4);
4. Revocation of certification of conformity or accreditation of a specialized green enterprise under Article 60 (3);
5. Revocation of designation under Article 68 (3).

Article 81 (Delegation and Entrustment of Authority)

(1) The head of a central administrative agency may delegate part of his or her authority under this Act to the head of a local government or the head of an affiliated agency, as prescribed by Presidential Decree.

(2) The head of a central administrative agency may entrust part of the affairs under this Act to a public institution or an institution prescribed by Presidential Decree which is

specializing in coping with climate crisis, as prescribed by Presidential Decree.

Article 82 (Legal Fiction as Public Officials for Purposes of Applying Penalty Provisions)

Any of the following persons shall be deemed public officials in applying Articles 129 through 132 of the Criminal Act:

1. Members who are not public officials, among members of the Committee, local committees, or special committees or specialized committees under Article 19 (1) and (4);

2. A person engaged in the affairs entrusted under Article 81 (2).

Article 83 (Administrative Fines)

(1) Any of the following persons shall be subject to an administrative fine of not more than 10 million won:

1. A person who fails to submit data necessary for calculating greenhouse gas emissions in violation of Article 27 (2) or submits false data;

2. A person who fails to submit specifications in violation of Article 27 (3) (including submission after revising and supplementing statements pursuant to the latter part of that paragraph; hereinafter the same shall apply) or submits a false statement;

3. Any person who fails to implement an improvement order in violation of Article 27 (6).

(2) An administrative fine under paragraph (1) shall be imposed and collected by the head of a relevant administrative agency, as prescribed by Presidential Decree.

ADDENDA <Act No. 18469, Sep. 24, 2021>

Article 1 (Enforcement Date)

This Act shall enter into force six months after the date of its promulgation: Provided, That Articles 69 through 74 shall enter into force on January 1, 2022, Articles 53 and 68 shall enter into force on July 1, 2022, and Article 23 shall enter into force one year after the date of its promulgation.

Article 2 (Repeal of Other Statutes)

The Framework Act on Low Carbon, Green Growth shall be repealed.

Article 3 (Applicability to Timing for Formulating Plans)

(1) The national strategy under Article 7 (2) shall be formulated within one year from the date this Act enters into force.

(2) The first national framework plan under Article 10 (1) shall be formulated within one year from the date this Act enters into force.

(3) The first City/Do plan under Article 11 (1) shall be formulated within one year from the date the national framework plan under this Act is formulated.

(4) The first Si/Gun/Gu plan under Article 12 (1) shall be formulated within one year from the date the relevant City/Do plan under this Act is formulated.

(5) The first public institutions' adaptation measures for climate crisis under Article 41 (1) shall be formulated within one year from the date of this Act enters into force.

Article 4 (Applicability to Evaluation of Impacts of Climate Change)

Article 23 shall begin to apply to cases where a preparatory statement for assessment is prepared pursuant to Article 11 or 24 of the Environmental Impact Assessment Act after the enforcement date under the proviso of Article 1 of the Addenda.

Article 5 (Special Cases concerning External Verification Institutions)

Any external specialized institution that has obtained public confidence under Article 42 (10) of the previous Framework Act on Low Carbon, Green Growth as at the time this Act enters into force shall be deemed designated as an external specialized institution for verification referred to in Article 24-2 (1) of the Act on the Allocation and Trading of Greenhouse-Gas Emission Permits, limited to verification under Article 27 (3) of this Act.

Article 6 (Transitional Measures concerning National Framework Plans)

A master plan for coping with climate change formulated under the previous Framework Act on Low Carbon, Green Growth as at the time this Act enters into force shall be deemed a national framework plan under this Act until the national framework plan under this Act is formulated for the first time.

Article 7 (Transitional Measures concerning Adaptation Measures)

Adaptation measures for climate change formulated by the Government pursuant to the previous Framework Act on Low Carbon, Green Growth as at the time this Act enters into force shall be deemed climate crisis adaptation measures, detailed action plans for adaptation measures, and regional adaptation measures for climate crisis under this Act, until the first climate crisis adaptation measures, detailed action plans for adaptation measures, and regional adaptation measures for climate crisis are formulated under this Act.

Article 8 (Transitional Measures concerning Administrative Fines)

The provisions on administrative fines under the previous Framework Act on Low Carbon, Green Growth shall apply to any violations falling under Article 64 (1) 1, 2, or 4 of the previous Framework Act on Low Carbon, Green Growth that were committed before this Act enters into force.

Article 9 Omitted.

Article 10 (Relationship to Other Statutes or Regulations)

Where the previous Framework Act on Low Carbon, Green Growth or any provisions thereof are cited in any other statutes or regulations as at the time this Act enters into force, such citation shall be deemed a citation of this Act or relevant provisions of this Act in lieu of the previous provisions, if there are any provisions corresponding thereto in this Act.

Last updated : 2022-07-07

SPACE DEVELOPMENT PROMOTION ACT

Korea Legislation Research Institute

Act No. 7538, May 31, 2005
Amended by Act No. 8714, Dec. 21, 2007
Act No. 8852, Feb. 29, 2008
Act No. 9440, Feb. 6, 2009
Act No. 10087, Mar. 17, 2010
Act No. 10447, Mar. 9, 2011
Act No. 10775, jun. 7, 2011
Act No. 11690, Mar. 23, 2013
Act No. 12723, jun. 3, 2014
Act No. 12736, jun. 3, 2014
Act No. 13009, Jan. 20, 2015
Act No. 15243, Dec. 19, 2017
Act No. 17347, jun. 9, 2020
Act No. 17359, jun. 9, 2020
Act No. 18867, jun. 10, 2022

CHAPTER I GENERAL PROVISIONS

Article 1 (Purpose)

The purpose of this Act is to facilitate the peaceful use and scientific exploration of outer space and to contribute to national security, the sound growth of the national economy, and the betterment of citizens' lives by systematically promoting the development of outer space and by efficiently using and managing space objects.

Article 2 (Definitions)

The terms used in this Act are defined as follows: *<Amended on Jun. 3, 2014; Jan. 20, 2015; Jun. 10, 2022>*

1. The term "space development" means any of the following activities:
   (a) Research on the design, manufacturing, launch, operation, etc. of artificial space objects and development of technology therefor;
   (b) Use and exploration of outer space and activities to facilitate such activities;

2. The term "space development project" means projects for advancing space development and projects for facilitating the development of education, technology, informatization, industries, etc. related thereto;

3. The term "space object" means the following:
   (a) The term "artificial space object" means an object designed and manufactured for use in outer space (including a space launch vehicle, artificial satellite, spaceship, and the components thereof);
   (b) The term "natural space object" means an object (including a meteorite) formed naturally in outer space;
   (c) The term "meteorite" means a solid piece of debris from outer space, which has fallen to the Earth's surface attracted by the gravity of Earth;

3-2. The term "space launch vehicle" means an artificial space object (including a quasi-orbital launch vehicle which meets the performance prescribed by Presidential Decree and does not fall under weapons systems, such as missiles), which makes an artificial satellite, spaceship, etc. enter into outer space by self-propelled vehicles;

4. The term "space accident" means a breakdown, crash, collision, explosion, etc. of an artificial space object, which occurs in the course of launching (including preparation for launch, test launch, and unsuccessful launch) and operating the space object;

5. The term "satellite information" means information processed with images, voice, sound, data, or combinations thereof acquired using a satellite (including those obtained by processing or utilizing such information);

6. The term "dangers in space" means risks of crash, collision, etc. of space objects in outer space;

7. The term "space business entity" means a person who performs economic activities related to research, development, manufacturing, production, provision, distribution, etc. of the following:

   (a) Artificial space objects;
   (b) Apparatuses, devices, software, etc. related to artificial space objects;
   (c) Infrastructure, buildings, structures, etc. related to artificial space objects;
   (d) Services related to the utilization of artificial space objects;

8. The term "space industry cluster" means an area developed by interconnecting research institutes, enterprises, educational institutions, and scienceand technology-related institutions and organizations (hereinafter referred to as "research institutes, etc.") with the relevant support facilities (including an area developed by connecting at least two areas which are not adjacent to each other) to facilitate the convergence and integration of the space industry and the development in connection with related industries, as designated pursuant to

Article 22 (1).
[This Article Wholly Amended on Jun. 7, 2011]

Article 3 (Responsibilities of the Government)

(1) The Government shall observe any outer space-related treaty it has entered into with any other country or international organization and shall pursue the peaceful use of outer space.

(2) The Government shall establish and promote a comprehensive policy for space development.

[This Article Wholly Amended on Jun. 7, 2011]

Article 4 (Relationship to Other Statutes)

Except as otherwise provided in any other statute, the promotion of space development and the use and management of space objects shall be governed by the provisions of this Act.

[This Article Wholly Amended on Jun. 7, 2011]

CHAPTER II IMPLEMENTATION SYSTEM

Article 5 (Formulation of Master Plan for Promotion of Space Development)

(1) For the promotion of space development and the use, management, etc. of space objects, the Government shall formulate a master plan for the promotion of space development (hereinafter referred to as "master plan") which prescribes midand long-term policy objectives and basic direction-setting on space development every five years.

(2) A master plan shall include the following: *<Amended on Jun. 10, 2022>*

　1. Matters concerning objectives and direction-setting of space development policies;

2. Matters concerning systems and strategies to pursue space development;

3. Matters concerning plans to pursue space development;

4. Matters concerning the expansion of infrastructure necessary for space development;

5. Matters concerning financing and investment plans for space development;

6. Matters concerning research and development for space development;

7. Matters concerning the nurturing of professionals necessary for space development;

8. Matters concerning international cooperation for the invigoration of space development;

9. Matters concerning the promotion of space development projects;

9-2. Matters concerning the promotion of space development by the private sector;

9-3. Matters concerning the development, operation, etc. of the satellite navigation system;

10. Matters concerning the use and management of space objects;

11. Matters concerning the utilization of the results of space development;

12. Other matters prescribed by Presidential Decree related to the promotion of space development and the use and management of space objects.

(3) Where the Government intends to formulate or alter a master plan, it shall finalize the master plan following deliberations by the National Space Committee under Article 6 (1): Provided, That the foregoing shall not apply to cases that it alters insignificant matters prescribed by Presidential Decree.

(4) The Government shall officially announce a master plan

finalized pursuant to paragraph (3) without delay: Provided, That it may choose not to officially announce matters concerning national security in consultation with the heads of relevant central administrative agencies (including the Director of the National Intelligence Service; hereinafter the same shall apply).

(5) Detailed procedures concerning the formulation and alteration of a master plan shall be prescribed by Presidential Decree.

[This Article Wholly Amended on Jun. 3, 2014]

Article 5-2 (Formulation of Action Plan for Promotion of Space Development)

(1) In accordance with a master plan, the Minister of Science and ICT shall formulate and execute an action plan thereof every year in consultation with the heads of relevant central administrative agencies: Provided, That where necessary for national security, the head of a relevant central administrative agency may formulate a separate special action plan within the scope of the master plan in consultation with the heads of relevant central administrative agencies prescribed by Presidential Decree. *<Amended on Jul. 26, 2017>*

(2) Detailed procedures concerning the formulation and execution of an action plan under paragraph (1) shall be prescribed by Presidential Decree.

[This Article Newly Inserted on Jun. 3, 2014]

Article 5-3 (Formulation of Master Plan for Utilization of Satellite Information)

(1) In order to promote the dissemination and utilization of satellite information, the Government shall formulate a master plan for the utilization of satellite information (hereinafter referred to as "master plan for the utilization of satellite

information") every five years.

(2) A master plan for the utilization of satellite information shall include the following:

1. Matters concerning objectives and direction of policies for the dissemination and utilization of satellite information;

2. Matters concerning the acquisition of satellite information;

3. Matters concerning a system for the dissemination of satellite information and a plan for the utilization thereof;

4. Matters concerning the nurturing of professionals related to satellite information;

5. Matters concerning demand for, trends, research, and development of technologies utilizing satellite information;

6. Matters concerning the prevention of duplicate investments in equipment, facilities, etc. related to satellite information;

7. Matters concerning demand for and trends of the development of artificial satellites for the acquisition of satellite information;

8. Other matters concerning the promotion of the dissemination and utilization of satellite information.

(3) Where the Government intends to formulate or alter a master plan for the utilization of satellite information, it shall finalize the master plan following deliberations by the National Space Committee under Article 6 (1): Provided, That the foregoing shall not apply to cases that it alters insignificant matters prescribed by Presidential Decree.

(4) The Government shall officially announce a master plan finalized pursuant to paragraph (3) without delay: Provided, That it may choose not to officially announce matters concerning national security.

(5) Detailed procedures concerning the formulation and alteration of a master plan for the utilization of satellite information shall be prescribed by Presidential Decree.

[This Article Newly Inserted on Jun. 3, 2014]

Article 5-4 (Formulation of Action Plan for Utilization of Satellite Information)

(1) In accordance with a master plan for the utilization of satellite information, the Minister of Science and ICT shall formulate and execute an action plan thereof every year in consultation with the heads of relevant central administrative agencies. *<Amended on Jul. 26, 2017>*

(2) Detailed procedures concerning the formulation and execution of an action plan under paragraph (1) shall be prescribed by Presidential Decree.

[This Article Newly Inserted on Jun. 3, 2014]

Article 6 (National Space Committee)

(1) The National Space Committee (hereinafter referred to as the "Committee") shall be established under the control of the President to deliberate on matters concerning space development, including the formulation of master plans.

(2) The Committee shall deliberate on the following: Provided, That the deliberation by the Committee on the matter falling under subparagraph 6 may be omitted, if necessary for national security, etc.: *<Amended on Jun. 3, 2014; Jun. 10, 2022>*

1. Matters concerning a master plan, a comprehensive plan for the utilization of satellite information, and a master plan for preparing against dangers in space under Article 15 (1) (hereafter referred to as "master plan, etc." in this paragraph);

2. Matters concerning the coordination of important policies of the Government with major duties of relevant central administrative agencies (including the National Intelligence Service; hereinafter the same shall apply) in relation to a

master plan, etc.;

3. Important matters concerning the designation, operation, etc. of institutions specializing in space development prescribed in Article 7;

4. Matters concerning the use, management, and evaluation of the outcomes of space development projects;

5. Matters concerning financing and investment plans for space development projects;

6. Matters concerning permission to launch space launch vehicles;

7. Matters concerning the correction of space development prescribed in Article 19 (2);

7-2. Matters concerning the designation of a space industry cluster and the cancellation of such designation under Article 22;

8. Other matters the chairperson brings to the Committee for deliberations.

(3) The Committee shall be comprised of up to 16 members, including one chairperson. *<Amended on Aug. 10, 2021>*

(4) The Prime Minister shall serve as the chairperson of the Committee, and the Minister of Science and ICT as the vice chairperson, and the following persons shall become the members thereof: *<Amended on Mar. 9, 2011; Mar. 23, 2013; Jul. 26, 2017; Aug. 10, 2021>*

1. The Minister of Economy and Finance, the Minister of Foreign Affairs, the Minister of National Defense, the Minister of Trade, Industry and Energy, and the Director of National Intelligence Service;

2. Persons with abundant knowledge and experience relating to the field of outer space who are commissioned by the President.

(5) Working committees for the promotion of space development

and working committees for the utilization of satellite information shall be established under the Committee, which shall be headed by the Vice Minister of Science and ICT in order to efficiently conduct the duties of the Committee: Provided, That the working committee for the space development for security shall be established with the Vice Minister of National Defense and one vice-chairperson of the National Intelligence Service as the joint-chairperson to deliberate on matters deemed inevitable for national security. *<Amended on Mar. 23, 2013; Jun. 3, 2014; Jul. 26, 2017; Aug. 10, 2021>*

(6) Matters necessary for the composition and operation of the Committee, the working committee for the promotion of space development, the working committee for the utilization of satellite information, and the working committee for the space development for security shall be prescribed by Presidential Decree. *<Amended on Jun. 3, 2014; Aug. 10, 2021>*

[This Article Wholly Amended on Jun. 7, 2011]

Article 6-2 Deleted. *<Jun. 10, 2022>*

Article 7 (Designation of Institution Specializing in Space Development)

(1) The Minister of Science and ICT may designate and support specialized institutions for promoting space development projects systematically and efficiently (hereinafter referred to as "institution specializing in space development"). *<Amended on Mar. 23, 2013; Jul. 26, 2017>*

(2) Each institution specializing in space development shall carry out the following activities: *<Amended on Jan. 20, 2015>*

  1. Execution of space development projects based on master plans;

  2. Comprehensively performing activities for the development,

launch, operation, etc. of artificial space objects;

3. Other duties prescribed by Presidential Decree with regard to space development projects.

(3) Matters necessary for criteria for designation of and details of support for institutions specializing in space development shall be prescribed by Presidential Decree.

[This Article Wholly Amended on Jun. 7, 2011]

CHAPTER III SPACE OBJECTS AND SPACE LAUNCH VEHICLES

Article 8 (Domestic Registration of Artificial Space Objects)

(1) Any citizen (including any corporation; hereinafter the same shall apply) of the Republic of Korea who intends to launch an artificial space object (excluding space launch vehicles; hereafter the same shall apply in this Article and Articles 9 and 10) in Korea or overseas shall file a preliminary registration with the Minister of Science and ICT, as prescribed by Presidential Decree, by no later than 180 days before the scheduled date of launch. *<Amended on Mar. 23, 2013; Jan. 20, 2015; Jul. 26, 2017>*

(2) Any person who is not a citizen of the Republic of Korea shall file preliminary registration with the Minister of Science and ICT in accordance with paragraph (1), if he or she falls under any of the following subparagraphs: *<Amended on Mar. 23, 2013; Jul. 26, 2017>*

1. When he or she intends to launch a space object from an area or structure situated within the territory or jurisdiction of the Republic of Korea;

2. When he or she intends to launch a space object from outside the Republic of Korea using a space launch vehicle

owned by the Government or a citizen of the Republic of Korea.

(3) Any person intending to file preliminary registration of an artificial space object in accordance with paragraphs (1) and (2) shall attach a launch plan stating the following: *<Amended on Mar. 9, 2011; Jan. 20, 2015>*

1. Purpose of use of the artificial space object;
2. Ownership or licensee of the artificial space object;
3. Basic orbit of the artificial space object;
4. Fulfillment of the liability for damages in the event of space accidents;
5. Other matters concerning the launch, use, and management of artificial space objects, prescribed by Presidential Decree;
6. Deleted; *<Mar. 9, 2011>*
7. Deleted; *<Mar. 9, 2011>*
8. Deleted; *<Mar. 9, 2011>*
9. Deleted. *<Mar. 9, 2011>*

(4) When the Minister of Science and ICT finds, after examining a launch plan referred to in paragraph (3), that the applicant is unable to bear the liability for damages referred to in Article 14, he or she may require the applicant to rectify and supplement such plan. *<Amended on Mar. 23, 2013; Jul. 26, 2017>*

(5) Any person who has completed preliminary registration of an artificial space object in accordance with paragraphs (1) and (2) shall file registration of the artificial space object with the Minister of Science and ICT, as prescribed by Presidential Decree, within 90 days from the date on which the artificial space object is successfully placed into orbit: Provided, That the foregoing shall not apply to artificial space objects registered with foreign countries under an agreement with the Government of the launching State pursuant to the Convention on Registration of Objects Launched into Outer Space.

<Amended on Mar. 23, 2013; Jan. 20, 2015; Jul. 26, 2017>

(6) If any detail prescribed in the subparagraphs of paragraph (3) is modified, the person who has completed preliminary registration under paragraphs (1) and (2) or person who has obtained registration of an artificial space object in accordance with paragraph (5) shall notify the Minister of Science and ICT thereof within 15 days from the time such fact comes to his/ her knowledge. *<Amended on Mar. 23, 2013; Jan. 20, 2015; Jul. 26, 2017>*

[This Article Wholly Amended on Jun. 7, 2011]

[Title Amended on Jan. 20, 2015]

Article 8-2 (Registration of Meteorites)

(1) The owner of a meteorite discovered in the Republic of Korea and a meteorite brought into the Republic of Korea from a foreign country may file an application for registration of the relevant meteorite with the Minister of Science and ICT. *<Amended on Jul. 26, 2017>*

(2) Where the Minister of Science and ICT checks the authenticity of a meteorite for which an application for registration is filed with him or her and it is verified as the meteorite, he or she shall issue a certificate of registration to an applicant for the registration thereof. *<Amended on Jul. 26, 2017; Jun. 9, 2020>*

(3) Where an alteration is made to already registered information, such as the transfer of ownership, due to the sale, transfer, division, etc. of a meteorite, a person in receipt of a certificate of registration pursuant to paragraph (2), shall report such alteration to the Minister of Science and ICT. *<Amended on Jul. 26, 2017>*

(4) Matters subject to registration under paragraph (1), to issue a certificate of registration under paragraph (2), and to file a report under paragraph (3) shall be prescribed by Presidential

Decree.
[This Article Newly Inserted on Jan. 20, 2015]

Article 8-3 (Prohibition on Taking Meteorites out of Republic of Korea)

(1) Any meteorite discovered in the Republic of Korea shall not be taken out of the Republic of Korea: Provided, That the foregoing shall not apply where a meteorite is taken out of the Republic of Korea for the purpose of scientific research approved by the Minister of Science and ICT. *<Amended on Jul. 26, 2017>*

(2) Necessary matters concerning procedures, etc. for taking a meteorite out of the Republic of Korea under the proviso of paragraph (1) shall be prescribed by Presidential Decree.
[This Article Newly Inserted on Jan. 20, 2015]

Article 9 (International Registration of Artificial Space Objects)

(1) When the registration of an artificial space object is filed pursuant to Article 8 (5), the Minister of Science and ICT shall register such space object with the United Nations through the Minister of Foreign Affairs pursuant to the Convention on Registration of Objects Launched into Outer Space: Provided, That the foregoing shall not apply to satellites registered with the United Nations pursuant to Article 44 (1) of the Radio Waves Act. *<Amended on Mar. 23, 2013; Jan. 20, 2015; Jul. 26, 2017>*

(2) If any details of registration filed with the United Nations under the main body of paragraph (1) is modified due to expiration of life cycle of an artificial space object or other reasons, the Minister of Science and ICT shall notify the United Nations thereof through the Minister of Foreign Affairs. *<Amended on Mar. 23, 2013; Jan. 20, 2015; Jul. 26, 2017>*

[This Article Wholly Amended on Jun. 7, 2011]
[Title Amended on Jan. 20, 2015]

Article 10 (Artificial Space Objects and Management of Registers of Artificial Space Objects)

(1) The Minister of Science and ICT shall maintain and manage the registers of preliminary registration and registration of artificial space objects, as prescribed by Ordinance of the Ministry of Science and ICT. *<Amended on Feb. 29, 2008; Mar. 23, 2013; Jan. 20, 2015; Jul. 26, 2017>*

(2) The Minister of Science and ICT shall maintain and manage the registers of meteorites, as prescribed by Ordinance of the Ministry of Science and ICT. *<Newly Inserted on Jan. 20, 2015; Jul. 26, 2017>*

[Title Amended on Jan. 20, 2015]

Article 11 (Permission to Launch Space Launch Vehicles)

(1) Where a person intending to launch a space launch vehicle falls under any of the following subparagraphs, he or she shall obtain permission from the Minister of Science and ICT therefor. The same shall also apply to any modifications of permitted matters: Provided, That any modification to minor matters prescribed by Presidential Decree shall be reported within 30 days after such modification: *<Amended on Mar. 23, 2013; Jul. 26, 2017>*

1. When he or she intends to launch a space launch vehicle from an area or structure situated within the territory or jurisdiction of the Republic of Korea;

2. When he or she intends to launch a space launch vehicle owned by the Government or a citizen of the Republic of Korea from outside the Republic of Korea.

(2) Any person intending to obtain permission for launch

prescribed in paragraph (1) shall file an application with the Minister of Science and ICT along with a launch plan prescribed by Presidential Decree, such as a safety analysis report, an operation plan of the load thereon, and a plan for compensation for damages. *<Amended on Mar. 23, 2013; Jul. 26, 2017>*

(3) The Minister of Science and ICT shall take the following matters into consideration when granting permission for launch referred to in paragraph (1): *<Amended on Mar. 23, 2013; Jul. 26, 2017>*

1. Appropriateness of the purpose of use of the space launch vehicle;

2. Appropriateness of safety management for the space launch vehicle and other things used for the launch;

3. Financial ability, such as subscription to compensation liability insurance in preparation for the event of space accidents;

4. Other matters prescribed by Ordinance of the Ministry of Science and ICT, which are necessary for launch and preparation for launch, such as moving of the space launch vehicle.

(4) The Minister of Science and ICT may attach necessary conditions to permission referred to in paragraph (1) when granting such permission. *<Amended on Mar. 23, 2013; Jul. 26, 2017>*

(5) Where the Minister of Science and ICT receives a report on modifications according to the proviso of paragraph (1), he or she shall accept the report if the details thereof are deemed in compliance with this Act as a result of review. *<Newly Inserted on Dec. 19, 2017>*

[This Article Wholly Amended on Jun. 7, 2011]

Article 12 (Grounds for Disqualification)

None of the following persons may obtain permission to launch space launch vehicles referred to in Article 11: *<Amended on Jun. 3,*

2014; Jun. 9, 2020; Apr. 20, 2021>

1. A person under adult guardianship;
2. A bankrupt who has not been reinstated yet;
3. A person for whom three years have not passed since his or her imprisonment with labor for violating this Act declared by a court was completely executed (including cases where the execution is deemed completed)or exempted;
4. A person who is under the suspension of the execution of his or her imprisonment with labor for violating this Act;
5. A corporation, the representative of which falls under any of subparagraphs 1 through 4.

[This Article Wholly Amended on Jun. 7, 2011]

Article 13 (Revocation of Permission for Launch, and Hearings)

(1) In any of the following cases, the Minister of Science and ICT may revoke permission to launch a space launch vehicle: *<Amended on Mar. 23, 2013; Jul. 26, 2017>*

1. Where launch is delayed for one year or longer from the scheduled date of permitted launch without good cause;
2. Where permission for launch is obtained by fraud or other improper means;
3. Where the head of a central relevant administrative agency requests the revocation of permission for launch in anticipation of a serious threat to national security;
4. Where a problem is detected in the safety management of a space launch vehicle before launch, such as leakage of fuel from the space launch vehicle and defects in telecommunications systems;
5. Where no permission for modification is obtained, in violation of the latter part of Article 11 (1);
6. Where a person who has obtained permission to launch a space launch vehicle falls under any subparagraph of

Article 12: Provided, That the foregoing shall not apply to cases falling under subparagraph 5 of Article 12, if the representative is replaced and appointed within three months from the date on which he or she becomes falling under the grounds for disqualification.

(2) The Minister of Science and ICT shall hold a hearing when he or she intends to revoke permission to launch space launch vehicles under paragraph (1): Provided, That hearings may be omitted in cases falling under paragraph (1) 3 and 4. *<Amended on Mar. 23, 2013; Jul. 26, 2017>*

[This Article Wholly Amended on Jun. 7, 2011]

Article 14 (Liability for Damages Caused by Space Accidents)

Any person who has launched a space object pursuant to Articles 8 and 11 shall hold the liability for damages arising from space accidents caused by the artificial space object. In such cases, the scope of compensation for damages, limitation of liabilities and other relevant matters shall be prescribed by other Acts. *<Amended on Jan. 20, 2015>*

[This Article Wholly Amended on Jun. 7, 2011]

Article 14-2 (Rescue of Astronauts)

When an astronaut aboard an artificial space object of a foreign country makes an emergency landing or is in distress or has an accident in the territory of the Republic of Korea or nearby international waters, the Government shall render all possible assistance to such astronaut and return the astronaut to the launching State or the State of registry or to an international organization, whichever is responsible for the launch of the relevant artificial space object. *<Amended on Jan. 20, 2015>*

[This Article Wholly Amended on Jun. 7, 2011]

[Moved from Article 22 <Jun. 10, 2022>]

Article 14-3 (Return of Artificial Space Objects)

If an artificial space object of a foreign country crashes or makes an emergency landing onto the territory of the Republic of Korea, the Government shall safely return the artificial space object to the launching State, the State of registry, or an international organization, whichever is responsible for the launch of the relevant space object. *<Amended on Jan. 20, 2015>*

[This Article Wholly Amended on Jun. 7, 2011]

[Title Amended on Jan. 20, 2015]

[Moved from Article 23 <Jun. 10, 2022>]

CHAPTER IV PREPARATION FOR DANGERS IN SPACE

Article 15 (Formulation of Master Plan for Preparing against Dangers in Space)

(1) In order to provide against dangers in space, the Government shall formulate a master plan for preparing against dangers in space (hereinafter referred to as "master plan for preparing against dangers in space") which prescribes midand long-term policy objectives and basic direction on securing preparation against dangers in space every 10 years.

(2) A master plan for preparing against dangers in space shall include the following:

1. Matters concerning environmental protection and surveillance of space;

2. Matters concerning forecasts and alarms of dangers in space;

3. Matters concerning research and development for the prevention of and preparing against dangers in space;

4. Matters concerning international cooperation for the prevention of and preparing against dangers in space;

5. Other matters necessary to provide against dangers in space.

(3) Where the Government intends to formulate or alter a master plan for preparing against dangers in space, it shall finalize the master plan following deliberations by the Committee: Provided, That the foregoing shall not apply to cases where it alters insignificant matters prescribed by Presidential Decree.

(4) The Government shall officially announce a master plan finalized pursuant to paragraph (3) without delay: Provided, That it may choose not to officially announce matters concerning national security.

(5) Detailed procedures concerning the formulation and alteration of a master plan for preparing against dangers in space shall be prescribed by Presidential Decree.

[This Article Newly Inserted on Jun. 3, 2014]

Article 15-2 (Formulation of Action Plan for Preparing against Dangers in Space)

(1) In accordance with a master plan for preparing against dangers in space, the Minister of Science and ICT shall formulate and execute an action plan thereof every year in consultation with the heads of relevant central administrative agencies. *<Amended on Jul. 26, 2017>*

(2) Detailed procedures concerning the formulation and execution of an action plan under paragraph (1) shall be prescribed by Presidential Decree.

[This Article Newly Inserted on Jun. 3, 2014]

Article 15-3 (Designation of Space Environment Surveillance Agency)

(1) The Minister of Science and ICT may designate a space environment surveillance agency which will conduct the following affairs for the efficient establishment and operation of a system for the prevention of and preparation against

dangers in space: *<Amended on Jul. 26, 2017>*

1. Establishment and operation of a system for issuing forecasts and alarms of dangers in space;
2. Establishment and operation of an international cooperation system for the prevention of and preparation against dangers in space;
3. In addition to matters provided in subparagraphs 1 and 2, affairs prescribed by Presidential Decree in relation to the prevention of and preparation against dangers in space.

(2) The Minister of Science and ICT may subsidize all or part of the expenses incurred in conducting affairs under the subparagraphs of paragraph (1) to a space environment surveillance agency designated pursuant to the aforesaid paragraph within the budget. *<Amended on Jul. 26, 2017>*

(3) Where necessary to prevent and prepare against dangers in space, the Minister of Science and ICT may establish and operate Headquarters for Countermeasures against Dangers in Space headed by the Vice Minister of Science and ICT. *<Amended on Jul. 26, 2017>*

(4) Criteria for designation of a space environment surveillance agency and matters necessary for the composition, operation, etc. of Headquarters for Countermeasures against Dangers in Space shall be prescribed by Presidential Decree.

[This Article Newly Inserted on Jun. 3, 2014]

Article 16 (Composition of Space Accident Investigation Committee)

(1) If space accidents prescribed by Presidential Decree occur, the Minister of Science and ICT may establish a Space Accident Investigation Committee under his/her jurisdiction to investigate space such accidents. *<Amended on Mar. 9, 2011; Mar. 23, 2013; Jul. 26, 2017>*

(2) The Space Accident Investigation Committee shall be comprised of not less than five but not more than 11 members, including one chairperson, and the members thereof shall be commissioned by the Minister of Science and ICT from among persons who satisfy the qualifications prescribed in Presidential Decree, whereas the chairperson thereof shall be appointed by the Minister of Science and ICT among the Committee members: Provided, That as for matters prescribed by Presidential Decree in view of national security, a separate space accident investigation committee may be organized as prescribed by Presidential Decree. <Amended on Mar. 9, 2011; Mar. 23, 2013; Jul. 26, 2017; Jun. 9, 2020>

(3) The Space Accident Investigation Committee may investigate any of the following persons to carry out its duties. In such cases, persons subject to such investigation shall comply therewith unless they have justifiable grounds to the contrary: <Amended on Mar. 9, 2011; Jan. 20, 2015>

1. A person who has filed preliminary registration or registration of an artificial space object under Article 8;

2. A person who has obtained permission to launch space objects under Article 11;

3. Other persons involved in artificial space objects, such as manufacturers of artificial space objects and testers of the performance of artificial space objects.

(4) The chairperson of Space Accident Investigation Committee may request the heads of relevant administrative agencies to cooperate for the control of access to areas of space accidents and other matters necessary for investigations. In such cases, the heads of relevant administrative agencies so requested shall cooperate unless they have justifiable grounds to the contrary. <Amended on Mar. 9, 2011>

(5) Matters necessary for the timing of organization, operation,

etc. of the Space Accident Investigation Committee other than the matters prescribed in paragraphs (1) through (4) shall be prescribed by Presidential Decree. *<Amended on Mar. 9, 2011>*
[This Article Wholly Amended on Jun. 7, 2011]
[Title Amended on Mar. 9, 2011]

Article 17 (Dissemination and Utilization of Satellite Information)

(1) The Minister of Science and ICT may adopt measures necessary to facilitate the dissemination and utilization of satellite information acquired by satellites developed in accordance with master plans, such as the designation and establishment of an organization exclusively dedicated to such activities. In such cases, he or she shall consult with the Minister of Land, Infrastructure and Transport about national spatial data under the Framework Act on National Spatial Data Infrastructure, and with the heads of relevant central administrative agencies about national security. *<Amended on Mar. 23, 2013; Jun. 3, 2014; Jul. 26, 2017>*

(2) The Minister of Science and ICT may subsidize expenses incurred in conducting activities of an organization exclusively dedicated to activities under paragraph (1) and promoting the dissemination and utilization of satellite information within the budget. *<Amended on Mar. 23, 2013; Jun. 3, 2014; Jul. 26, 2017>*

(3) The Government shall endeavor not to invade privacy during utilization of satellite information.

(4) In order to efficiently deal with the dissemination and utilization of satellite information under paragraph (1), the following matters shall be prescribed by Presidential Decree: *<Newly Inserted on Jun. 3, 2014>*

1. Establishment of an integrated system for the dissemination and utilization of satellite information;
2. Receipt, processing and disclosure of satellite information;

3. Reproduction and sale of satellite information;
4. Inspection of the present status of the utilization of satellite information;
5. Security affairs of satellite information;
6. Other matters necessary for the dissemination and utilization of satellite information.

[This Article Wholly Amended on Jun. 7, 2011]
[Title Amended on Jun. 3, 2014]

CHAPTER V FACILITATION OF SPACE DEVELOPMENT

Article 18 (Facilitation of Space Development by Private Sector)

(1) The Minister of Science and ICT shall formulate and implement strategies for invigorating space development and investment in research and development in the private sector and for fostering enterprises related to space development in accordance with a master plan. *<Amended on Jun. 10, 2022>*

(2) The Minister of Science and ICT may request the heads of the relevant central administrative agencies to render cooperation necessary for formulating and implementing strategies under paragraph (1). *<Amended on Mar. 23, 2013; Jul. 26, 2017; Jun. 10, 2022>*

[This Article Wholly Amended on Jun. 7, 2011]
[Title Amended on Jun. 10, 2022]

Article 18-2 (Opening and Utilization of Space Development Infrastructure)

(1) The State and local governments may open space development infrastructure held by the following institutions to space business entities and may require them to utilize such infrastructure in order to facilitate the space development by the private sector:

1. A public enterprise under Article 5 (4) 1 of the Act on the Management of Public Institutions;
2. A local public enterprise under the Local Public Enterprises Act;
3. A government-funded science and technology research institute under the Act on the Establishment, Operation and Fostering of Government-Funded Science and Technology Research Institutes;
4. A local government-invested research institute under the Act on the Establishment and Operation of Local Government-Invested Research Institutes;
5. A specific research institute under the Specific Research Institutes Support Act;
6. A research institute specializing in manufacturing technology under Article 42 (1) of the Industrial Technology Innovation Promotion Act;
7. Other institutions prescribed by Presidential Decree which have space development infrastructure deemed necessary for opening and utilization by the Minister of Science and ICT.

(2) The Minister of Science and ICT may request the institutions under the subparagraphs of paragraph (1) to submit the records of opening and utilization of infrastructure for space development.

(3) Except as provided in paragraphs (1) and (2), matters necessary for procedures, etc. for opening and utilization of space development infrastructure shall be prescribed by Presidential Decree.

[This Article Newly Inserted on Jun. 10, 2022]

Article 18-3 (Methods of Promotion of Space Development Projects)

(1) In order to efficiently promote a master plan, the Government

may enter into an agreement with an institution or organization prescribed in each subparagraph of Article 14 (1) of the Basic Research Promotion and Technology Development Support Act to implement space development projects.

(2) The Government may conclude a contract with an institution or organization under paragraph (1) to require it to manufacture a product of the same quality, performance, etc. with products to which technology developed through a space development project applies or any product similar thereto

(3) The Government may contribute to an institution or organization implementing space development projects (hereinafter referred to as "institution implementing space development projects") all or part of the expenses incurred in implementing space development projects by entering into an agreement under paragraph (1).

(4) Where necessary to effectively perform a space development project, an institution implementing space development projects may have another institution or organization perform part of the relevant project.

(5) Except as provided in this Act, the Act on Contracts to Which the State Is a Party shall apply to the following contracts:

1. Where the Government implements a space development project under a contract pursuant to paragraph (2), the contract;

2. Where an institution implementing space development projects requires other institutions or organizations to perform part of the space development project pursuant to paragraph (4), the contract therefor;

3. A contract for the purchase of research facilities, equipment, materials, etc. or services which is concluded by an institution implementing space development projects.

(6) When the Government or an institution implementing space development projects concludes a contract under the subparagraphs of paragraph (5), it shall require the other party to the contract that delays performance of the contract without good cause to pay a penalty for delay, as prescribed by Presidential Decree.

(7) Except as provided in paragraphs (1) through (6), matters necessary for procedures, etc. for promoting a space development project shall be prescribed by Presidential Decree.

[This Article Newly Inserted on Jun. 10, 2022]

Article 18-4 (Dissemination of Outcomes of Space Development Projects and Promotion of Technology Transfer)

(1) The Minister of Science and ICT shall formulate and implement policies on the following in order to disseminate the outcomes of space development projects and promote technology transfer:

1. Management and distribution of information on the outcomes of space development projects and technology transfer;

2. Fostering of organizations established within research institutes, etc. related to the dissemination of the outcomes of space development projects and technology transfer;

3. Exchange and cooperation of human resources, technology, infrastructure, etc. between research institutes, etc.;

4. Other matters that the Minister of Science and ICT deems necessary for the dissemination of the outcomes of space development projects and the promotion of technology transfer.

(2) The Minister of Science and ICT may implement projects based on the policies provided in the subparagraphs of paragraph (1).

(3) The Minister of Science and ICT may require research

institutes, etc. to perform projects implemented pursuant to paragraph (2) and may fully or partially contribute or subsidize to cover expenses incurred in performing such projects.

(4) The head of a research institute, etc. may dispatch researchers or employees under his or her control to an enterprise, etc. intending to transfer technologies for a certain period in order to facilitate the transfer of technologies arising from space development projects.

[This Article Newly Inserted on Jun. 10, 2022]

Article 18-5 (Facilitation of Business Start-Ups)

The Government may provide necessary support to facilitate business start-ups related to space development.

[This Article Newly Inserted on Jun. 10, 2022]

Article 18-6 (Training of Professional Human Resources)

The Minister of Science and ICT shall formulate and implement the following policies to foster professional human resources necessary for space development:

1. Identifying of demand for professional human resources and an outlook for midto long-term supply and demand;
2. Support for development and dissemination of educational programs for training professional human resources;
3. Support for job creation for professional human resources;
4. Educational support for space development-related technology (hereinafter referred to as "space technology") which is implemented by educational institutions, including schools at all levels;
5. Other policies necessary for training professional human resources.

[This Article Newly Inserted on Jun. 10, 2022]

Article 18-7 (Designation of New Space Technology)

(1) The Minister of Science and ICT may designate technology that is deemed domestically new and advanced and deemed needed to be disseminated and utilized, as new space technology (hereinafter referred to as "new space technology") from among the following space technology:

1. Space technology first developed in Korea;
2. Space technology introduced from abroad and learned and improved;
3. Space technology that can create new added value by applying to other fields.

(2) A person who intends to obtain designation of new space technology pursuant to paragraph (1) shall file an application for designation with the Minister of Science and ICT, as prescribed by Presidential Decree.

(3) The Minister of Science and ICT may request the following persons to preferentially purchase the products manufactured or produced by using the new space technology:

1. A State agency or local government;
2. A public institution under the Act on the Management of Public Institutions;
3. A person who receives financial support, such as contributions and subsidies, from the State or a local government.

(2) Where new space technology designated pursuant to paragraph (1) falls under any of the following cases, the Minister of Science and ICT may revoke such designation: Provided, That the Minister shall revoke the designation in cases falling under subparagraph 1 and 2:

1. Where it is designated by fraud or other improper means;
2. Where it is impossible to utilize the technology, owing to any substantial defects of its content;
3. Where the need for dissemination and utilization of the

relevant new space technology ceases to exist due to changes, etc. in the technological environment.

(5) Except as provided in paragraphs (1) through (4), matters necessary for methods for the designation or revocation of designation of new space technology or utilization thereof, preferential purchase of such technology, etc. shall be prescribed by Presidential Decree.

[This Article Newly Inserted on Jun. 10, 2022]

Article 19 (Suspension and Correction of Space Development)

(1) When the Minister of Science and ICT receives a request from the Minister of National Defense during a war or upheaval, or in any emergency situation similar thereto to suspend a space development activity being carried out by a citizen of the Republic of Korea for the purpose of undertaking military operations, he or she shall issue an order to the citizen to suspend the space development activity. *<Amended on Mar. 23, 2013; Jul. 26, 2017>*

(2) When the Minister of Science and ICT receives a request from the head of a relevant central administrative agency to take corrective measures with regard to space development activities performed by a citizen of the Republic of Korea in view of the maintenance of public order or national security, he or she may issue an order to the citizen to correct the space development activity after deliberation by the Committee. *<Amended on Mar. 23, 2013; Jul. 26, 2017>*

[This Article Wholly Amended on Jun. 7, 2011]

Article 20 (Requests for Assistance or Cooperation in Space Development)

(1) If the Minister of Science and ICT deems it necessary for promoting space development, he or she may request the

heads of relevant central administrative agencies or the heads of local governments to assist with and cooperate for the following. In such cases, the heads of the relevant central administrative agencies or the heads of the local governments so requested shall comply therewith in the absence of good cause: *<Amended on Mar. 23, 2013; Jan. 20, 2015; Jul. 26, 2017>*

1. Matters concerning the control of access to surrounding areas (including territorial waters and airspace) for the launch of artificial space objects in Korea;
2. Matters concerning telecommunications, fire-fighting, emergency rescue and salvage, safety management, etc.

(2) When the Minister of Science and ICT makes a request for assistance or cooperation referred to in paragraph (1), he or she shall limit the assistance or cooperation to the minimum extent necessary for space development. *<Amended on Mar. 23, 2013; Jul. 26, 2017>*

[This Article Wholly Amended on Jun. 7, 2011]

Article 20-2 (Compensation for Damages Caused by Launched Space Objects)

(1) The State and local governments shall compensate persons who have sustained a loss caused by access control referred to in Article 20 (1) 1.

(2) Matters necessary for standards, procedure, methods of payment, etc. of compensation for a loss referred to in paragraph (1) shall be prescribed by Presidential Decree.

[This Article Newly Inserted on Jun. 7, 2011]

[Title Amended on Jan. 20, 2015]

Article 21 (Implementation of Space Development Projects Related to National Security)

(1) When the Minister of Science and ICT implements a

space development project related to national security, he
or she shall consult in advance with the heads of relevant
central administrative agencies. *<Amended on Mar. 23, 2013; Jul.
26, 2017>*

(2) Matters necessary for the formulation and implementation
of security measures for space development projects
referred to in paragraph (1) shall be prescribed by
Presidential Decree.

[This Article Wholly Amended on Jun. 7, 2011]

Article 22 (Designation of Space Industry Cluster)

(1) Where the Minister of Science and ICT deems it necessary
to create a specific area as a space industry cluster, he or she
may designate such area as a space industry cluster after
consultation with the head of the relevant central administrative agency and the competent Special Metropolitan City
Mayor, Metropolitan City Mayor, Special Self-Governing City
Mayor, Do Governor, or Special Self-Governing Province
Governor (hereinafter referred to as "Mayor/Do Governor")
and following deliberation by the Committee.

(2) Where a space industry cluster designated pursuant to
paragraph (1) falls under any of the following cases, the
Minister of Science and ICT may fully or partially cancel its
designation after consultation with the head of the relevant
central administrative agency and the competent Mayor/Do
Governor and following deliberation by the Committee:

1. Where it is impossible to or it is anticipated to be
impossible to attain the objectives of the designation of a
space industry cluster;

2. Where it is necessary to cancel the designation of a space
industry cluster for the public interest due to unexpected
changes in circumstances at the time of designation of the

space industry cluster.

(3) Except as provided in paragraphs (1) and (2), matters necessary for the designation of designation of a space industry cluster, cancellation thereof, etc. shall be prescribed by Presidential Decree.

[This Article Newly Inserted on Jun. 10, 2022]

[Previous Article 22 moved to Article 14-2 <*Jun. 10, 2022*>]

Article 23 (Financial Support)

The State and local governments may subsidize or lend necessary expenses within the budget to research institutes, etc. located in a space industry cluster in order to foster and support the space industry.

[This Article Newly Inserted on Jun. 10, 2022]

[Previous Article 23 moved to Article 14-3 <*Jun. 10, 2022*>]

CHAPTER VI SUPPLEMENTARY PROVISIONS

Article 24 (Collection of Data and Surveys of Actual Conditions on Space Development)

(1) The Minister of Science and ICT may collect data on space development and aerospace industries or survey the actual conditions thereof in order to promote space development systematically and efficiently. *<Amended on Mar. 23, 2013; Jul. 26, 2017>*

(2) If the Minister of Science and ICT deems it necessary for the survey on the actual conditions of Korea referred to in paragraph (1), he or she may request relevant administrative agencies, research institutes, educational institutions, and enterprises to provide him or her with data or to make a statement of opinions. *<Amended on Mar. 23, 2013; Jul. 26, 2017>*

(3) Matters necessary for the details, timing, procedure, etc. of collection of data and surveys of actual conditions referred to in paragraph (1) shall be prescribed by Presidential Decree.

[This Article Wholly Amended on Jun. 7, 2011]

Article 25 (Confidentiality)

No person who is engaging or has engaged in duties prescribed in this Act shall divulge any confidential information he or she has learned in the course of performing his or her duties or use it for purposes, other than the purpose of this Act.

[This Article Wholly Amended on Jun. 7, 2011]

Article 26 (Entrustment of Authority)

The Minister of Science and ICT may entrust the following duties among his/her duties under this Act to government-funded science and technological research institutions established under the Act on the Establishment, Operation and Fostering of Government-Funded Science and Technology Research Institutes or to relevant specialized institutions, as prescribed by Presidential Decree: *<Amended on Mar. 23, 2013; Jan. 20, 2015; Jul. 26, 2017>*

1. Matters concerning the registration of meteorites under Article 8-2 and matters concerning the management of the registers of meteorites under Article 10 (2);

2. Examination of safety related to permission or permission for modification referred to in the former and latter parts of Article 11 (1);

3. Matters concerning the collection of data on space development and aerospace industries and survey of the actual conditions thereof referred to in Article 24.

[This Article Wholly Amended on Jun. 7, 2011]

CHAPTER VII PENALTY PROVISIONS

Article 27 (Penalty Provisions)

(1) Any person who launches a space object without permission or permission for modification referred to in the former and latter parts of Article 11 (1) shall be punished by imprisonment with labor for not more than five years or by a fine not exceeding 50 million won.

(2) Any of the following persons shall be punished by imprisonment with labor for not more than three years or by a fine not exceeding 30 million won: *<Amended on Jan. 20, 2015>*

   1. A person who takes a meteorite out of the Republic of Korea, in violation of Article 8-3;

   2. A person who fails to comply with an order for suspension or correction referred to in Article 19;

   3. A person who violates Article 25.

[This Article Wholly Amended on Jun. 7, 2011]

Article 28 (Joint Penalty Provisions)

When a representative of a corporation, or an agent, employee, or other servant of a corporation or individual commits an offense under Article 27 in connection with the business of the corporation or individual, not only shall such offender be punished, but also the corporation or individual shall be punished by a fine under the relevant provisions: Provided, That the same shall not apply where such corporation or individual has not been negligent in giving due attention and supervision concerning the relevant duties to prevent such offense.

[This Article Wholly Amended on Jun. 7, 2011]

Article 29 (Administrative Fines)

(1) Any of the following persons shall be subject to an administ-

rative fine not exceeding 10 million won: *<Amended on Jan. 20, 2015>*

1. A person who fails to file preliminary registration of an artificial space object, in violation of Article 8 (1) or (2);
2. A person who fails to file registration of an artificial space object, in violation of Article 8 (5);
3. A person who fails to report modified matters, in violation of the proviso of Article 11 (1).

(2) Any of the following persons shall be punished by an administrative fine not exceeding five million won:

1. A person who fails to give notice of modification within 15 days or give such notice by falsehood, in violation of Article 8 (6);
2. A person who refuses, interferes with, or evades the investigation of an accident referred to in Article 16 (3).

(3) The Minister of Science and ICT shall impose and collect administrative fines referred to in paragraphs (1) and (2), as prescribed by Presidential Decree. *<Amended on Mar. 23, 2013; Jul. 26, 2017>*

[This Article Wholly Amended on Jun. 7, 2011]

ADDENDA *<Act No. 7538, May 31, 2005>*

(1) (Enforcement Date) This Act shall enter into force six months after the date of its promulgation.

(2) (Transitional Measures concerning Master Plans for Promotion of Space Development) The medium-and long-term master plans for space development deliberated by the National Science and Technology Council prescribed in Article 9 of the Framework Act on Science and Technology shall be construed as a master plan for the promotion of space development until the master plan for the promotion of space development is established pursuant to Article 5.

(3) (Transitional Measures concerning Registration of Space Objects) The space objects already registered by the Republic of Korea with the United Nations as at the time this Act enters into force shall be deemed registered pursuant to Article 8.

ADDENDA <*Act No. 8714, Dec. 21, 2007*>
(1) (Enforcement Date) This Act shall enter into force six months after the date of its promulgation.
(2) Omitted.

ADDENDA <*Act No. 8852, Feb. 29, 2008*>
Article 1 (Enforcement Date)
This Act shall enter into force on the date of its promulgation. Provided, That...
Articles 2 through 7 Omitted.

ADDENDA <*Act No. 9440, Feb. 6, 2009*>
Article 1 (Enforcement Date)
This Act shall enter into force six months after the date of its promulgation.
Articles 2 through 4 Omitted.

ADDENDUM <*Act No. 10087, Mar. 17, 2010*>
This Act shall enter into force on the date of its promulgation.

ADDENDUM <*Act No. 10447, Mar. 9, 2011*>
This Act shall enter into force on the date of its promulgation: Provided, That the amended provisions of Articles 6 (4), 6-2, 8 (3) and 16 shall enter into force three months after the date of its promulgation.

ADDENDA *<Act No. 10775, Jun. 7, 2011>*

(1) (Enforcement Date) This Act shall enter into force on the date of its promulgation.

(2) (Applicability to Persons Eligible for Compensation for Damages Caused by Launched Space Objects) The amended provisions of Article 20-2 shall also apply to those who have sustained a loss caused by access control for the launch of space objects during the period from August 1, 2009 to the date preceding the date on which this Act enters into force.

ADDENDA *<Act No. 11690, Mar. 23, 2013>*

Article 1 (Enforcement Date)

(1) This Act shall enter into force on the date of its promulgation.

(2) Omitted.

Articles 2 through 7 Omitted.

ADDENDA *<Act No. 12723, Jun. 3, 2014>*

Article 1 (Enforcement Date)

This Act shall enter into force six months after the date of its promulgation: Provided, That the amended provision of subparagraph 1 of Article 12 shall enter into force on the date of its promulgation.

Article 2 (Transitional Measures concerning Incompetents, etc.)

Notwithstanding the amended provision of subparagraph 1 of Article 12, the former provision shall apply to a person who has been already declared incompetent or quasi-incompetent at the time the aforesaid amended provision enters into force and in whose case the effect of declaration of incompetent or quasi-incompetent is maintained pursuant to the amended provisions of Article 2 of Addenda to the Civil Act (Act No. 10429).

ADDENDA *<Act No. 12736, Jun. 3, 2014>*

Article 1 (Enforcement Date)

This Act shall enter into force one year after the date of its promulgation.

Articles 2 through 4 Omitted.

ADDENDUM *<Act No. 13009, Jan. 20, 2015>*

This Act shall enter into force six months after the date of its promulgation.

ADDENDA *<Act No. 14839, Jul. 26, 2017>*

Article 1 (Enforcement Date)

(1) This Act shall enter into force on the date of its promulgation. Provided, That the provisions amending any Act that was promulgated before this Act enters into force but has yet to enter into force, among the Acts amended pursuant to Article 5 of the Addenda, shall enter into force on the respective date the relevant Act enters into force.

Articles 2 through 6 Omitted.

ADDENDA *<Act No. 15243, Dec. 19, 2017>*

Article 1 (Enforcement Date)

This Act shall enter into force on the date of its promulgation.

Article 2 (Case of Application concerning Report of Modifications to Space Launch Vehicles)

The amended provisions of Article 11 (5) shall apply beginning with the case where a report of modifications is filed after this Act enters into force.

ADDENDUM *<Act No. 17347, Jun. 9, 2020>*

This Act shall enter into force on the date of its promulgation.

ADDENDUM *<Act No. 17359, Jun. 9, 2020>*

This Act shall enter into force on the date of its promulgation.

ADDENDA *<Act No. 18077, Apr. 20, 2021>*

Article 1 (Enforcement Date)

This Act shall enter into force one year after the date of its promulgation.

Article 2 (Transitional Measure concerning Grounds for Disqualification for Permission to Launch Space Launch Vehicles)

Notwithstanding the amended provisions of subparagraph 3 of Article 12, the previous provisions shall apply to persons who obtain permission to launch space launch vehicles before this Act enters into force.

ADDENDUM *<Act No. 18375, Aug. 10, 2021>*

This Act shall enter into force three months after the date of its promulgation.

ADDENDUM *<Act No. 18867, Jun. 10, 2022>*

This Act shall enter into force six months after the date of its promulgation.

Last updated : 2023-02-15

Judicial Decisions in Pubic International Law (2022)

JANG Jiyong
High Court Judge
Suwon High Court, Suwon, Korea

Korea's amended Act on Private International Law, which includes detailed rules on international jurisdiction, entered into force starting on July 5, 2022.

1. Applicable Law

1-1. CISG

Supreme Court Decision 2021Da269388 Decided January 13, 2022 [Price of Goods]

【Main Issues and Holdings】

[1] With respect to cases involving foreign factors, even if no allegation exists in relation to applicable laws, whether or not a court shall be obliged to deliberate and investigate the laws applicable to legal relations in accordance with the International Convention or private international law (affirmative).

[2] Whether the "United Nations Convention on Contracts for the

International Sale of Goods (CISG)" shall apply to contracts of sale
of goods between corporations of the Kingdom of the Netherlands
and those of the Republic of Korea as a priority (affirmative); and
whether applicable laws determined in accordance with private
international law of the jurisdiction shall apply to the matters that are
excluded from the application of the CISG or are not directly
regulated by the CISG (affirmative).

[3] Whether implicit agreement on applicable laws may be recognized according to Article 25(1) of the Act on Private International
Law even if there is no explicit agreement thereon (affirmative); and
whether the implicit agreement on applicable laws may be recognized
on the sole basis of the circumstance that the parties did not contest
applicable laws in the litigation procedures (negative).

【Summary of Decision】

[1] A foreign law as the law applicable to any legal relation which
involves foreign elements is not a matter of fact but a legal matter,
and a court should investigate the contents thereof ex officio. Thus,
with respect to cases involving foreign elements, even if no
allegation exists in relation to the applicable law, a court shall be
obliged to deliberate and investigate the law applicable to legal
relations thereof in accordance with the International Convention or
the Private International Law by giving the parties opportunities to
state their opinion through the active exercise of the right to request
elucidation or having them submit necessary materials.

[2] The international treaties that the Republic of Korea joined are
generally applied in preference to the Civil Act, Commercial Act, or
Act on Private International Law. Since both the Kingdom of the
Netherlands and the Republic of Korea joined the United Nations
Convention on Contracts for the International Sale of Goods (Vienna,
1980) (hereinafter "CISG"), the CISG preferentially applies to
contracts for the sale of goods between corporations of the Kingdom

of the Netherlands and those of the Republic of Korea pursuant to Article 1(1) of the CISG. The CISG regulates matters such as the formation of a contract for the international sale of goods, the obligations of the seller and buyer, the passing of risk, the scope of compensation for damages, etc., but excludes product liability from its application and does not stipulate the validity of a contract, the effect of the contract on the ownership of goods, the extinctive prescription thereof, etc. Meanwhile, neither the Kingdom of the Netherlands nor the Republic of Korea has ever joined the United Nations Convention on the Limitation Period in the International Sale of Goods (New York, 1974). As such, applicable laws determined in accordance with the private international law of the jurisdiction apply to the matters that are excluded from the application of the CISG or are not directly regulated by the CISG.

[3] Article 25(1) of the Act on Private International Law provides that "a contract shall be governed by the law which the parties choose explicitly or implicitly: Provided, That the implicit choice shall be limited to the case which the implicit choice can be reasonably recognized by the content of the contract and all other circumstances," while Article 26(1) of the Act on Private International Law stipulates that "in case the parties to a contract do not choose the applicable law, the contract shall be governed by the law of the country which is most closely connected with the contract," and Article 26(2)1 of the Act on Private International Law provides that in case of assignment contracts, the law of the country where the principal business office is located in case the assignor is a corporation shall be presumed to be most closely connected. Article 25(1) of the Act on Private International Law allows the parties to freely choose the applicable law of a contract but limits implicit choice to cases in which the implicit choice can be reasonably recognized by the details of the contract and all other circumstances to prevent such choice from being unfairly extended; thus, even if

there is no explicit agreement on the applicable law, the implicit agreement on the applicable law may be recognized. However, implicit agreement on the applicable law cannot be found on the sole basis of the circumstance that the parties did not contest the applicable law in the litigation procedures.

1-2. Korean law: Assumption of obligation

Supreme Court Decision 2019Da201662 Decided July 28, 2022 〔Stock Return〕

〔Facts〕

A, a Korean national, concludes a lease contract with company B to lend stocks of the foreign company C which was established by Swiss law. When C was merged into the foreign company D, A made a claim against D asserting that C concurrently assumed the obligations of company B to return the stock to A, and requesting D's return of the stock.

〔Main Issues and Holdings〕

[1] Assumption of obligation in Article 34 of the Act on Private International Law includes not only exempt assumption of obligation but concurrent assumption of obligation (affirmative); the law applicable to the obligation of the assignee to the creditor when a concurrent assumption of obligation is made by an agreement between the creditor, the debtor and assignee (law applicable to the legal relationship between the creditor and the debtor).

[2] The law applicable to the contractual obligation under Article 25(1) of the Act on Private International Law (the law which the debtor chose explicitly or implicitly when the debtor concluded a contract with the creditor); considerations when granting implicit choice of the applicable law.

[3] Korean law was implicitly chosen by A and B as the law applicable to the stock lease contract; therefore, Korean law governs the legal relationship of stock return claimed by A against D which merged C.

1-3. Korean Law: Formation of marriage

Supreme Court Decision 2007Meu1224 Decided January 27, 2022 【Nullity of Marriage, Alimony】

【Facts】

The plaintiff, a Korean man, married the defendant in Vietnam in September 2015 and they spent about 20 days together in Vietnam. After the plaintiff returned to Korea and reported the marriage in February 2016, the defendant entered Korea in June 2016. The defendant left home around August 2016 and the plaintiff claimed mainly nullity of marriage, preliminarily divorce.

【Main Issues and Holdings】

[1] The law applicable to a decision on the requirements for the formation of marriage (law of the nationality of each party); whether article 36(1) of the Act on Private International Law regulates the types of litigation on the dissolution of marriage or legal effect of the status after the litigation (affirmative); the law applicable to the litigation on the dissolution of marriage when a Korean national claims the dissolution of marriage on the ground that marriage was not established due to the lack of an agreement to marry (Korean Civil Act).

[2] The meaning of "no agreement to marry" in Article 815(1) of the Korean Civil Act as a cause for nullity of marriage / Matters to be considered especially when determining whether there was an agreement to marriage between a Korean national and a Vietnamese spouse.

【Summary of Decision】

[1] Article 36(1) of the Act on Private International Law provides that "the requirements for the formation of a marriage shall be governed by the law of the nationality of each party." The law applicable to decide on the requirements for the formation of marriage is the Korean Civil Act for Korean nationals and Vietnam Marriage and Family Law for Vietnamese nationals.

Article 815(1) of the Korean Civil Act provides that "where there is no agreement between the parties to marry, the marriage is null and void" and the Vietnam Marriage and Family Law constitutes that "the marriage is voluntarily decided by the man and woman." If a Korean national intended to marry but has not reached an agreement with the Vietnamese national concerned to marry, the requirements for the formation of marriage cannot be fulfilled under either the Korean Civil Act or the Vietnam Marriage and Family Act.

Article 36(1) of the Act on Private International Law regulates the applicable law to determine substantial requirements for the formation of marriage, not the types of litigation on the dissolution of marriage due to defects in the requirements or legal effect of the status after the litigation. Courts may therefore apply the Korean Civil Act to determine the nullity of marriage for the litigation claims the dissolution of marriage on the ground that marriage was not established due to the lack of agreement to marry.

[2] "Where there is no agreement between the parties to marry" as one of the causes for marriage anulment stipulated in Article 815(1) of the Korean Civil Act means there is no mutual consent between the parties intending to create any mental and physical bond recognized as a married couple by social norms. The family court should examine and determine in the specifics whether the other spouse had no intention of marriage at the time of the marriage registration, or his/her intent to maintain the marriage vanished

afterward. This decision is made by considering many factors such as motive or circumstances of the marriage, and no conclusion that the other spouse had no intention to marry at the time of the marriage registration should be readily made on the sole basis of some circumstances revealed during the marriage, such as neglecting efforts to maintain the marriage, or words or actions demonstrating the intention to terminate the marriage relationship.

When a Korean national marries a Vietnamese spouse, it is common for the spouse to complete the procedures for the establishment of a marriage stipulated in the statutes of Vietnam, after which the foreign spouse registers a marriage in accordance with the Civil Act of Korea, completing the marriage through the procedure of entering Korea with a visa issued for the purpose of a marriage and cohabitation pursuant to the Immigration Act of Korea. Differences in the aspect of married life may arise from differences in language, culture, and custom, necessitating that the family court take account of such circumstances in a careful determination of whether the foreign spouse had any intent to marry.

2. Recognition of threefold damage award by a Hawaiian court

Supreme Court Decision 2018Da231550 Decided March 11, 2022 【Judgment of Execution】

【Main Issues and Holdings】

[1] Method of determining whether the approval of a final and conclusive judgment rendered by a foreign court or a judgment acknowledged to have the same force (hereinafter "final judgment, etc.") may give rise to an outcome contrary to sound morals or other social order of the Republic of Korea When determining the

requirements for recognition of a final judgment, etc. stipulated in Article 217-2(1) of the Civil Procedure Act, whether the stability or predictability of the international trade order as well as domestic circumstances should be considered (affirmative); and whether the approval of a judgment rendered by a foreign court can be denied for the simple reason that no statute prescribing on the same subject as the statutes applied in a judgment rendered by a foreign court exists in the legislative system of the Republic of Korea (negative). [2] Where a judgment is rendered by a foreign court ordering compensation for damage exceeding the scope of compensatory damage, and the act cited as the cause of such compensation is in the regulatory realm of a statute allowing compensation for damage in excess of the scope of compensatory damage in the Republic of Korea, whether the approval of the judgment rendered by a foreign court is markedly contrary to the basic order of the statutes related to compensation for damage and thus impermissible (negative); in such a case, whether the approval of a judgment rendered by a foreign court can be denied on the sole basis of the fact that the foreign statutes applied in a judgment rendered by a foreign court contain the substance automatically deeming the specific multiples of the actual amount of damage as the final amount of compensation for damage (negative); and the standard for determining whether a court should approve the whole or part of a judgment rendered by a foreign court ordering compensation for damage exceeding the scope of compensatory damage.

【Summary of Decision】

[1] To permit the judgment of execution in relation to a final judgment rendered by a foreign court, etc., the requirements for recognition thereof should be satisfied. Article 217(1)3 of the Civil Procedure Act provides as a requirement for the approval of a final judgment rendered by a foreign court that the approval of a final

judgment rendered by a foreign court, etc. should not undermine sound morals or other social order of the Republic of Korea. Herein, whether the approval of a final judgment, etc. may give rise to a result being against sound morals or other social order of the Republic of Korea should be determined by examining the effect of the approval of a final judgment, etc. on basic moral convictions and social order that our domestic legal order intends to protect, in light of the degree of relevance between the cases dealt with in such final judgment, etc. and those of the Republic of Korea. Article 217-2(1) of the Civil Procedure Act prescribes that "[w]here final judgment, etc. on compensation for damage give rise to a result markedly contrary to the basic order of the statutes of the Republic of Korea or international treaties entered into by the Republic of Korea, a court shall not approve the whole or part of such final judgment, etc." This provision envisions limitations on the approval of a judgment rendered by a foreign court to the proper extent where the substance of a foreign court's judgment ordering compensation for damage exceeding the scope of compensatory damage in Article 217(1)3 of the Civil Procedure Act reach an unacceptable extent in light of the basic principle, ideology, structure, etc. of the compensation system recognized in the statutes of the Republic of Korea or international treaties entered into by the Republic of Korea. Moreover, when determining such requirements for recognition, the stability or predictability of the international trade order as well as domestic circumstances should be considered, and the approval of a judgment rendered by a foreign court should not be denied immediately for the simple reason that no statutes providing for the same subjects as the statutes applied in a judgment rendered by a foreign court exist in the legislative system of the Republic of Korea. [2] The basic principle of the compensation system of the Republic of Korea was originally to return the victim, etc. back to the state before such damage arises by making up for the actual damage inflicted upon the victim, etc. With respect to compensation for damage caused by a prime contractor's unfair act, compensation for damage exceeding the scope of compensatory damage to the extent not exceeding three times the actual damage was introduced to the "Fair Transactions in Subcontracting Act" for the first time in 2011 (Article 35). Subsequently, with regard to the illegal cartel conduct of business entities, a provision on compensation for damage exceeding the scope of compensatory damage to the extent not exceeding three times the actual damage was introduced to the "Monopoly Regulation and Fair Trade Act", and, further, a provision allowing compensation for damage exceeding the scope of compensatory damage to the extent not exceeding three to five times the damage with respect to certain types of acts was introduced through the amendment of individual statutes in the areas such as personal information, labor relations, intellectual property, consumer protection, etc. As such, the purpose of allowing compensation for damage exceeding the scope of compensatory damage in an individual statute is to inhibit the occurrence of unlawful acts and substantially compensate for the damage inflicted upon the victim through such compensation. As above, in light of compensation jurisprudence in the Republic of Korea, which is based on compensatory damage in principle and allows damage payments exceeding the scope of compensatory damage depending on special circumstances corresponding thereto in certain areas through individual Statutes, where an act that was deemed to be the cause of compensation for damage in a judgment rendered by a foreign court ordering compensation for damage exceeding the scope of compensatory damage belongs to the regulatory realm of individual statutes allowing compensation for damage exceeding the scope of compensatory damage in the Republic of Korea, it is not found that the approval of a judgment rendered by a foreign court as markedly contrary to the basic order of the statutes related to compensation for damage and thus impermissible. In such a case, even if the foreign statutes applied in a judgment rendered by a foreign court contain the contents that the specific multiples of the actual amount of damage is automatically fixed as the final amount of compensation for damage, the approval of the judgment rendered by a foreign court cannot be denied on the sole basis of such provisions and should be determined in consideration of the upper limit of the amount of compensation stipulated in the related statutes of the Republic of Korea. In short, whether a court should approve the whole or part of a judgment rendered by a foreign court ordering compensation for damage exceeding the scope of compensatory damage should be individually determined after a comprehensive consideration of the following circumstances: the relations between the corresponding judgment rendered by a foreign court and the statutes related thereto in the Republic of Korea; whether an act that was deemed as the cause of compensation for damage in the judgment rendered by a foreign court is in the legislative realm of individual statutes allowing compensation for damage exceeding the scope of compensatory damage in the Republic of Korea; and if such act belongs thereto, the difference between compensation for damage recognized in the judgment rendered by a foreign court and the prescription by the aforementioned individual statutes, particularly the upper limit of the amount of compensation, etc., premised on the basic principle, ideology, structure, etc. of the compensation system of the Republic of Korea.

Treaties/Agreements Concluded by the Republic of Korea

Treaties/Agreements
Concluded by the Republic of Korea

The Editorial Board
ILA Korean Branch

1. BILATERAL AGREEMENTS

https://www.mofa.go.kr/www/wpge/m_3834/contents.do

2. MULTILATERAL AGREEMENTS

https://www.mofa.go.kr/www/wpge/m_3835/contents.do

INDEX

AUTHOR GUIDELINES AND STYLE SHEET

I. SUBMISSION

Manuscripts should be submitted in Microsoft Word and electronically sent to ilakoreanbranch@gmail.com

II. GENERAL TERMS AND PEER-REVIEW SYSTEM OF PUBLICATION

All manuscripts are subject to initial evaluation by the KYIL Editorial Board and subsequently sent out to independent reviewers for a peer review. The Editorial Board accepts manuscripts on a rolling basis and will consider requests for an expedited review in appropriate cases.

III. FORMATING

1. ABSTRACT

Please include an abstract (no more than 150 words) at the beginning of an article.

2. TEXT

Main Text: Times New Roman, font size 12, 1.5 spacing
Endnotes: Times New Roman, font size 12, single spacing

3. CITING REFERENCE

The KYIL requires endnotes with subsequent numbering; the initial endnote should be indicated with '*,' if it is necessary to provide explanatory information about the manuscript.

Please include a reference list for all works the are cited at the end of the manuscript.

IV. NOTES

1. BOOKS

P. Malanczuk, *Akehurst's Modern Introduction to International Law*, 7th ed. (New York: Eoutledge, 1997), p. 1.

2. ARTICLES

Chao Wang, *China's Preferential Trade Remedy Approaches: A New Haven School Perspective*, Vol.21 No.1, Asia Pacific Law Review, (2013), p. 103.

3. ARTICLES IN COLLECTIONS

J. Paulsson & Z. Douglas, *Indirect Expropriation in Investment Treaty Arbitrations, in* Arbitration Foreign Investment Disputes 148 (N. Horn & S. Kroll eds., Kluwer Law International, 2004).

4. ARTICLES IN NEWSPAPER

YI Whan-Woo, *Korea, New Zealand embrace free trade pact*, Korea Times, November 14, 2014.

5. UNPUBLISHED MATERIALS

PARK Jung-Won, *Minority Rights Constraints on a State's Power to Regulate Citizenship under International Law*, Ph.D thesis (2006), on file with author.

6. WORKING PAPERS AND REPORTS

OECD, *'Indirect Expropriation' and the 'Right to Regulate' in International Investment Law*, OECD Working Paper, 2014/09.

7. INTERNET SOURCES

C. Schreuer, The Concept of Expropriation under the ETC and Other Investment Protection Treaties (2005), http://www.univie,ac,at/intlaw/pdf/csunpuyblpaper_3pdf. [Accessed on September 22, 2015]

V. GUIDELINE FOR AUTHORS

1. ARTICLE

Manuscripts must be in the form of a regular paper including endnotes and references. The length for an articles should not exceed 10,000 words in English excluding notes and references.

2. SPECIAL REPORT

Manuscripts for Special Report must be in the form of a descriptive report which covers the international law issues related to Korea in the past 5 years. Special Report must include author's comments with less than 10 endnotes and 5 references. The length for a special report should be no more the 5,000 words.

3. RECENT DEVELOPMENT

Manuscripts must cover the trends in international law related to Korea in the preceding year. Recent Development must be in the form of a short report, including less than 5 endnotes. The length for Recent Development should be no more than 2,000 words.